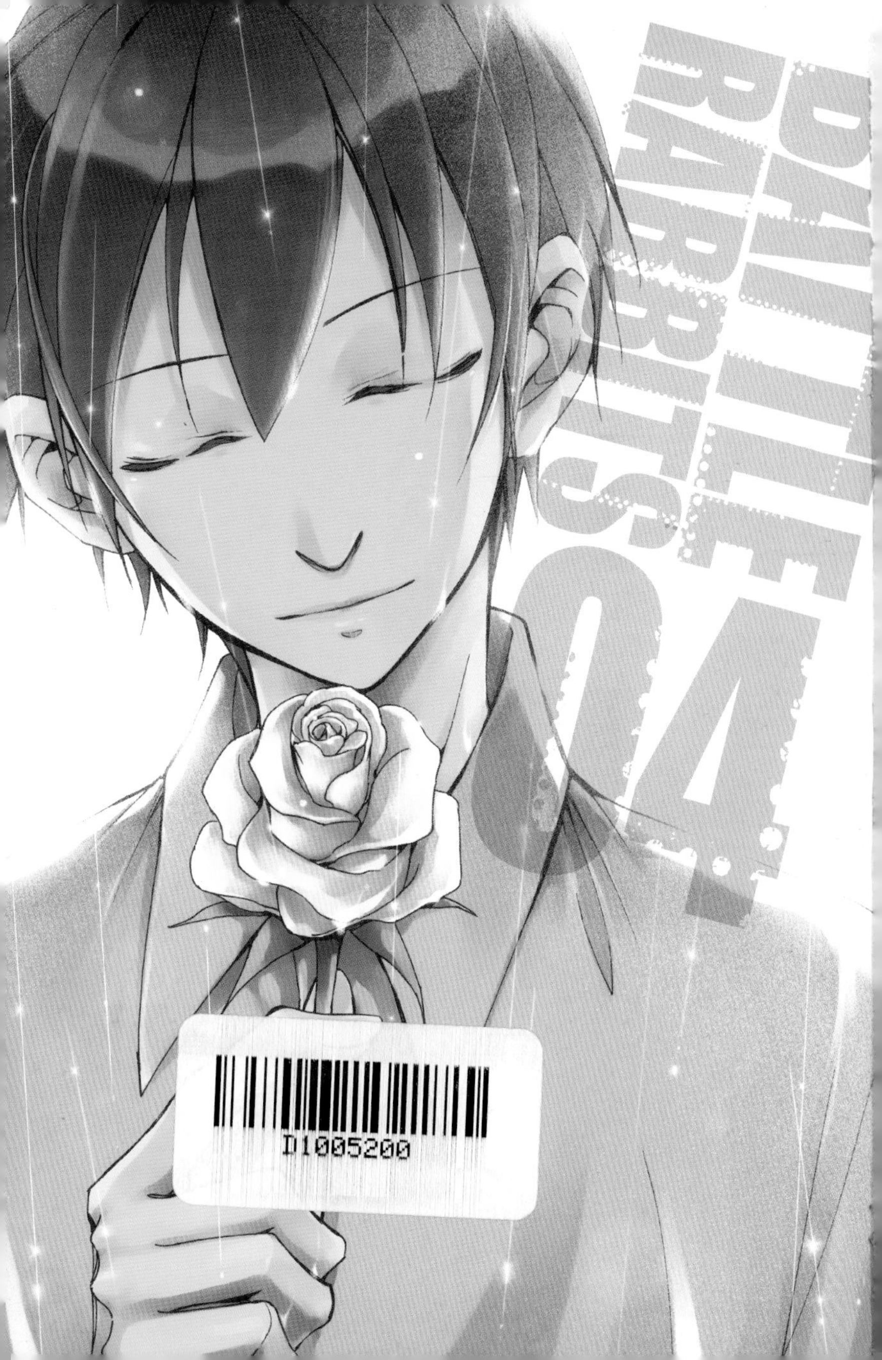
BATTLE RABBITS
04

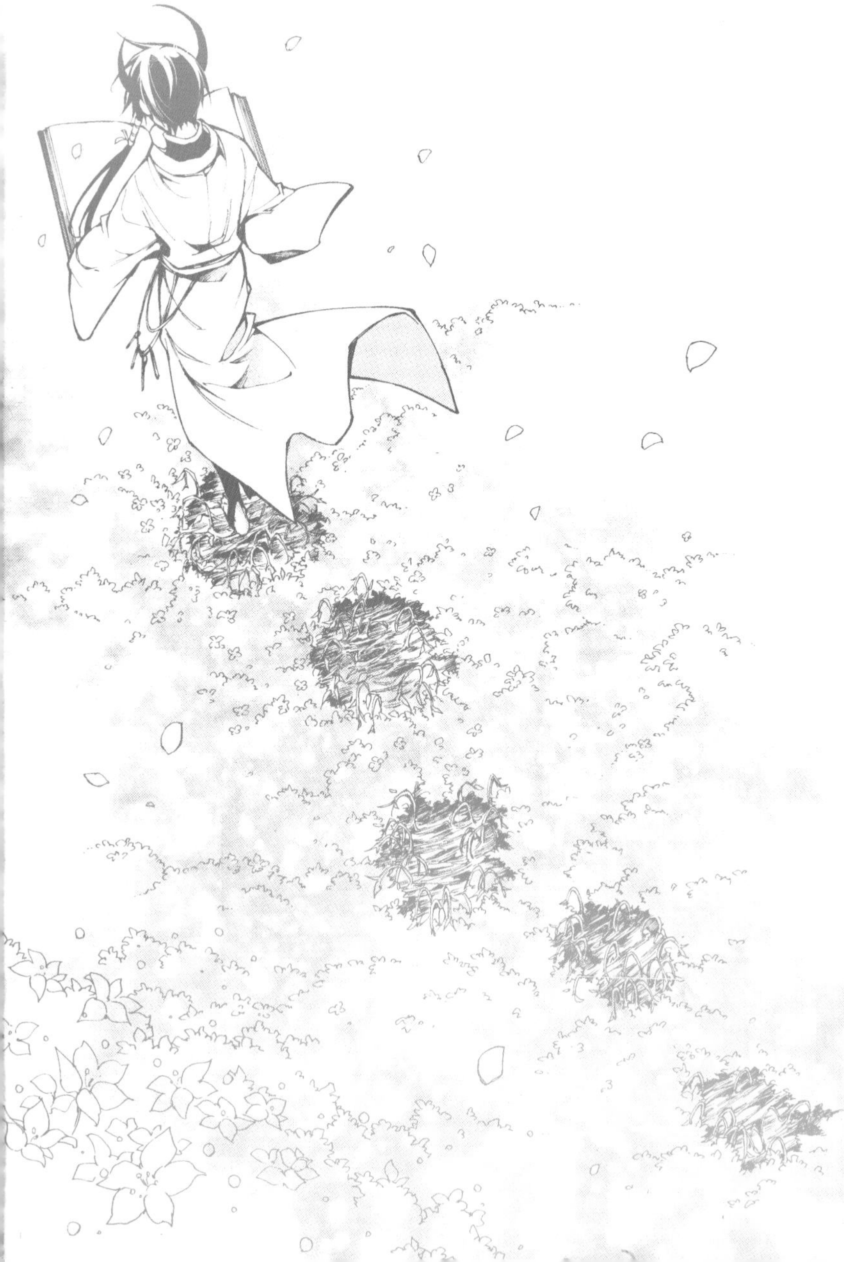

BATTLE RABBITS

バトラビッツ

04

BATTLE RABBITS CHARACTERS

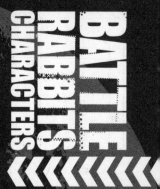

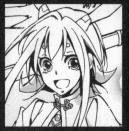

Domyoji Mao

A girl that was dispatched from the moon to protect the Earth. She adores Kaguya and serves as his bodyguard.

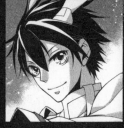

Kokuryuu Kaguya

A high school freshman who was raised without any knowledge that he was a citizen of the moon. He lost his family when he was very young.

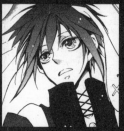

Kagura Nureha

A specialist with the ability to repair all of the body's cells by using an advanced medical technique.

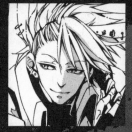

Kurogane Iori

A member of the elite Battle Rabbits force "Genou" with Hijiri, Izumi and Nureha. His abilities are unknown.

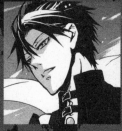

Takanomiya Hijiri

The Commander-in-Chief of the Earth Defense Force. He coerced Kaguya into joining their organization, and is responsible for his strict training.

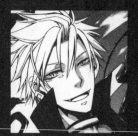

Shinigami (Death)

The otherworldly presence who manages the dead in the realm between worlds and keeps the balance of the world by collecting souls.

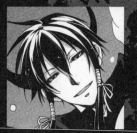

Rasetsu

An alien with the power to control ogres who feed on negative feelings. With this ability, he has destroyed many planets.

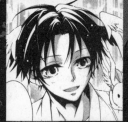

Teito

The leader of the first Genou, 1,200 years ago. Like Kaguya, he was able to absorb evil power into his Rabi-Jewel.

The Story So Far

After a human possessed by an ogre attacked Kaguya, he became aware of the Battle Rabbits--citizens of the moon who have protected the Earth and its people since ancient times. Kaguya overcame numerous challenges and became much stronger, when suddenly Rasetsu appeared before him. Rasetsu's purpose is to destroy the Earth. Just before disappearing into another dimension, however, he claims that the symbol on Kaguya's chest proves that Kaguya is just like him.

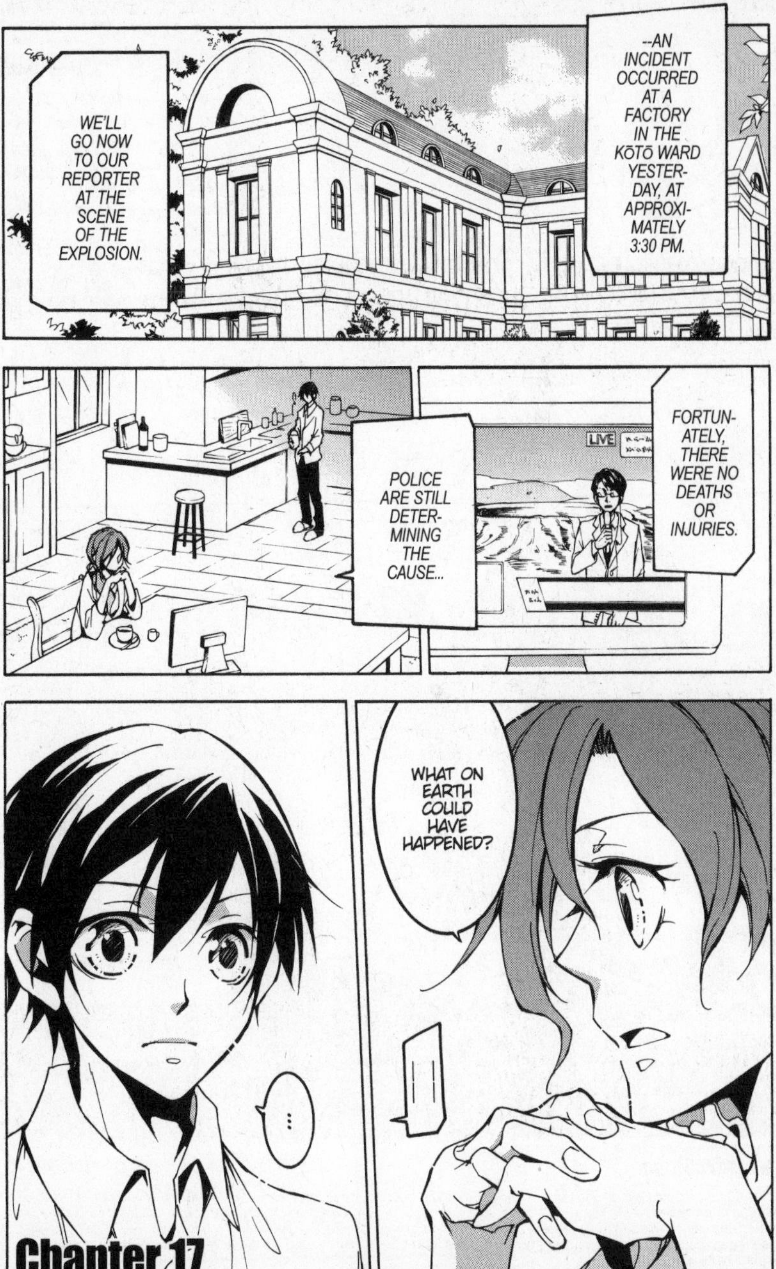
--AN INCIDENT OCCURRED AT A FACTORY IN THE KŌTŌ WARD YESTERDAY, AT APPROXIMATELY 3:30 PM.
WE'LL GO NOW TO OUR REPORTER AT THE SCENE OF THE EXPLOSION.
FORTUNATELY, THERE WERE NO DEATHS OR INJURIES.
LIVE
POLICE ARE STILL DETERMINING THE CAUSE...
WHAT ON EARTH COULD HAVE HAPPENED?
--
...
Chapter 17

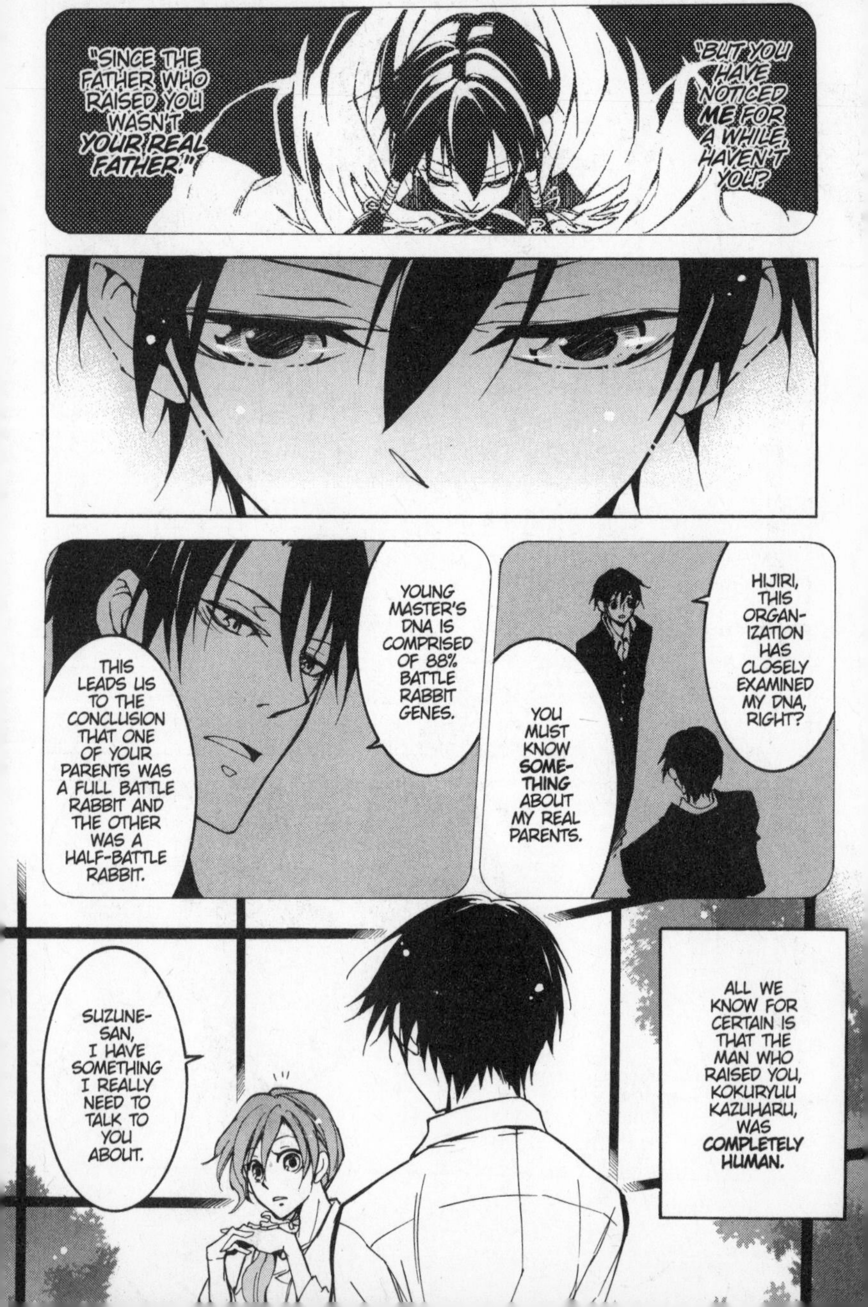
"BUT YOU HAVE NOTICED ME FOR A WHILE, HAVEN'T YOU?
SINCE THE FATHER WHO RAISED YOU WASN'T YOUR REAL FATHER."
HIJIRI, THIS ORGAN-IZATION HAS CLOSELY EXAMINED MY DNA, RIGHT?
YOU MUST KNOW SOMETHING ABOUT MY REAL PARENTS.
YOUNG MASTER'S DNA IS COMPRISED OF 88% BATTLE RABBIT GENES.
THIS LEADS US TO THE CONCLUSION THAT ONE OF YOUR PARENTS WAS A FULL BATTLE RABBIT AND THE OTHER WAS A HALF-BATTLE RABBIT.
ALL WE KNOW FOR CERTAIN IS THAT THE MAN WHO RAISED YOU, KOKURYUU KAZUHARU, WAS COMPLETELY HUMAN.
SUZUNE-SAN, I HAVE SOMETHING I REALLY NEED TO TALK TO YOU ABOUT.

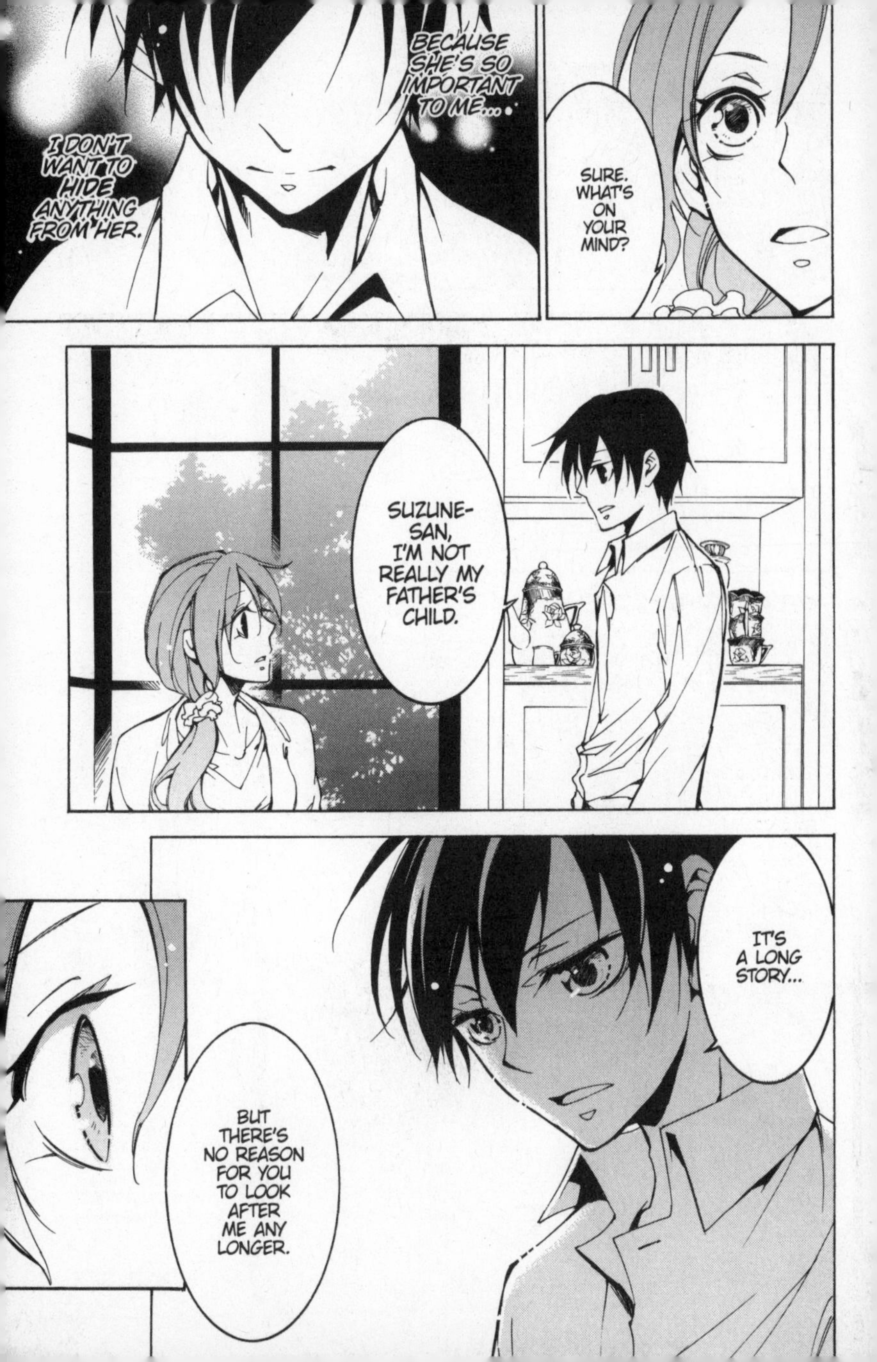
SURE. WHAT'S ON YOUR MIND?
BECAUSE SHE'S SO IMPORTANT TO ME...
I DON'T WANT TO HIDE ANYTHING FROM HER.
SUZUNE-SAN, I'M NOT REALLY MY FATHER'S CHILD.
IT'S A LONG STORY...
BUT THERE'S NO REASON FOR YOU TO LOOK AFTER ME ANY LONGER.

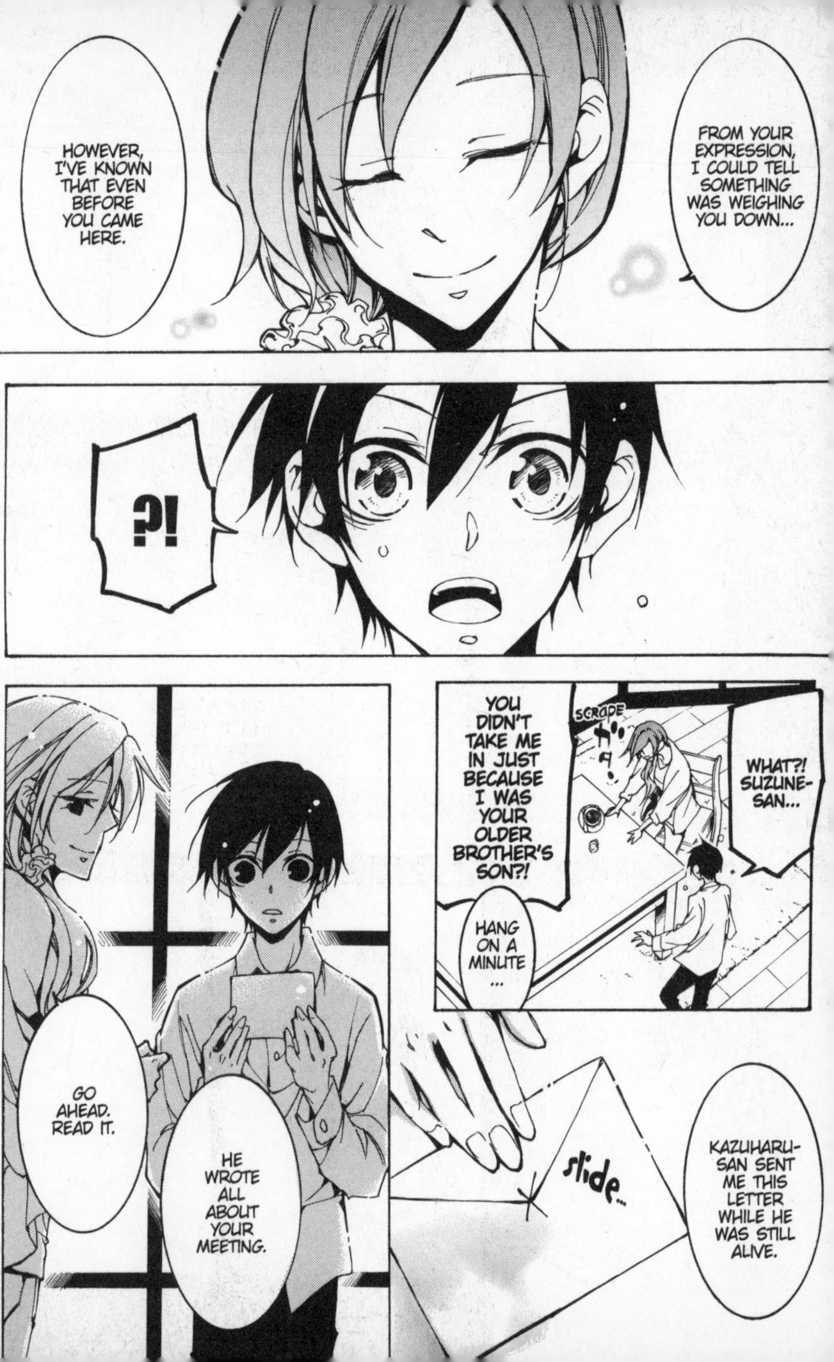
FROM YOUR EXPRESSION, I COULD TELL SOMETHING WAS WEIGHING YOU DOWN...
HOWEVER, I'VE KNOWN THAT EVEN BEFORE YOU CAME HERE.
?!
WHAT?! SUZUNE-SAN...
SCRAPE
YOU DIDN'T TAKE ME IN JUST BECAUSE I WAS YOUR OLDER BROTHER'S SON?!
HANG ON A MINUTE ...
KAZUHARU-SAN SENT ME THIS LETTER WHILE HE WAS STILL ALIVE.
slide...
HE WROTE ALL ABOUT YOUR MEETING.
GO AHEAD. READ IT.

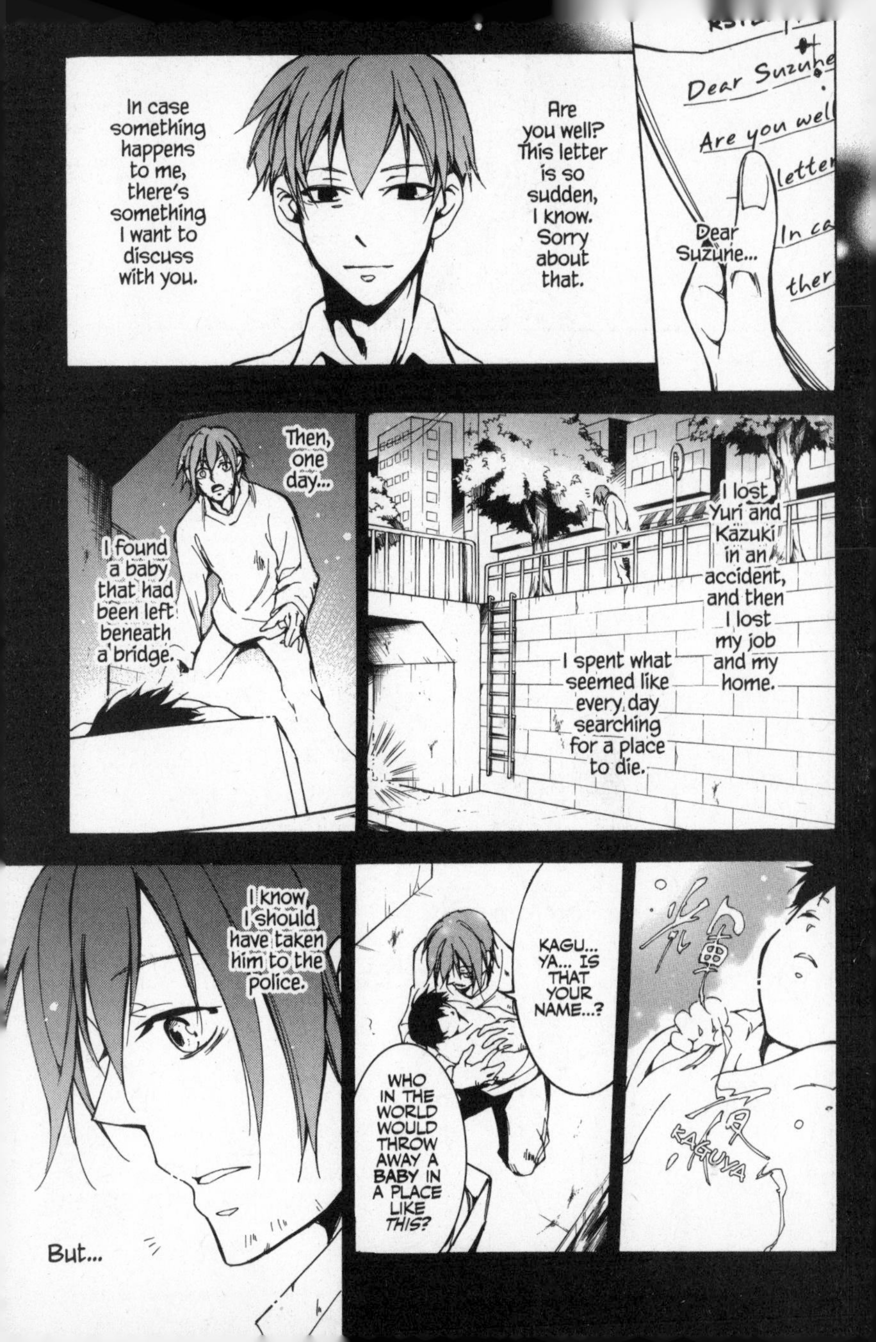
Dear Suzune...
Are you well? This letter is so sudden, I know. Sorry about that.
In case something happens to me, there's something I want to discuss with you.
I lost Yuri and Kazuki in an accident, and then I lost my job and my home.
I spent what seemed like every day searching for a place to die.
Then, one day...
I found a baby that had been left beneath a bridge.
KAGUYA
KAGU... YA... IS THAT YOUR NAME...?
WHO IN THE WORLD WOULD THROW AWAY A BABY IN A PLACE LIKE *THIS?*
I know I should have taken him to the police.
But...

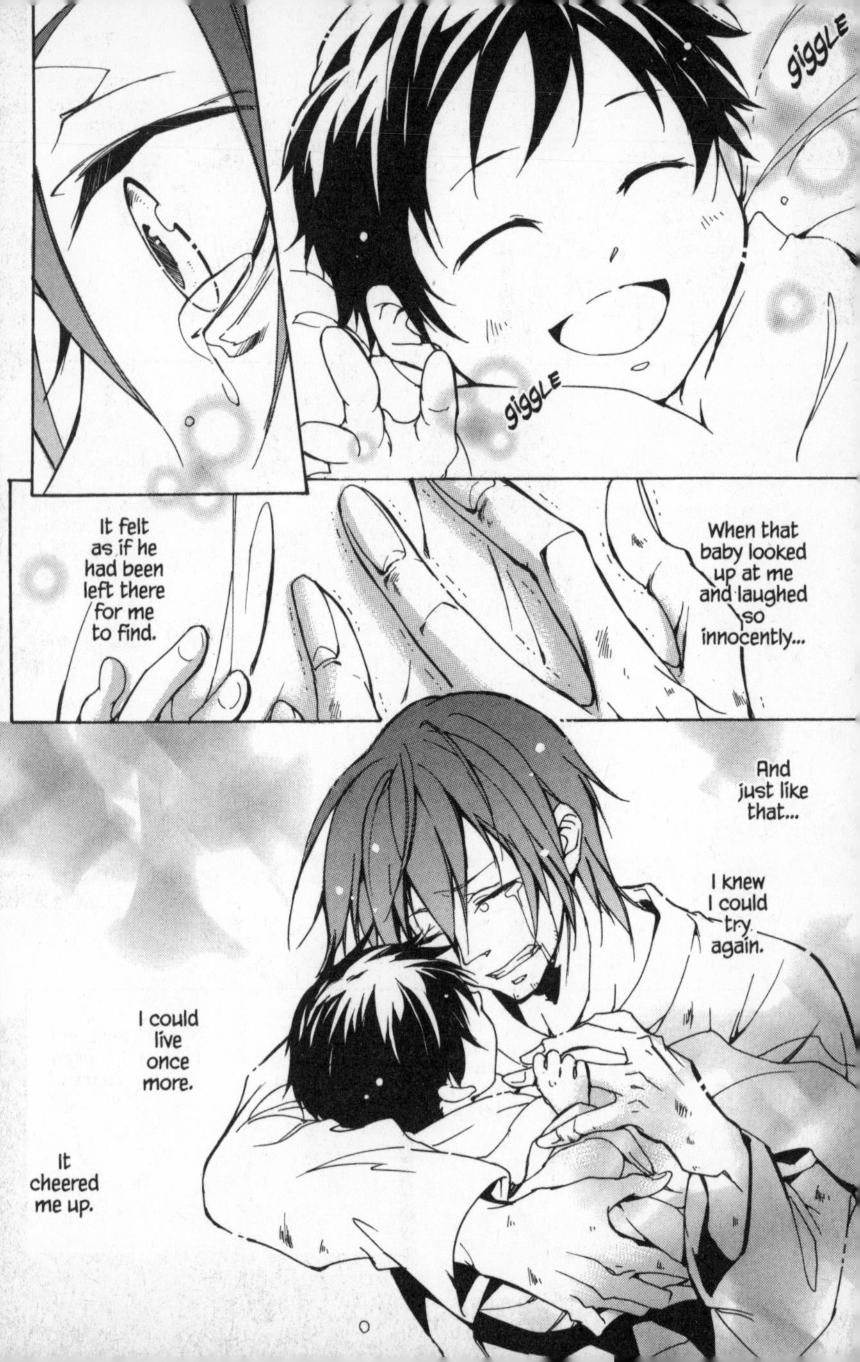
giggle
giggle
When that baby looked up at me and laughed so innocently...
It felt as if he had been left there for me to find.
And just like that...
I knew I could try again.
I could live once more.
It cheered me up.

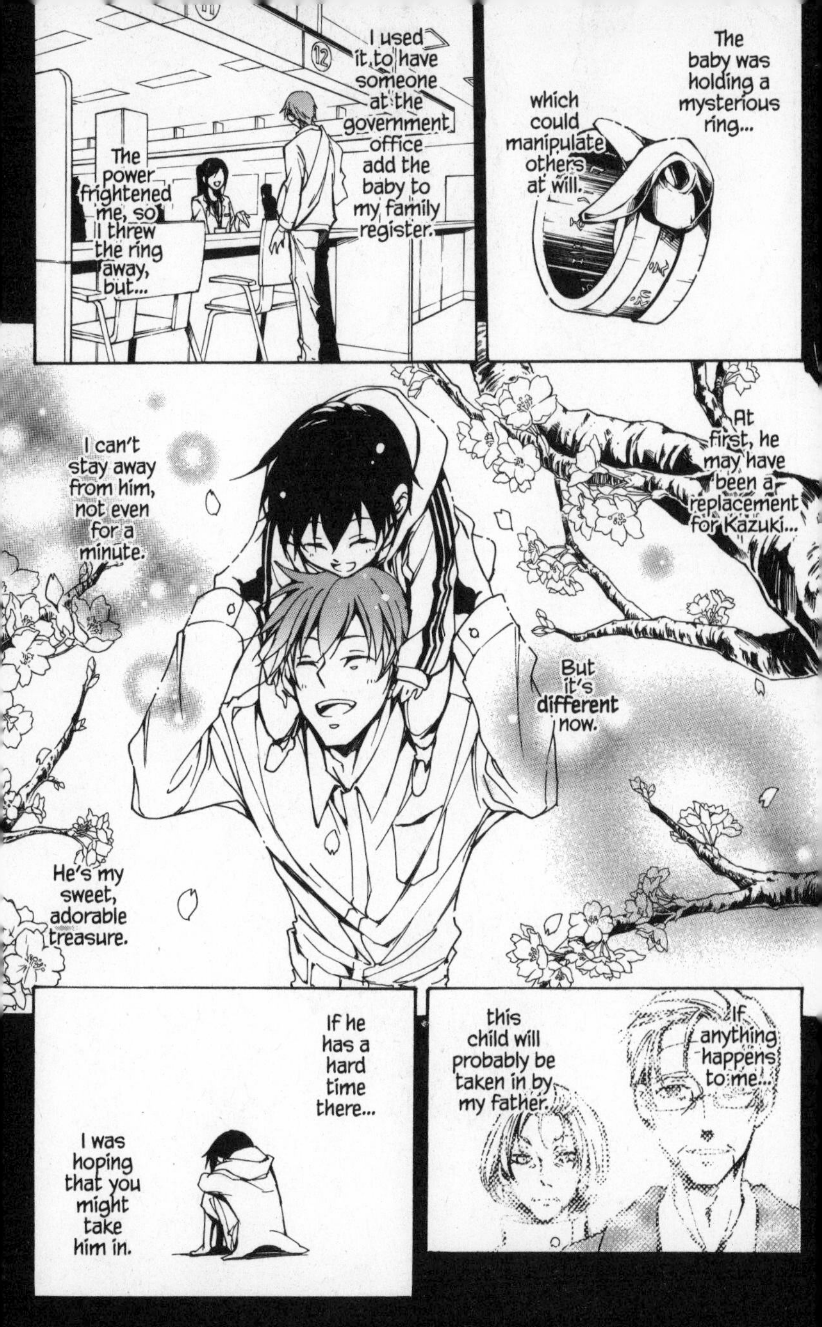
The baby was holding a mysterious ring...
which could manipulate others at will.
I used it to have someone at the government office add the baby to my family register.
The power frightened me, so I threw the ring away, but...
At first, he may have been a replacement for Kazuki...
I can't stay away from him, not even for a minute.
But it's different now.
He's my sweet, adorable treasure.
If anything happens to me...
this child will probably be taken in by my father.
If he has a hard time there...
I was hoping that you might take him in.

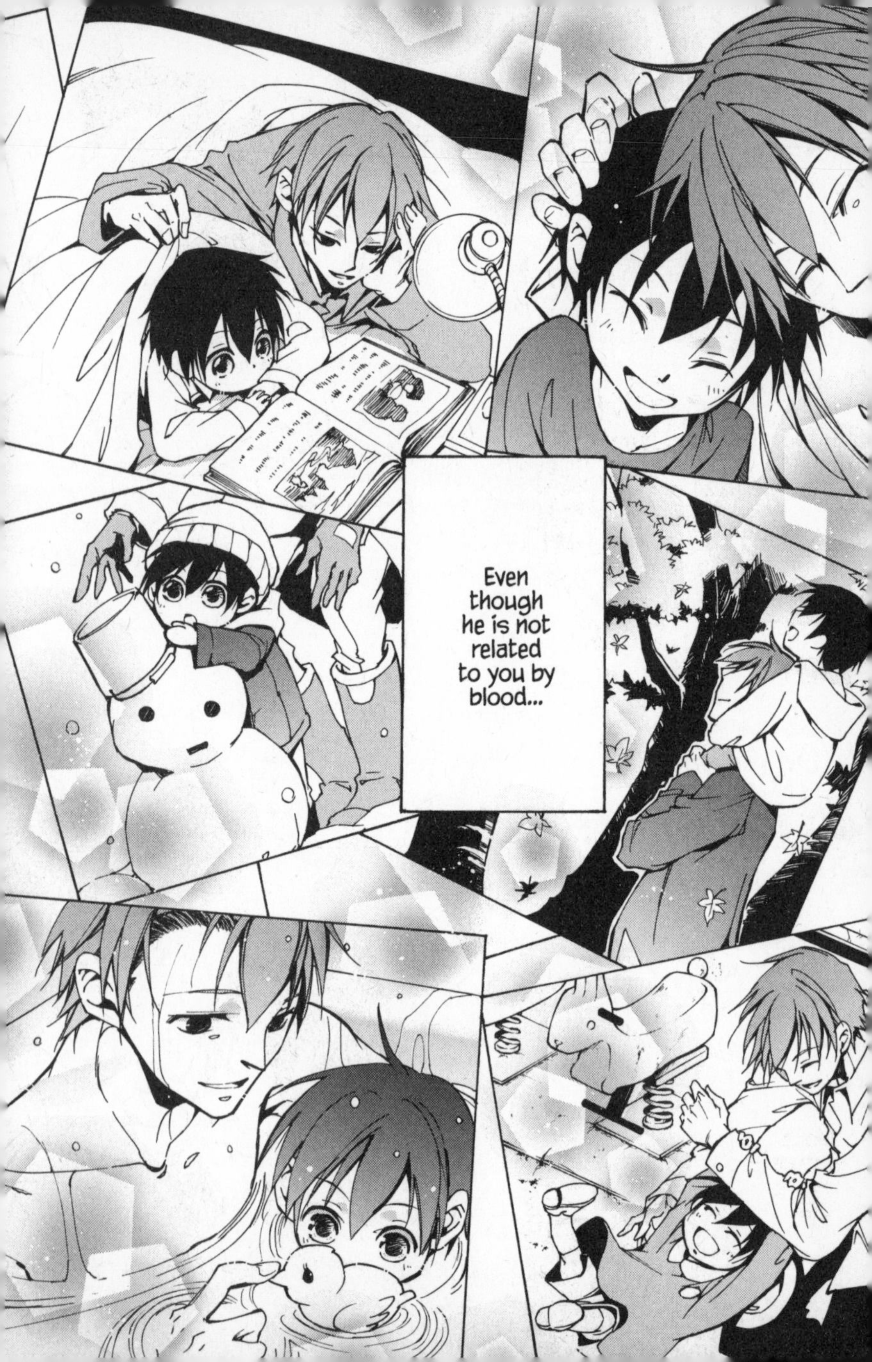
Even though he is not related to you by blood...

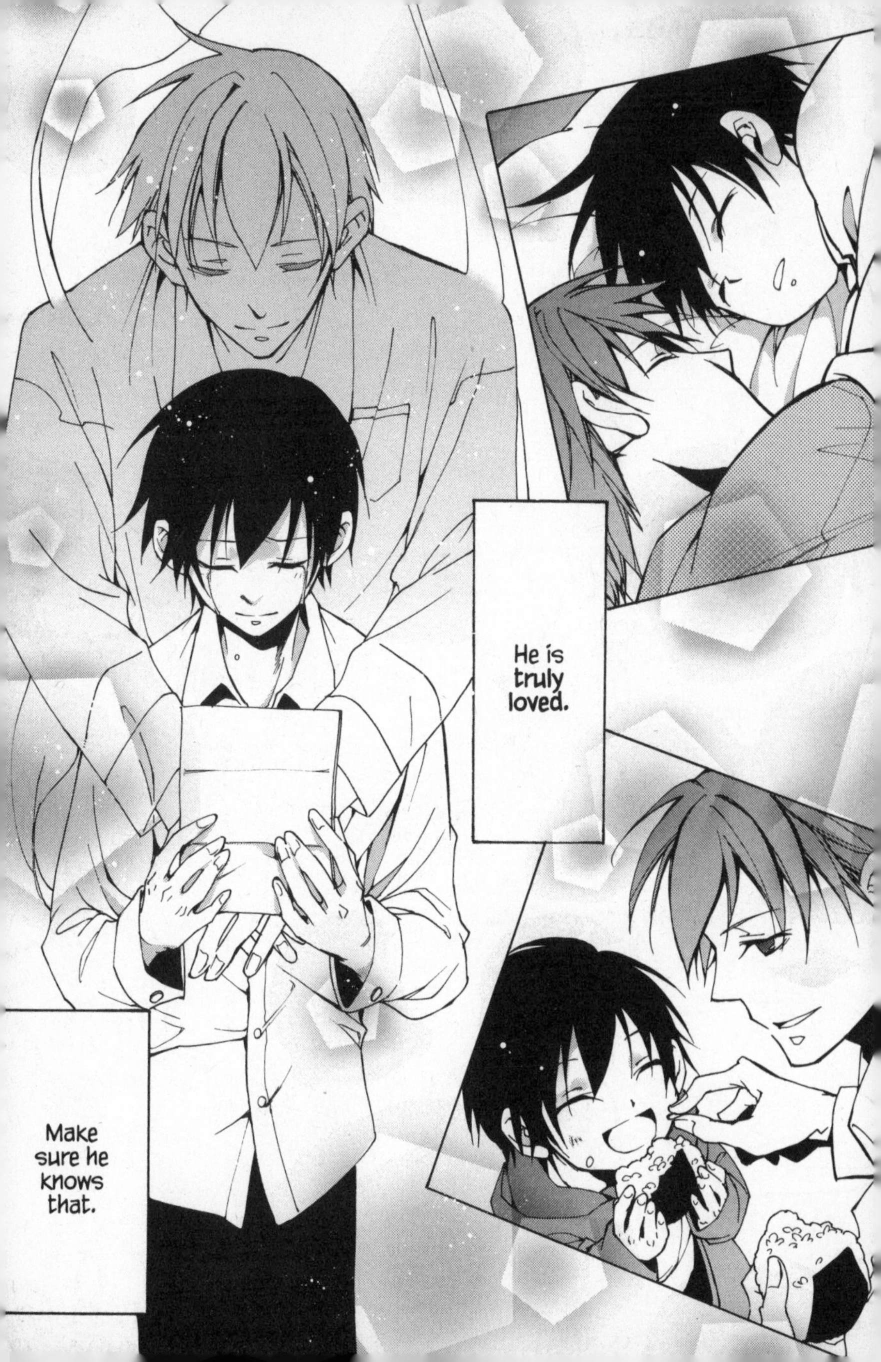
He is truly loved.
Make sure he knows that.

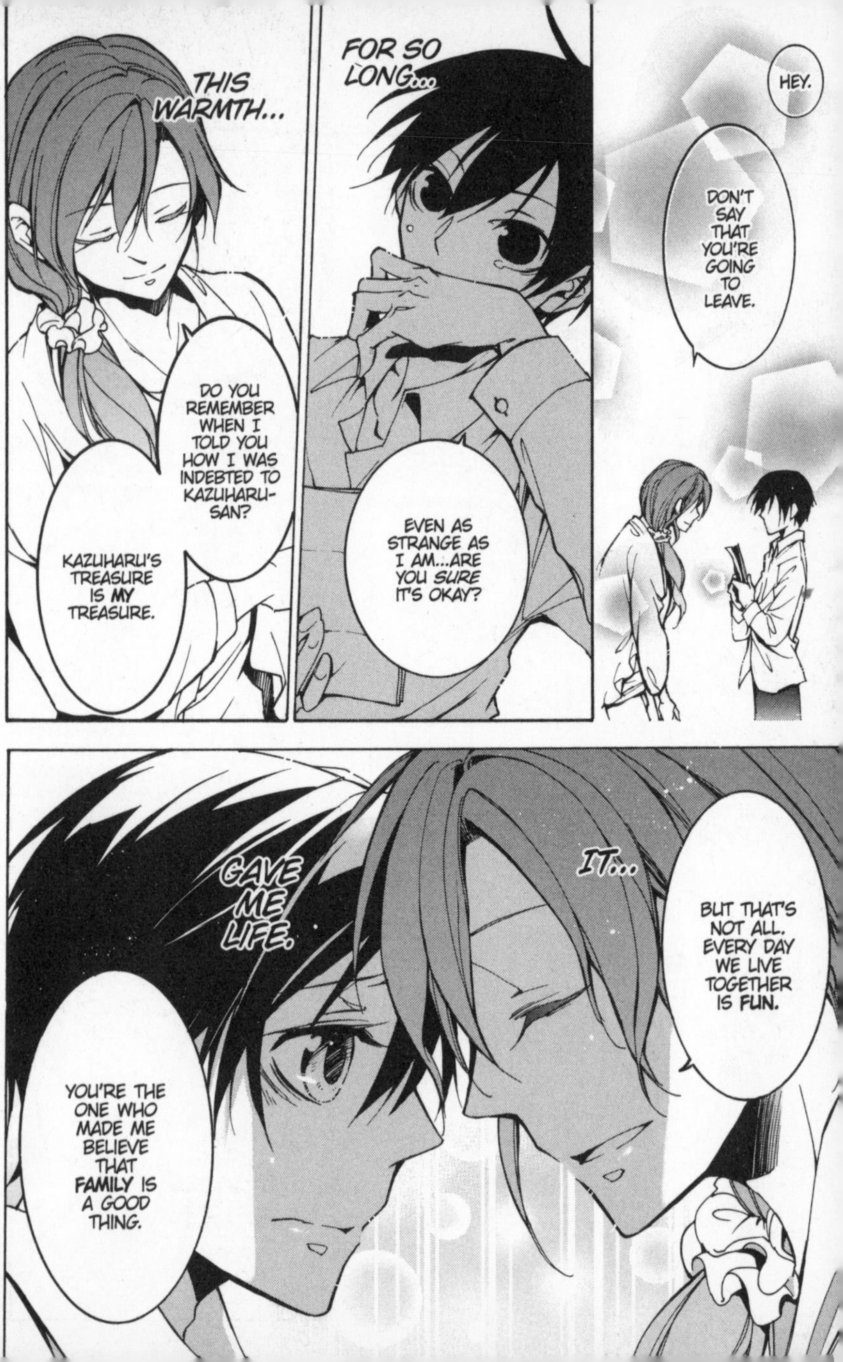
HEY.
DON'T SAY THAT YOU'RE GOING TO LEAVE.
FOR SO LONG...
EVEN AS STRANGE AS I AM...ARE YOU *SURE* IT'S OKAY?
THIS WARMTH...
DO YOU REMEMBER WHEN I TOLD YOU HOW I WAS INDEBTED TO KAZUHARU-SAN?
KAZUHARU'S TREASURE IS **MY** TREASURE.
BUT THAT'S NOT ALL. EVERY DAY WE LIVE TOGETHER IS **FUN**.
IT...
GAVE ME LIFE.
YOU'RE THE ONE WHO MADE ME BELIEVE THAT **FAMILY** IS A GOOD THING.

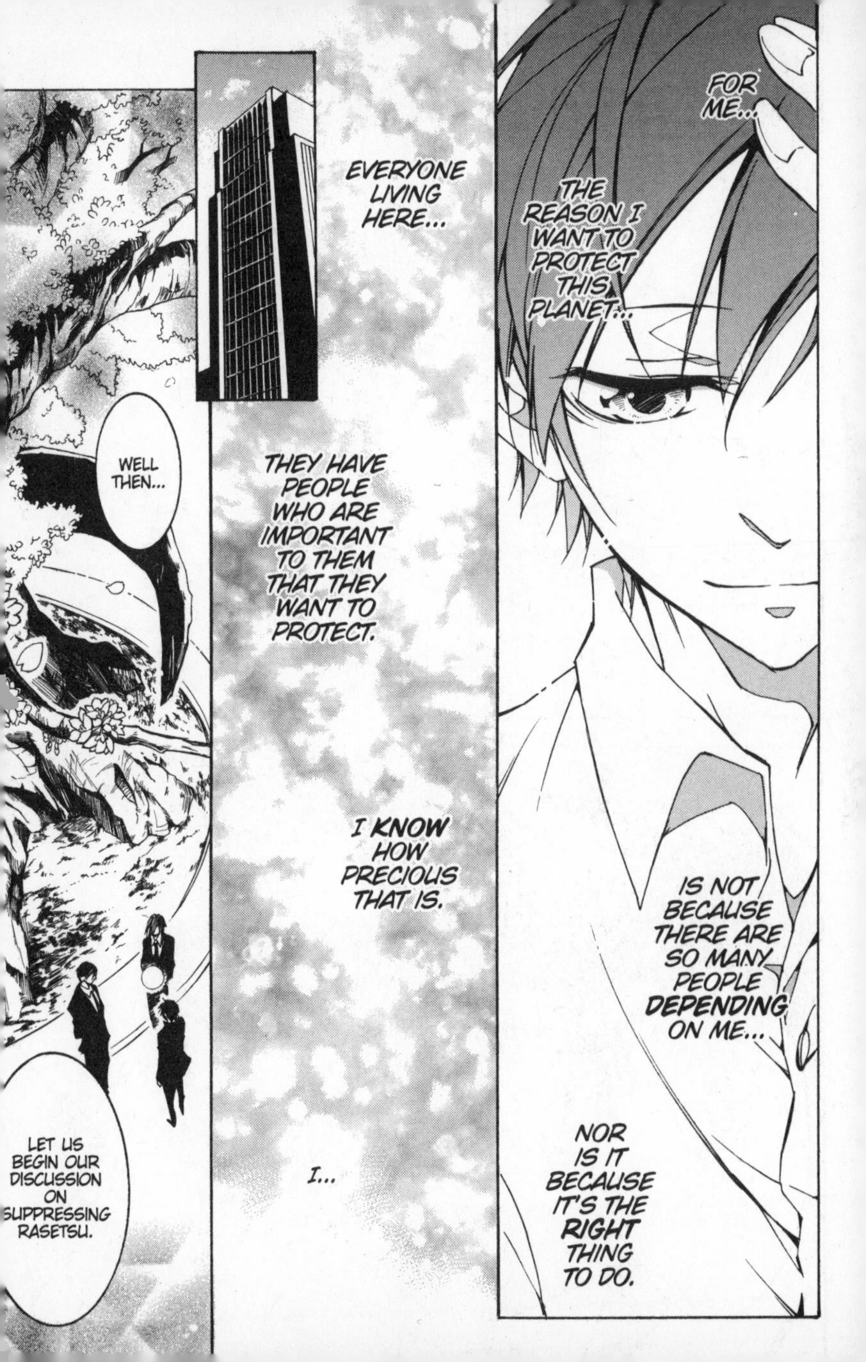
FOR ME...
THE REASON I WANT TO PROTECT THIS PLANET...
IS NOT BECAUSE THERE ARE SO MANY PEOPLE DEPENDING ON ME...
NOR IS IT BECAUSE IT'S THE RIGHT THING TO DO.
EVERYONE LIVING HERE...
THEY HAVE PEOPLE WHO ARE IMPORTANT TO THEM THAT THEY WANT TO PROTECT.
I KNOW HOW PRECIOUS THAT IS.
I...
WELL THEN...
LET US BEGIN OUR DISCUSSION ON SUPPRESSING RASETSU.

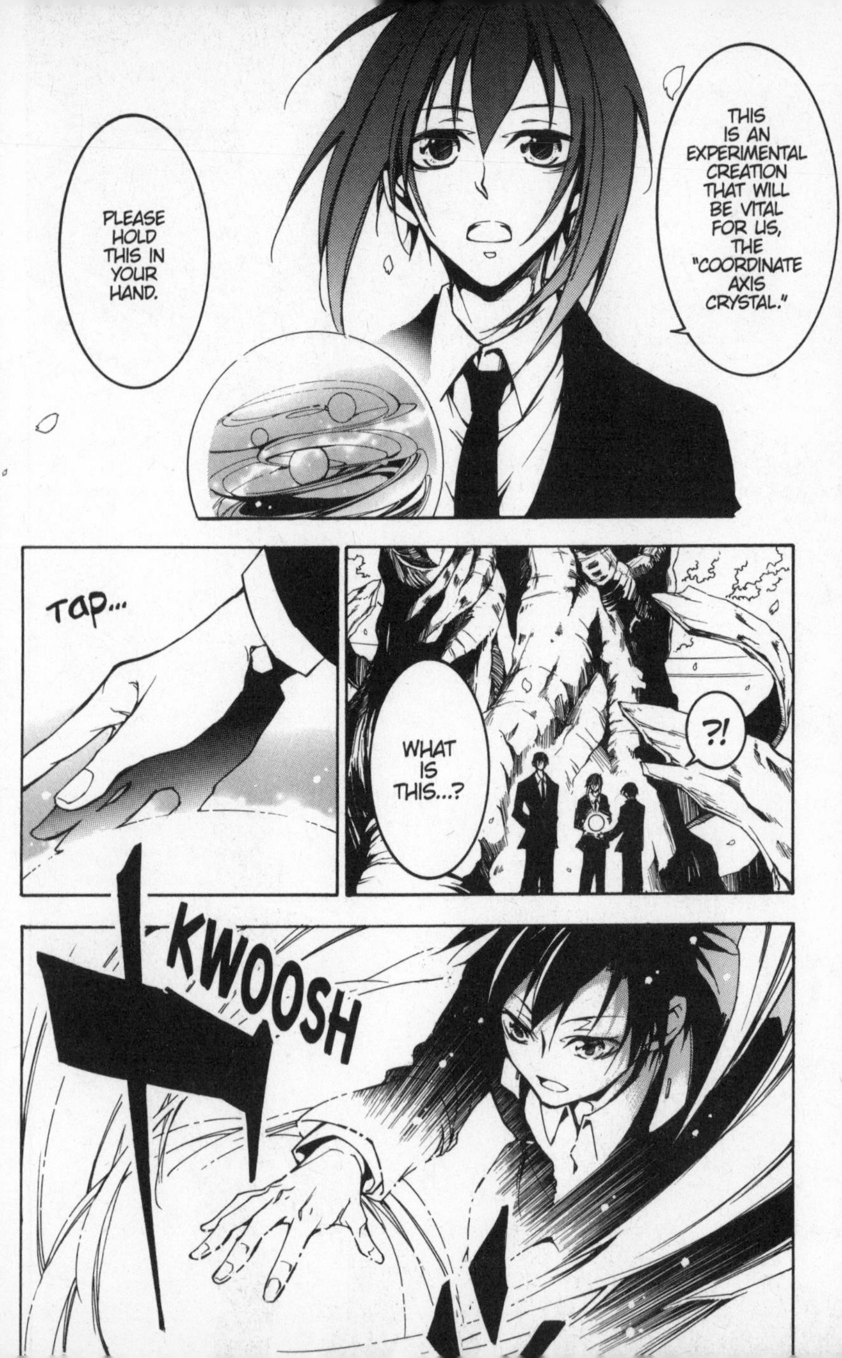
THIS IS AN EXPERIMENTAL CREATION THAT WILL BE VITAL FOR US, THE "COORDINATE AXIS CRYSTAL."
PLEASE HOLD THIS IN YOUR HAND.
?!
WHAT IS THIS...?
tap...
KWOOSH

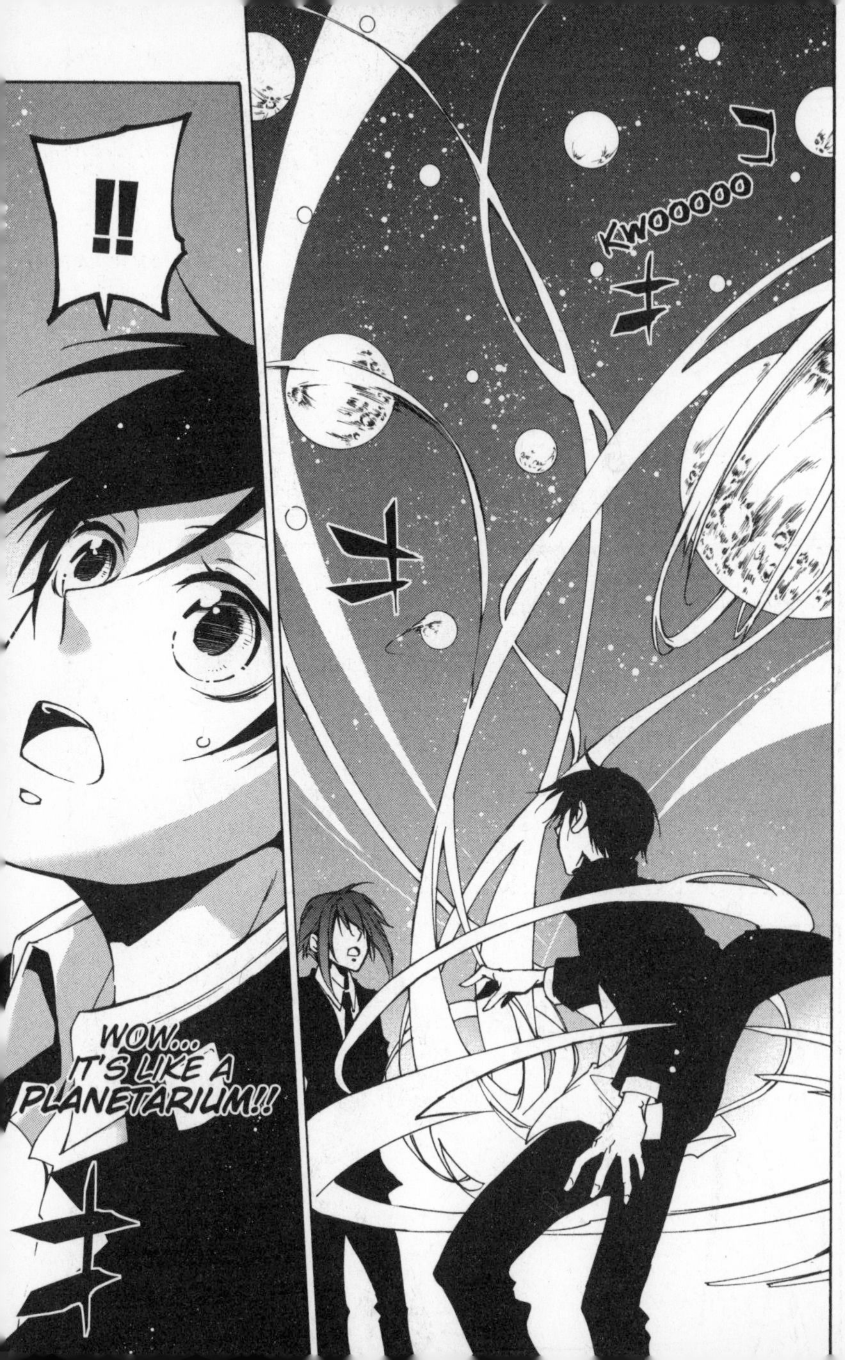
KWOOOOO
!!
WOW... IT'S LIKE A PLANETARIUM!!

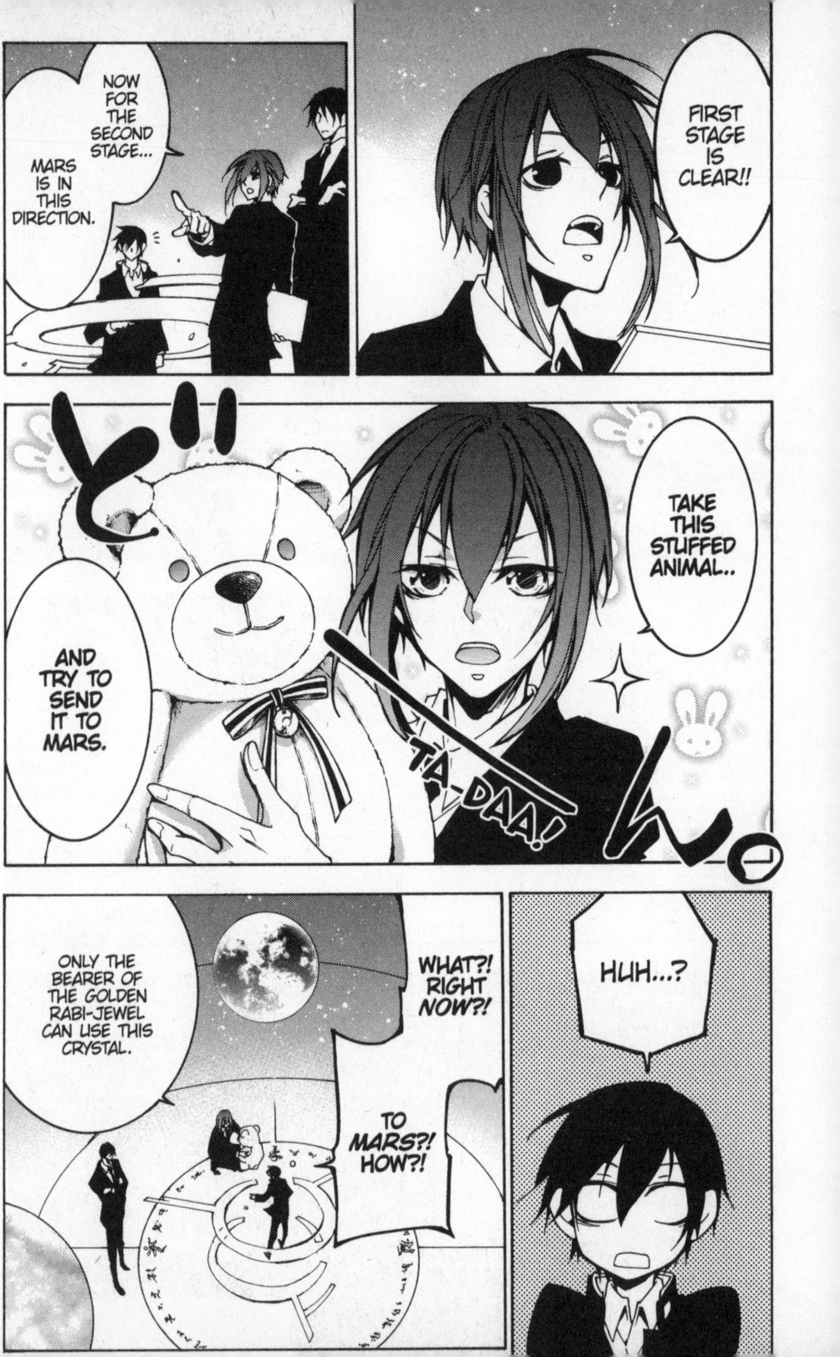
FIRST STAGE IS CLEAR!!
NOW FOR THE SECOND STAGE...
MARS IS IN THIS DIRECTION.
TAKE THIS STUFFED ANIMAL..
AND TRY TO SEND IT TO MARS.
TA-DAA!
HUH...?
WHAT?! RIGHT NOW?!
TO MARS?! HOW?!
ONLY THE BEARER OF THE GOLDEN RABI-JEWEL CAN USE THIS CRYSTAL.

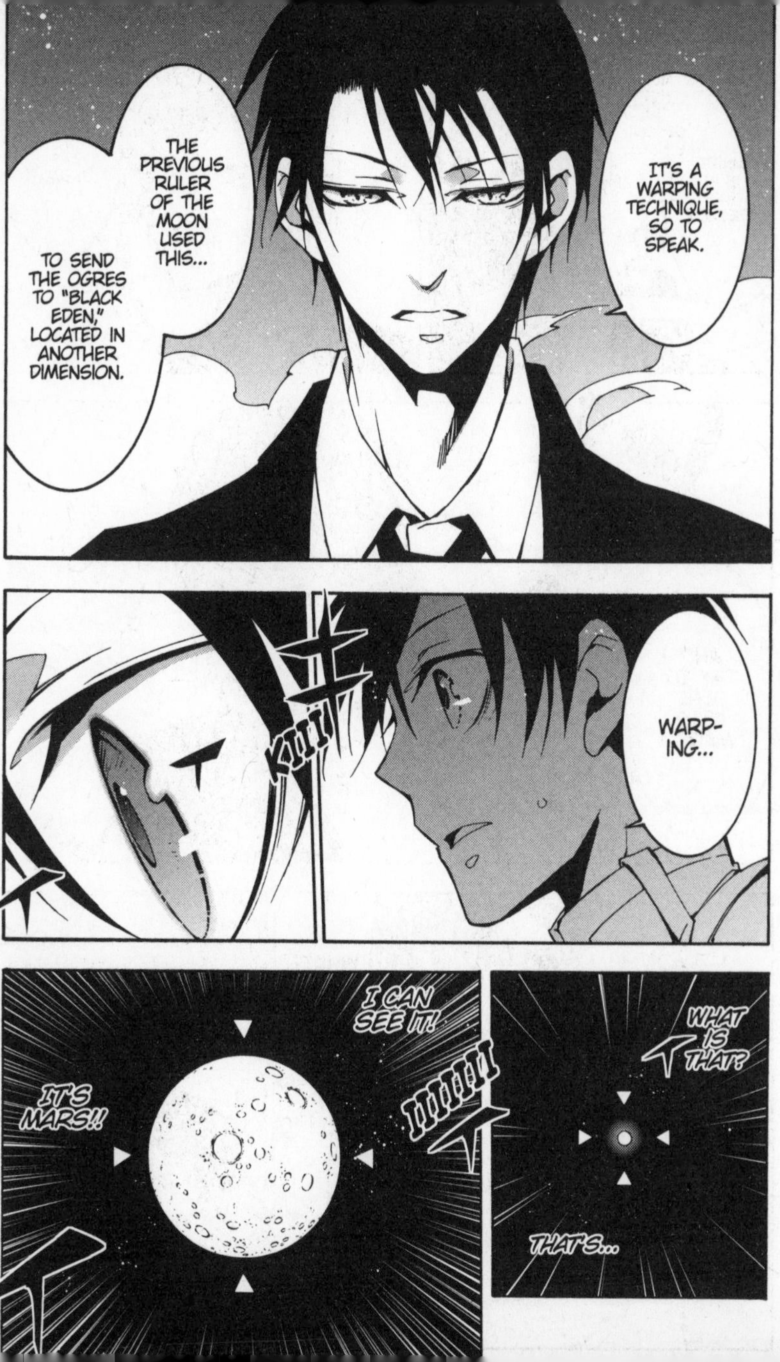
IT'S A WARPING TECHNIQUE, SO TO SPEAK.
THE PREVIOUS RULER OF THE MOON USED THIS...
TO SEND THE OGRES TO "BLACK EDEN," LOCATED IN ANOTHER DIMENSION.
WARP-ING...
KIIII
WHAT IS THAT?
THAT'S...
I CAN SEE IT!
IIIIIIII
IT'S MARS!!

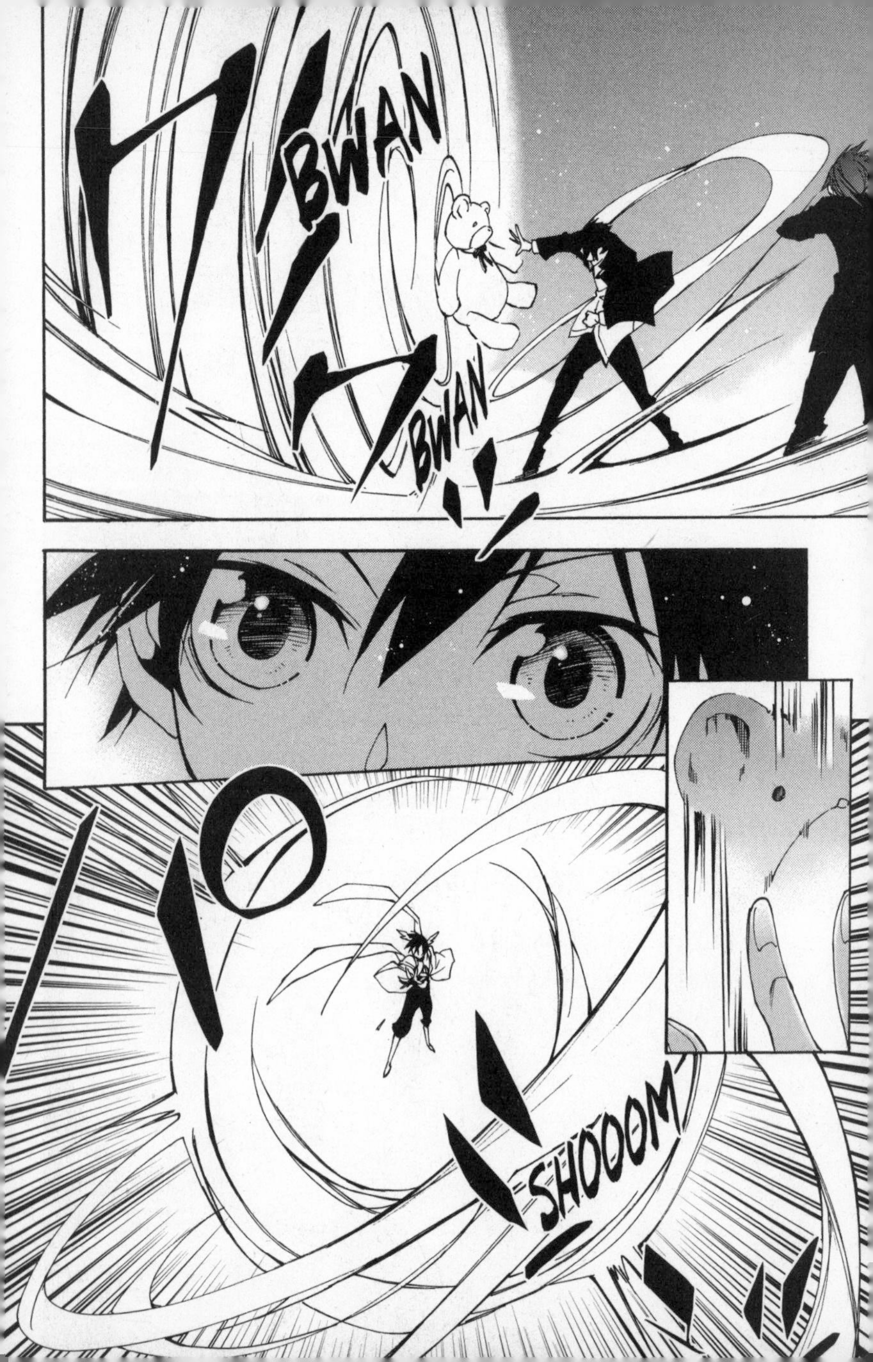
BWAN
BWAN
SHOOOM

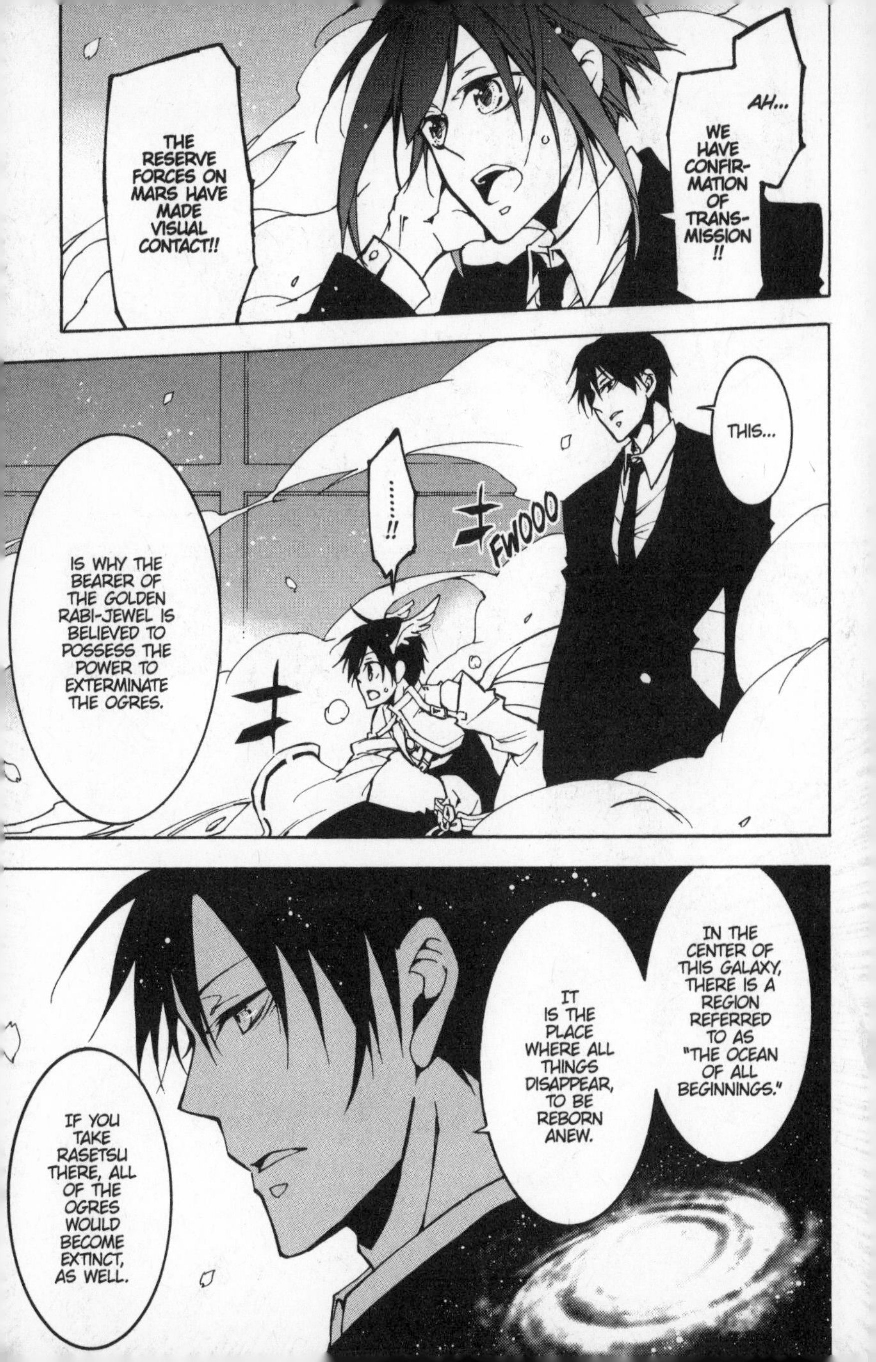
AH... WE HAVE CONFIRMATION OF TRANSMISSION!!
THE RESERVE FORCES ON MARS HAVE MADE VISUAL CONTACT!!
THIS...
......!!
FWOOO
IS WHY THE BEARER OF THE GOLDEN RABI-JEWEL IS BELIEVED TO POSSESS THE POWER TO EXTERMINATE THE OGRES.
IN THE CENTER OF THIS GALAXY, THERE IS A REGION REFERRED TO AS "THE OCEAN OF ALL BEGINNINGS."
IT IS THE PLACE WHERE ALL THINGS DISAPPEAR, TO BE REBORN ANEW.
IF YOU TAKE RASETSU THERE, ALL OF THE OGRES WOULD BECOME EXTINCT, AS WELL.

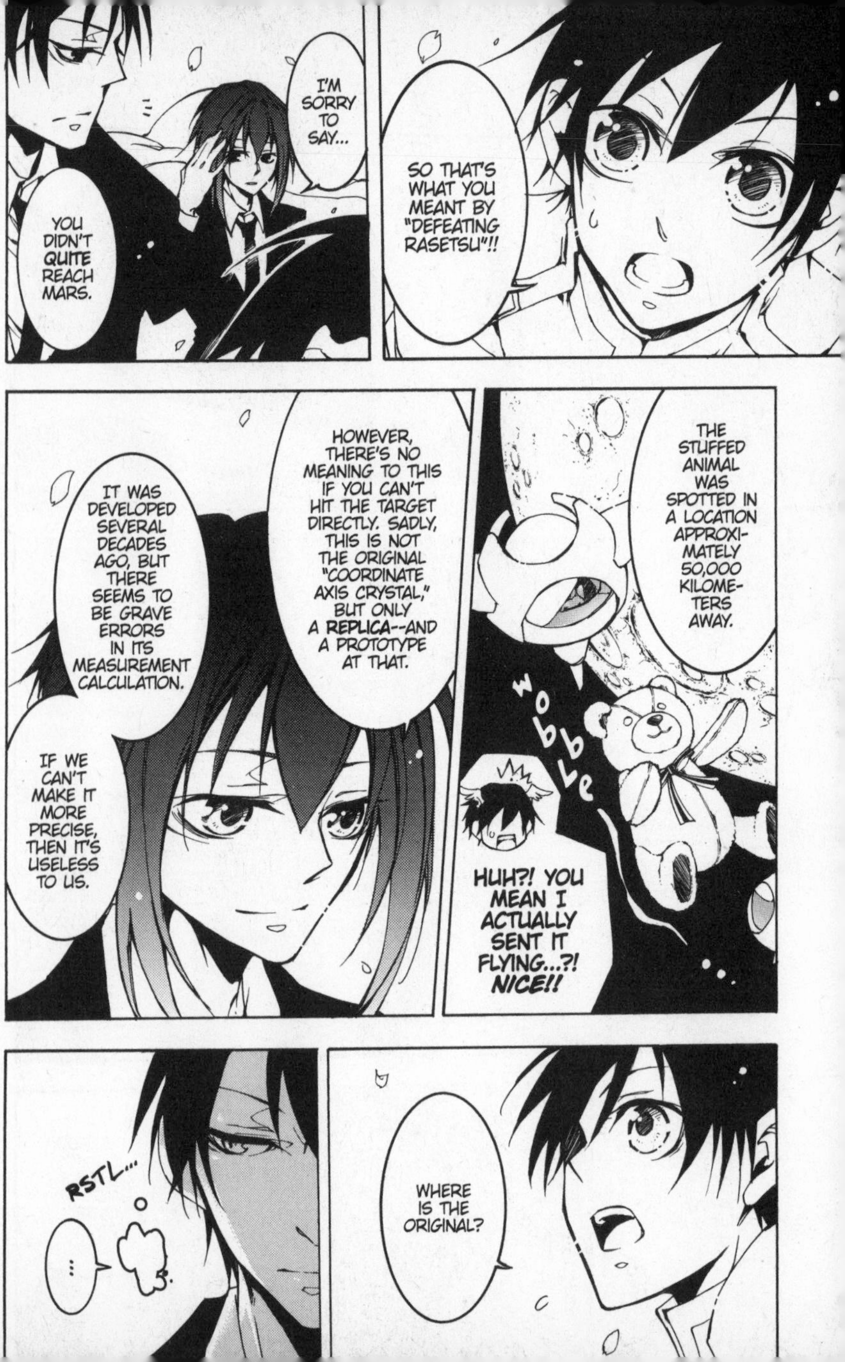
SO THAT'S WHAT YOU MEANT BY "DEFEATING RASETSU"!!
I'M SORRY TO SAY...
YOU DIDN'T QUITE REACH MARS.
THE STUFFED ANIMAL WAS SPOTTED IN A LOCATION APPROXI-MATELY 50,000 KILOME-TERS AWAY.
wobble
HUH?! YOU MEAN I ACTUALLY SENT IT FLYING...?! NICE!!
HOWEVER, THERE'S NO MEANING TO THIS IF YOU CAN'T HIT THE TARGET DIRECTLY. SADLY, THIS IS NOT THE ORIGINAL "COORDINATE AXIS CRYSTAL," BUT ONLY A REPLICA--AND A PROTOTYPE AT THAT.
IT WAS DEVELOPED SEVERAL DECADES AGO, BUT THERE SEEMS TO BE GRAVE ERRORS IN ITS MEASUREMENT CALCULATION.
IF WE CAN'T MAKE IT MORE PRECISE, THEN IT'S USELESS TO US.
WHERE IS THE ORIGINAL?
RSTL...
...

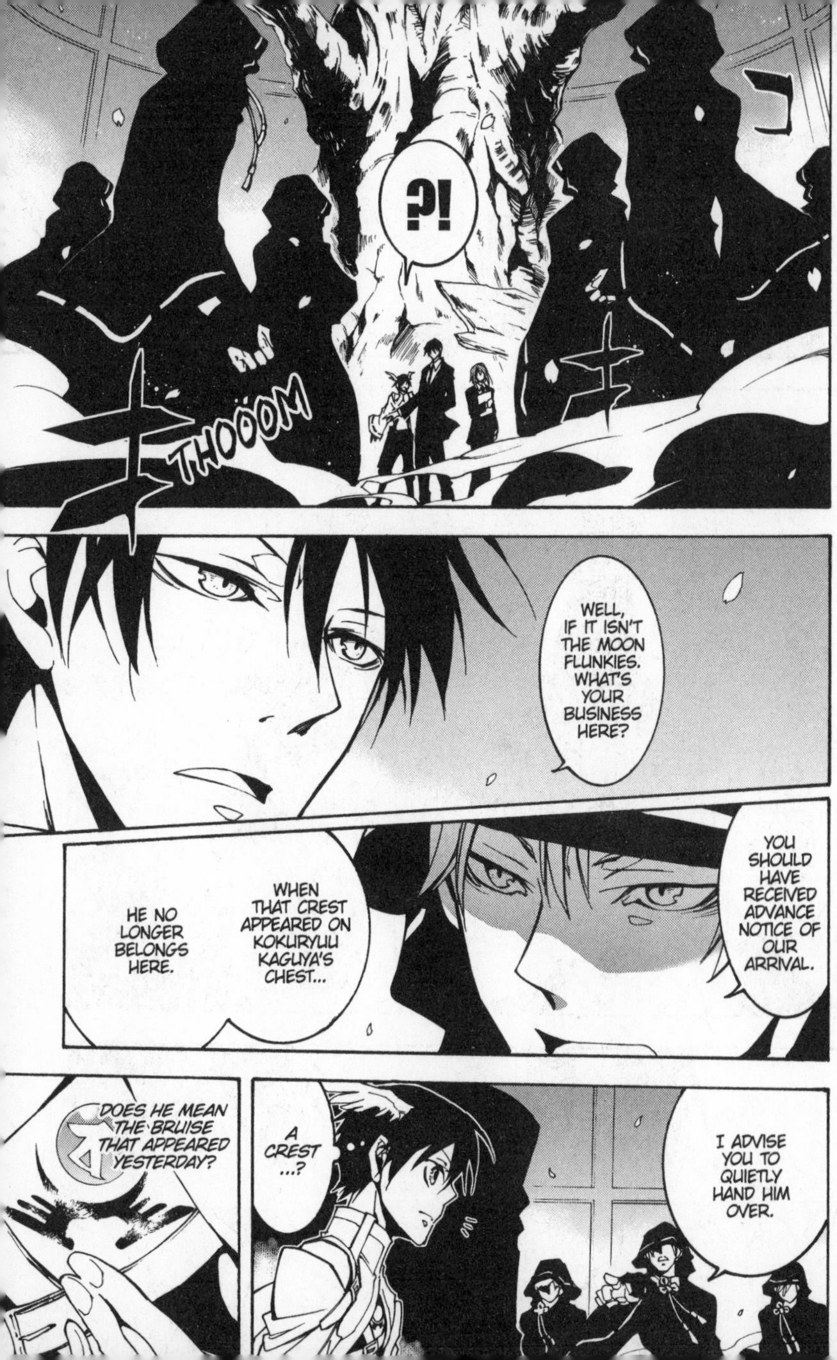
?!
THOOOM
WELL, IF IT ISN'T THE MOON FLUNKIES. WHAT'S YOUR BUSINESS HERE?
YOU SHOULD HAVE RECEIVED ADVANCE NOTICE OF OUR ARRIVAL.
WHEN THAT CREST APPEARED ON KOKURYUU KAGUYA'S CHEST...
HE NO LONGER BELONGS HERE.
I ADVISE YOU TO QUIETLY HAND HIM OVER.
A CREST ...?
DOES HE MEAN THE BRUISE THAT APPEARED YESTERDAY?

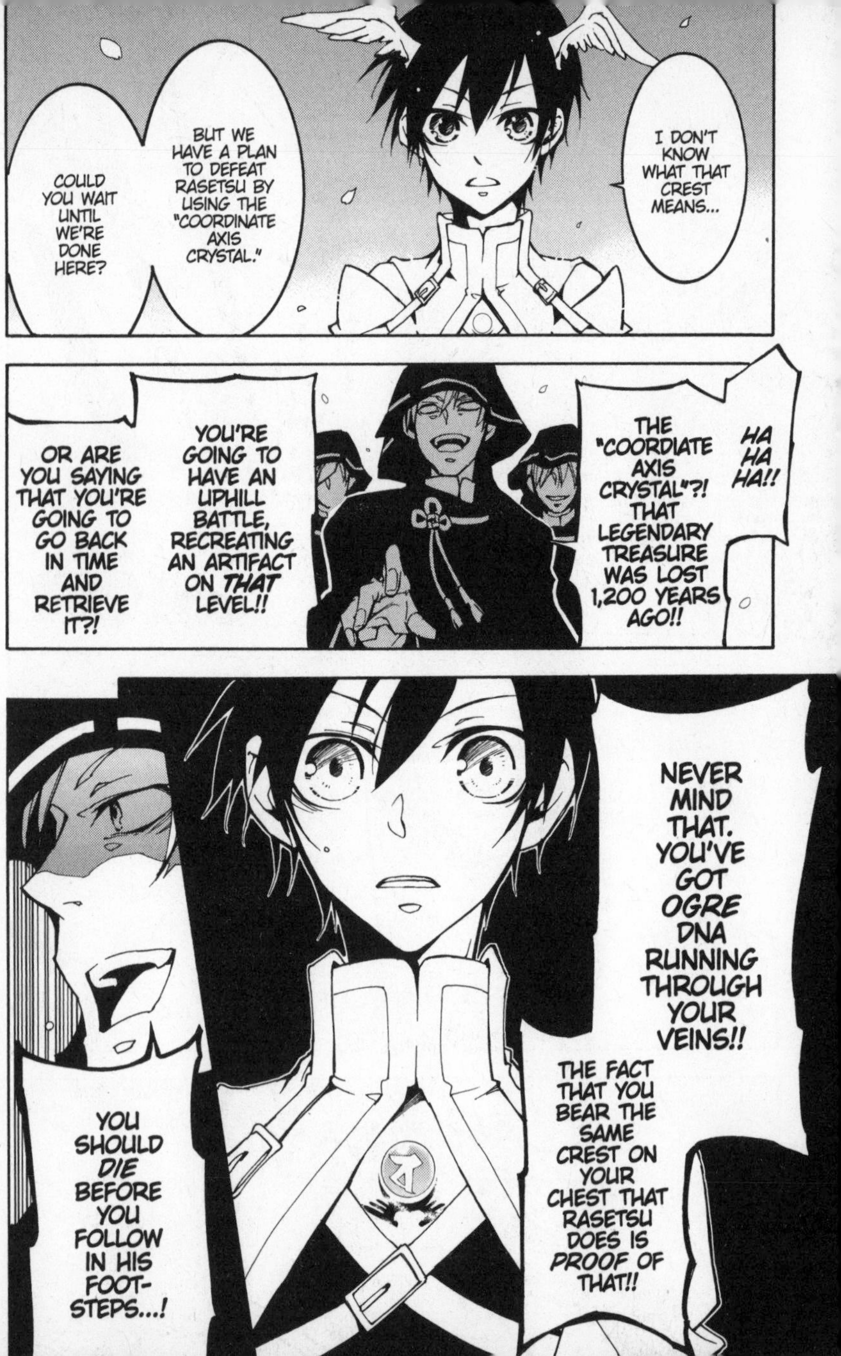
I DON'T KNOW WHAT THAT CREST MEANS...
BUT WE HAVE A PLAN TO DEFEAT RASETSU BY USING THE "COORDINATE AXIS CRYSTAL."
COULD YOU WAIT UNTIL WE'RE DONE HERE?
HA HA HA!!
THE "COORDIATE AXIS CRYSTAL"?! THAT LEGENDARY TREASURE WAS LOST 1,200 YEARS AGO!!
YOU'RE GOING TO HAVE AN UPHILL BATTLE, RECREATING AN ARTIFACT ON *THAT* LEVEL!!
OR ARE YOU SAYING THAT YOU'RE GOING TO GO BACK IN TIME AND RETRIEVE IT?!
NEVER MIND THAT. YOU'VE GOT *OGRE* DNA RUNNING THROUGH YOUR VEINS!!
THE FACT THAT YOU BEAR THE SAME CREST ON YOUR CHEST THAT RASETSU DOES IS *PROOF* OF THAT!!
YOU SHOULD *DIE* BEFORE YOU FOLLOW IN HIS FOOT-STEPS...!

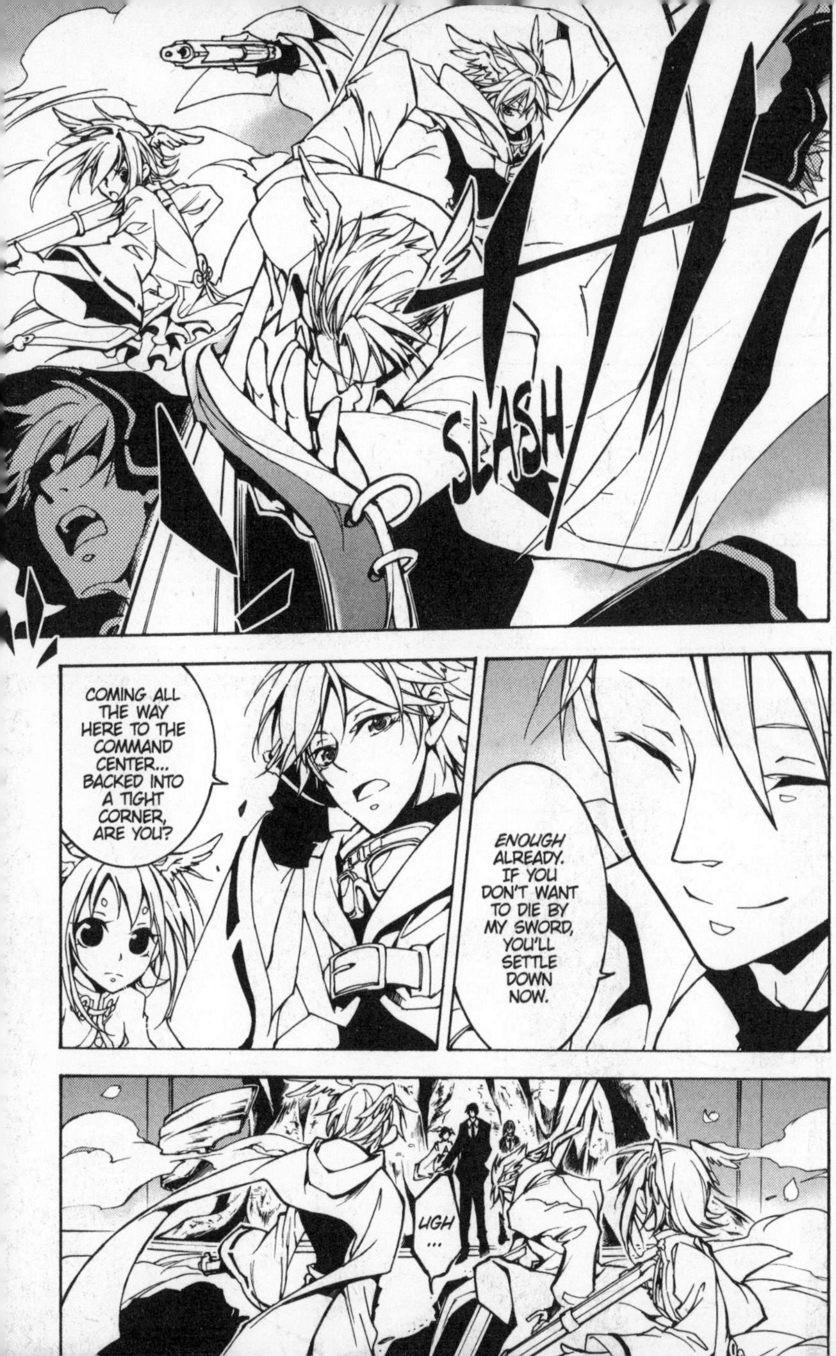
SLASH
ENOUGH ALREADY. IF YOU DON'T WANT TO DIE BY MY SWORD, YOU'LL SETTLE DOWN NOW.
COMING ALL THE WAY HERE TO THE COMMAND CENTER... BACKED INTO A TIGHT CORNER, ARE YOU?
UGH ...

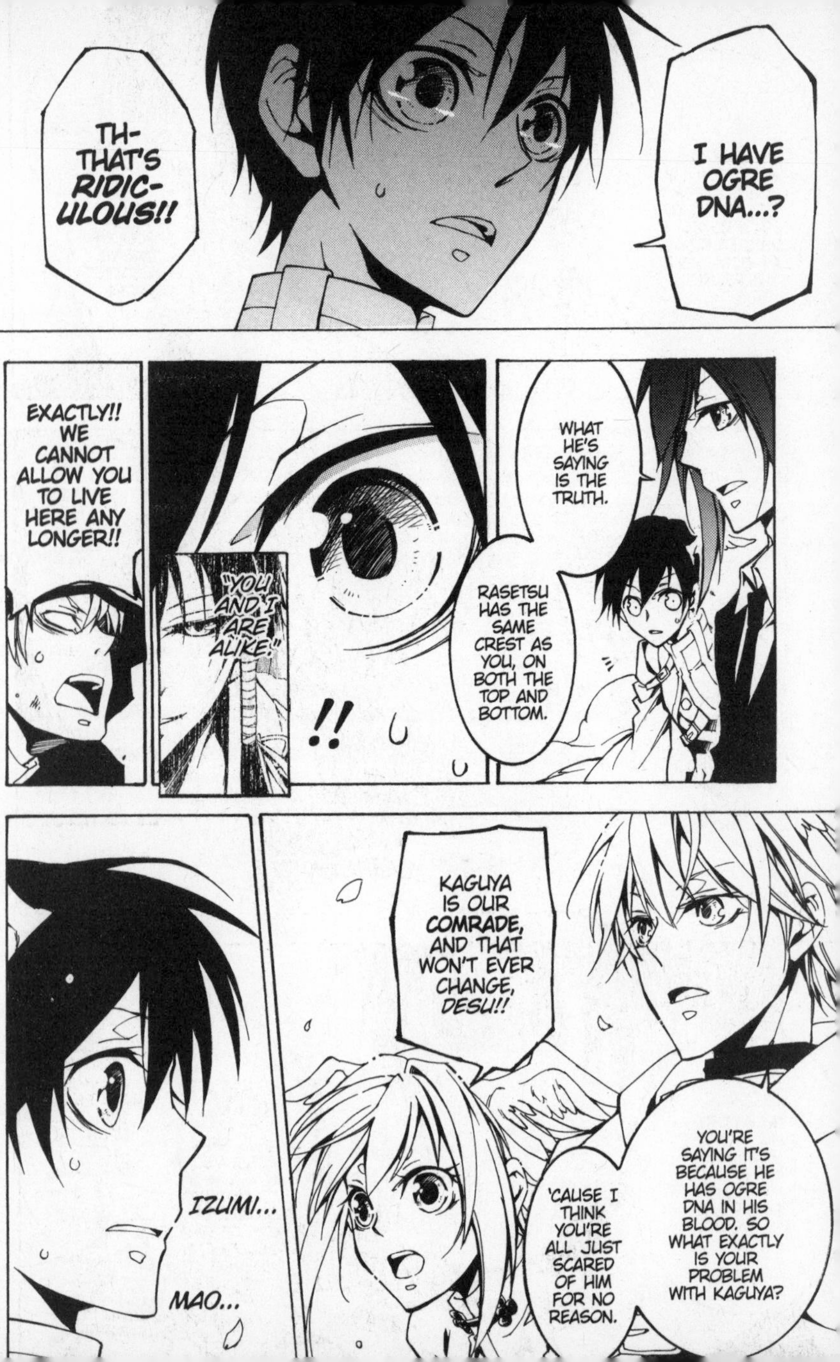
I HAVE OGRE DNA...?
TH-THAT'S RIDICULOUS!!
WHAT HE'S SAYING IS THE TRUTH.
RASETSU HAS THE SAME CREST AS YOU, ON BOTH THE TOP AND BOTTOM.
!!
"YOU AND I ARE ALIKE."
EXACTLY!! WE CANNOT ALLOW YOU TO LIVE HERE ANY LONGER!!
KAGUYA IS OUR COMRADE, AND THAT WON'T EVER CHANGE, DESU!!
YOU'RE SAYING IT'S BECAUSE HE HAS OGRE DNA IN HIS BLOOD. SO WHAT EXACTLY IS YOUR PROBLEM WITH KAGUYA?
'CAUSE I THINK YOU'RE ALL JUST SCARED OF HIM FOR NO REASON.
IZUMI...
MAO...

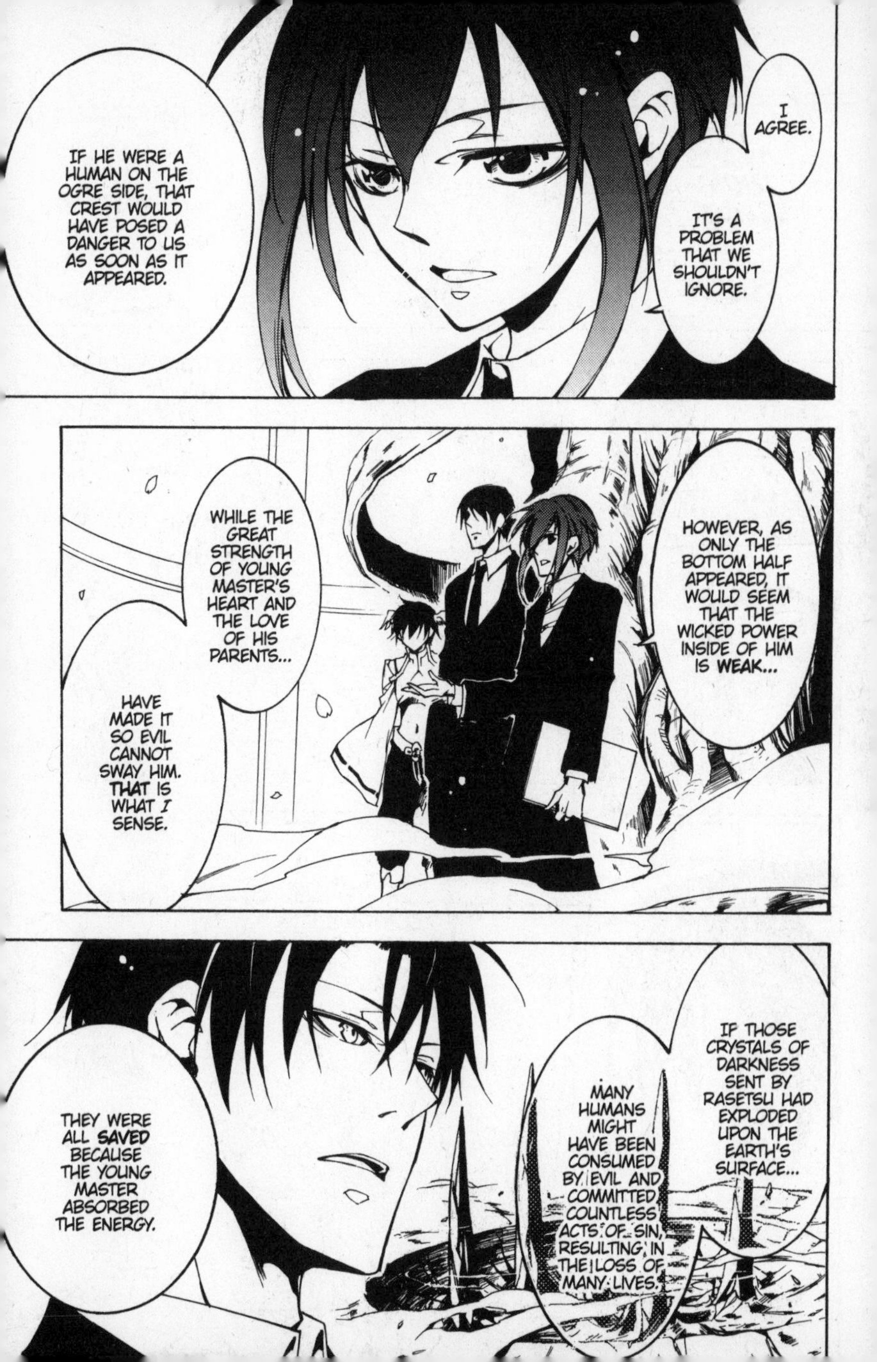
I AGREE.
IT'S A PROBLEM THAT WE SHOULDN'T IGNORE.
IF HE WERE A HUMAN ON THE OGRE SIDE, THAT CREST WOULD HAVE POSED A DANGER TO US AS SOON AS IT APPEARED.
HOWEVER, AS ONLY THE BOTTOM HALF APPEARED, IT WOULD SEEM THAT THE WICKED POWER INSIDE OF HIM IS WEAK...
WHILE THE GREAT STRENGTH OF YOUNG MASTER'S HEART AND THE LOVE OF HIS PARENTS...
HAVE MADE IT SO EVIL CANNOT SWAY HIM. THAT IS WHAT I SENSE.
IF THOSE CRYSTALS OF DARKNESS SENT BY RASETSU HAD EXPLODED UPON THE EARTH'S SURFACE...
MANY HUMANS MIGHT HAVE BEEN CONSUMED BY EVIL AND COMMITTED COUNTLESS ACTS OF SIN, RESULTING IN THE LOSS OF MANY LIVES.
THEY WERE ALL SAVED BECAUSE THE YOUNG MASTER ABSORBED THE ENERGY.

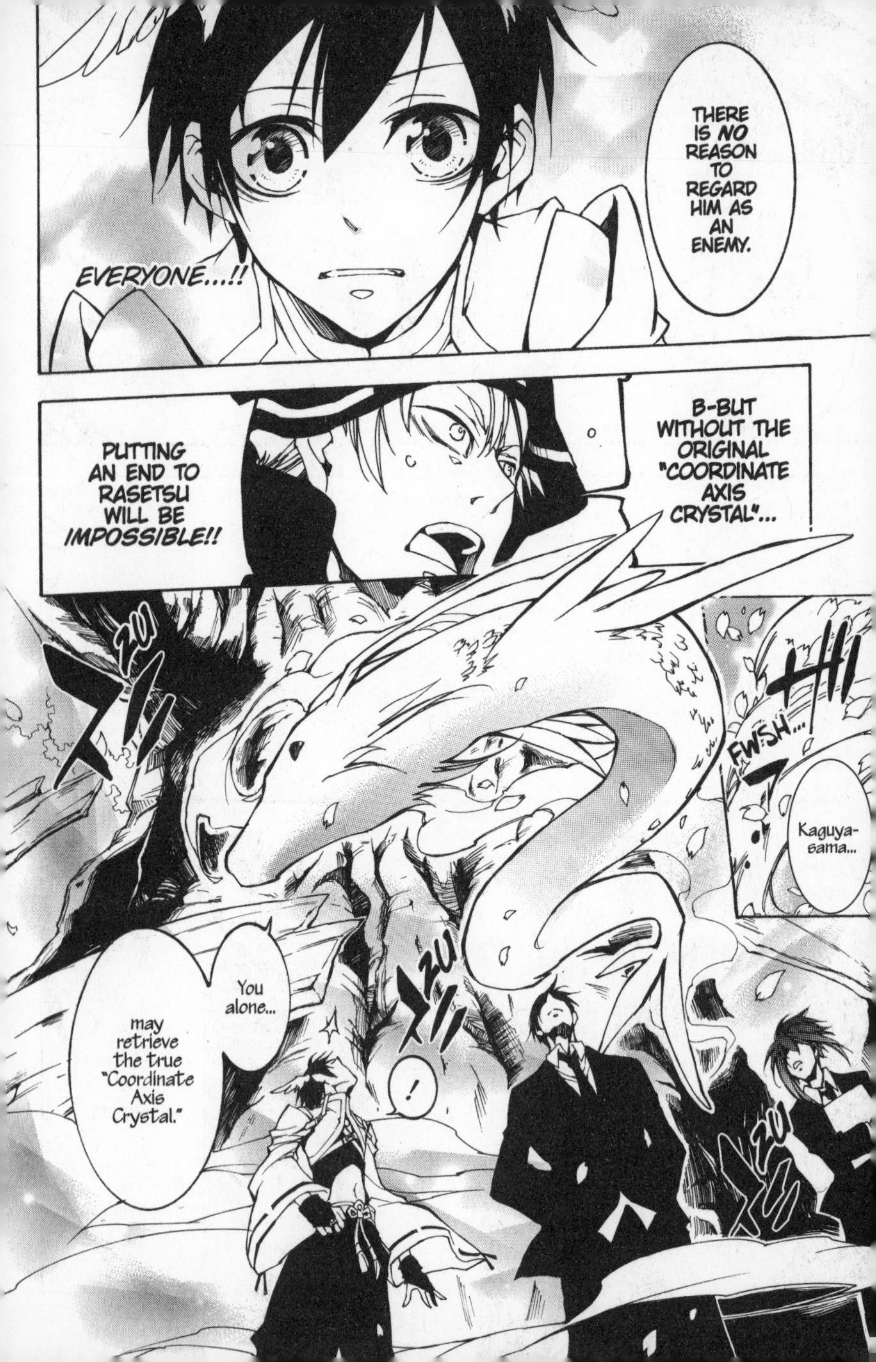
THERE IS NO REASON TO REGARD HIM AS AN ENEMY.
EVERYONE...!!
B-BUT WITHOUT THE ORIGINAL "COORDINATE AXIS CRYSTAL"...
PUTTING AN END TO RASETSU WILL BE IMPOSSIBLE!!
FWSH...
Kaguya-sama...
ZU
ZU
ZU
!
You alone...
may retrieve the true "Coordinate Axis Crystal."

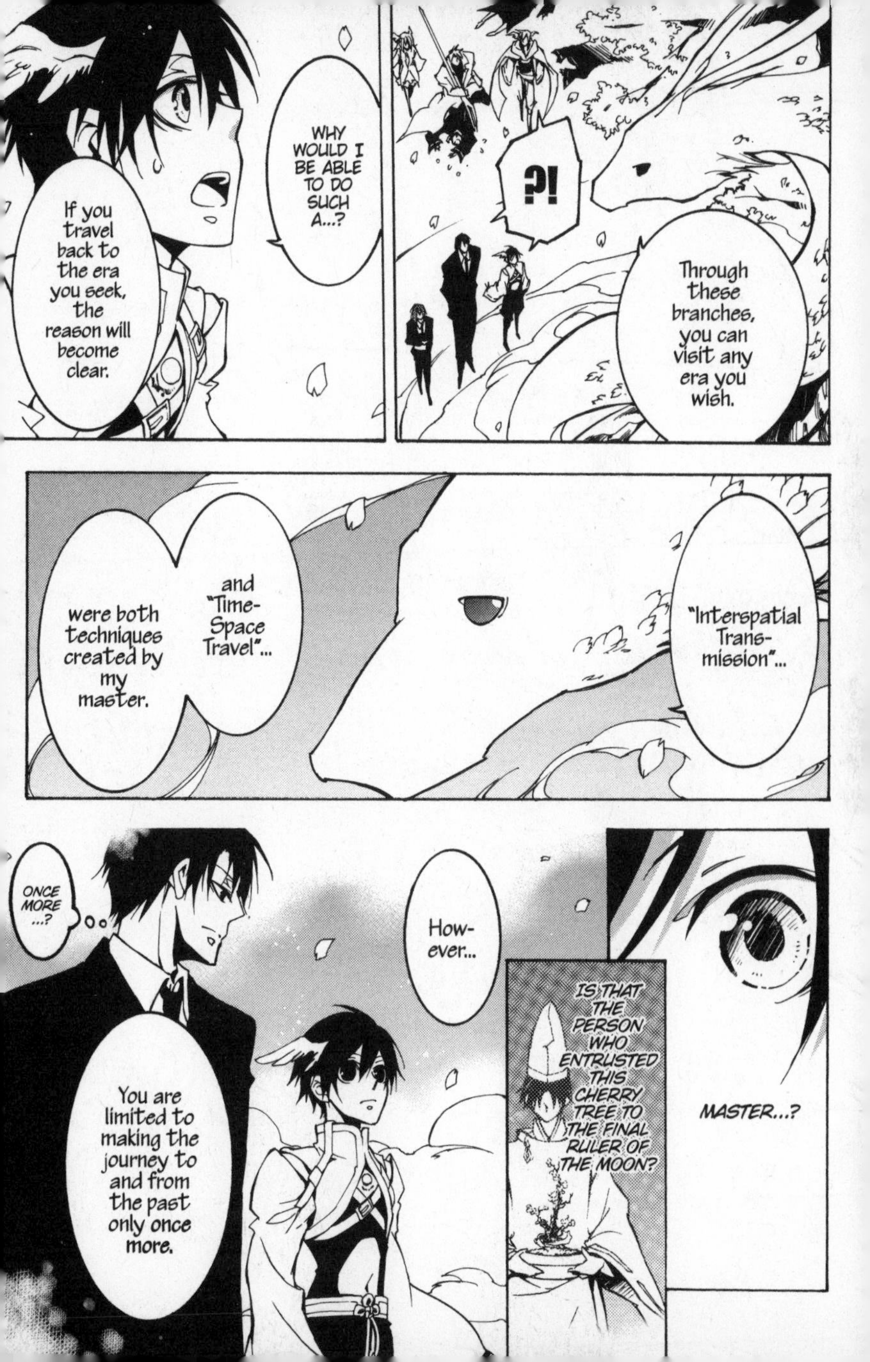
?!
Through these branches, you can visit any era you wish.
WHY WOULD I BE ABLE TO DO SUCH A...?
If you travel back to the era you seek, the reason will become clear.
"Interspatial Trans-mission"...
and "Time-Space Travel"...
were both techniques created by my master.
MASTER...?
IS THAT THE PERSON WHO ENTRUSTED THIS CHERRY TREE TO THE FINAL RULER OF THE MOON?
How-ever...
You are limited to making the journey to and from the past only once more.
ONCE MORE ...?

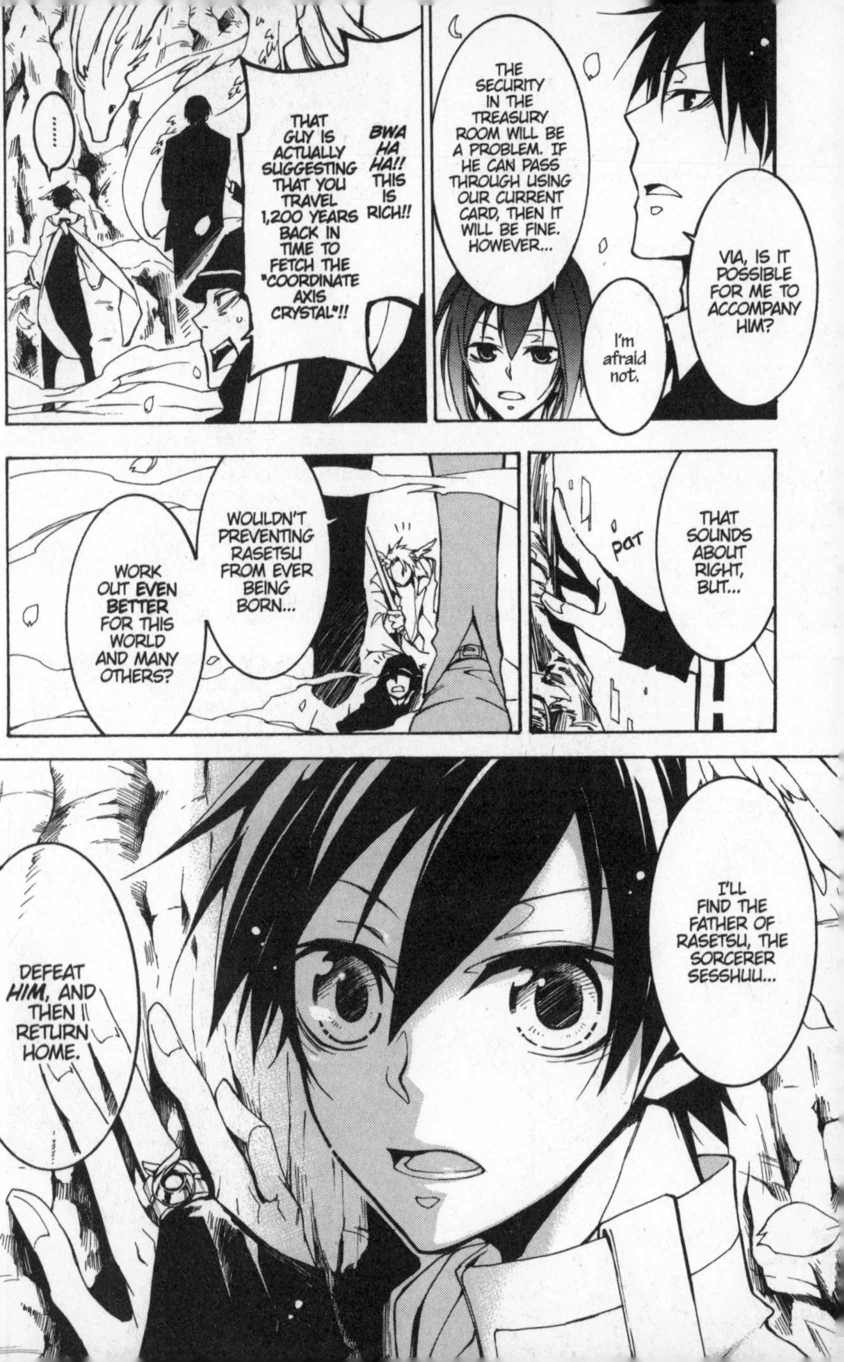
THE SECURITY IN THE TREASURY ROOM WILL BE A PROBLEM. IF HE CAN PASS THROUGH USING OUR CURRENT CARD, THEN IT WILL BE FINE. HOWEVER...
VIA, IS IT POSSIBLE FOR ME TO ACCOMPANY HIM?
I'm afraid not.
BWA HA HA!! THIS IS RICH!!
THAT GUY IS ACTUALLY SUGGESTING THAT YOU TRAVEL 1,200 YEARS BACK IN TIME TO FETCH THE "COORDINATE AXIS CRYSTAL"!!
......
pat
THAT SOUNDS ABOUT RIGHT, BUT...
WOULDN'T PREVENTING RASETSU FROM EVER BEING BORN...
WORK OUT **EVEN** BETTER FOR THIS WORLD AND MANY OTHERS?
I'LL FIND THE FATHER OF RASETSU, THE SORCERER SESSHUU...
DEFEAT ***HIM***, AND THEN RETURN HOME.

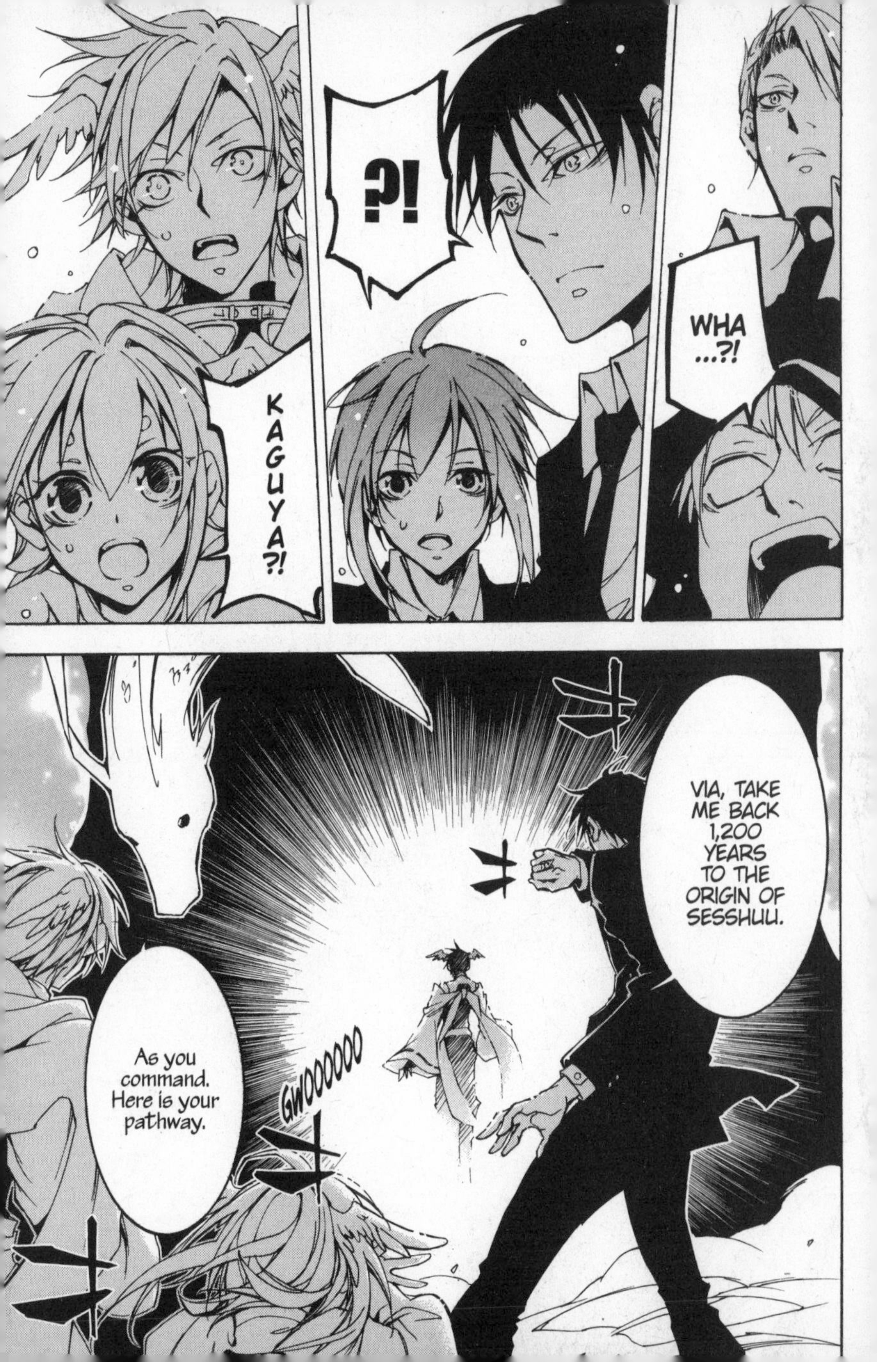
WHA ...?!
?!
KAGUYA?!
VIA, TAKE ME BACK 1,200 YEARS TO THE ORIGIN OF SESSHUU.
GWOOOOOO
As you command. Here is your pathway.

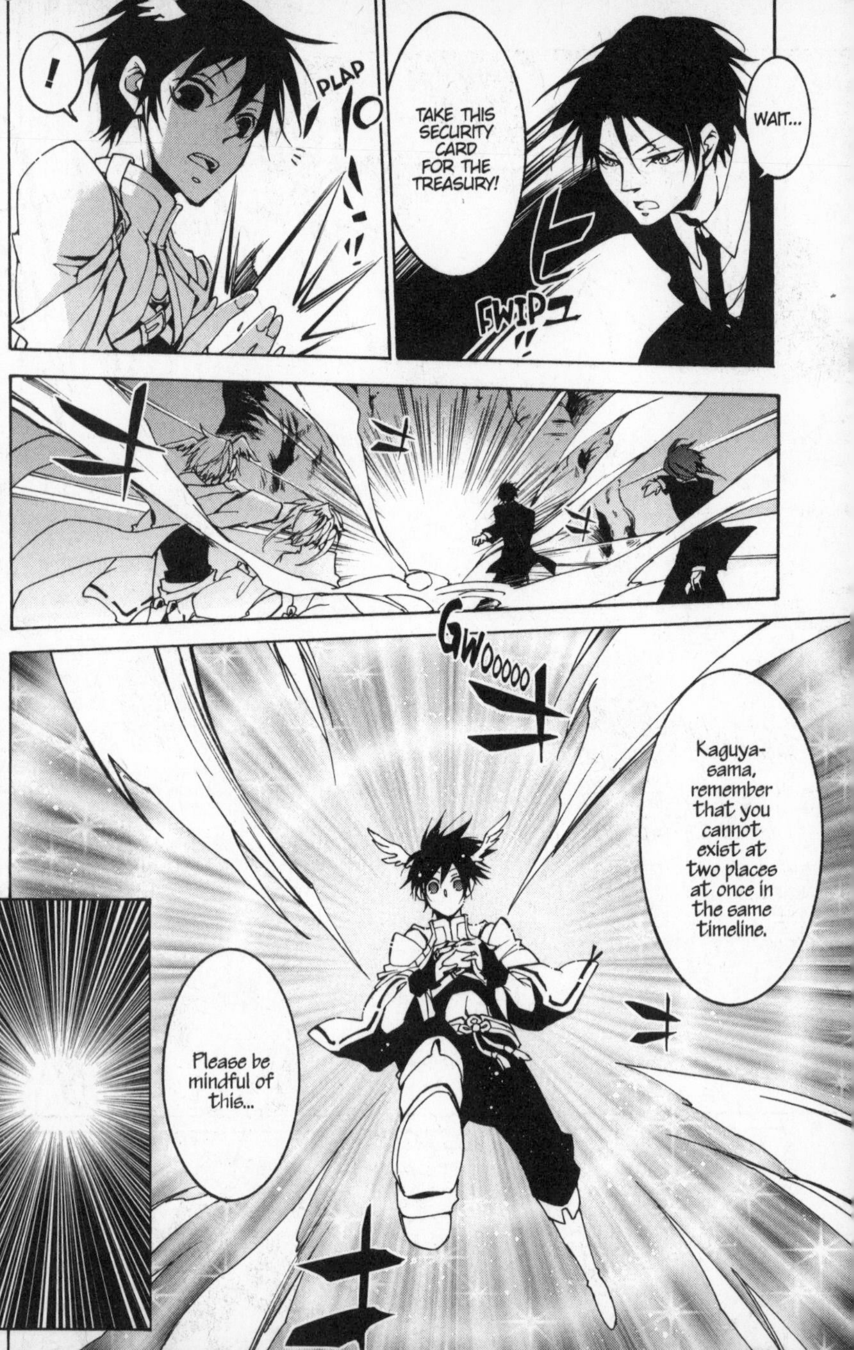
WAIT...
TAKE THIS SECURITY CARD FOR THE TREASURY!
FWIP
PLAP
!
GWOOOOO
Kaguya-sama, remember that you cannot exist at two places at once in the same timeline.
Please be mindful of this...

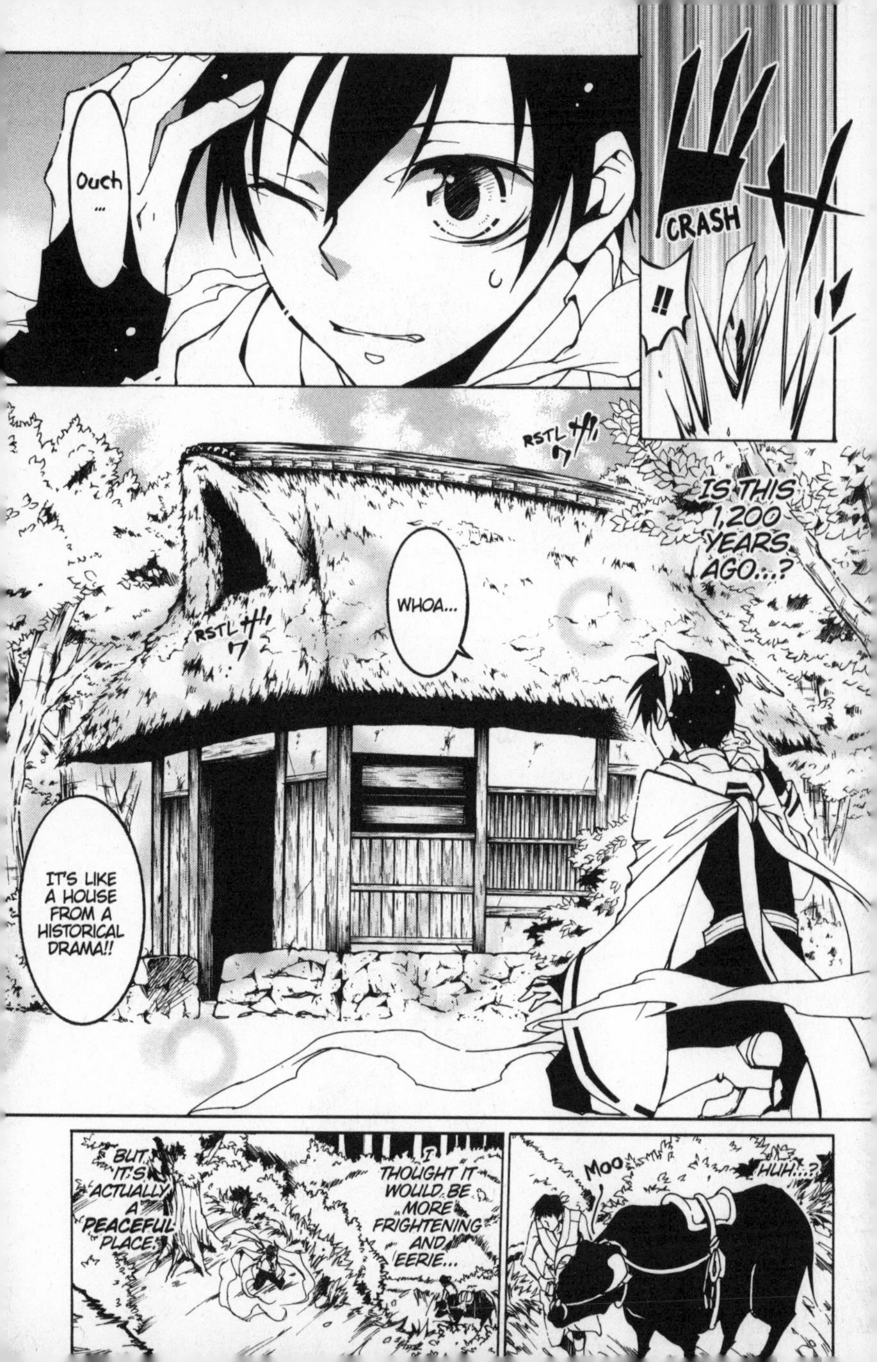
CRASH
!!
Ouch
...
IS THIS 1,200 YEARS AGO...?
RSTL
WHOA...
RSTL
IT'S LIKE A HOUSE FROM A HISTORICAL DRAMA!!
HUH...?
Moo
I THOUGHT IT WOULD BE MORE FRIGHTENING AND EERIE...
BUT IT'S ACTUALLY A PEACEFUL PLACE.

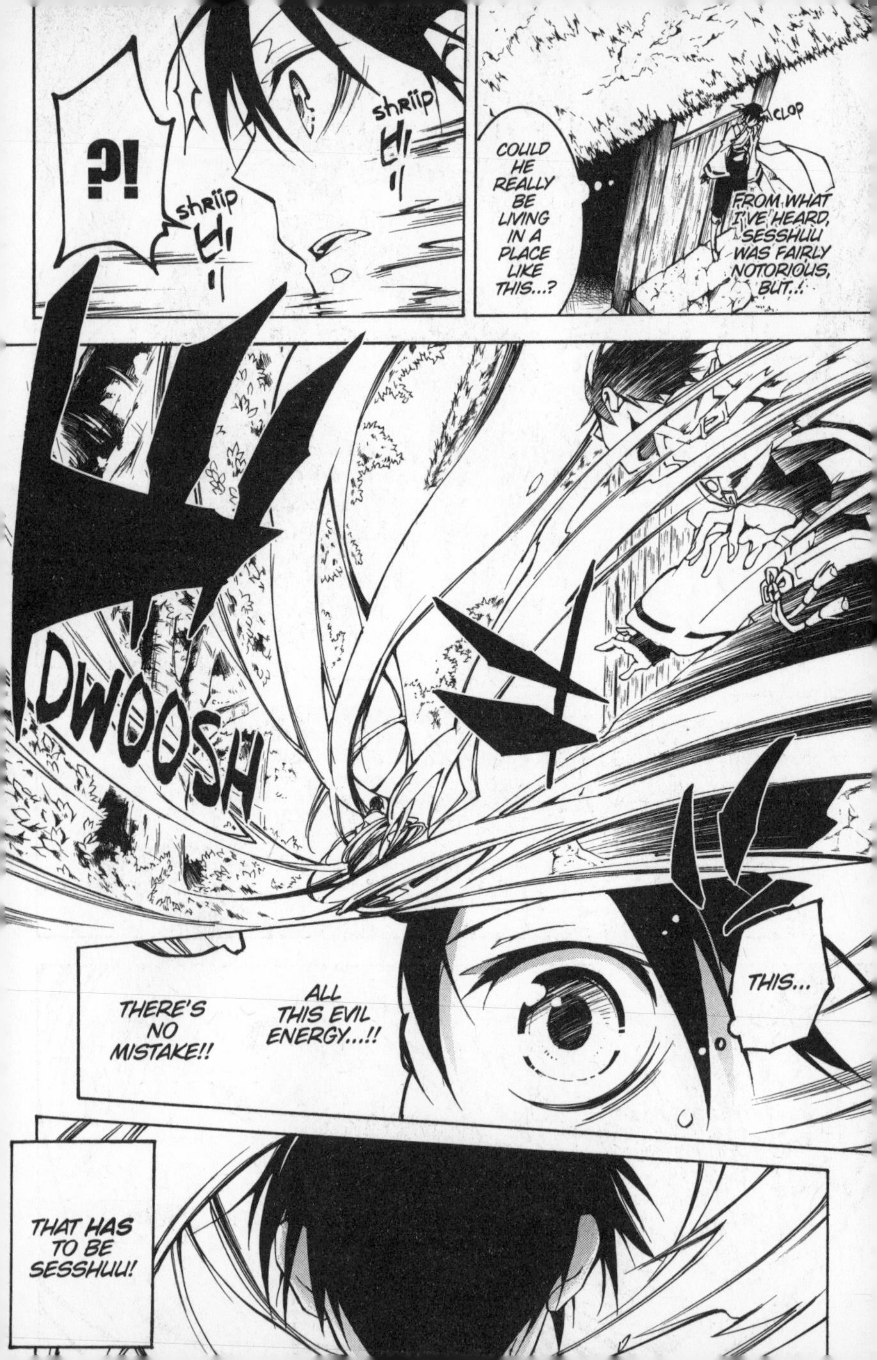
CLOP
FROM WHAT I'VE HEARD, SESSHUU WAS FAIRLY NOTORIOUS, BUT...
COULD HE REALLY BE LIVING IN A PLACE LIKE THIS...?
shriip
shriip
?!
DWOOSH
THIS...
ALL THIS EVIL ENERGY...!!
THERE'S NO MISTAKE!!
THAT HAS TO BE SESSHUU!

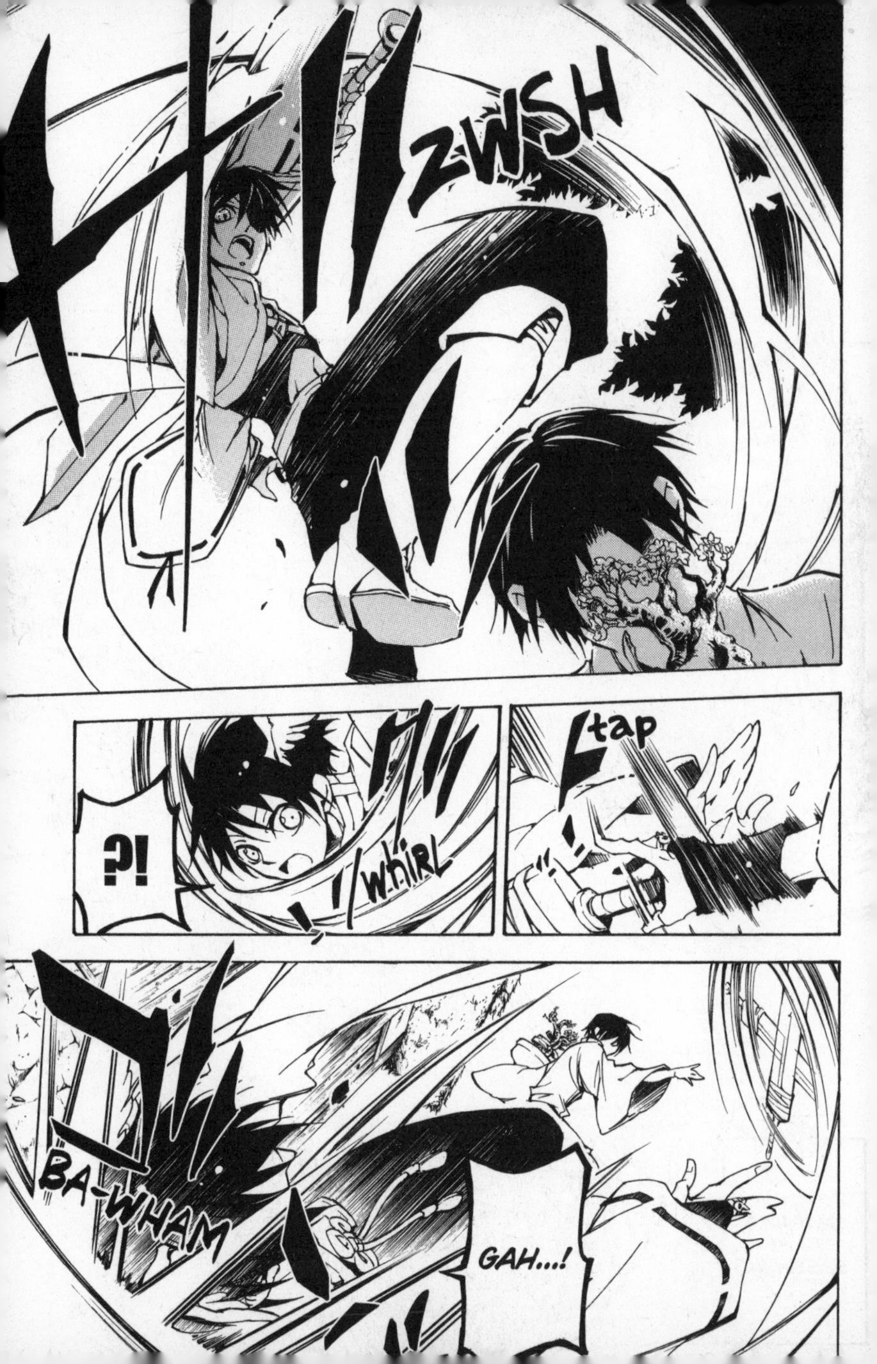
ZWSH
tap
whirl
?!
BA-WHAM
GAH...!

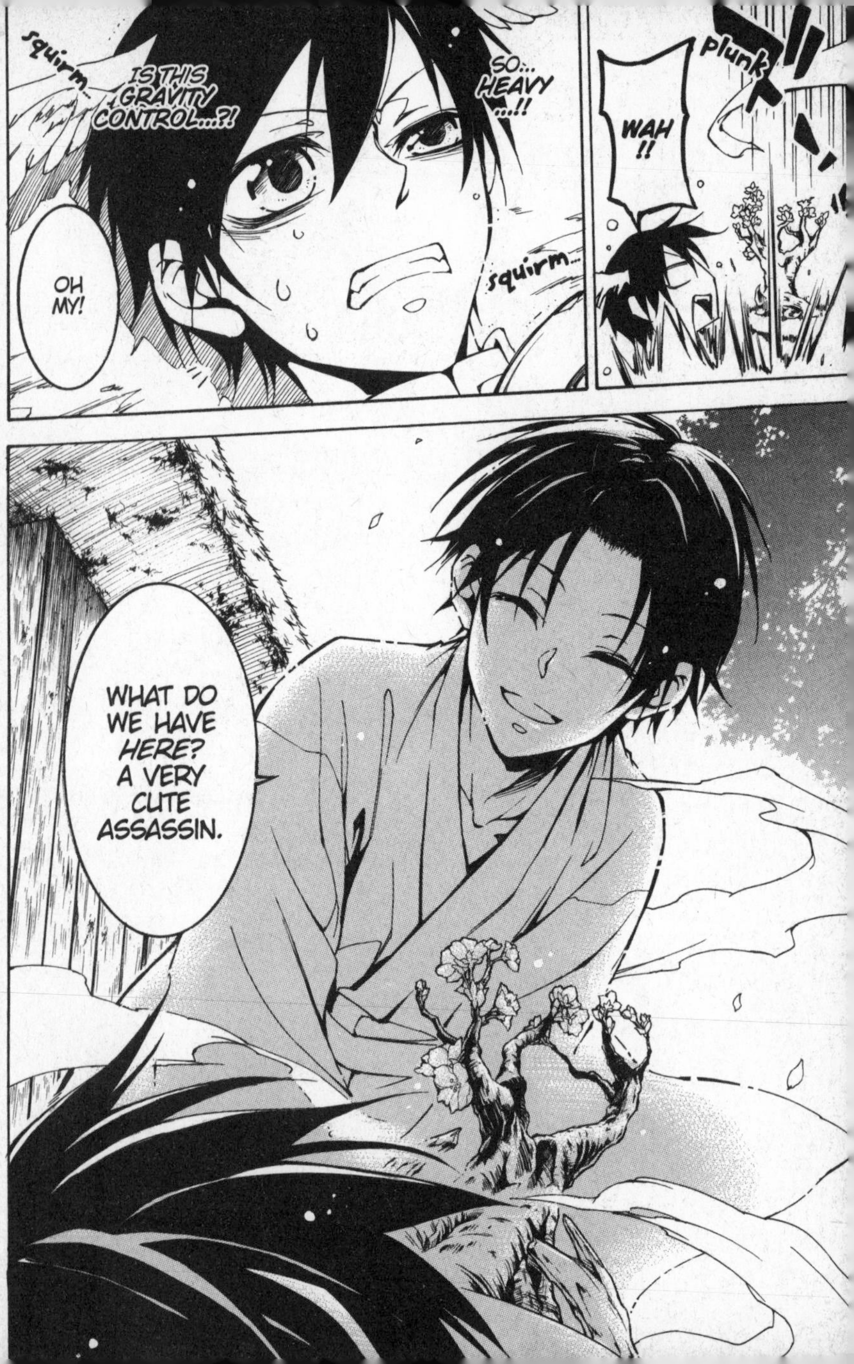
plunk
WAH !!
SO... HEAVY ...!!
IS THIS GRAVITY CONTROL...?!
squirm...
squirm...
OH MY!
WHAT DO WE HAVE HERE? A VERY CUTE ASSASSIN.

Chapter 18

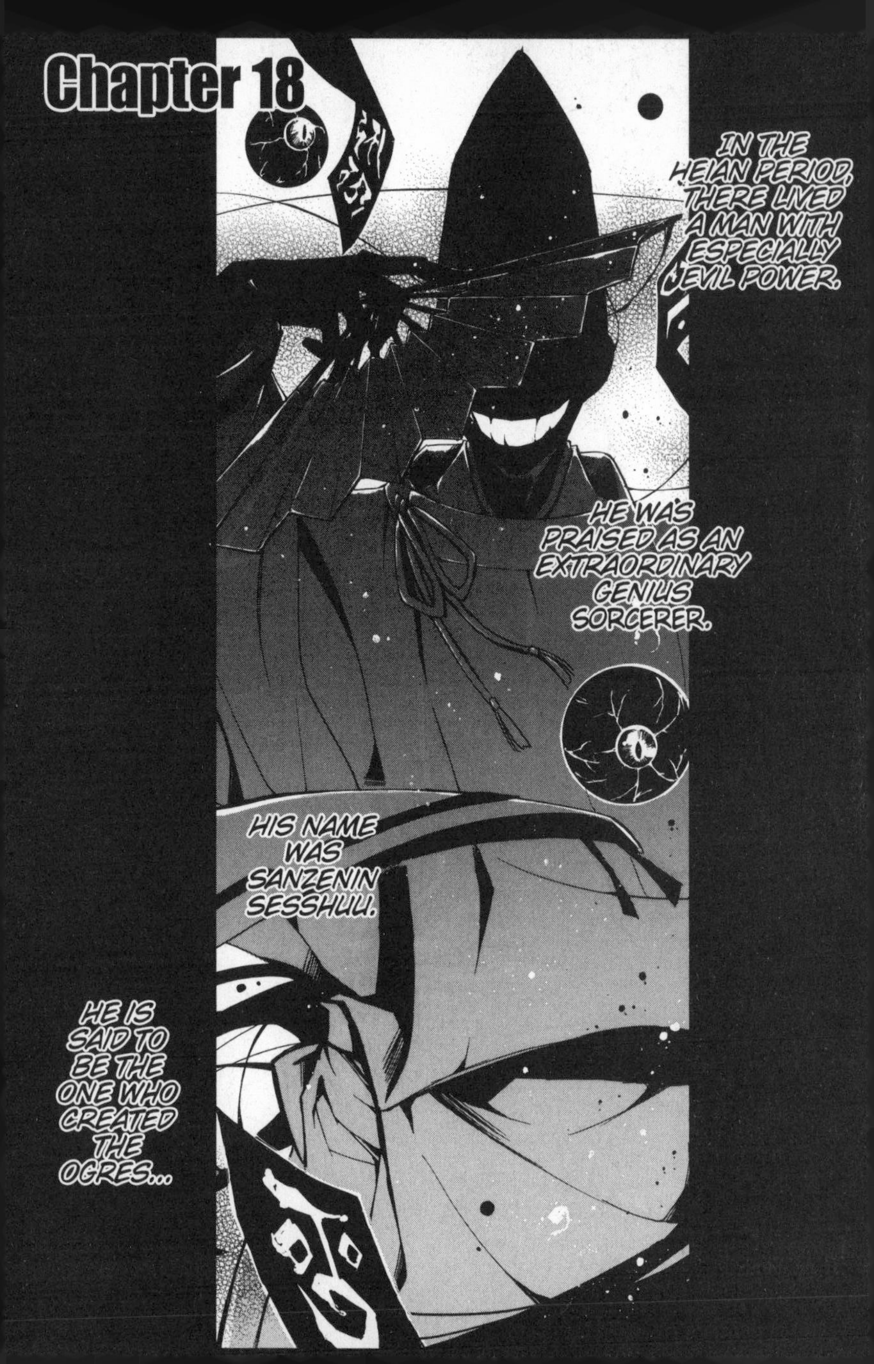
IN THE HEIAN PERIOD, THERE LIVED A MAN WITH ESPECIALLY EVIL POWER.
HE WAS PRAISED AS AN EXTRAORDINARY GENIUS SORCERER.
HIS NAME WAS SANZENIN SESSHUU.
HE IS SAID TO BE THE ONE WHO CREATED THE OGRES...

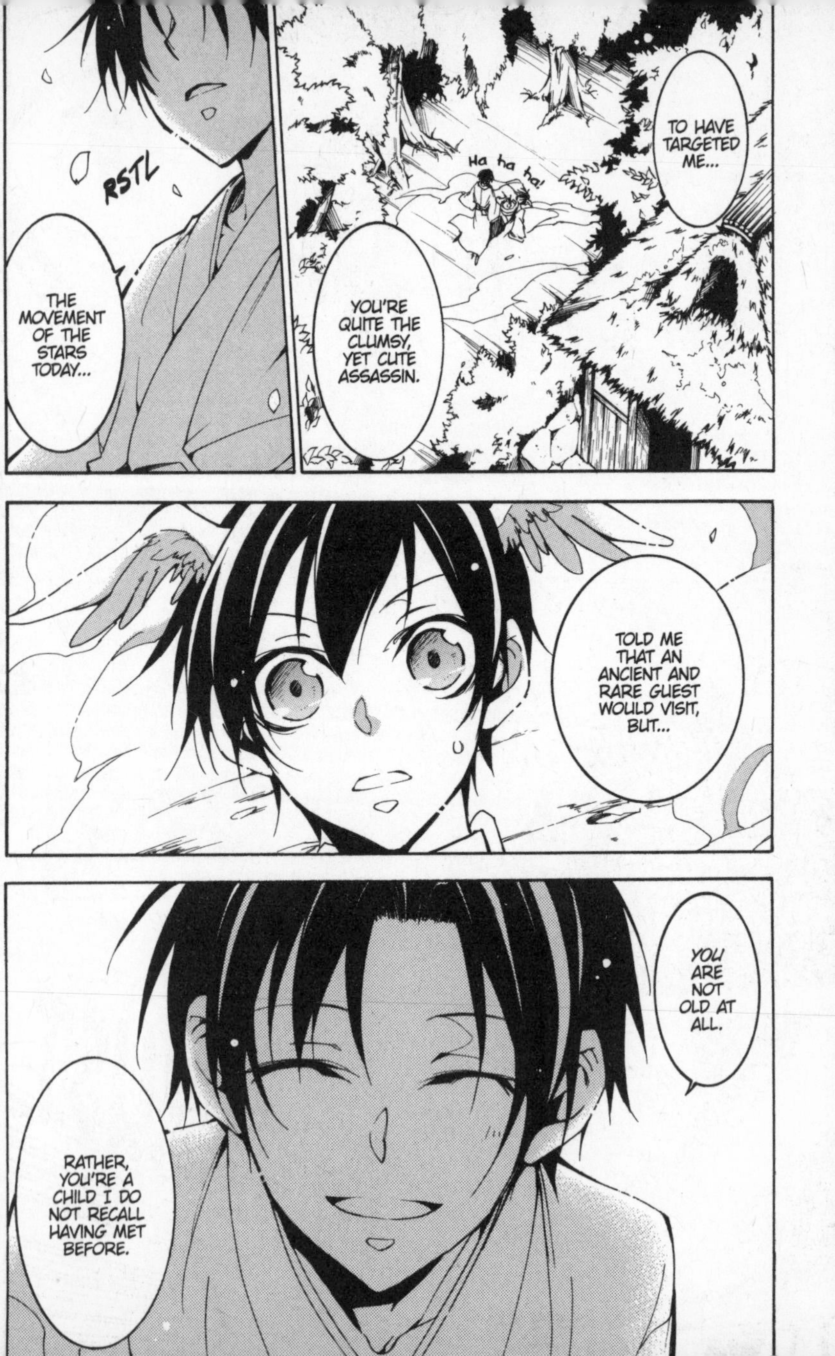
TO HAVE TARGETED ME...
Ha ha ha!
YOU'RE QUITE THE CLUMSY, YET CUTE ASSASSIN.
RSTL
THE MOVEMENT OF THE STARS TODAY...
TOLD ME THAT AN ANCIENT AND RARE GUEST WOULD VISIT, BUT...
YOU ARE NOT OLD AT ALL.
RATHER, YOU'RE A CHILD I DO NOT RECALL HAVING MET BEFORE.

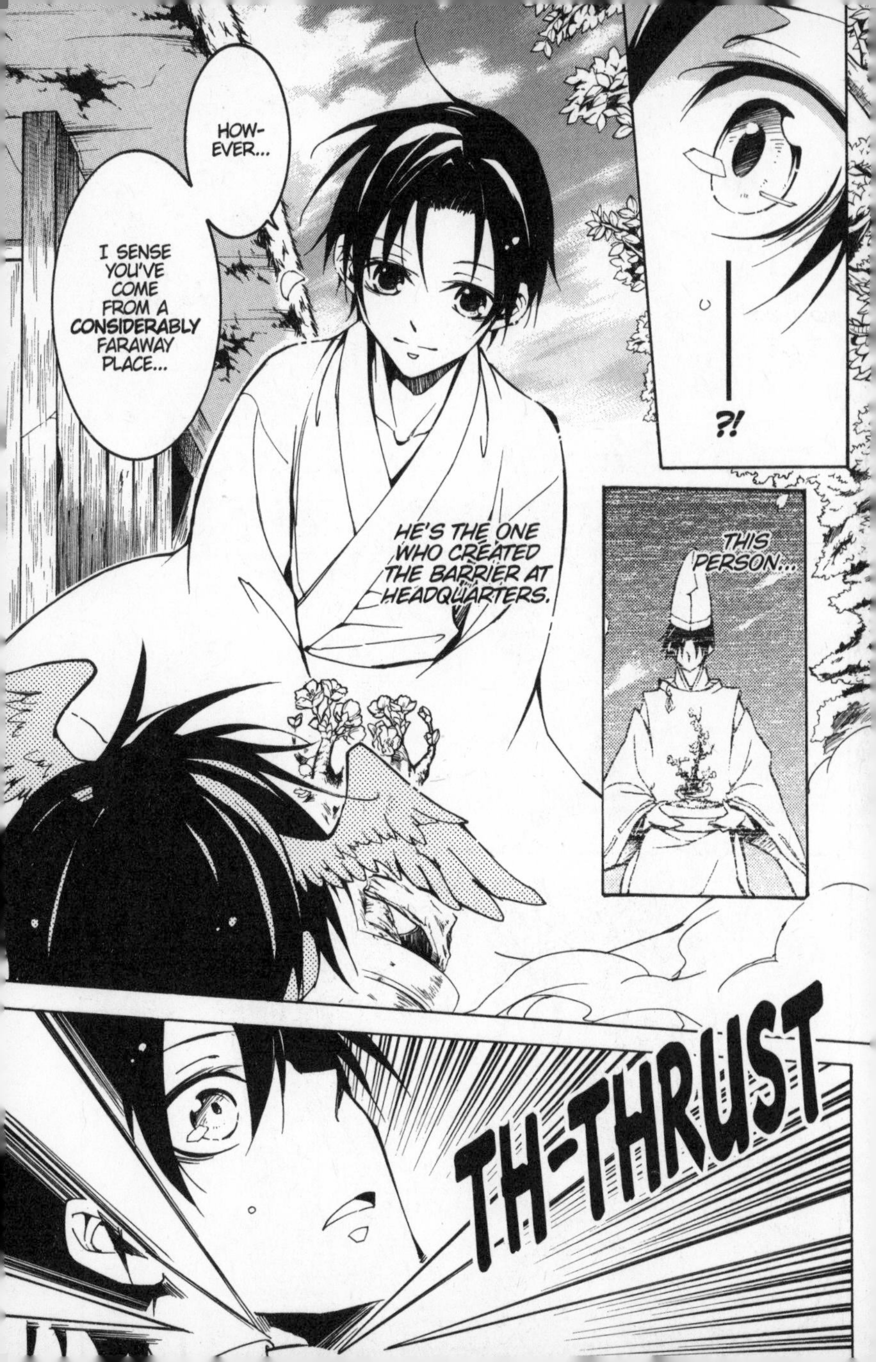
?!
THIS PERSON...
HOW-EVER...
I SENSE YOU'VE COME FROM A CONSIDERABLY FARAWAY PLACE...
HE'S THE ONE WHO CREATED THE BARRIER AT HEADQUARTERS.
TH-THRUST

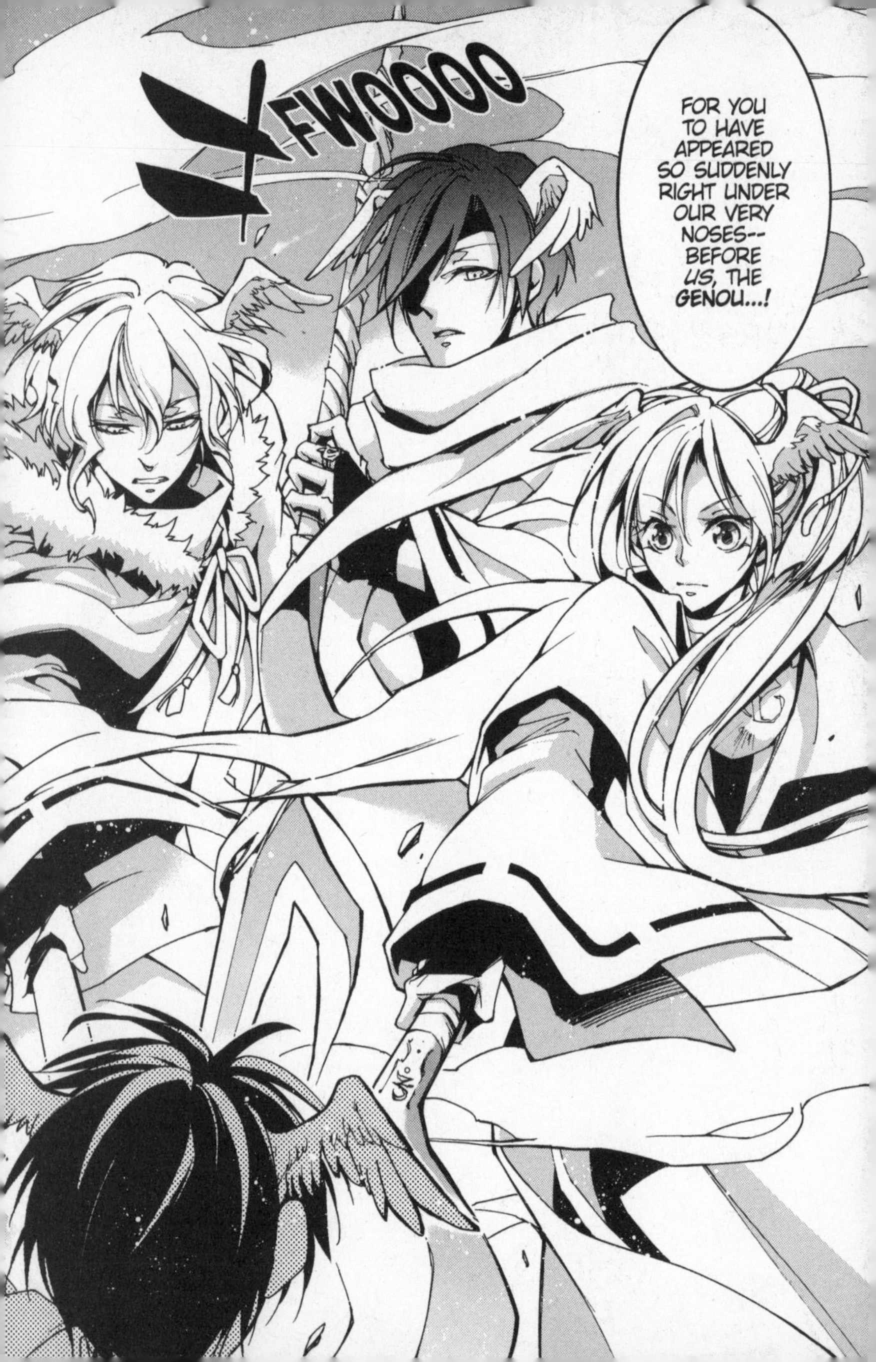
FWOOOO
FOR YOU TO HAVE APPEARED SO SUDDENLY RIGHT UNDER OUR VERY NOSES-- BEFORE US, THE GENOU...!

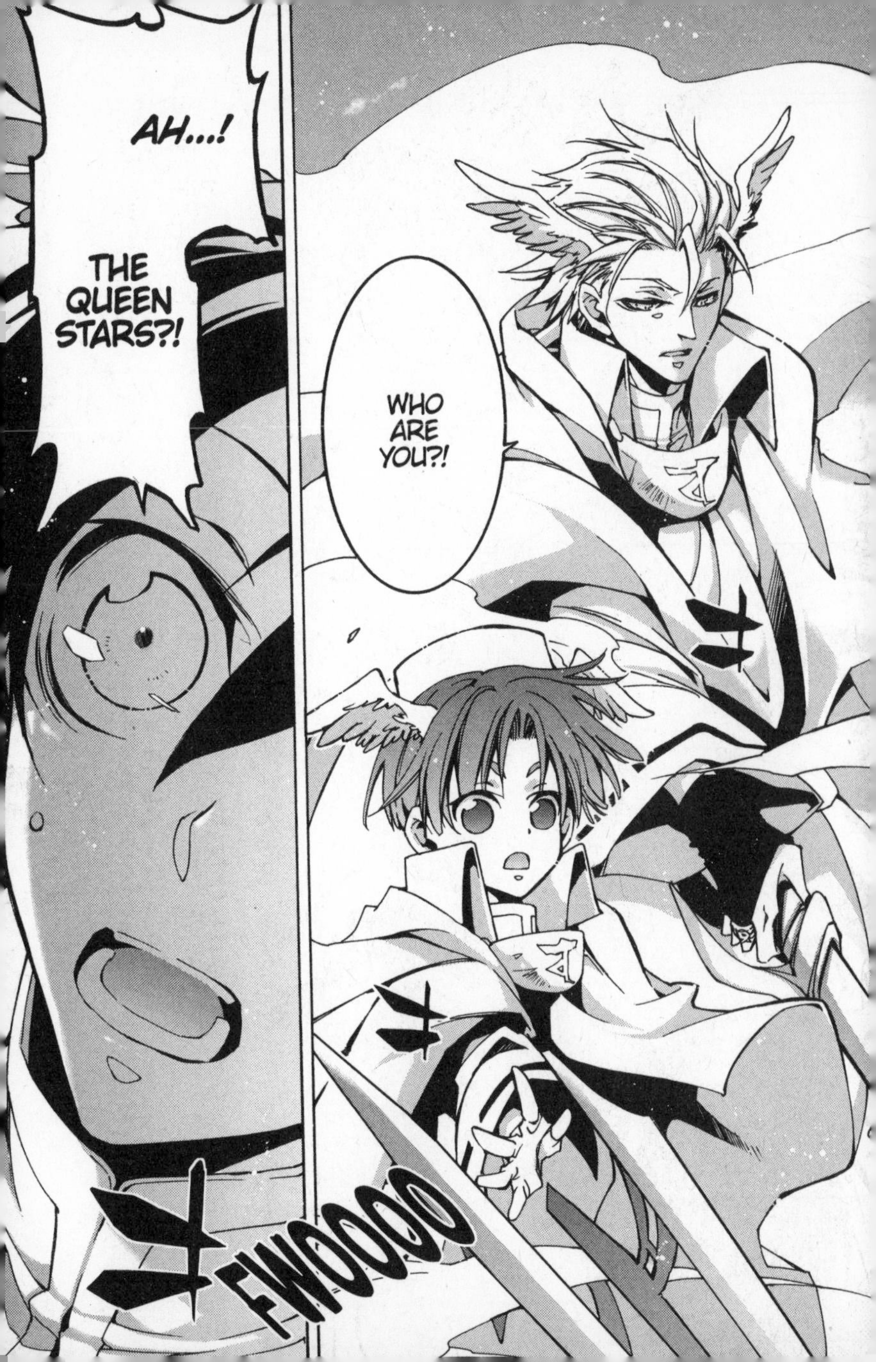
WHO ARE YOU?!
AH...!
THE QUEEN STARS?!
FWOOOO

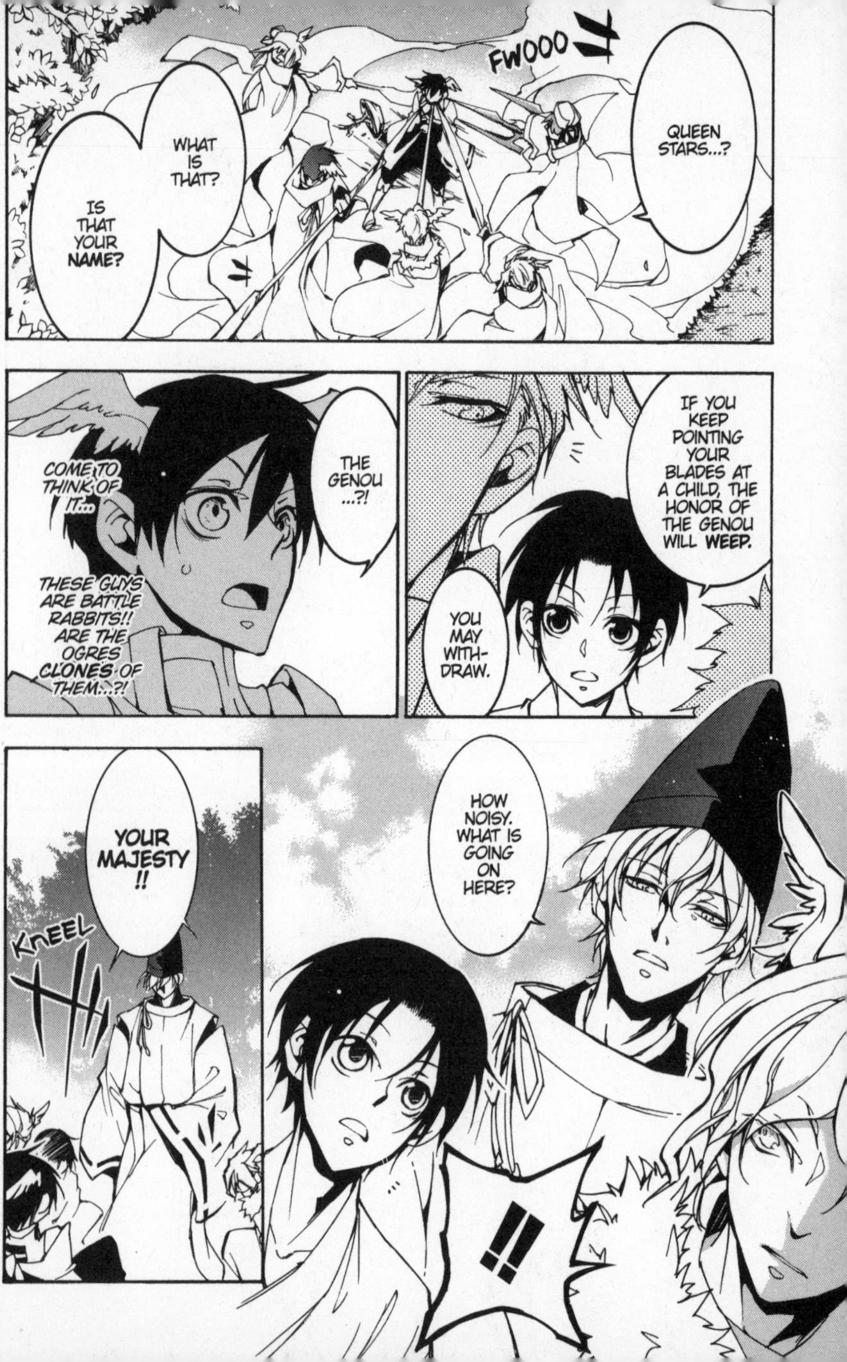
QUEEN STARS...?
FWOOO
WHAT IS THAT?
IS THAT YOUR NAME?
IF YOU KEEP POINTING YOUR BLADES AT A CHILD, THE HONOR OF THE GENOU WILL WEEP.
YOU MAY WITH-DRAW.
THE GENOU ...?!
COME TO THINK OF IT...
THESE GUYS ARE BATTLE RABBITS!! ARE THE OGRES CLONES OF THEM...?!
HOW NOISY. WHAT IS GOING ON HERE?
!!
YOUR MAJESTY !!
KnEEL

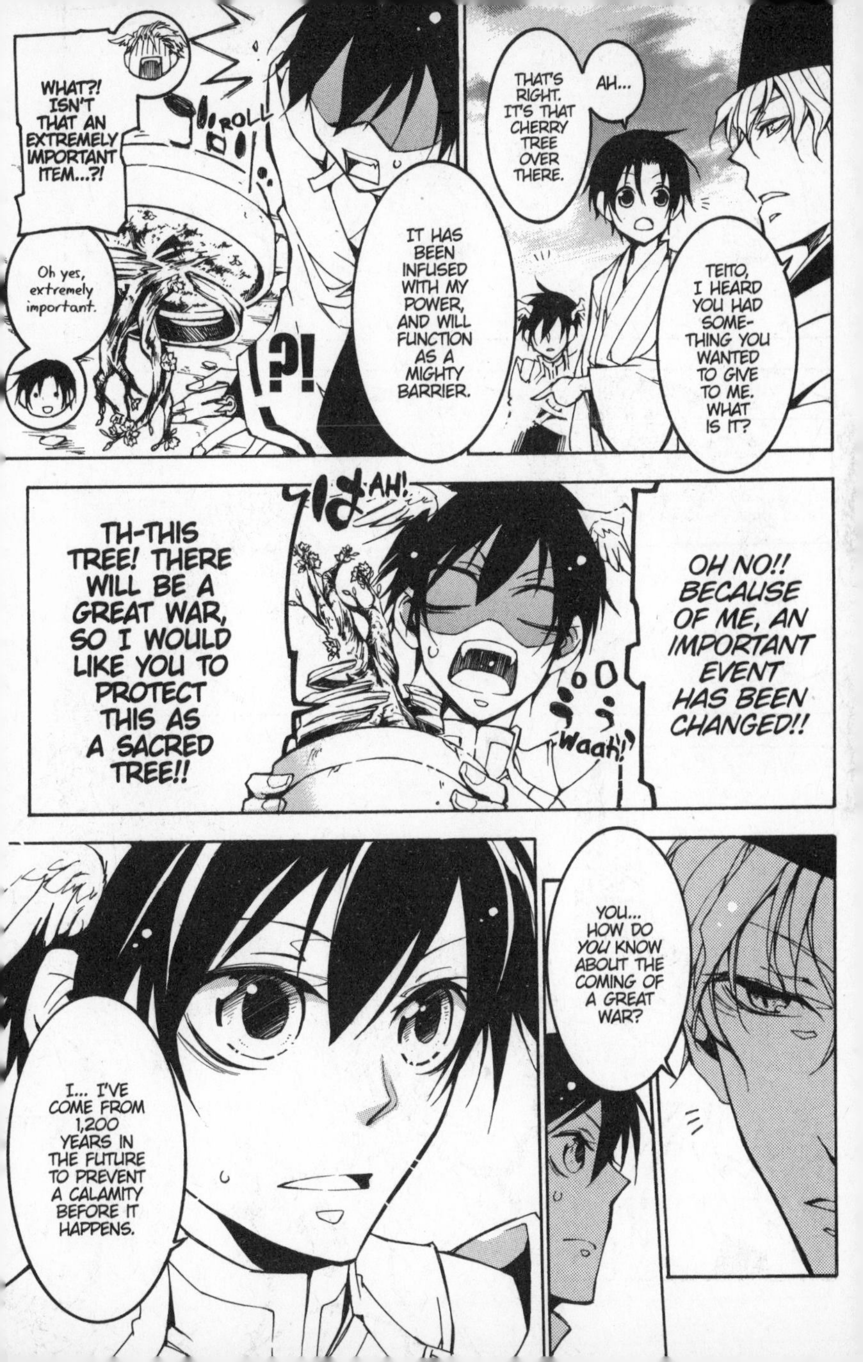

TEITO, I HEARD YOU HAD SOME-THING YOU WANTED TO GIVE TO ME. WHAT IS IT?
AH...
THAT'S RIGHT. IT'S THAT CHERRY TREE OVER THERE.
IT HAS BEEN INFUSED WITH MY POWER, AND WILL FUNCTION AS A MIGHTY BARRIER.
ROLL
?!
WHAT?! ISN'T THAT AN EXTREMELY IMPORTANT ITEM...?!
Oh yes, extremely important.
OH NO!! BECAUSE OF ME, AN IMPORTANT EVENT HAS BEEN CHANGED!!
AH!
Waah!
TH-THIS TREE! THERE WILL BE A GREAT WAR, SO I WOULD LIKE YOU TO PROTECT THIS AS A SACRED TREE!!
YOU... HOW DO YOU KNOW ABOUT THE COMING OF A GREAT WAR?
I... I'VE COME FROM 1,200 YEARS IN THE FUTURE TO PREVENT A CALAMITY BEFORE IT HAPPENS.

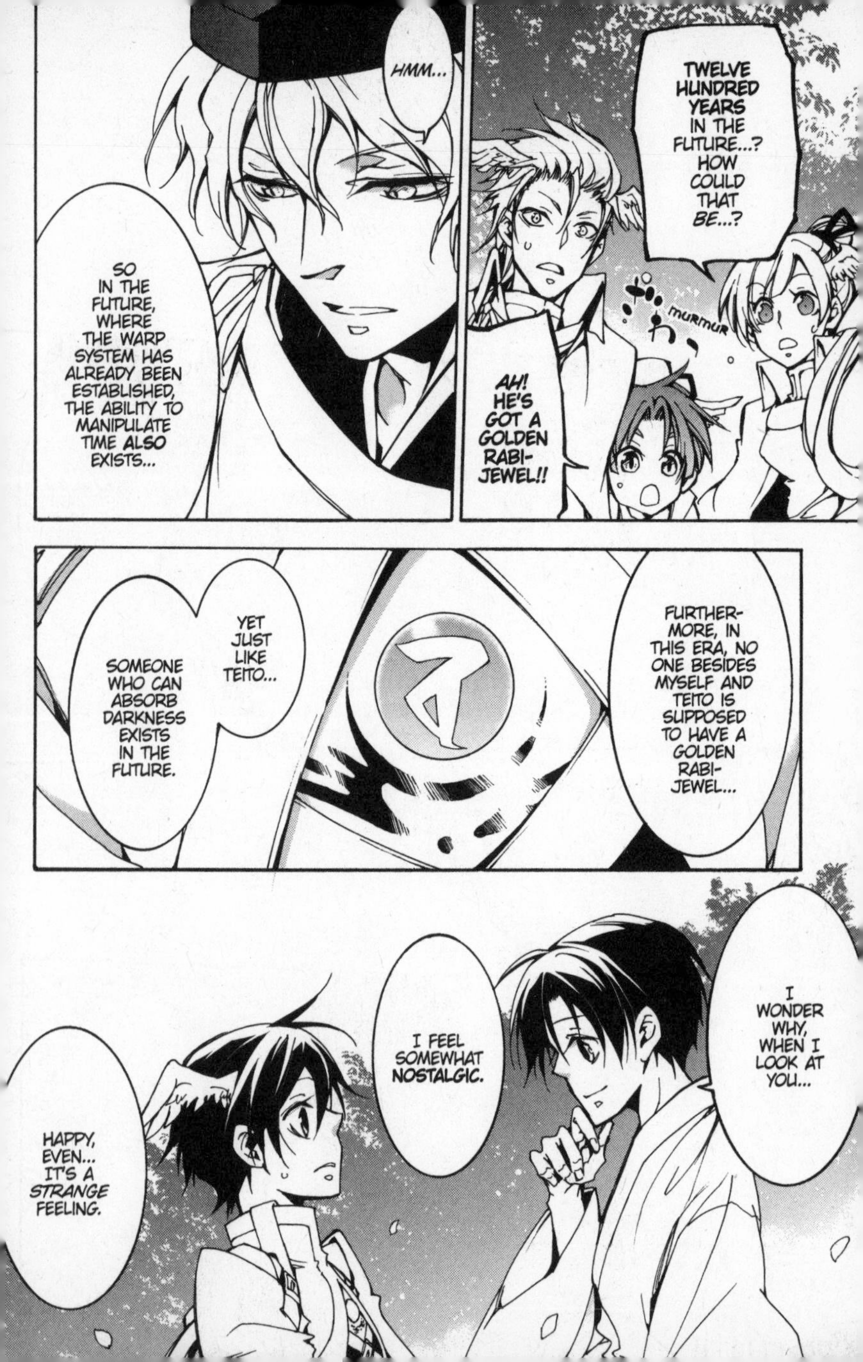

TWELVE HUNDRED YEARS IN THE FUTURE...? HOW COULD THAT BE...?
murmur
AH! HE'S GOT A GOLDEN RABI-JEWEL!!
HMM...
SO IN THE FUTURE, WHERE THE WARP SYSTEM HAS ALREADY BEEN ESTABLISHED, THE ABILITY TO MANIPULATE TIME ALSO EXISTS...
FURTHERMORE, IN THIS ERA, NO ONE BESIDES MYSELF AND TEITO IS SUPPOSED TO HAVE A GOLDEN RABI-JEWEL...
YET JUST LIKE TEITO...
SOMEONE WHO CAN ABSORB DARKNESS EXISTS IN THE FUTURE.
I WONDER WHY, WHEN I LOOK AT YOU...
I FEEL SOMEWHAT NOSTALGIC.
HAPPY, EVEN... IT'S A STRANGE FEELING.

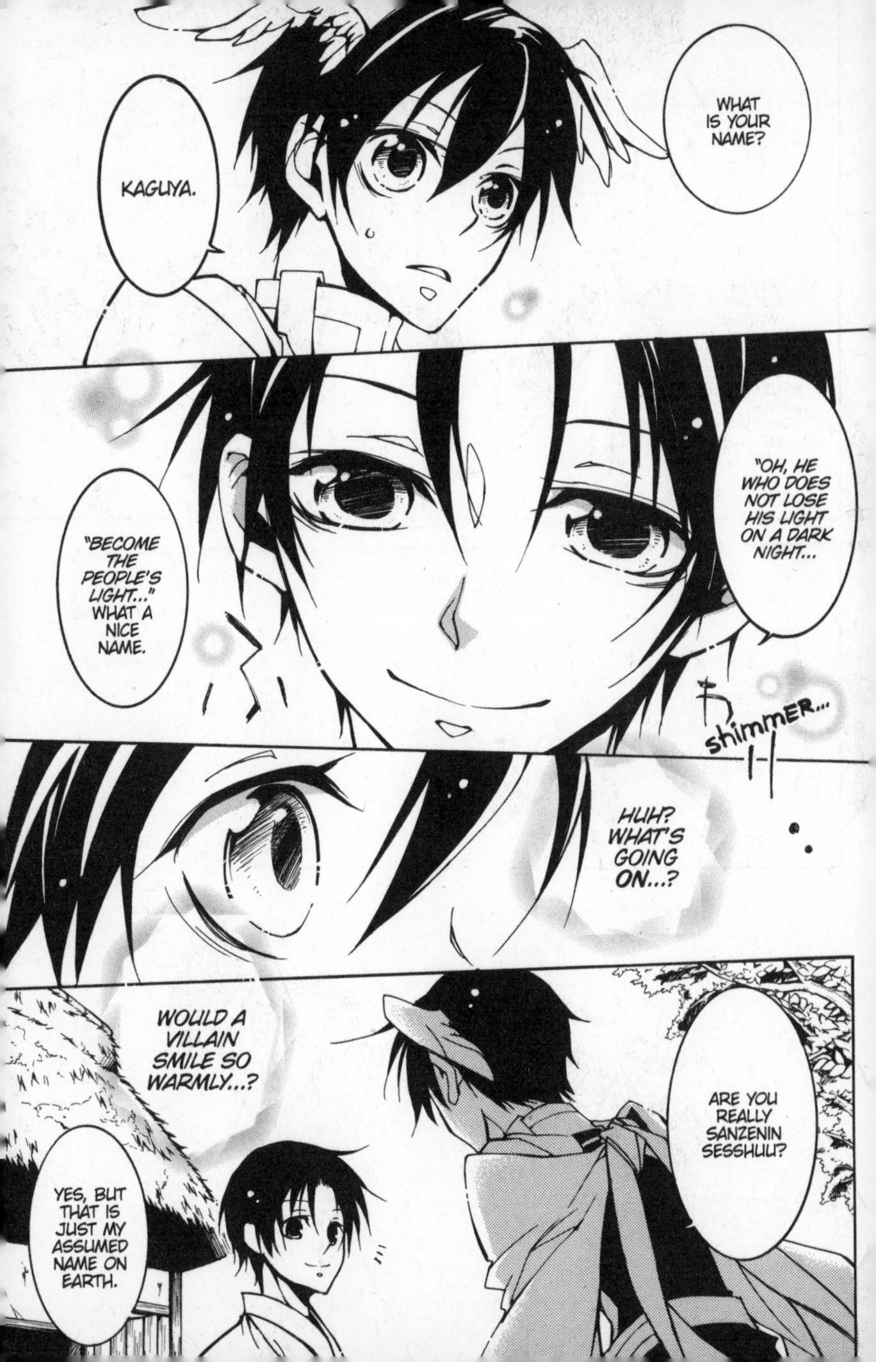
WHAT IS YOUR NAME?
KAGUYA.
"OH, HE WHO DOES NOT LOSE HIS LIGHT ON A DARK NIGHT...
"BECOME THE PEOPLE'S LIGHT..." WHAT A NICE NAME.
shimmER...
HUH? WHAT'S GOING ON...?
ARE YOU REALLY SANZENIN SESSHUU?
WOULD A VILLAIN SMILE SO WARMLY...?
YES, BUT THAT IS JUST MY ASSUMED NAME ON EARTH.

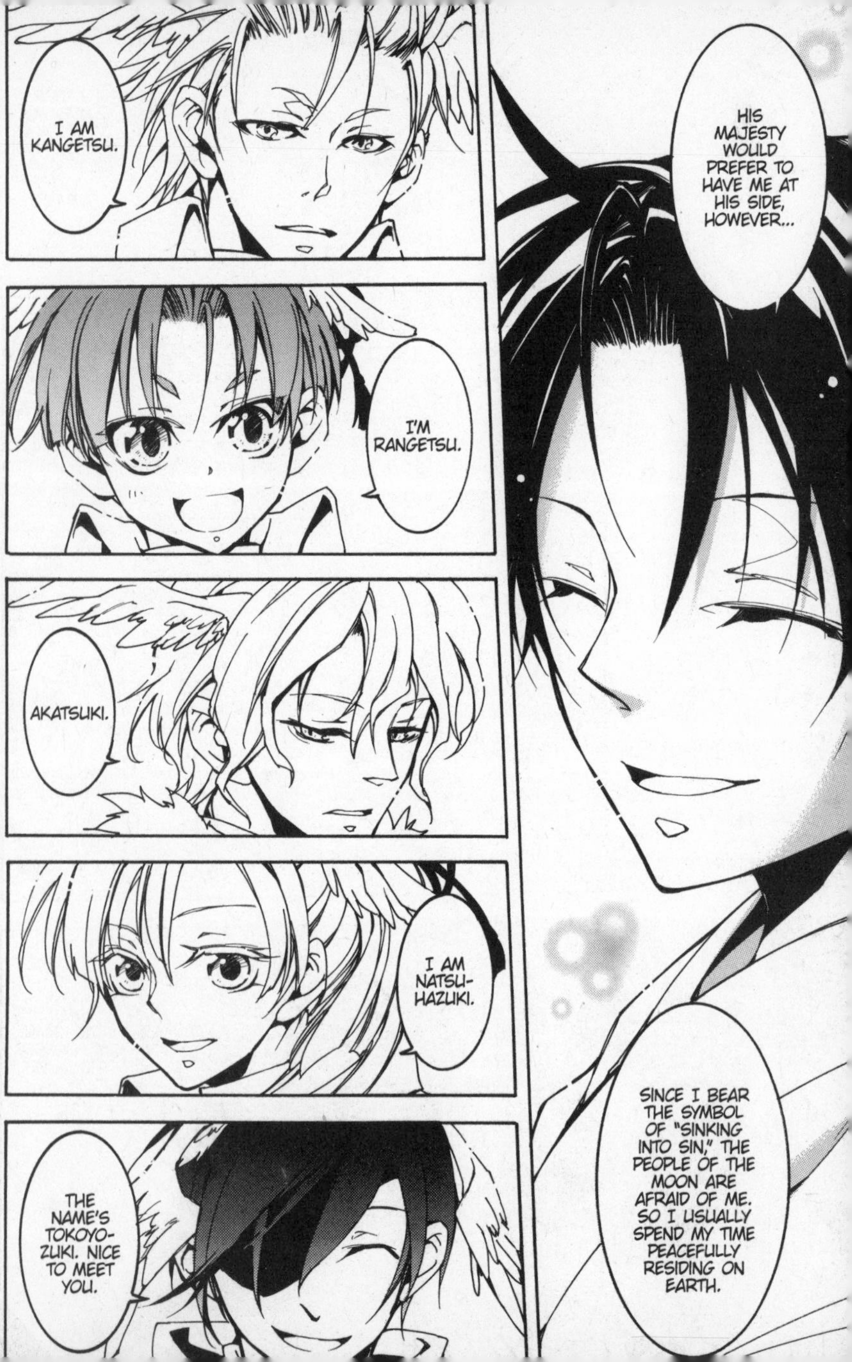
HIS MAJESTY WOULD PREFER TO HAVE ME AT HIS SIDE, HOWEVER...
SINCE I BEAR THE SYMBOL OF "SINKING INTO SIN," THE PEOPLE OF THE MOON ARE AFRAID OF ME. SO I USUALLY SPEND MY TIME PEACEFULLY RESIDING ON EARTH.
I AM KANGETSU.
I'M RANGETSU.
AKATSUKI.
I AM NATSU-HAZUKI.
THE NAME'S TOKOYO-ZUKI. NICE TO MEET YOU.

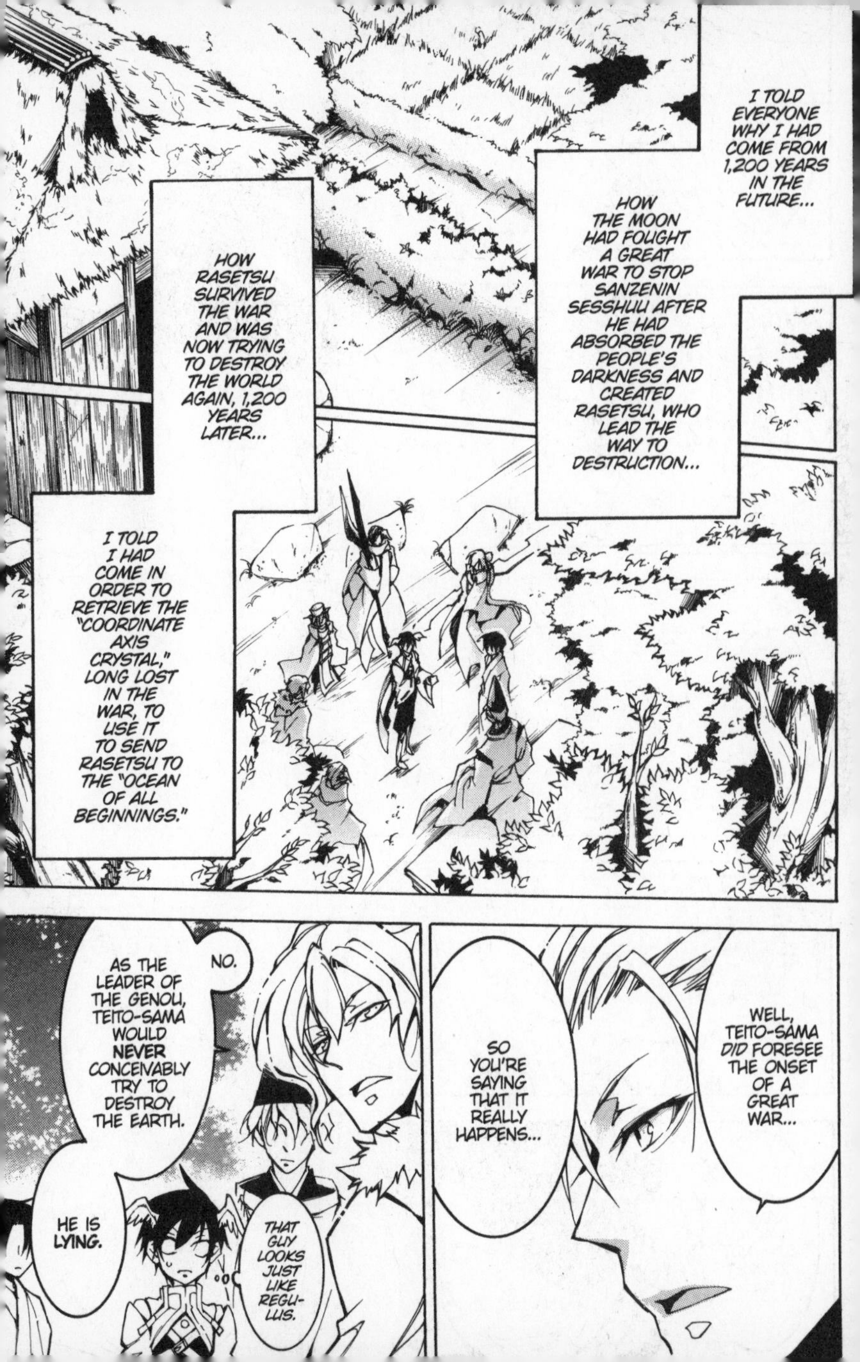
I TOLD EVERYONE WHY I HAD COME FROM 1,200 YEARS IN THE FUTURE...
HOW THE MOON HAD FOUGHT A GREAT WAR TO STOP SANZENIN SESSHUU AFTER HE HAD ABSORBED THE PEOPLE'S DARKNESS AND CREATED RASETSU, WHO LEAD THE WAY TO DESTRUCTION...
HOW RASETSU SURVIVED THE WAR AND WAS NOW TRYING TO DESTROY THE WORLD AGAIN, 1,200 YEARS LATER...
I TOLD I HAD COME IN ORDER TO RETRIEVE THE "COORDINATE AXIS CRYSTAL," LONG LOST IN THE WAR, TO USE IT TO SEND RASETSU TO THE "OCEAN OF ALL BEGINNINGS."
WELL, TEITO-SAMA DID FORESEE THE ONSET OF A GREAT WAR...
SO YOU'RE SAYING THAT IT REALLY HAPPENS...
NO.
AS THE LEADER OF THE GENOU, TEITO-SAMA WOULD **NEVER** CONCEIVABLY TRY TO DESTROY THE EARTH.
THAT GUY LOOKS JUST LIKE REGULUS.
HE IS **LYING.**

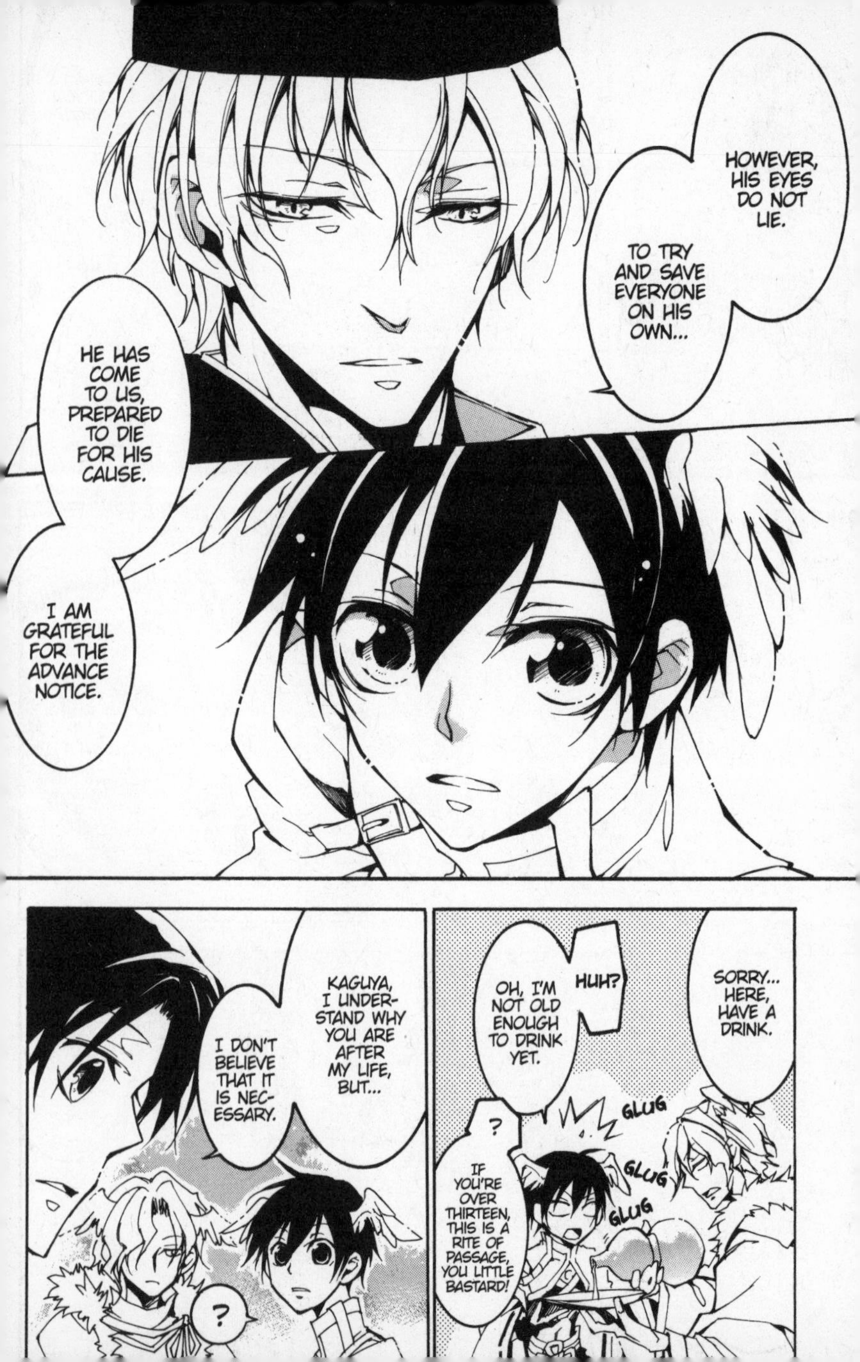
HOWEVER, HIS EYES DO NOT LIE.
TO TRY AND SAVE EVERYONE ON HIS OWN...
HE HAS COME TO US, PREPARED TO DIE FOR HIS CAUSE.
I AM GRATEFUL FOR THE ADVANCE NOTICE.
SORRY... HERE, HAVE A DRINK.
HUH?
OH, I'M NOT OLD ENOUGH TO DRINK YET.
GLUG
GLUG
GLUG
?
IF YOU'RE OVER THIRTEEN, THIS IS A RITE OF PASSAGE, YOU LITTLE BASTARD!
KAGUYA, I UNDER-STAND WHY YOU ARE AFTER MY LIFE, BUT...
I DON'T BELIEVE THAT IT IS NEC-ESSARY.
?

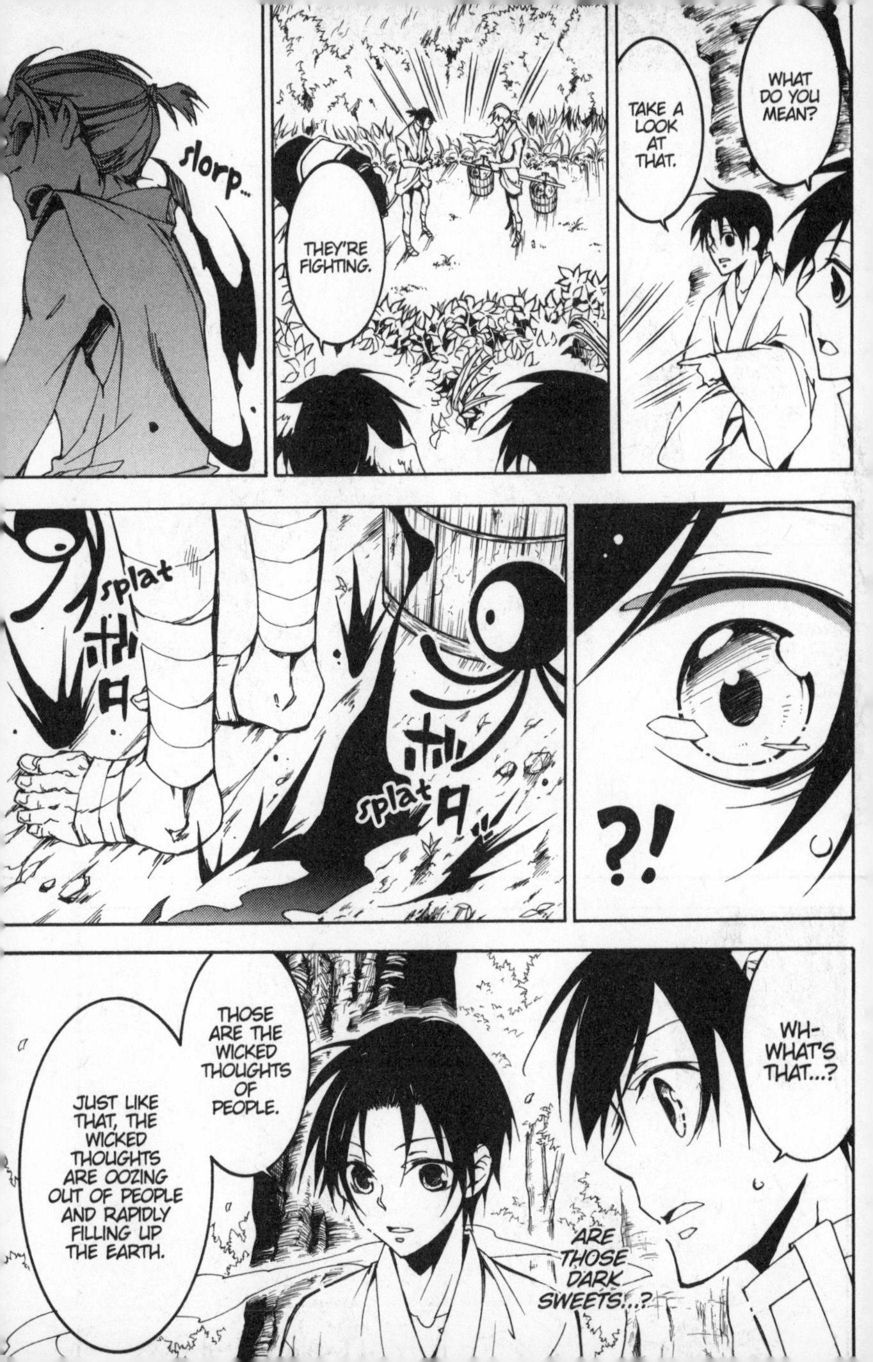
WHAT DO YOU MEAN?
TAKE A LOOK AT THAT.
THEY'RE FIGHTING.
slorp...
?!
splat
ボタ
splat
ボタ
WH- WHAT'S THAT...?
ARE THOSE DARK SWEETS...?
THOSE ARE THE WICKED THOUGHTS OF PEOPLE.
JUST LIKE THAT, THE WICKED THOUGHTS ARE OOZING OUT OF PEOPLE AND RAPIDLY FILLING UP THE EARTH.

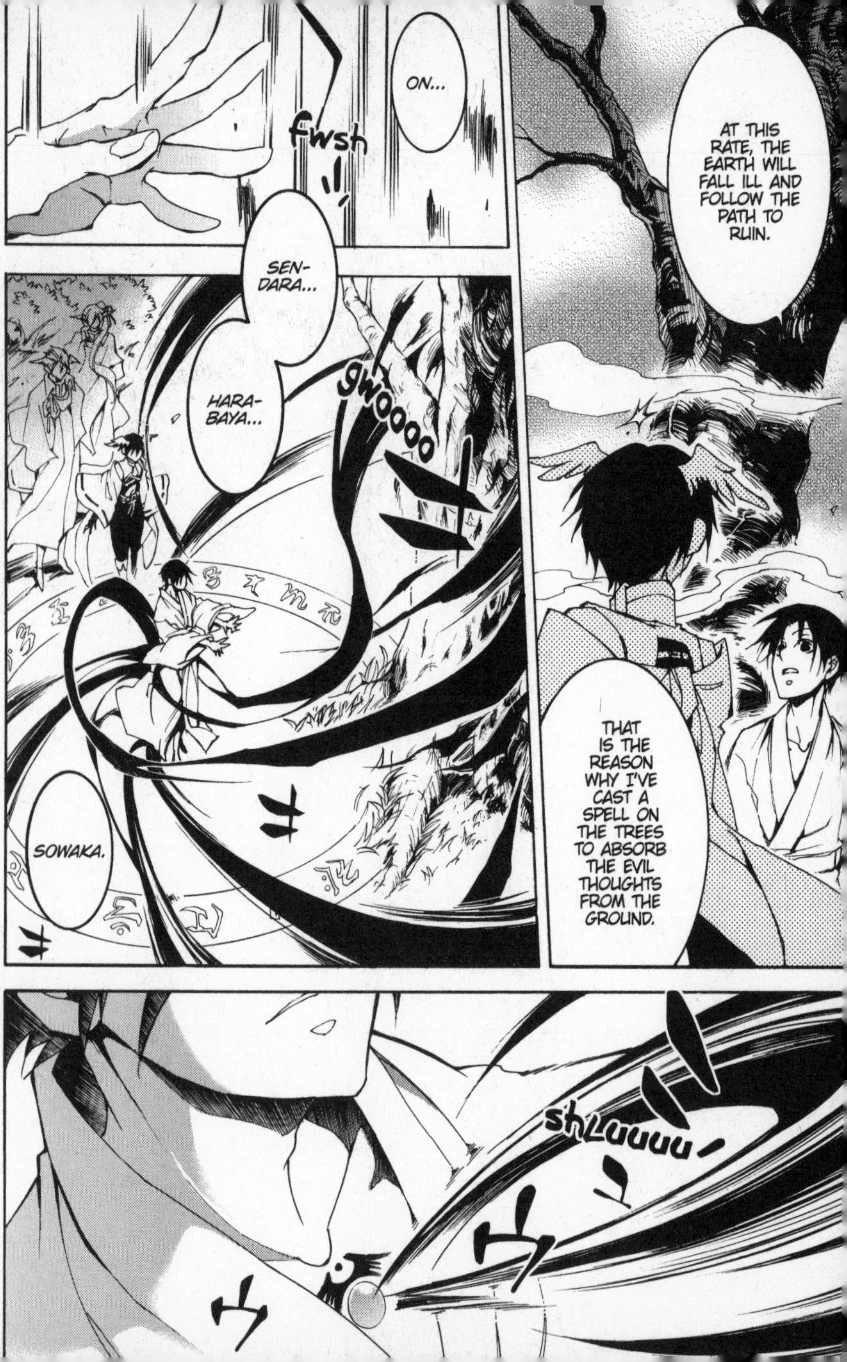
AT THIS RATE, THE EARTH WILL FALL ILL AND FOLLOW THE PATH TO RUIN.
THAT IS THE REASON WHY I'VE CAST A SPELL ON THE TREES TO ABSORB THE EVIL THOUGHTS FROM THE GROUND.
ON...
fwsh
SEN-DARA...
HARA-BAYA...
gwoooo
SOWAKA.
shluuuu-

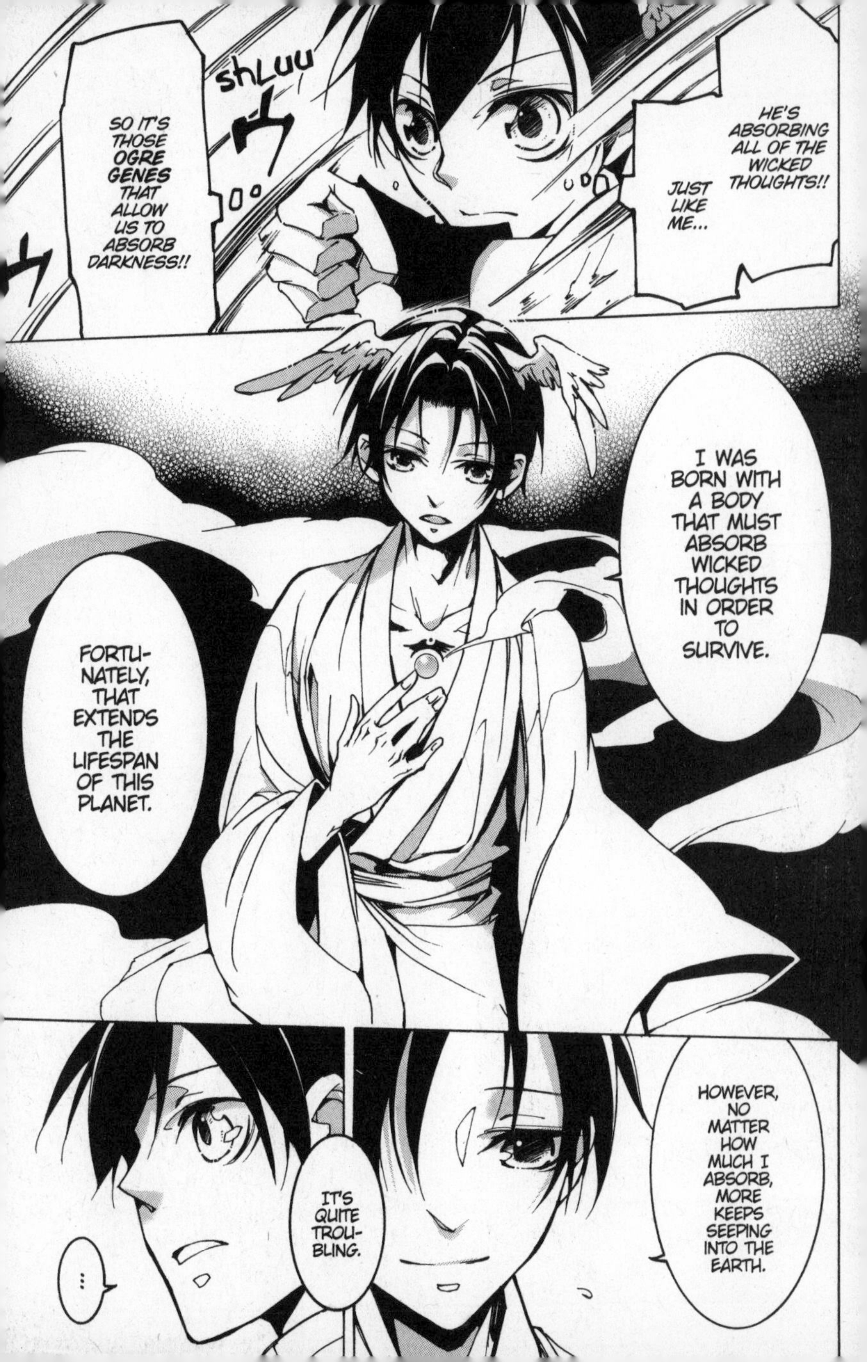
HE'S ABSORBING ALL OF THE WICKED THOUGHTS!!
JUST LIKE ME...
shLUU
SO IT'S THOSE OGRE GENES THAT ALLOW US TO ABSORB DARKNESS!!
I WAS BORN WITH A BODY THAT MUST ABSORB WICKED THOUGHTS IN ORDER TO SURVIVE.
FORTUNATELY, THAT EXTENDS THE LIFESPAN OF THIS PLANET.
HOWEVER, NO MATTER HOW MUCH I ABSORB, MORE KEEPS SEEPING INTO THE EARTH.
IT'S QUITE TROUBLING.
...

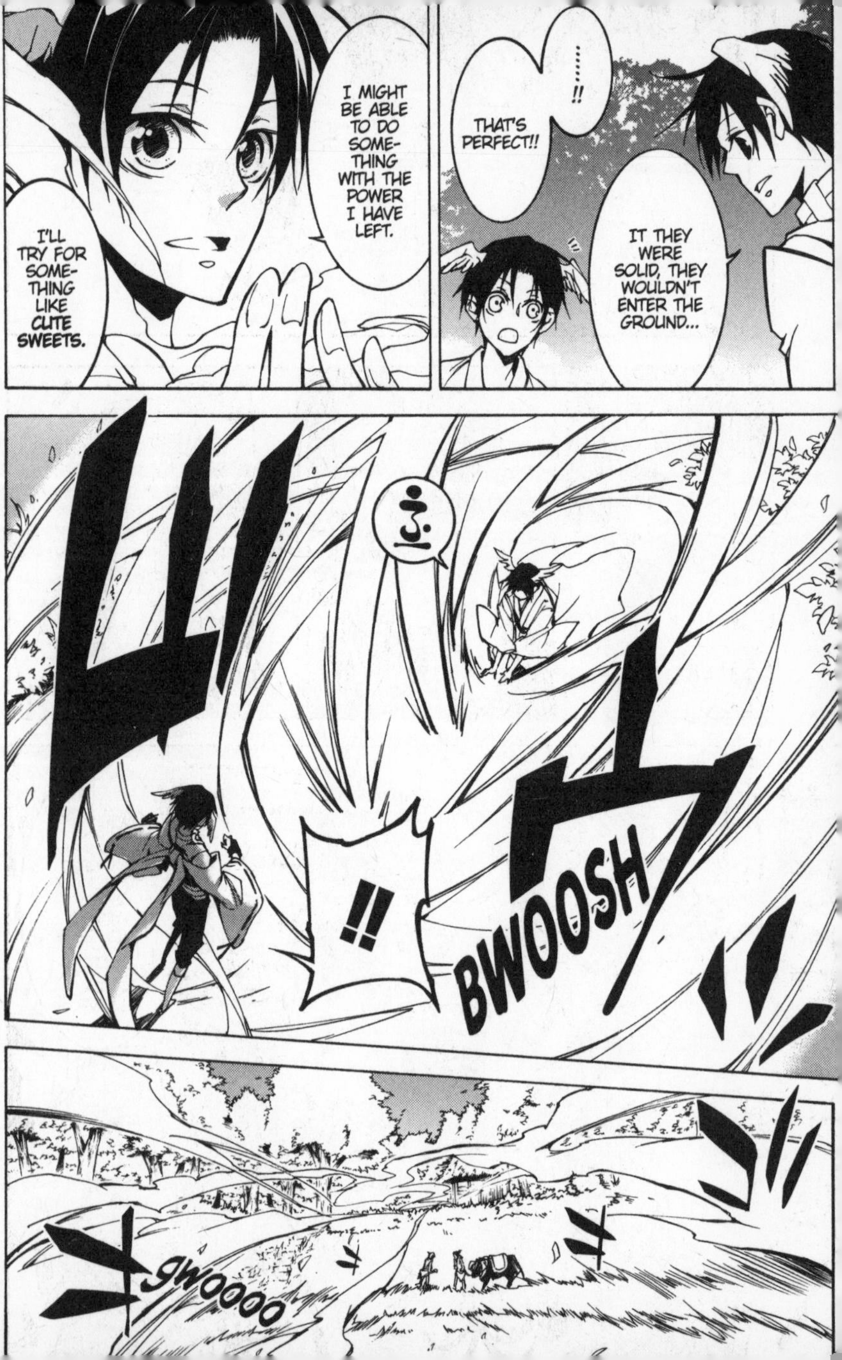
IT THEY WERE SOLID, THEY WOULDN'T ENTER THE GROUND...
......!!
THAT'S PERFECT!!
I MIGHT BE ABLE TO DO SOME-THING WITH THE POWER I HAVE LEFT.
I'LL TRY FOR SOME-THING LIKE CUTE SWEETS.
!!
BWOOSH
gwoooo

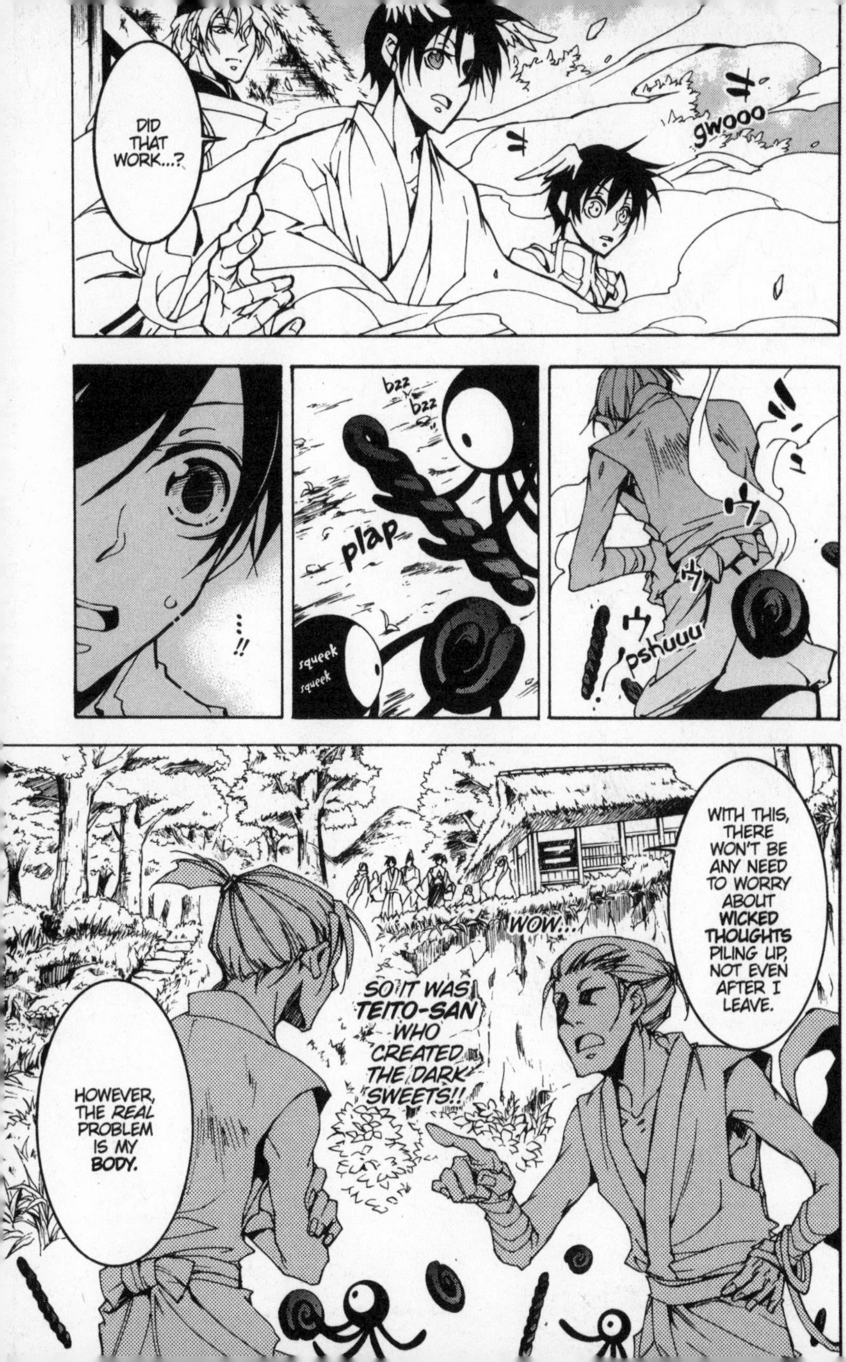
gwooo
DID THAT WORK...?
pshuuu
bzz bzz
plap
squeek squeek
...!!
WITH THIS, THERE WON'T BE ANY NEED TO WORRY ABOUT WICKED THOUGHTS PILING UP, NOT EVEN AFTER I LEAVE.
WOW...
SO IT WAS TEITO-SAN WHO CREATED THE DARK SWEETS!!
HOWEVER, THE REAL PROBLEM IS MY BODY.

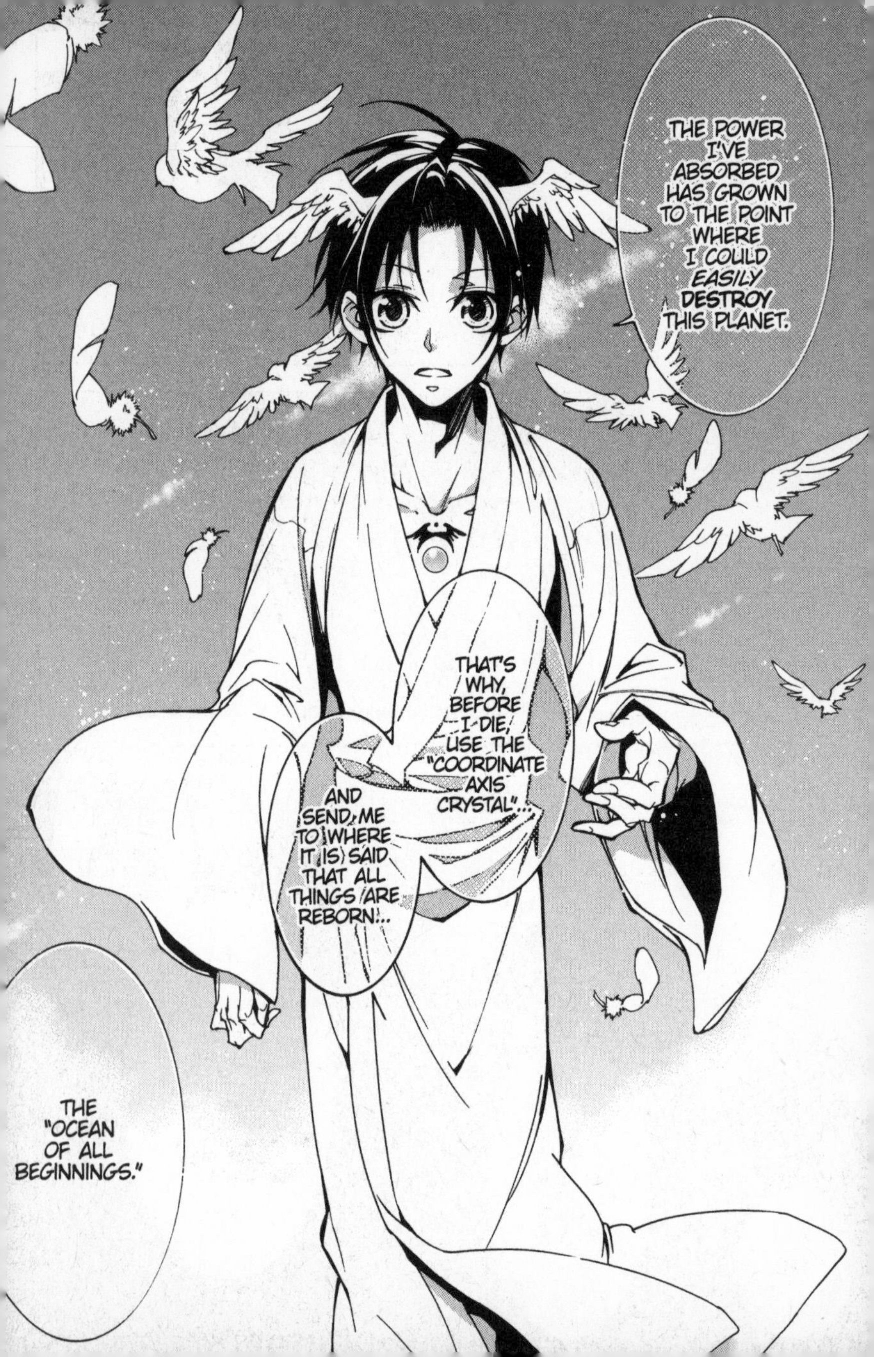
THE POWER I'VE ABSORBED HAS GROWN TO THE POINT WHERE I COULD *EASILY* DESTROY THIS PLANET.
THAT'S WHY, BEFORE I DIE, USE THE "COORDINATE AXIS CRYSTAL"...
AND SEND ME TO WHERE IT IS SAID THAT ALL THINGS ARE REBORN...
THE "OCEAN OF ALL BEGINNINGS."

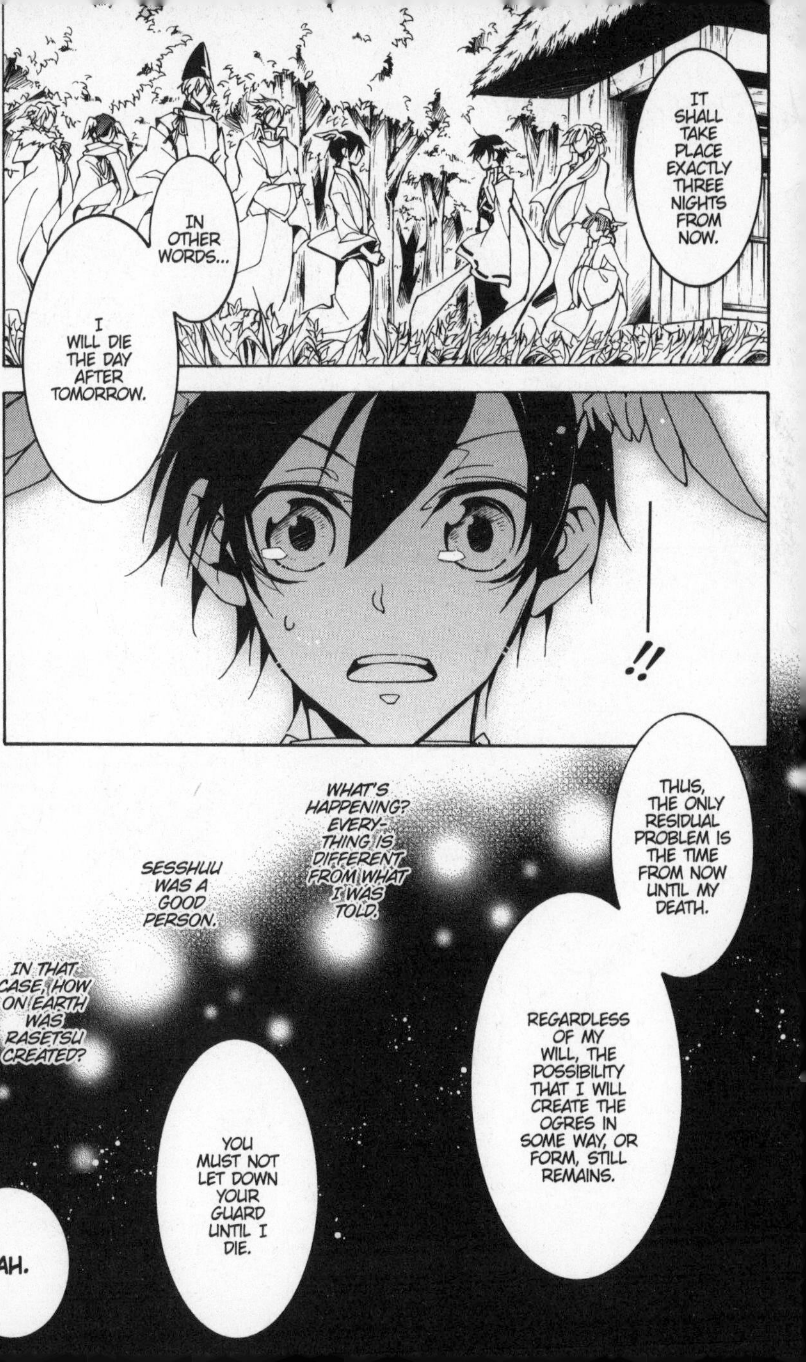
IT SHALL TAKE PLACE EXACTLY THREE NIGHTS FROM NOW.
IN OTHER WORDS...
I WILL DIE THE DAY AFTER TOMORROW.
!!
THUS, THE ONLY RESIDUAL PROBLEM IS THE TIME FROM NOW UNTIL MY DEATH.
REGARDLESS OF MY WILL, THE POSSIBILITY THAT I WILL CREATE THE OGRES IN SOME WAY, OR FORM, STILL REMAINS.
WHAT'S HAPPENING? EVERYTHING IS DIFFERENT FROM WHAT I WAS TOLD.
SESSHUU WAS A GOOD PERSON.
YOU MUST NOT LET DOWN YOUR GUARD UNTIL I DIE.
IN THAT CASE, HOW ON EARTH WAS RASETSU CREATED?
AH.

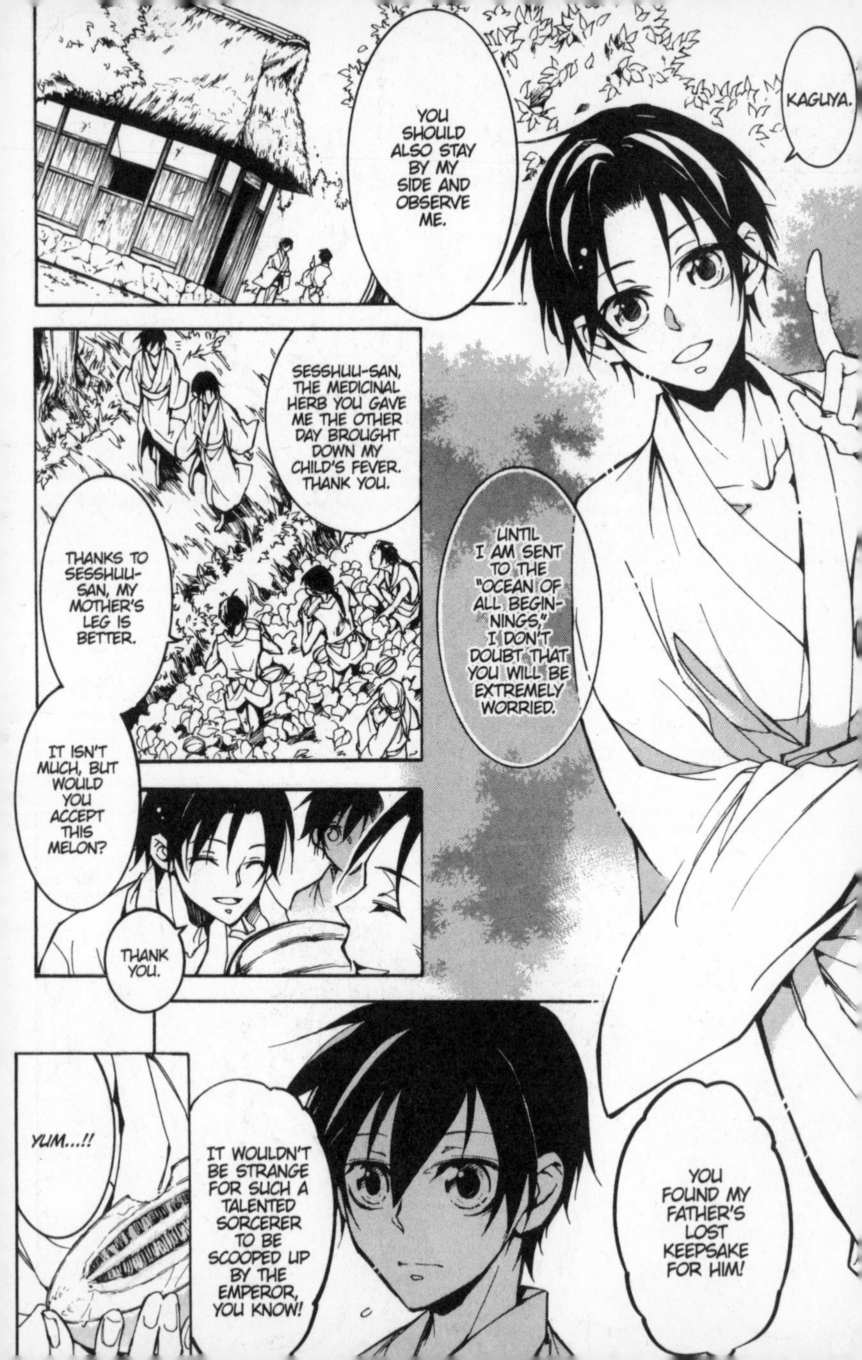
KAGUYA.
YOU SHOULD ALSO STAY BY MY SIDE AND OBSERVE ME.
UNTIL I AM SENT TO THE "OCEAN OF ALL BEGIN-NINGS," I DON'T DOUBT THAT YOU WILL BE EXTREMELY WORRIED.
SESSHUU-SAN, THE MEDICINAL HERB YOU GAVE ME THE OTHER DAY BROUGHT DOWN MY CHILD'S FEVER. THANK YOU.
THANKS TO SESSHUU-SAN, MY MOTHER'S LEG IS BETTER.
IT ISN'T MUCH, BUT WOULD YOU ACCEPT THIS MELON?
THANK YOU.
YOU FOUND MY FATHER'S LOST KEEPSAKE FOR HIM!
IT WOULDN'T BE STRANGE FOR SUCH A TALENTED SORCERER TO BE SCOOPED UP BY THE EMPEROR, YOU KNOW!
YUM...!!

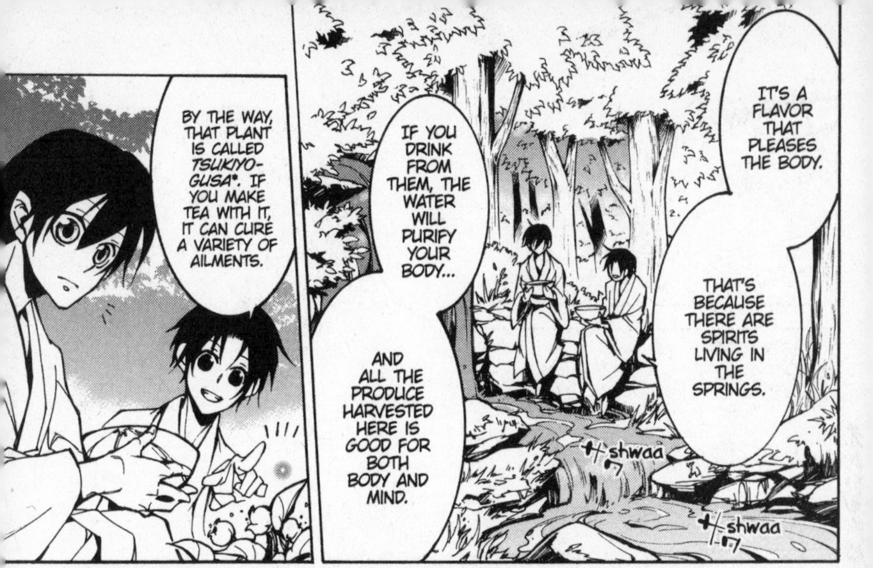
IT'S A FLAVOR THAT PLEASES THE BODY.
THAT'S BECAUSE THERE ARE SPIRITS LIVING IN THE SPRINGS.
IF YOU DRINK FROM THEM, THE WATER WILL PURIFY YOUR BODY...
AND ALL THE PRODUCE HARVESTED HERE IS GOOD FOR BOTH BODY AND MIND.
shwaa
shwaa
BY THE WAY, THAT PLANT IS CALLED *TSUKIYO-GUSA**. IF YOU MAKE TEA WITH IT, IT CAN CURE A VARIETY OF AILMENTS.

One of the common names for the oenothera tetraptera plant is tsukiyogusa, literally "moonlit night grass."

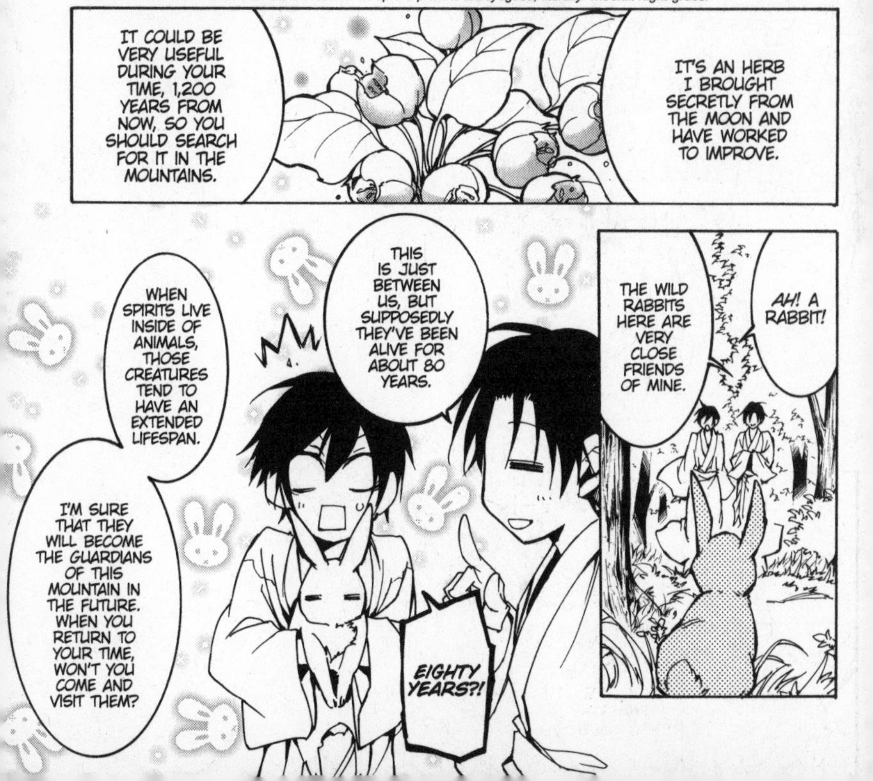
IT'S AN HERB I BROUGHT SECRETLY FROM THE MOON AND HAVE WORKED TO IMPROVE.
IT COULD BE VERY USEFUL DURING YOUR TIME, 1,200 YEARS FROM NOW, SO YOU SHOULD SEARCH FOR IT IN THE MOUNTAINS.
AH! A RABBIT!
THE WILD RABBITS HERE ARE VERY CLOSE FRIENDS OF MINE.
THIS IS JUST BETWEEN US, BUT SUPPOSEDLY THEY'VE BEEN ALIVE FOR ABOUT 80 YEARS.
WHEN SPIRITS LIVE INSIDE OF ANIMALS, THOSE CREATURES TEND TO HAVE AN EXTENDED LIFESPAN.
EIGHTY YEARS?!
I'M SURE THAT THEY WILL BECOME THE GUARDIANS OF THIS MOUNTAIN IN THE FUTURE. WHEN YOU RETURN TO YOUR TIME, WON'T YOU COME AND VISIT THEM?

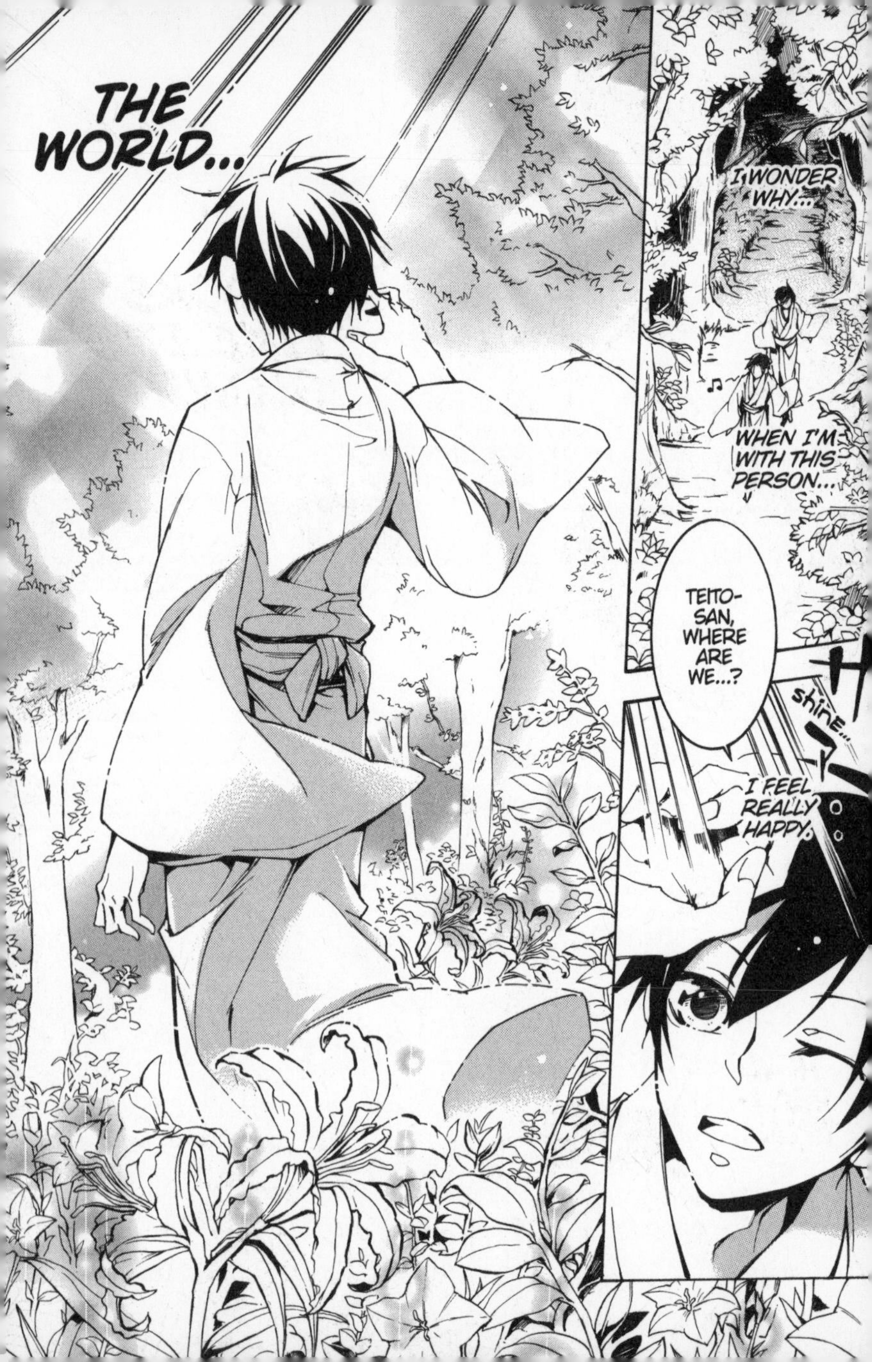
I WONDER WHY...
WHEN I'M WITH THIS PERSON...
TEITO-SAN, WHERE ARE WE...?
shine...
I FEEL REALLY HAPPY.
THE WORLD...

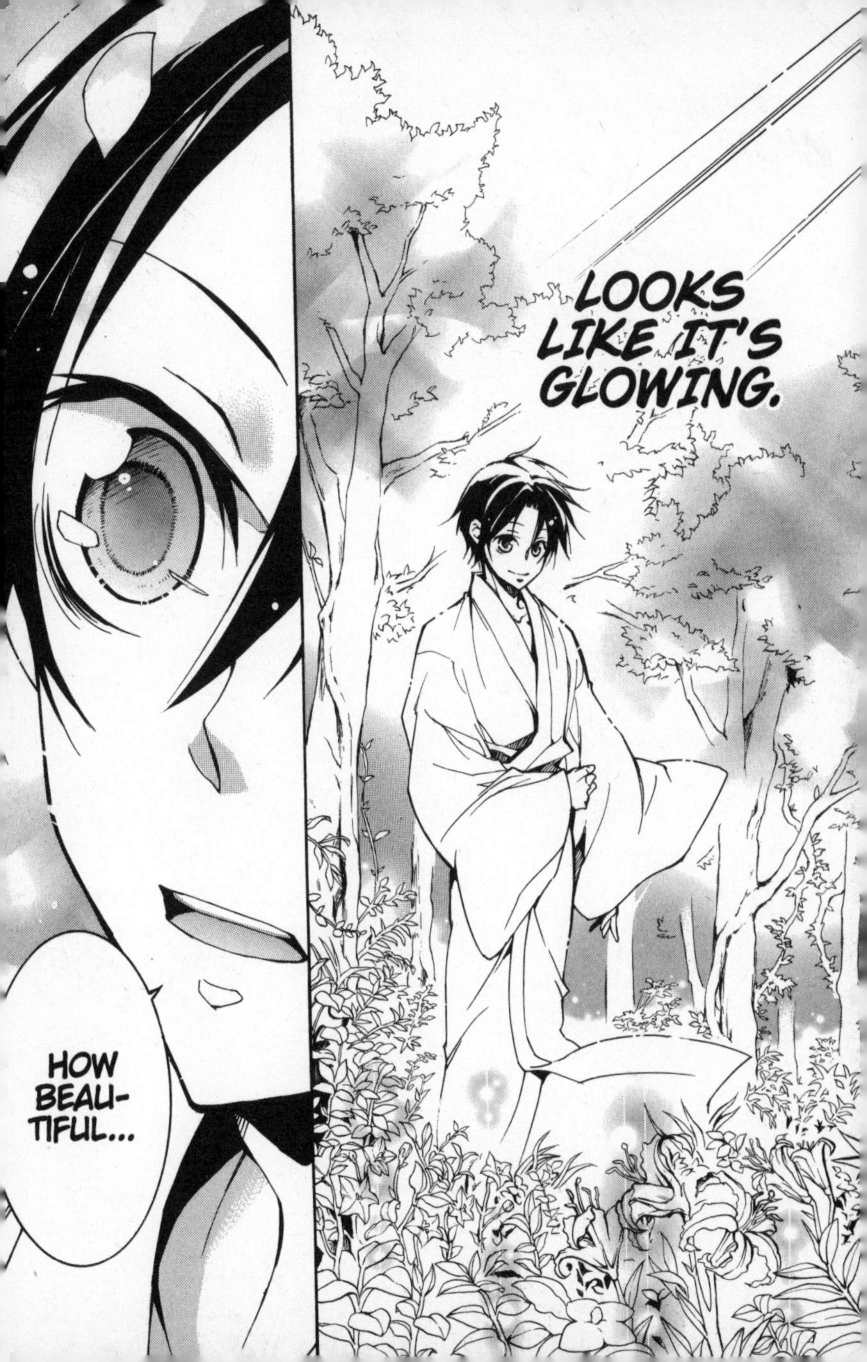
LOOKS LIKE IT'S GLOWING.
HOW BEAU-TIFUL...

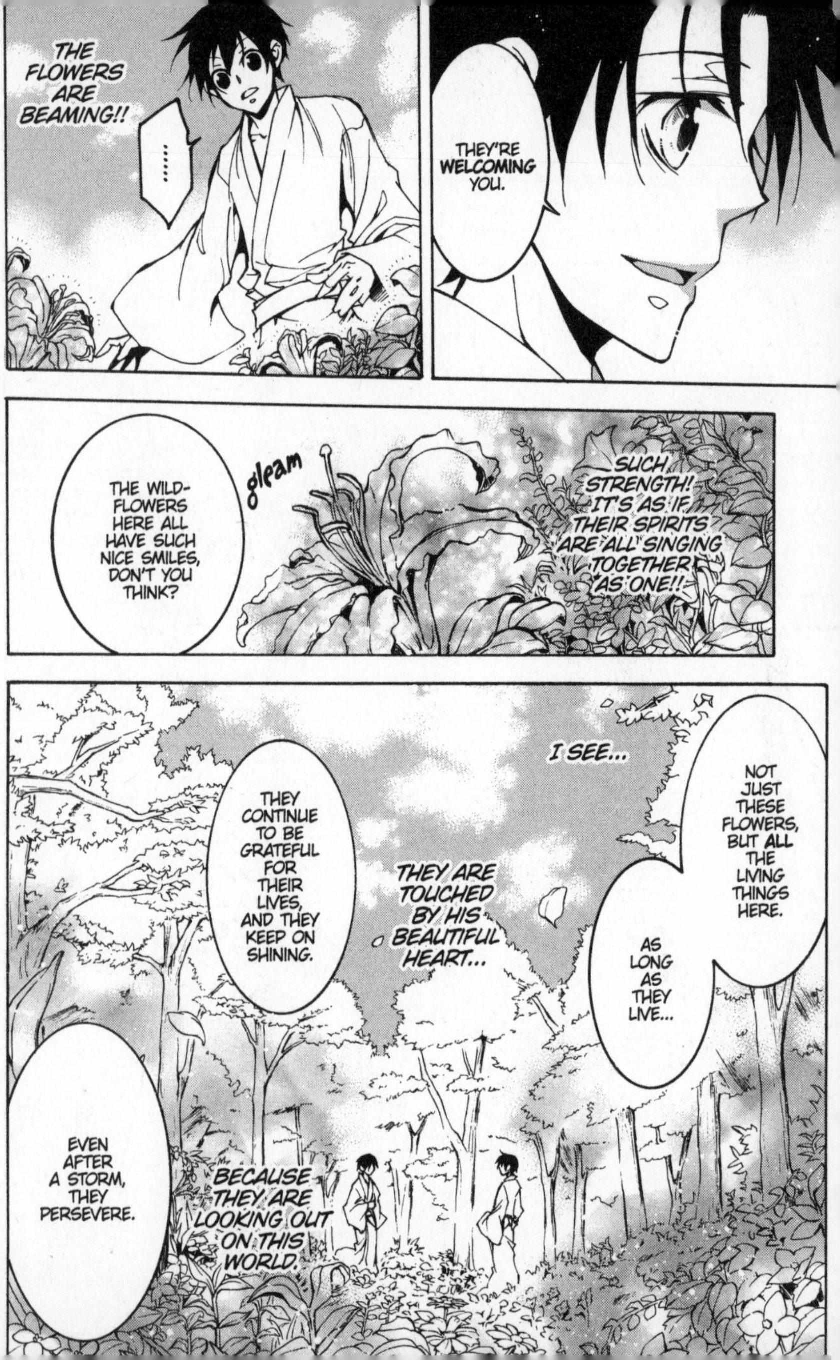
THEY'RE WELCOMING YOU.
THE FLOWERS ARE BEAMING!!
......
SUCH STRENGTH! IT'S AS IF THEIR SPIRITS ARE ALL SINGING TOGETHER AS ONE!!
gleam
THE WILD-FLOWERS HERE ALL HAVE SUCH NICE SMILES, DON'T YOU THINK?
NOT JUST THESE FLOWERS, BUT ALL THE LIVING THINGS HERE.
AS LONG AS THEY LIVE...
I SEE...
THEY CONTINUE TO BE GRATEFUL FOR THEIR LIVES, AND THEY KEEP ON SHINING.
THEY ARE TOUCHED BY HIS BEAUTIFUL HEART...
EVEN AFTER A STORM, THEY PERSEVERE.
BECAUSE THEY ARE LOOKING OUT ON THIS WORLD.

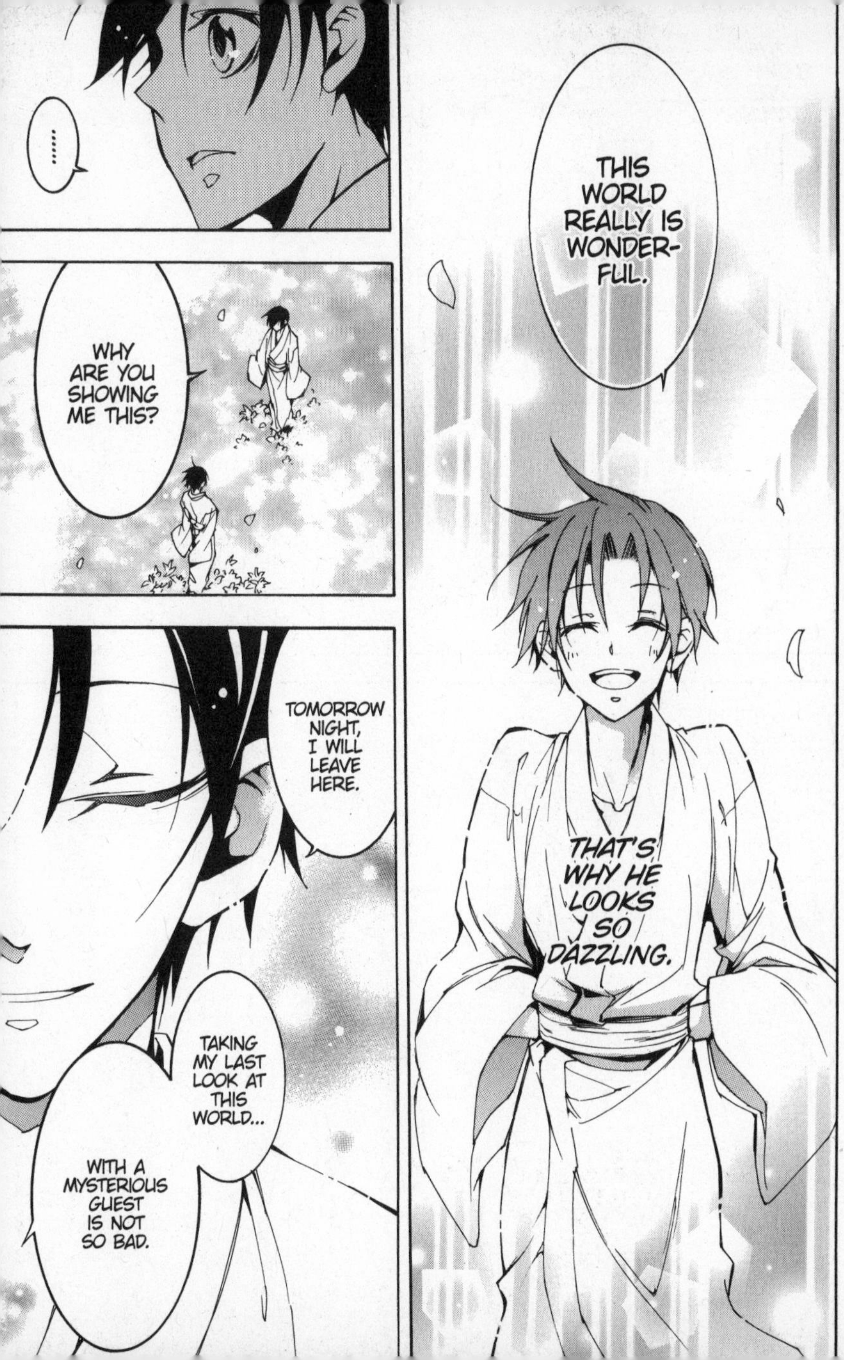
THIS WORLD REALLY IS WONDER-FUL.
THAT'S WHY HE LOOKS SO DAZZLING.
......
WHY ARE YOU SHOWING ME THIS?
TOMORROW NIGHT, I WILL LEAVE HERE.
TAKING MY LAST LOOK AT THIS WORLD...
WITH A MYSTERIOUS GUEST IS NOT SO BAD.

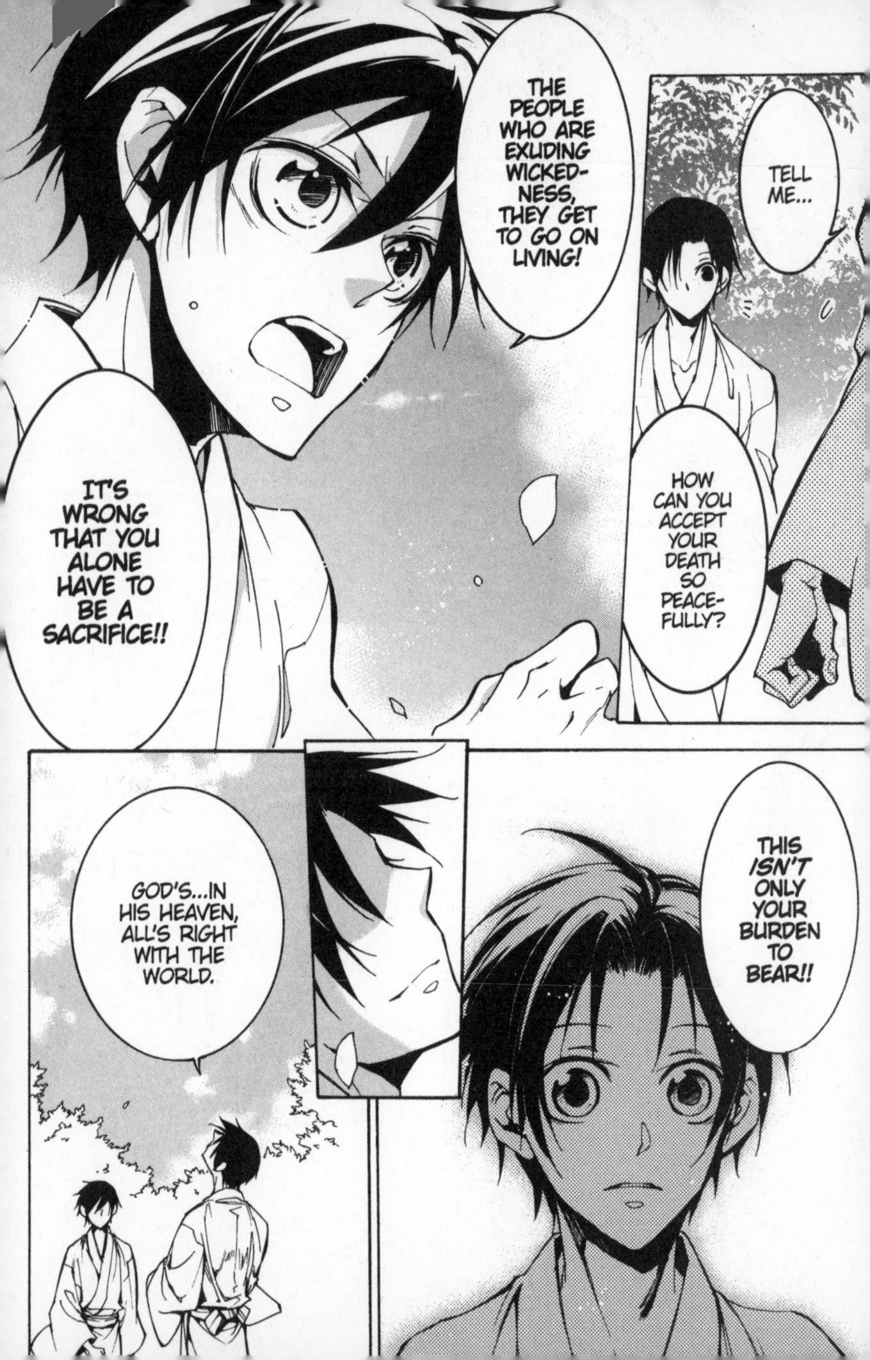
TELL ME...
HOW CAN YOU ACCEPT YOUR DEATH SO PEACE-FULLY?
THE PEOPLE WHO ARE EXUDING WICKED-NESS, THEY GET TO GO ON LIVING!
IT'S WRONG THAT YOU ALONE HAVE TO BE A SACRIFICE!!
THIS *ISN'T* ONLY YOUR BURDEN TO BEAR!!
GOD'S...IN HIS HEAVEN, ALL'S RIGHT WITH THE WORLD.

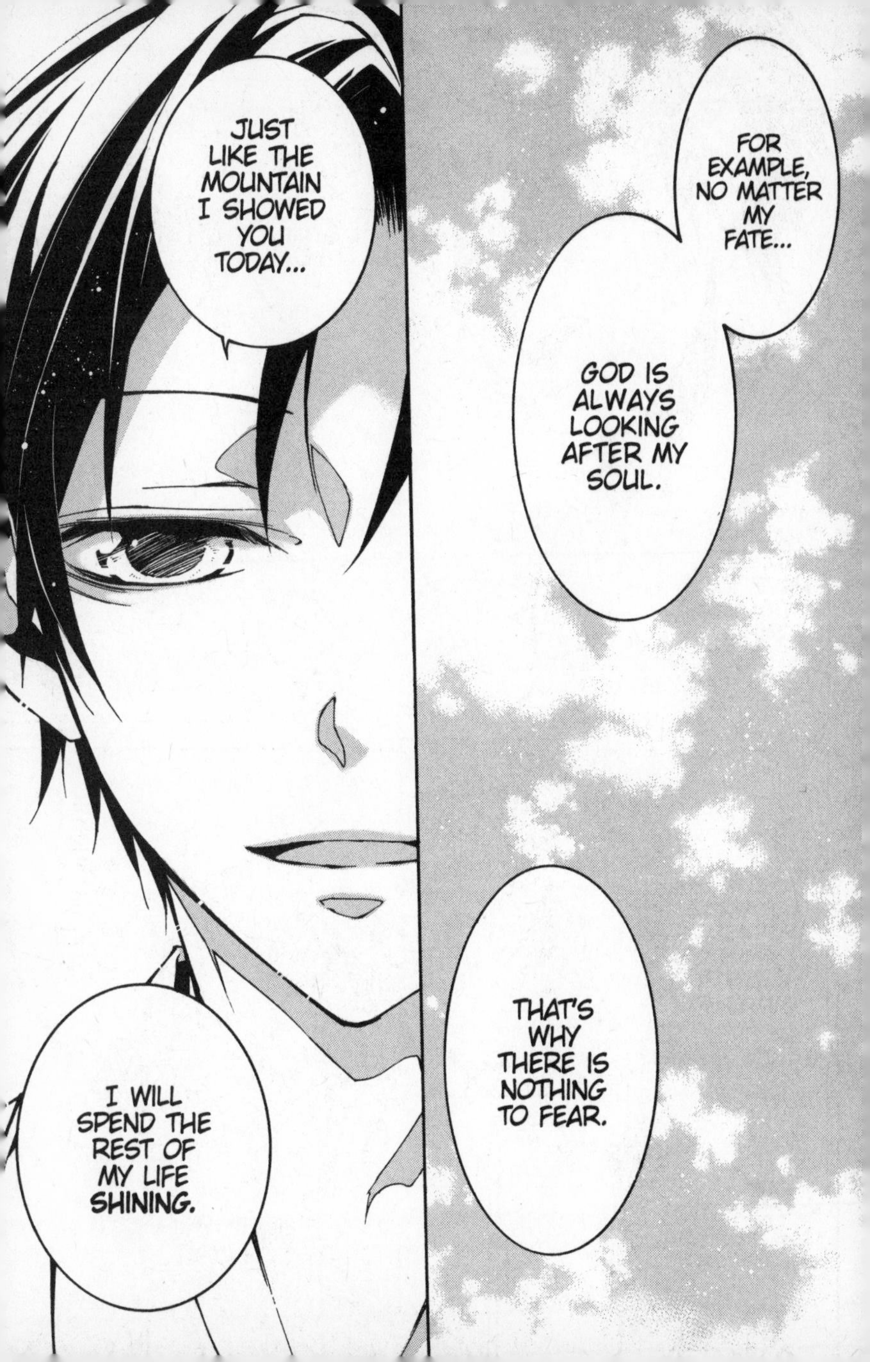
FOR EXAMPLE, NO MATTER MY FATE...
GOD IS ALWAYS LOOKING AFTER MY SOUL.
THAT'S WHY THERE IS NOTHING TO FEAR.
JUST LIKE THE MOUNTAIN I SHOWED YOU TODAY...
I WILL SPEND THE REST OF MY LIFE SHINING.

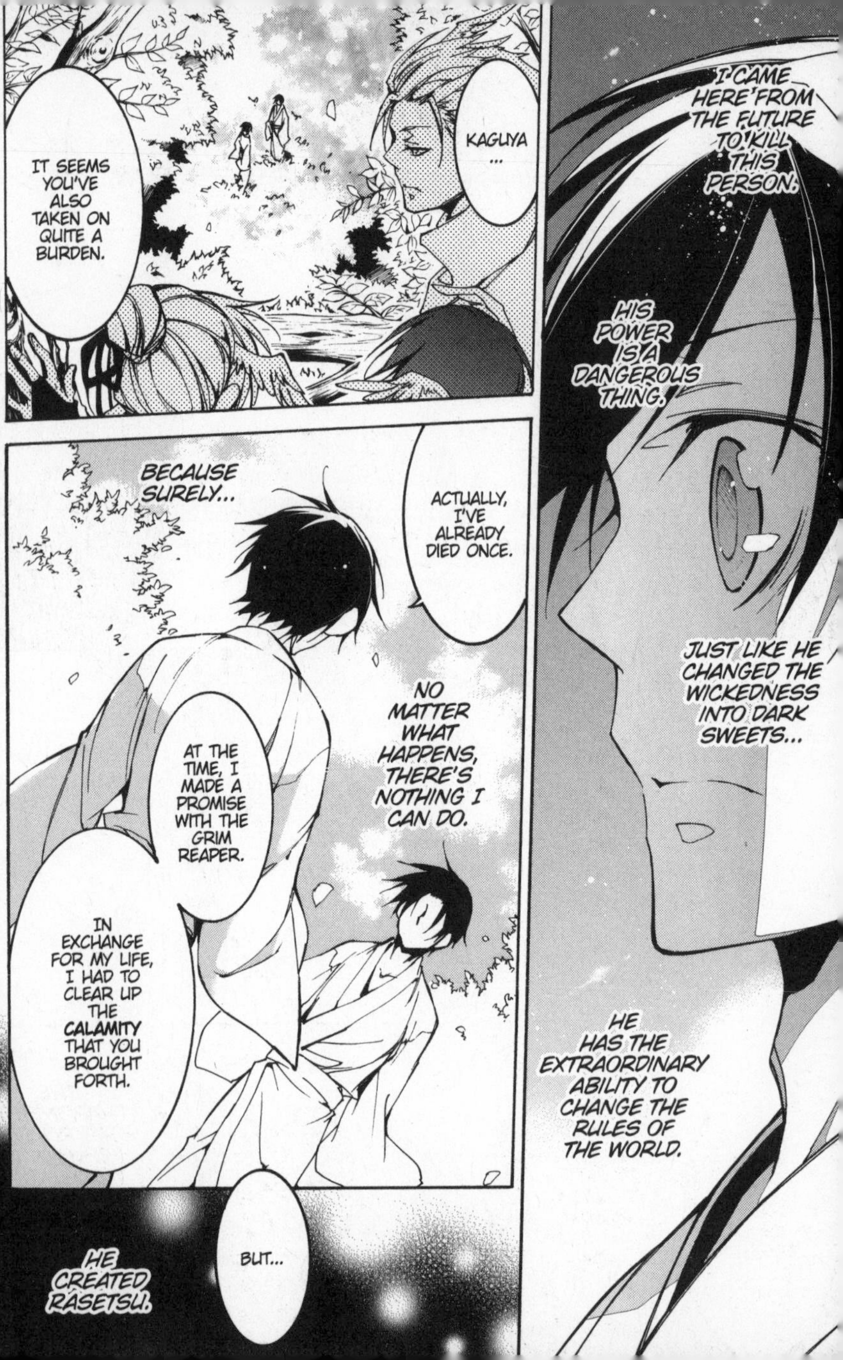
I CAME HERE FROM THE FUTURE TO KILL THIS PERSON.
HIS POWER IS A DANGEROUS THING.
JUST LIKE HE CHANGED THE WICKEDNESS INTO DARK SWEETS...
HE HAS THE EXTRAORDINARY ABILITY TO CHANGE THE RULES OF THE WORLD.
KAGUYA...
IT SEEMS YOU'VE ALSO TAKEN ON QUITE A BURDEN.
ACTUALLY, I'VE ALREADY DIED ONCE.
BECAUSE SURELY...
NO MATTER WHAT HAPPENS, THERE'S NOTHING I CAN DO.
AT THE TIME, I MADE A PROMISE WITH THE GRIM REAPER.
IN EXCHANGE FOR MY LIFE, I HAD TO CLEAR UP THE **CALAMITY** THAT YOU BROUGHT FORTH.
BUT...
HE CREATED RASETSU.

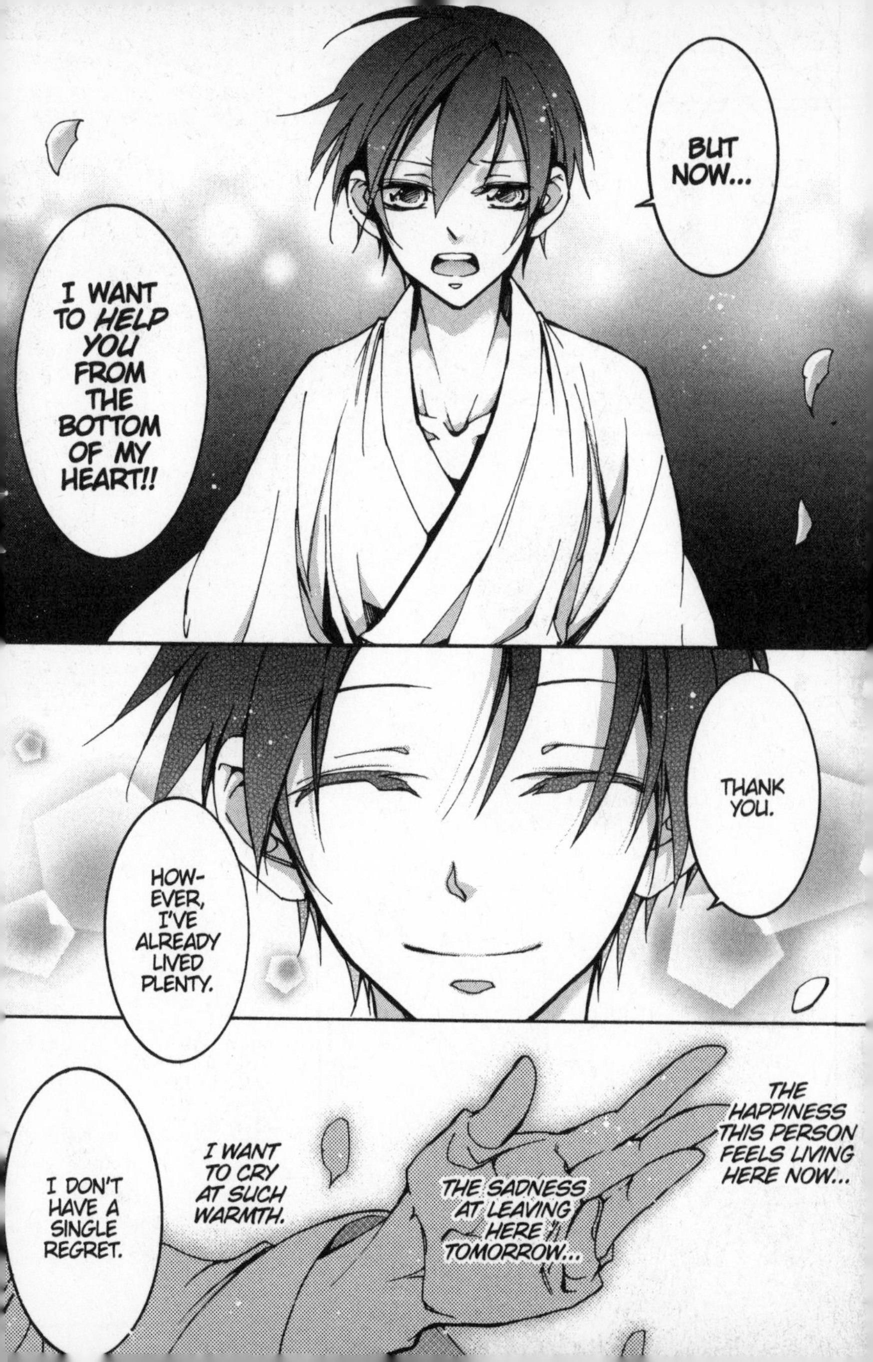
BUT NOW...
I WANT TO *HELP YOU* FROM THE BOTTOM OF MY HEART!!
THANK YOU.
HOW-EVER, I'VE ALREADY LIVED PLENTY.
THE HAPPINESS THIS PERSON FEELS LIVING HERE NOW...
THE SADNESS AT LEAVING HERE TOMORROW...
I WANT TO CRY AT SUCH WARMTH.
I DON'T HAVE A SINGLE REGRET.

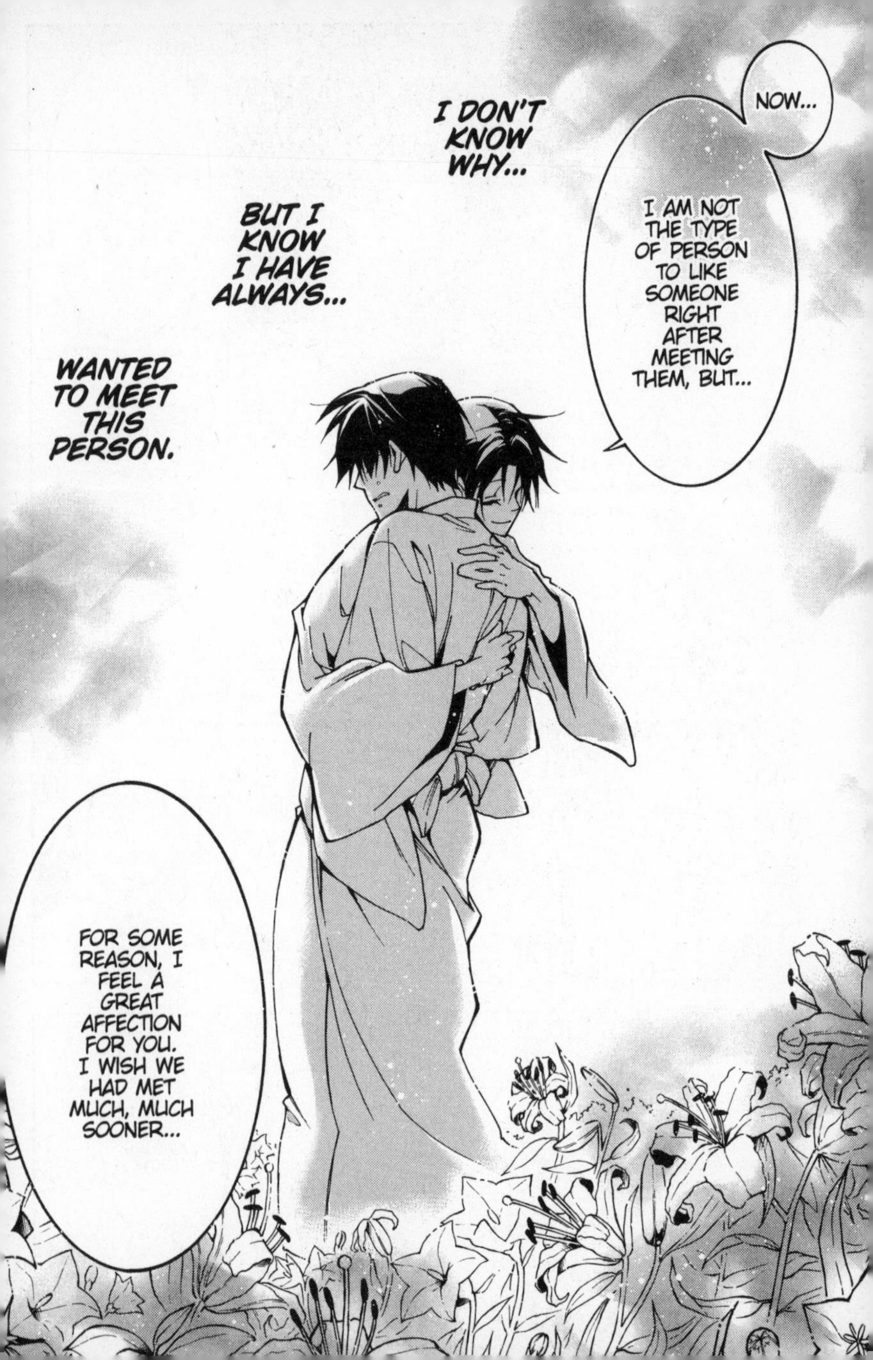
NOW...
I AM NOT THE TYPE OF PERSON TO LIKE SOMEONE RIGHT AFTER MEETING THEM, BUT...
I DON'T KNOW WHY...
BUT I KNOW I HAVE ALWAYS...
WANTED TO MEET THIS PERSON.
FOR SOME REASON, I FEEL A GREAT AFFECTION FOR YOU. I WISH WE HAD MET MUCH, MUCH SOONER...

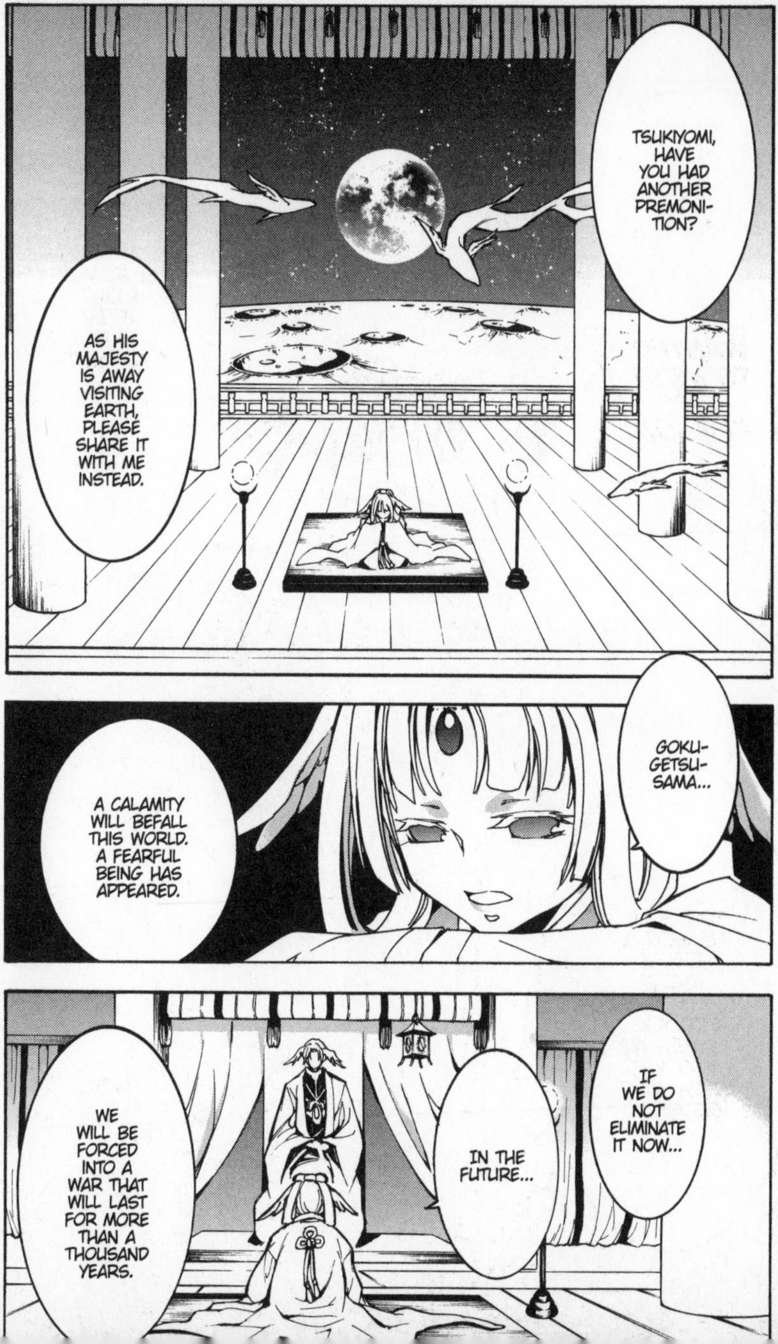
TSUKIYOMI, HAVE YOU HAD ANOTHER PREMONITION?
AS HIS MAJESTY IS AWAY VISITING EARTH, PLEASE SHARE IT WITH ME INSTEAD.
GOKU-GETSU-SAMA...
A CALAMITY WILL BEFALL THIS WORLD. A FEARFUL BEING HAS APPEARED.
IF WE DO NOT ELIMINATE IT NOW...
IN THE FUTURE...
WE WILL BE FORCED INTO A WAR THAT WILL LAST FOR MORE THAN A THOUSAND YEARS.

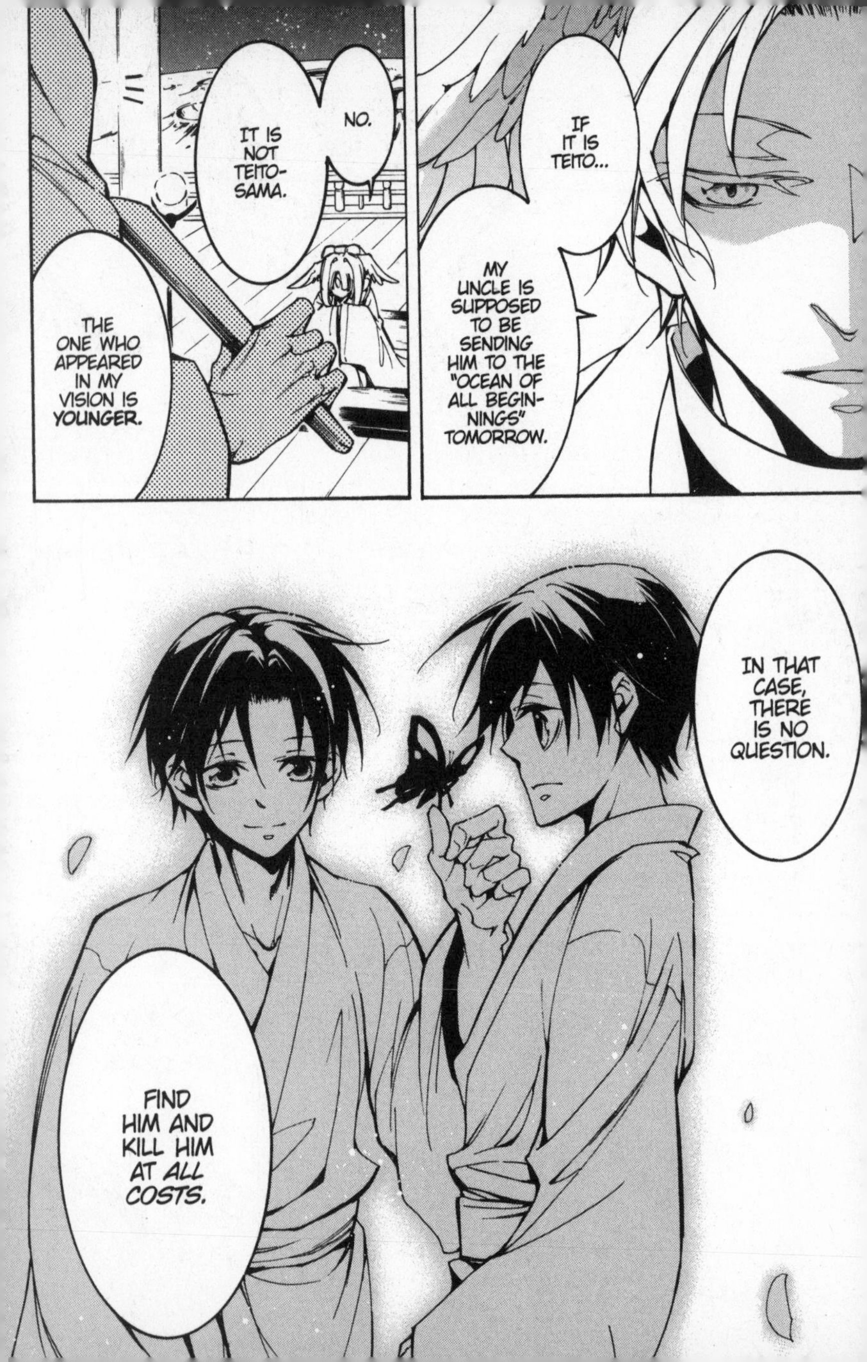
IF IT IS TEITO...
MY UNCLE IS SUPPOSED TO BE SENDING HIM TO THE "OCEAN OF ALL BEGINNINGS" TOMORROW.
NO.
IT IS NOT TEITO-SAMA.
THE ONE WHO APPEARED IN MY VISION IS YOUNGER.
IN THAT CASE, THERE IS NO QUESTION.
FIND HIM AND KILL HIM AT ALL COSTS.

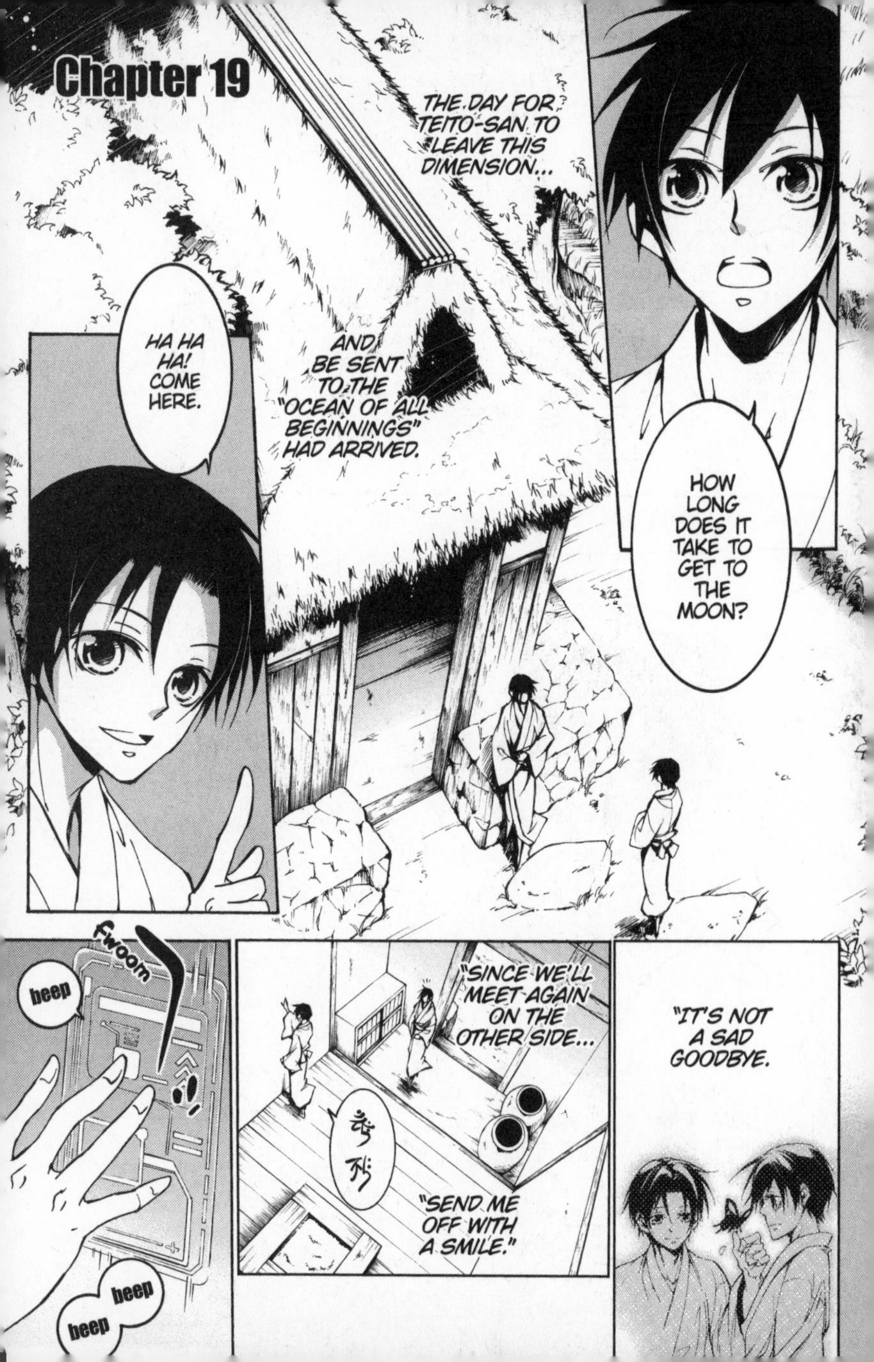
Chapter 19
THE DAY FOR TEITO-SAN TO LEAVE THIS DIMENSION...
AND BE SENT TO THE "OCEAN OF ALL BEGINNINGS" HAD ARRIVED.
HOW LONG DOES IT TAKE TO GET TO THE MOON?
HA HA HA! COME HERE.
"IT'S NOT A SAD GOODBYE.
"SINCE WE'LL MEET AGAIN ON THE OTHER SIDE...
"SEND ME OFF WITH A SMILE."
fwoom
beep
beep
beep

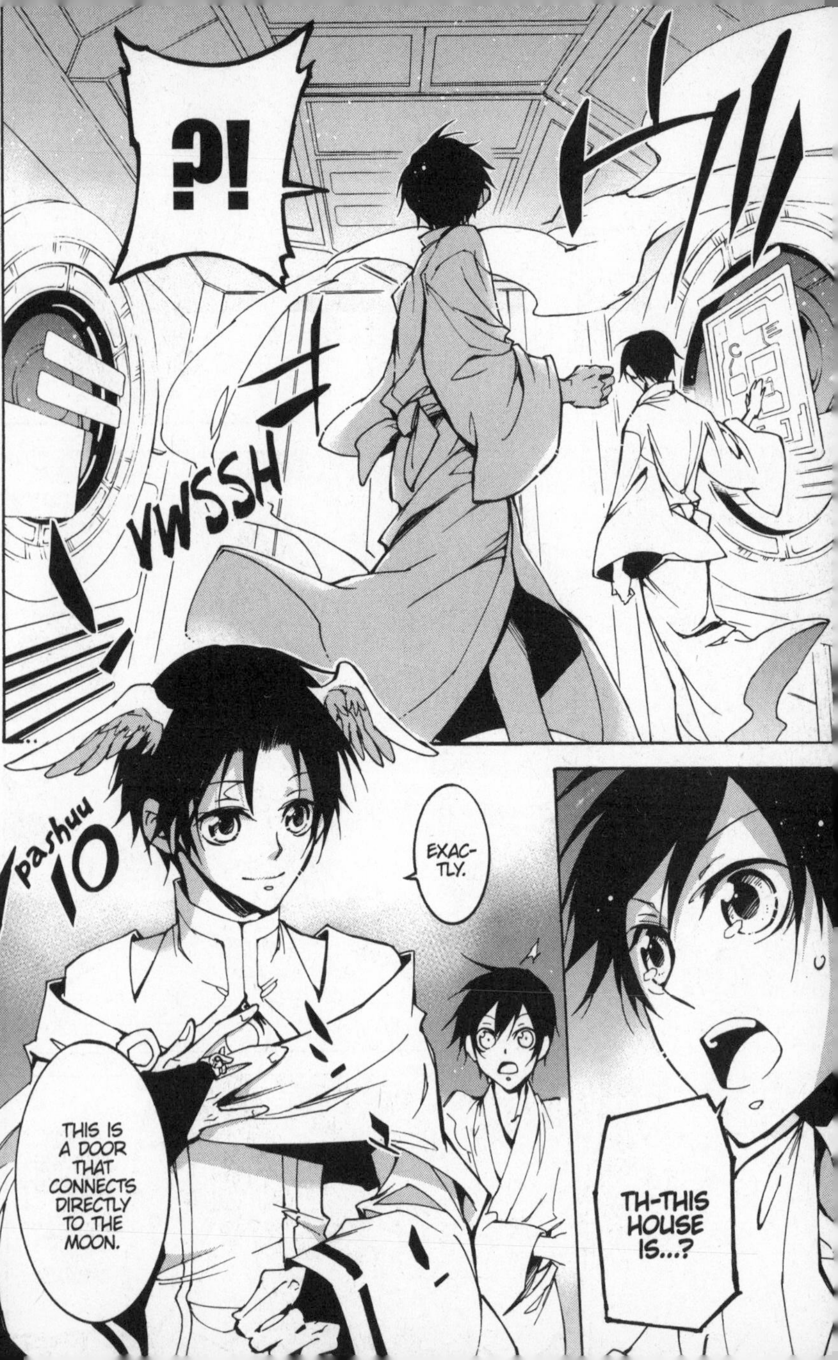
?!
VWSSH
TH-THIS HOUSE IS...?
EXACTLY.
pashuu
THIS IS A DOOR THAT CONNECTS DIRECTLY TO THE MOON.

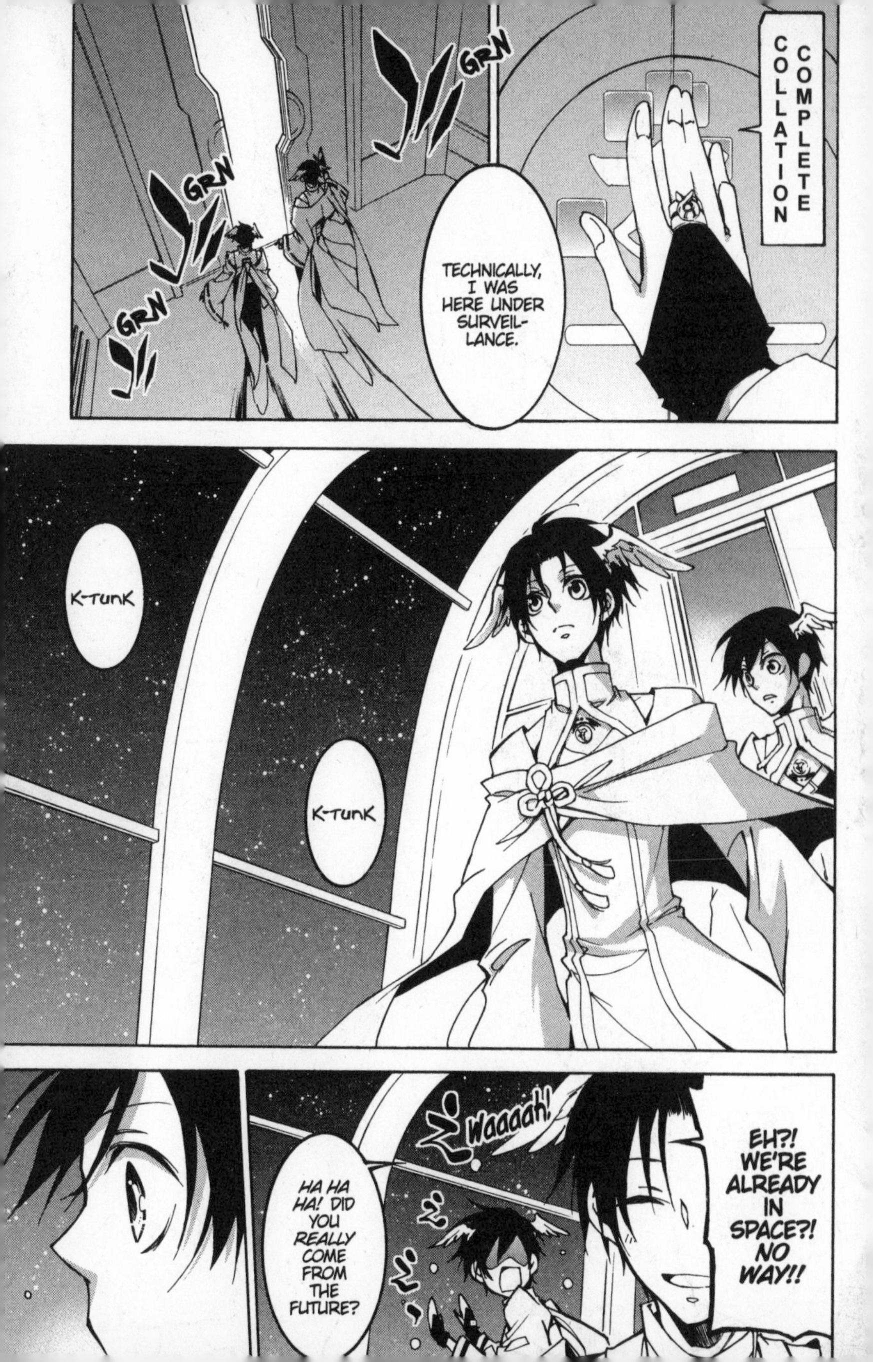
COLLATION COMPLETE
TECHNICALLY, I WAS HERE UNDER SURVEIL-LANCE.
GRN
GRN
GRN
K-TUNK
K-TUNK
EH?! WE'RE ALREADY IN SPACE?! NO WAY!!
WAAAAH!
HA HA HA! DID YOU REALLY COME FROM THE FUTURE?

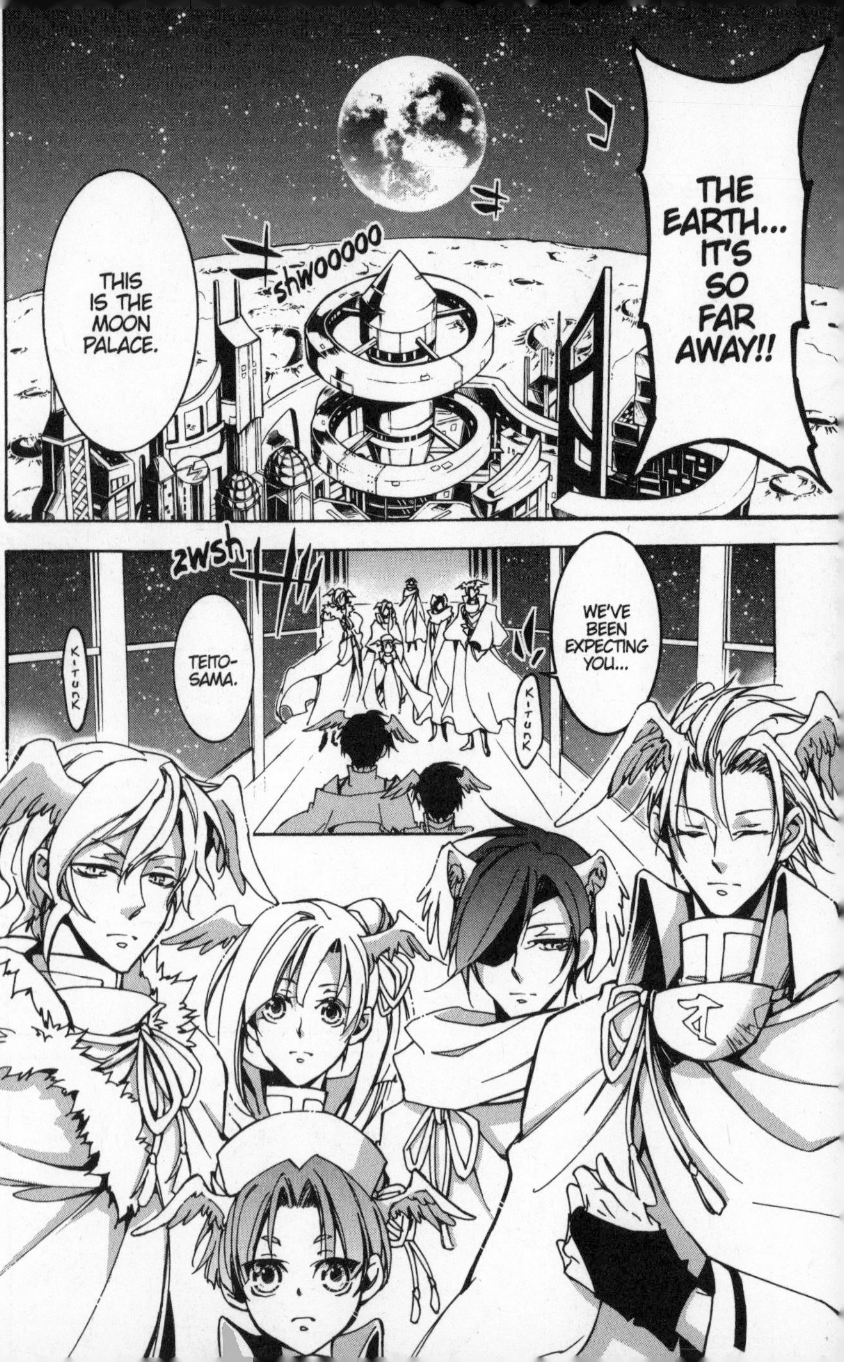
THE EARTH... IT'S SO FAR AWAY!!
shwooooo
THIS IS THE MOON PALACE.
WE'VE BEEN EXPECTING YOU...
K-TUNK
zwsh
TEITO-SAMA.
K-TUNK

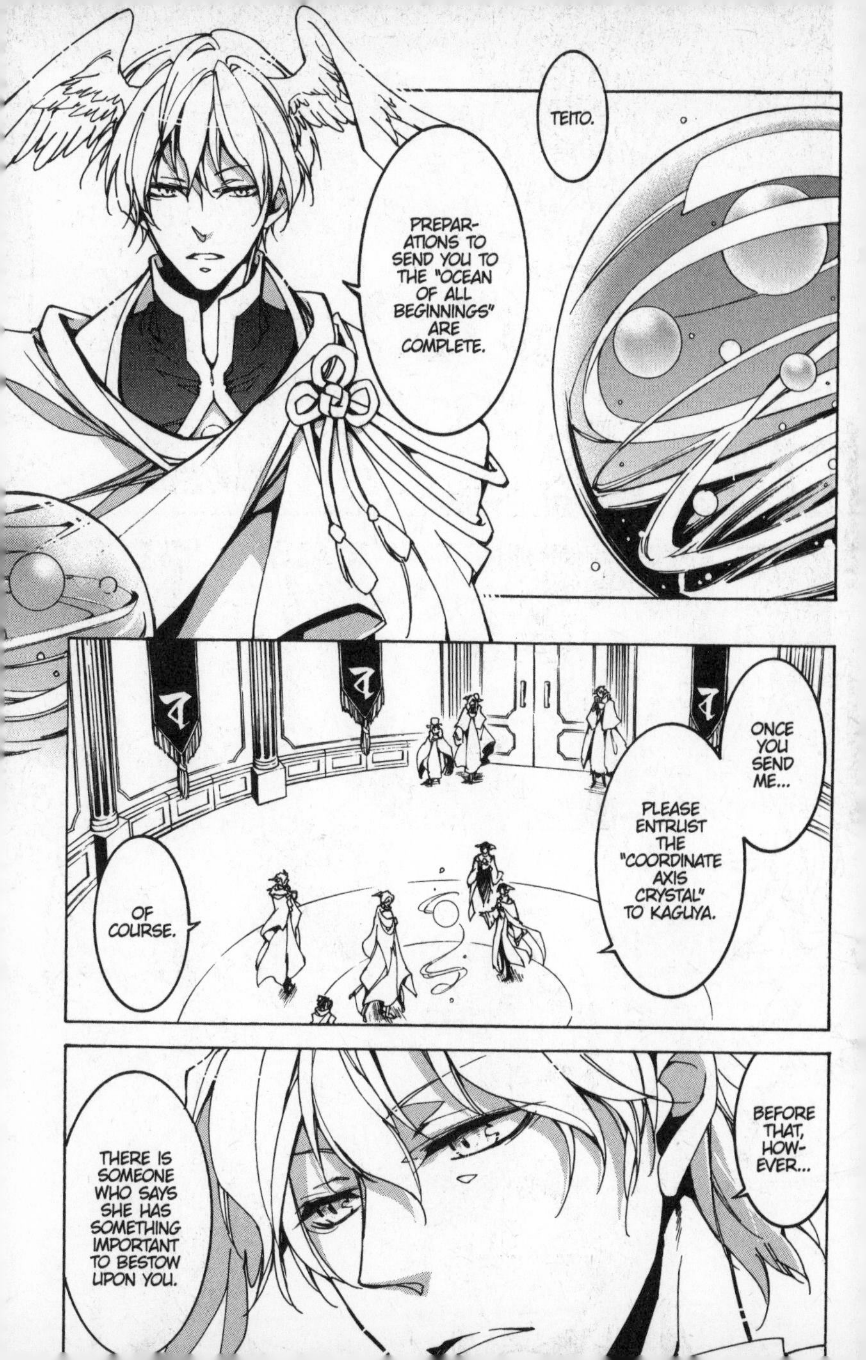
TEITO.
PREPAR-ATIONS TO SEND YOU TO THE "OCEAN OF ALL BEGINNINGS" ARE COMPLETE.
ONCE YOU SEND ME...
PLEASE ENTRUST THE "COORDINATE AXIS CRYSTAL" TO KAGUYA.
OF COURSE.
BEFORE THAT, HOW-EVER...
THERE IS SOMEONE WHO SAYS SHE HAS SOMETHING IMPORTANT TO BESTOW UPON YOU.

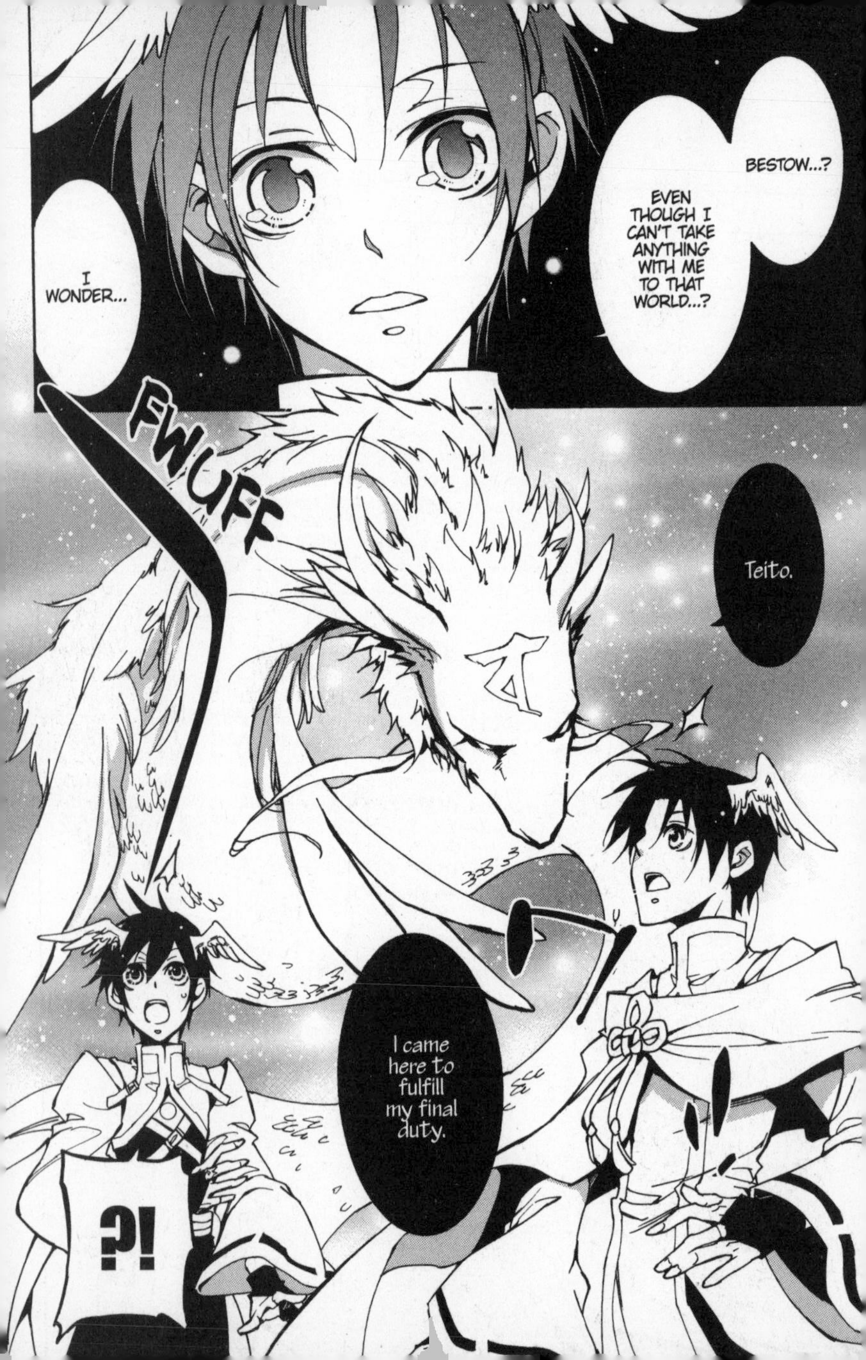
BESTOW...?
EVEN THOUGH I CAN'T TAKE ANYTHING WITH ME TO THAT WORLD...?
I WONDER...
FWUFF
Teito.
I came here to fulfill my final duty.
?!

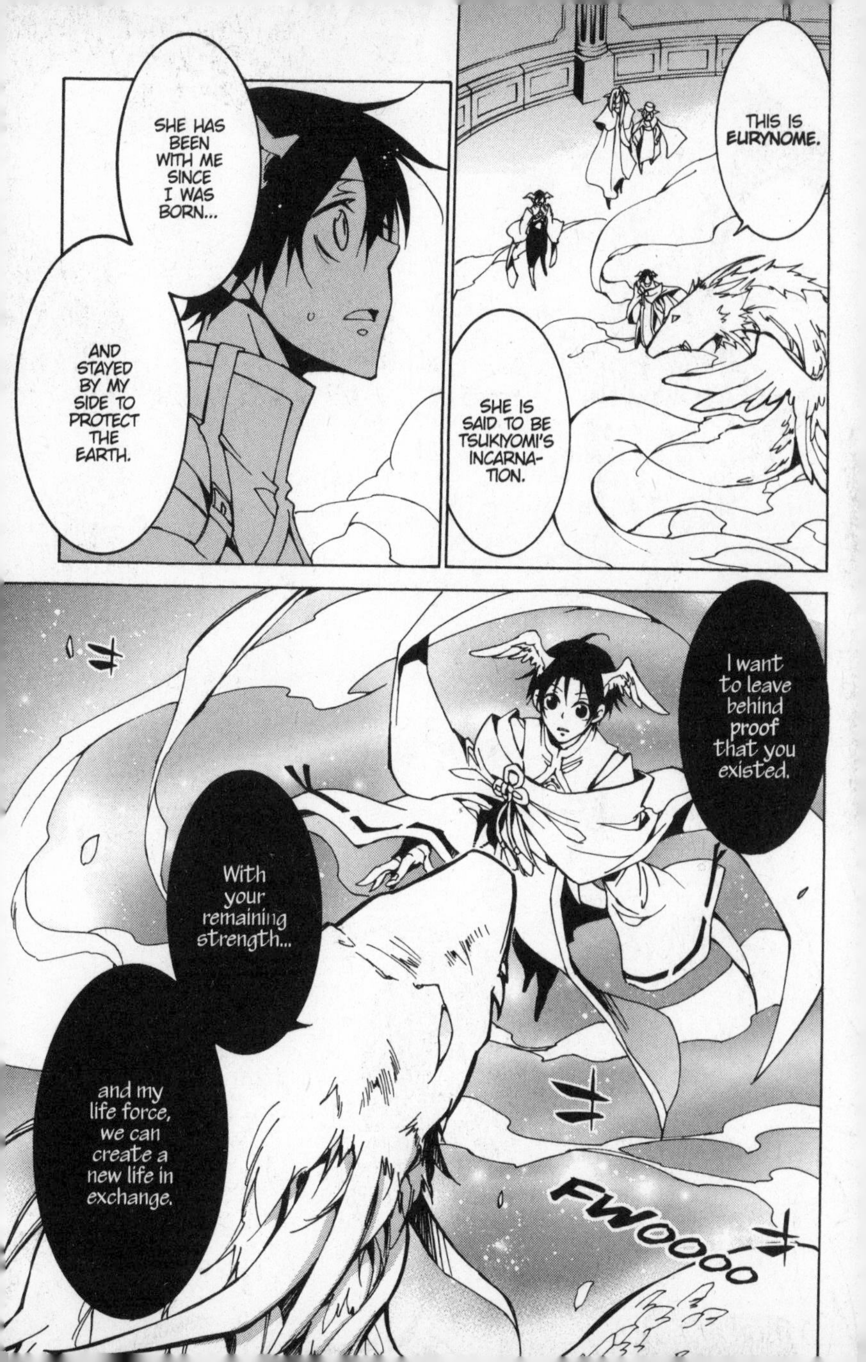
THIS IS EURYNOME.
SHE IS SAID TO BE TSUKIYOMI'S INCARNATION.
SHE HAS BEEN WITH ME SINCE I WAS BORN...
AND STAYED BY MY SIDE TO PROTECT THE EARTH.
I want to leave behind proof that you existed.
With your remaining strength...
and my life force, we can create a new life in exchange.
FWOOOOO

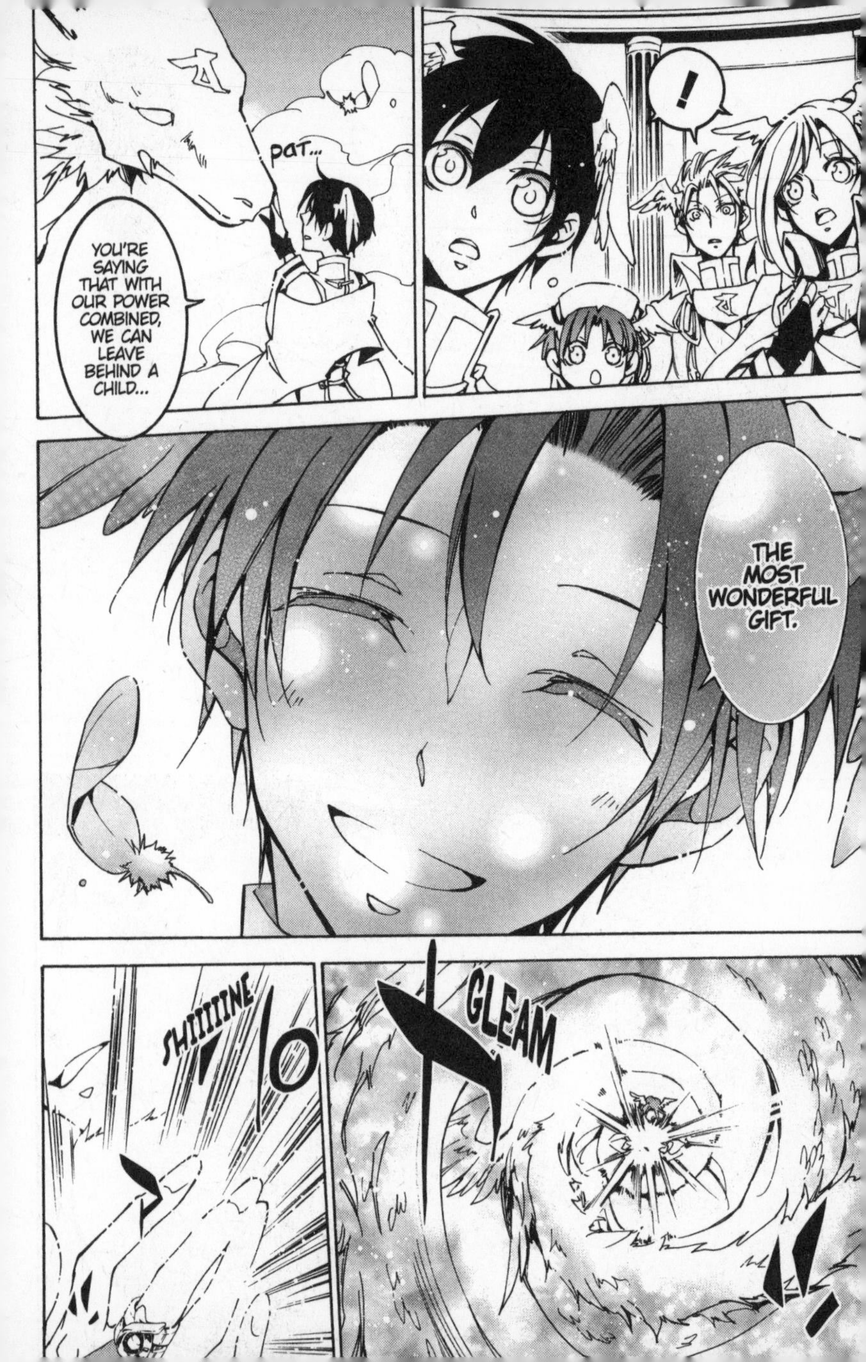
!
pat...
YOU'RE SAYING THAT WITH OUR POWER COMBINED, WE CAN LEAVE BEHIND A CHILD...
THE MOST WONDERFUL GIFT.
GLEAM
SHIIIIINE

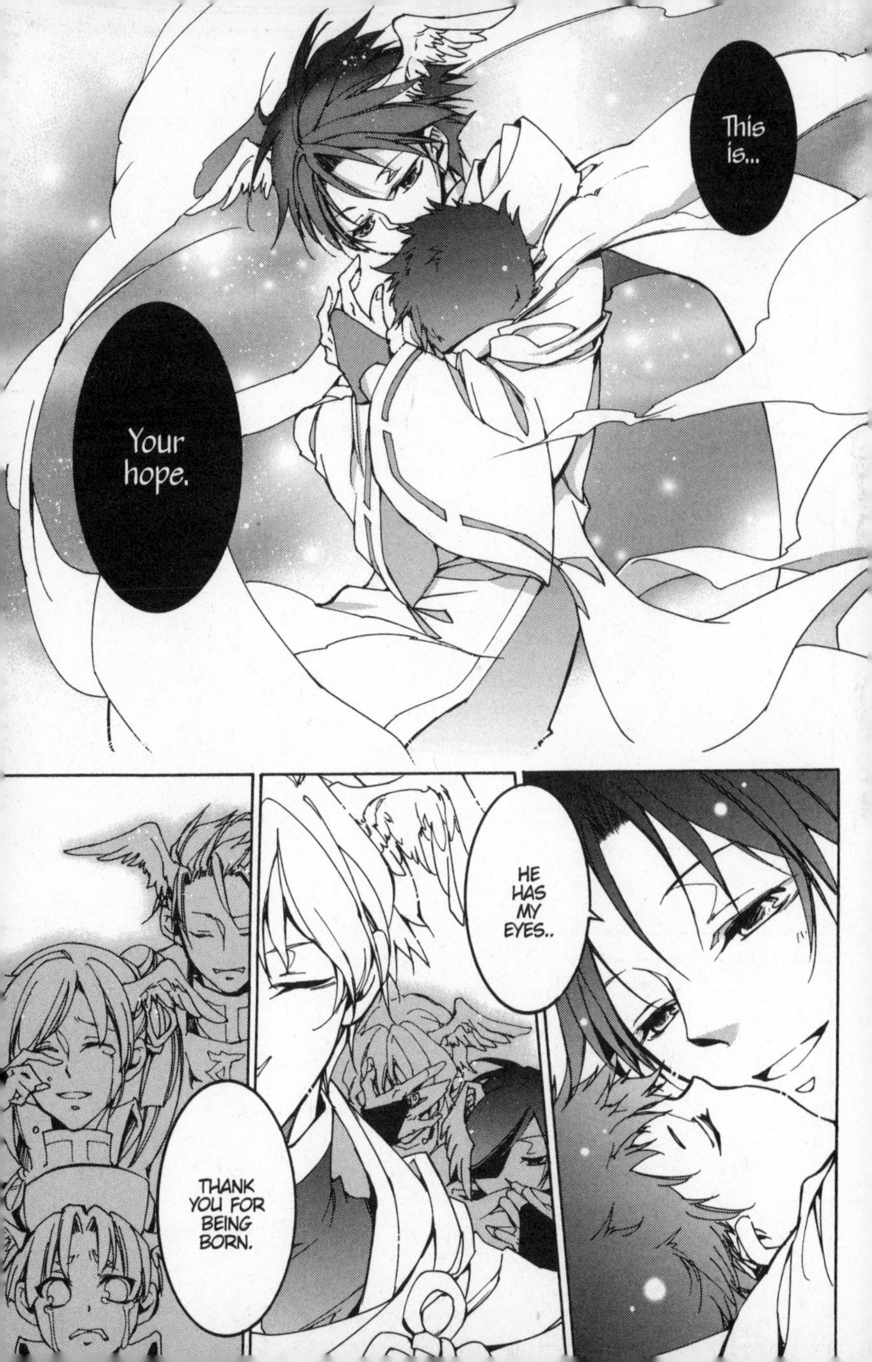
This is...
Your hope.
HE HAS MY EYES..
THANK YOU FOR BEING BORN.

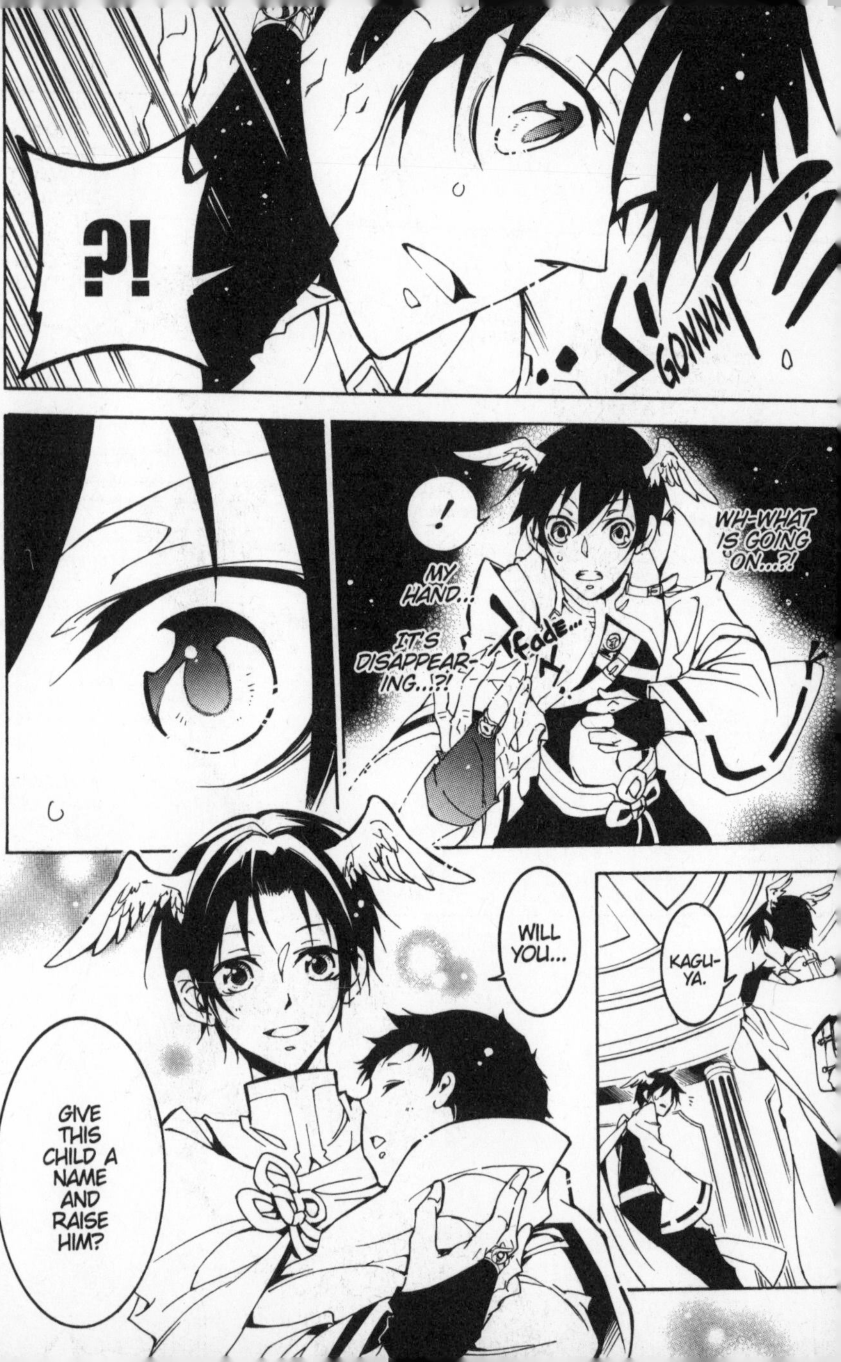
GONNN
?!
WH-WHAT IS GOING ON...?!
!
MY HAND...
IT'S DISAPPEARING...?!
fade...
KAGU-YA.
WILL YOU...
GIVE THIS CHILD A NAME AND RAISE HIM?

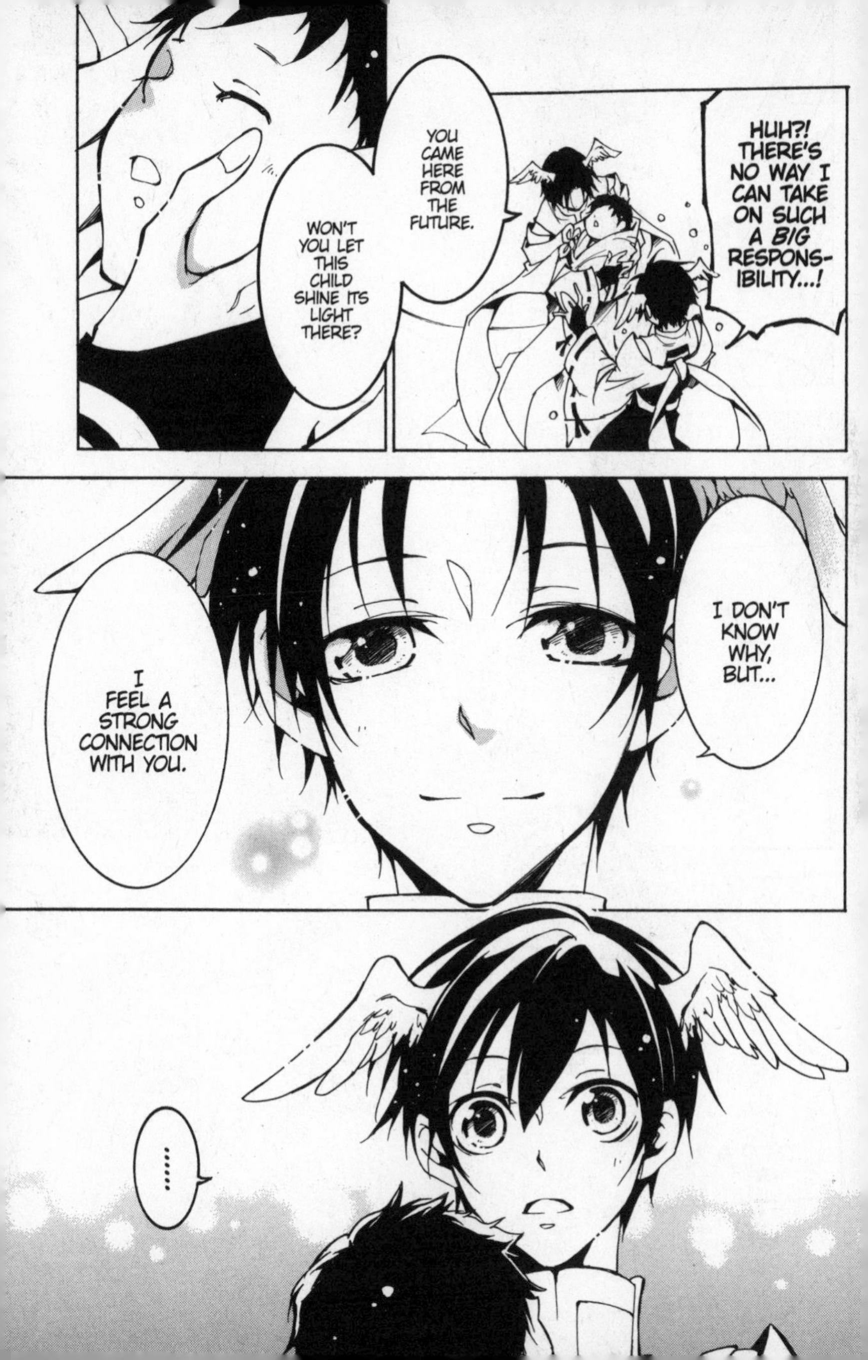
HUH?! THERE'S NO WAY I CAN TAKE ON SUCH A *BIG* RESPONSIBILITY...!
YOU CAME HERE FROM THE FUTURE.
WON'T YOU LET THIS CHILD SHINE ITS LIGHT THERE?
I DON'T KNOW WHY, BUT...
I FEEL A STRONG CONNECTION WITH YOU.
......

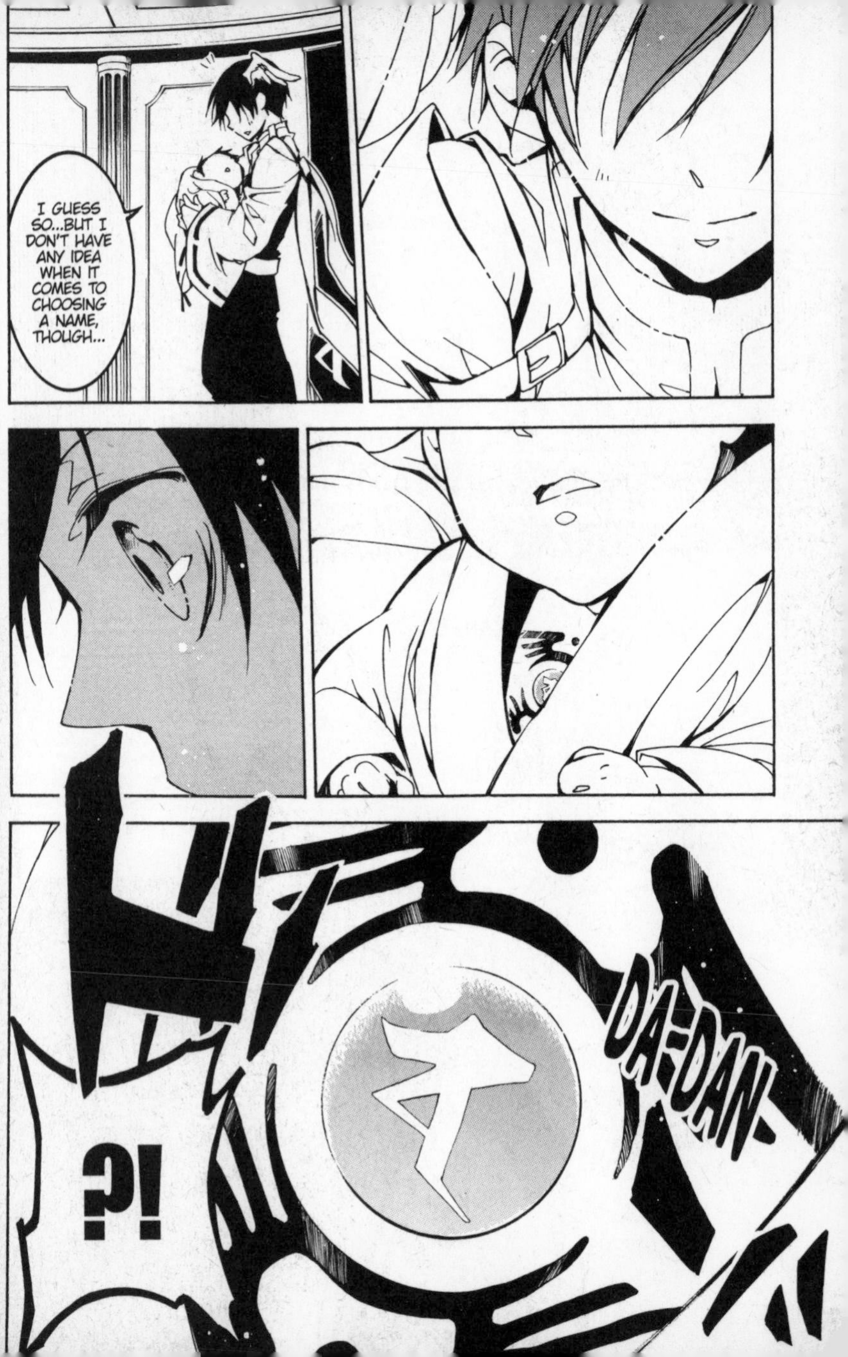
I GUESS SO...BUT I DON'T HAVE ANY IDEA WHEN IT COMES TO CHOOSING A NAME, THOUGH...
DA-DAN
?!

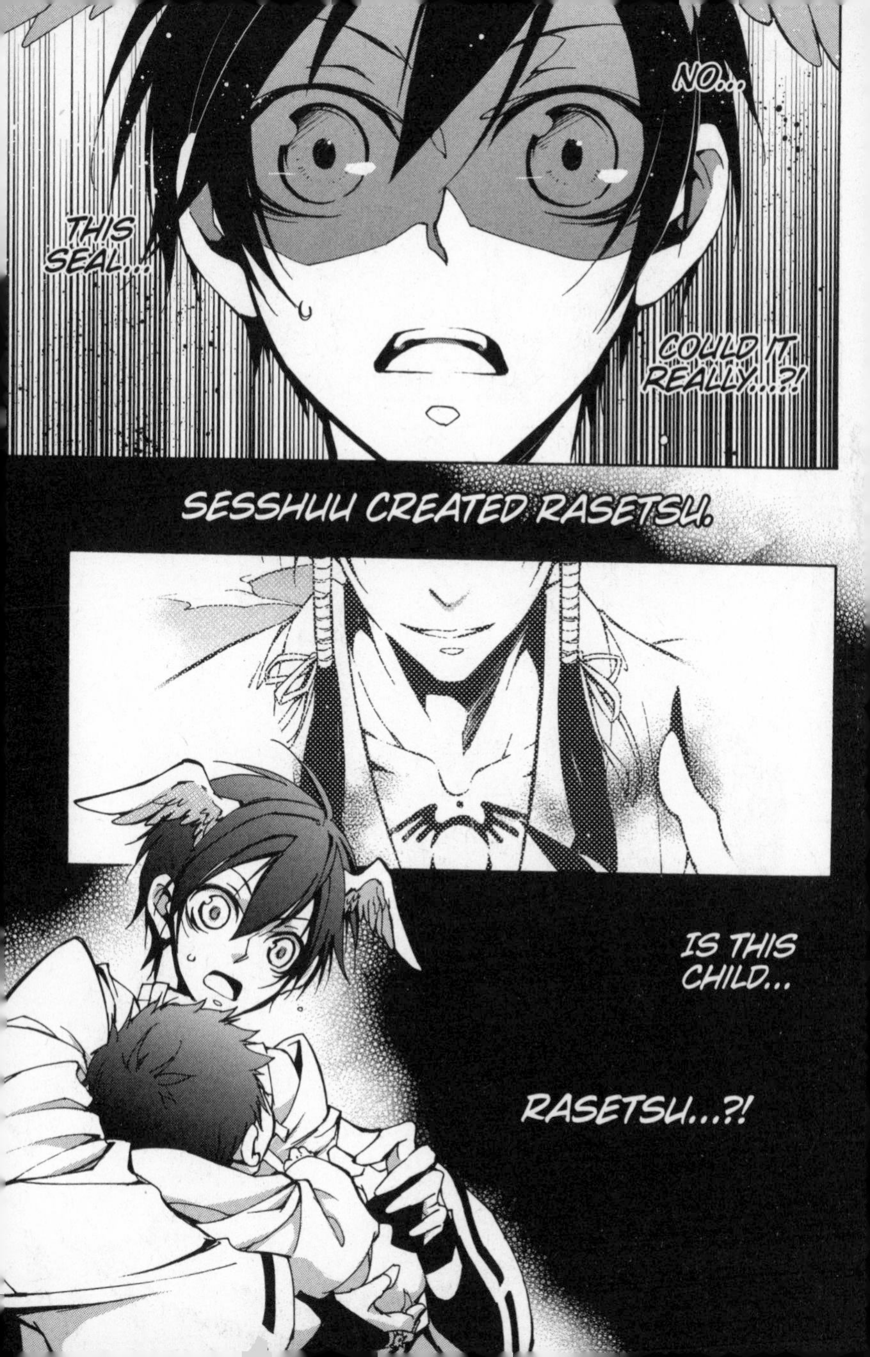
NO...
THIS SEAL...
COULD IT REALLY...?!
SESSHUU CREATED RASETSU.
IS THIS CHILD...
RASETSU...?!

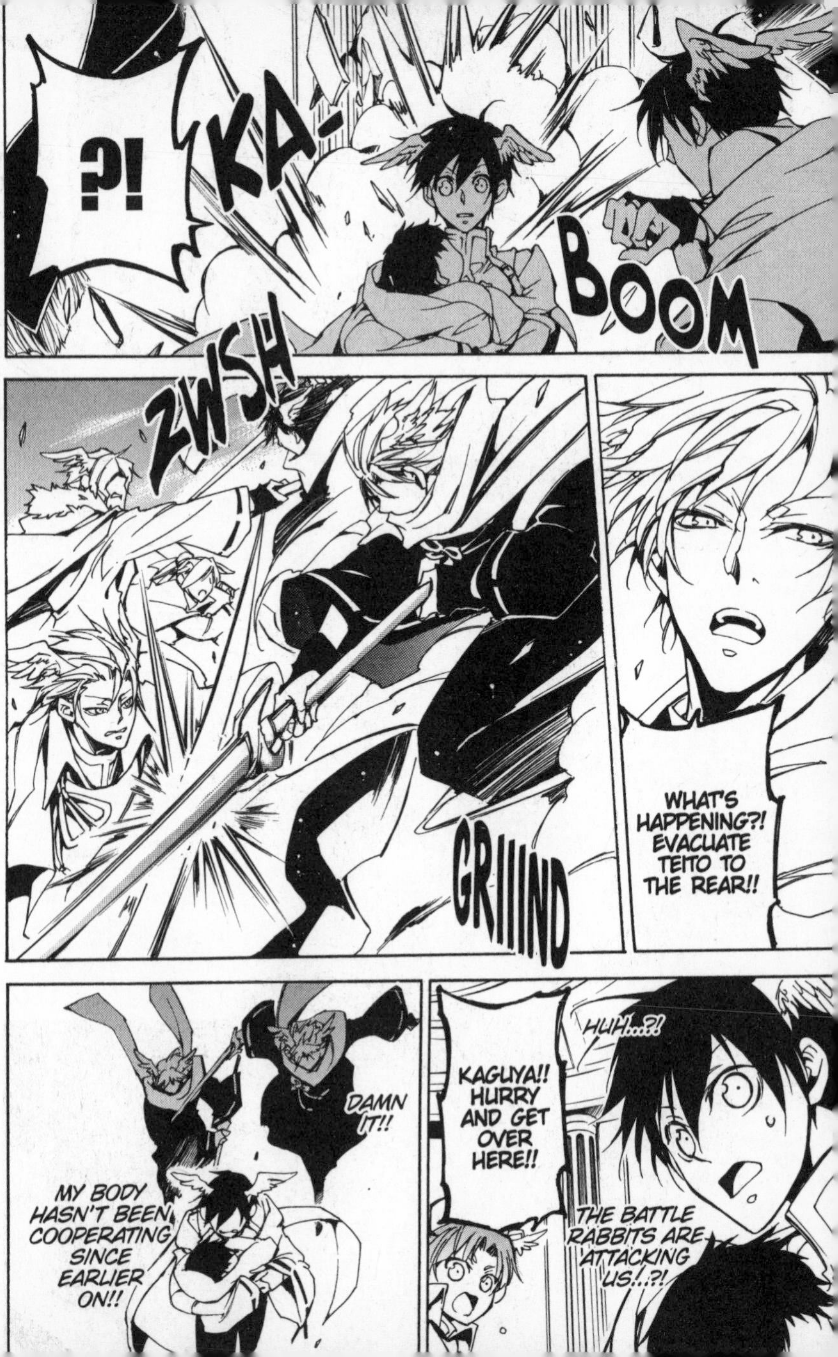
KA-
BOOM
?!
ZWSH
WHAT'S HAPPENING?! EVACUATE TEITO TO THE REAR!!
GRIIIND
HUH...?!
KAGUYA!! HURRY AND GET OVER HERE!!
THE BATTLE RABBITS ARE ATTACKING US...?!
DAMN IT!!
MY BODY HASN'T BEEN COOPERATING SINCE EARLIER ON!!

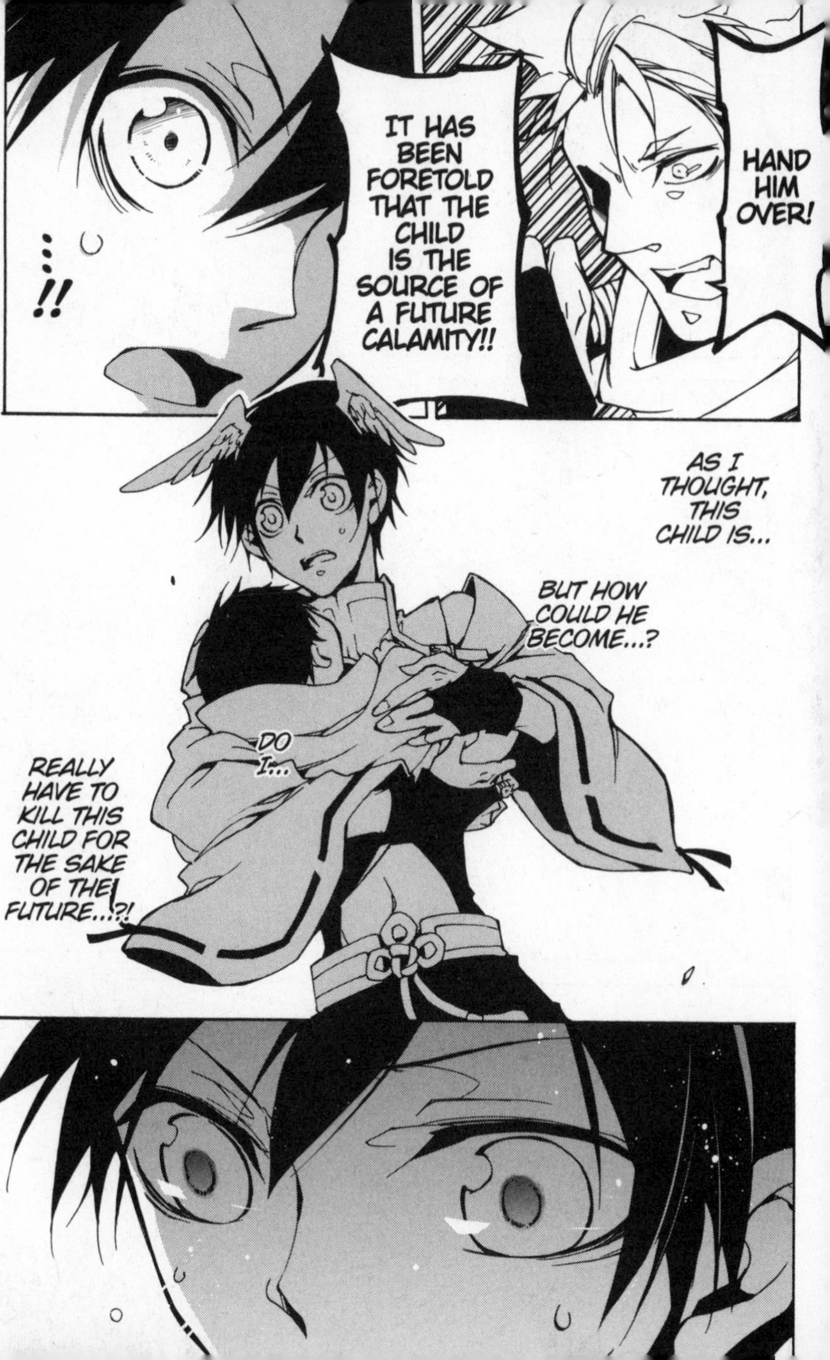
HAND HIM OVER!
IT HAS BEEN FORETOLD THAT THE CHILD IS THE SOURCE OF A FUTURE CALAMITY!!
...!!
AS I THOUGHT, THIS CHILD IS...
BUT HOW COULD HE BECOME...?
DO I...
REALLY HAVE TO KILL THIS CHILD FOR THE SAKE OF THE FUTURE...?!

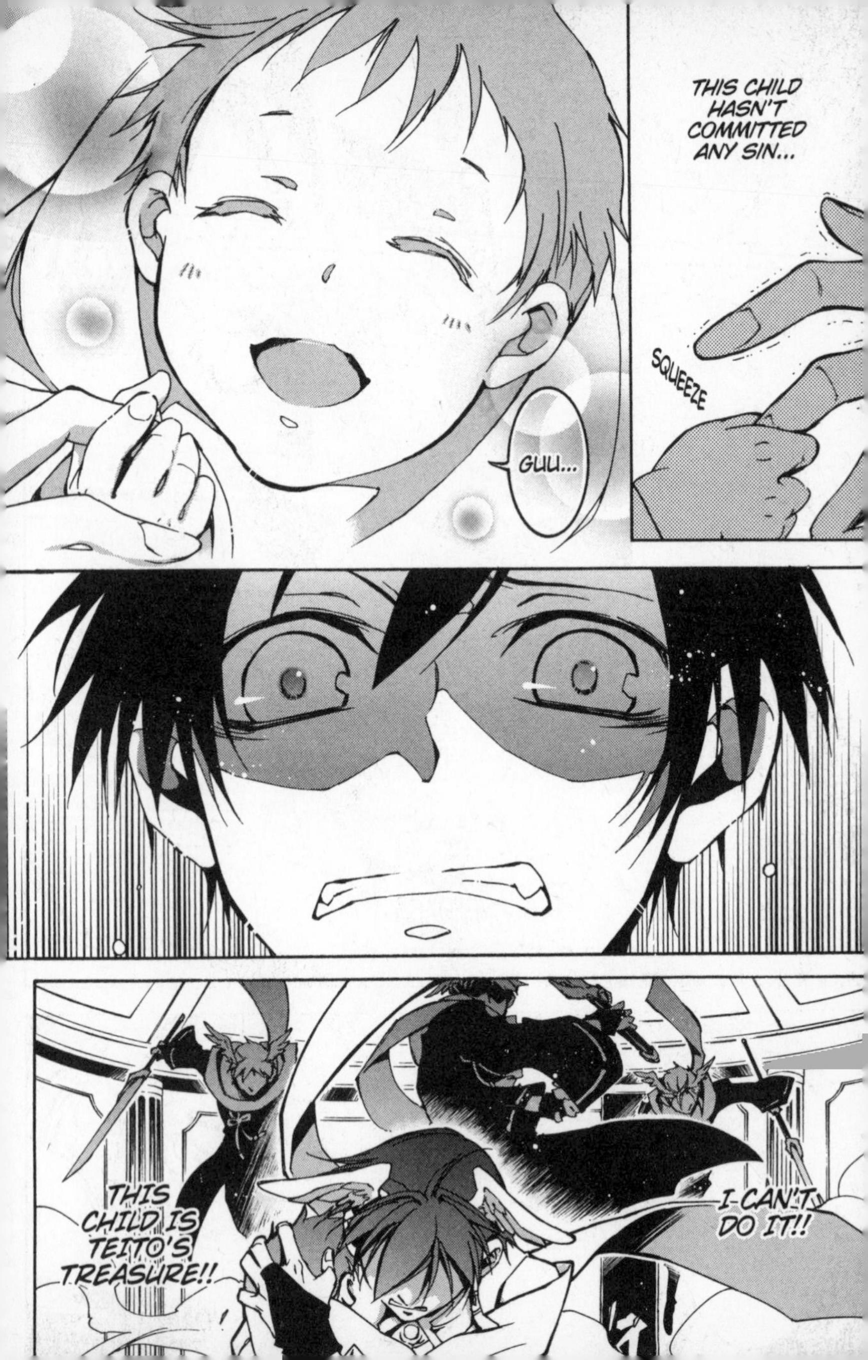
THIS CHILD HASN'T COMMITTED ANY SIN...
SQUEEZE
GUU...
I CAN'T DO IT!!
THIS CHILD IS TEITO'S TREASURE!!

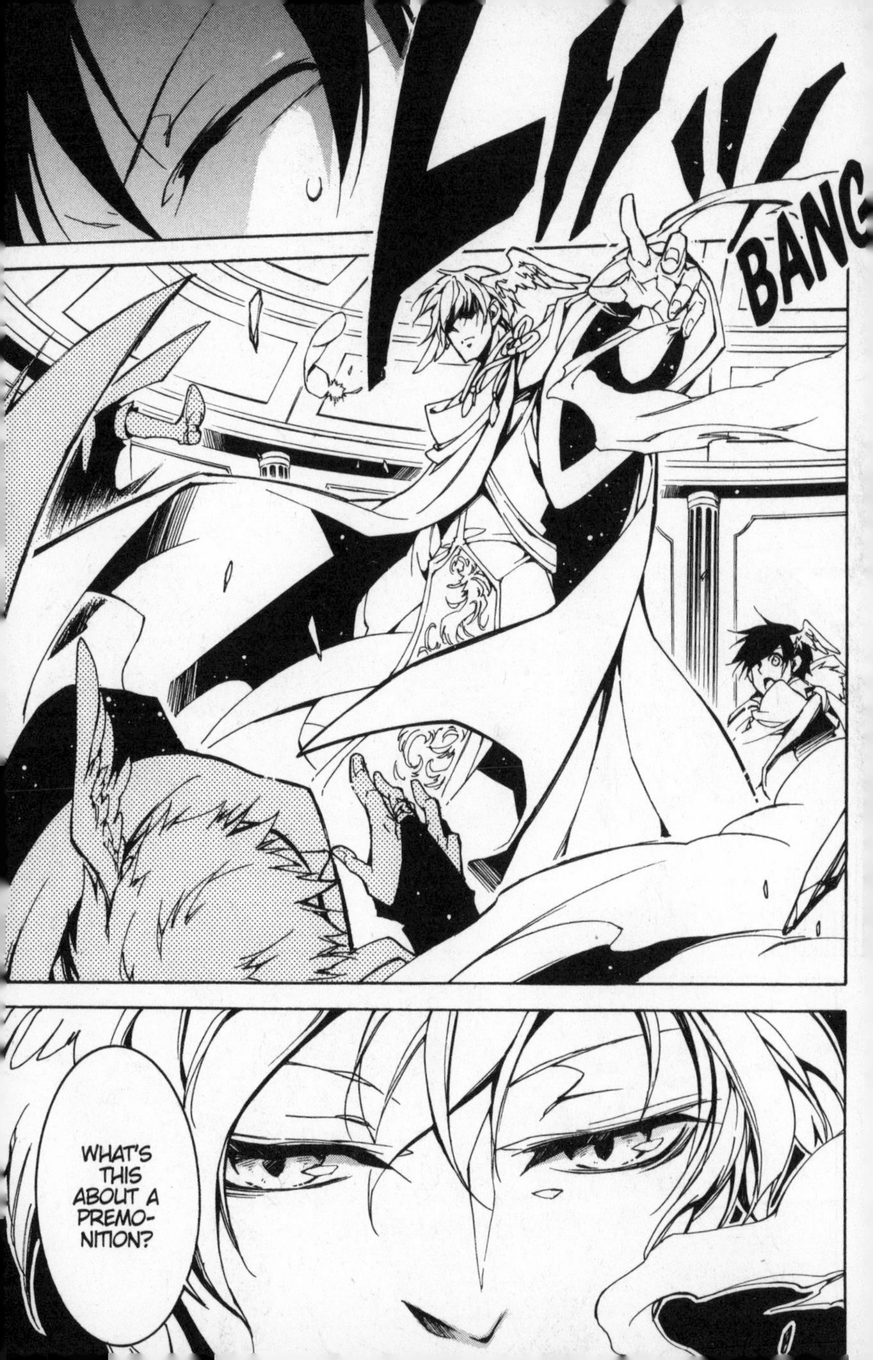
BANG
WHAT'S THIS ABOUT A PREMO-NITION?

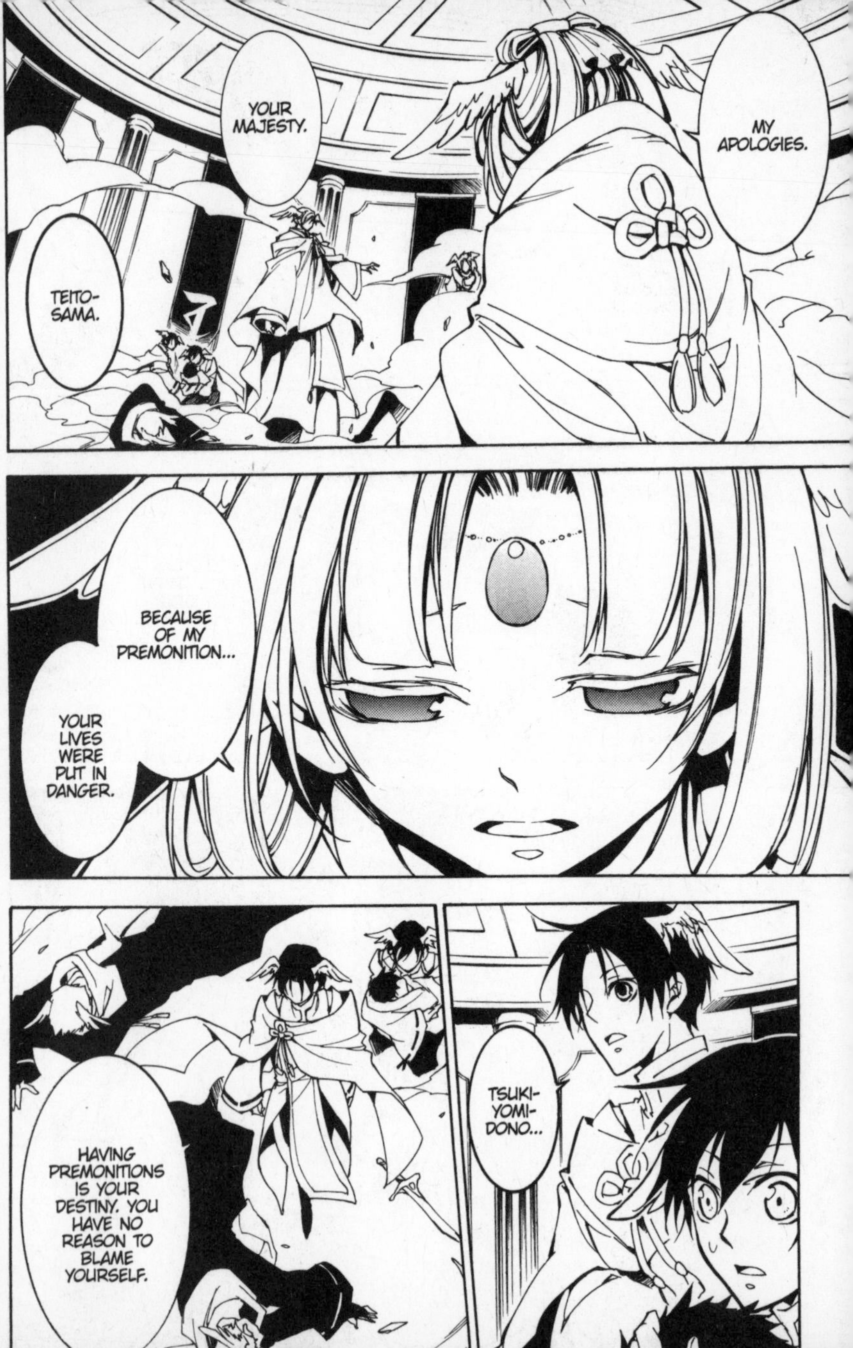
MY APOLOGIES.
YOUR MAJESTY.
TEITO-SAMA.
BECAUSE OF MY PREMONITION...
YOUR LIVES WERE PUT IN DANGER.
TSUKI-YOMI-DONO...
HAVING PREMONITIONS IS YOUR DESTINY. YOU HAVE NO REASON TO BLAME YOURSELF.

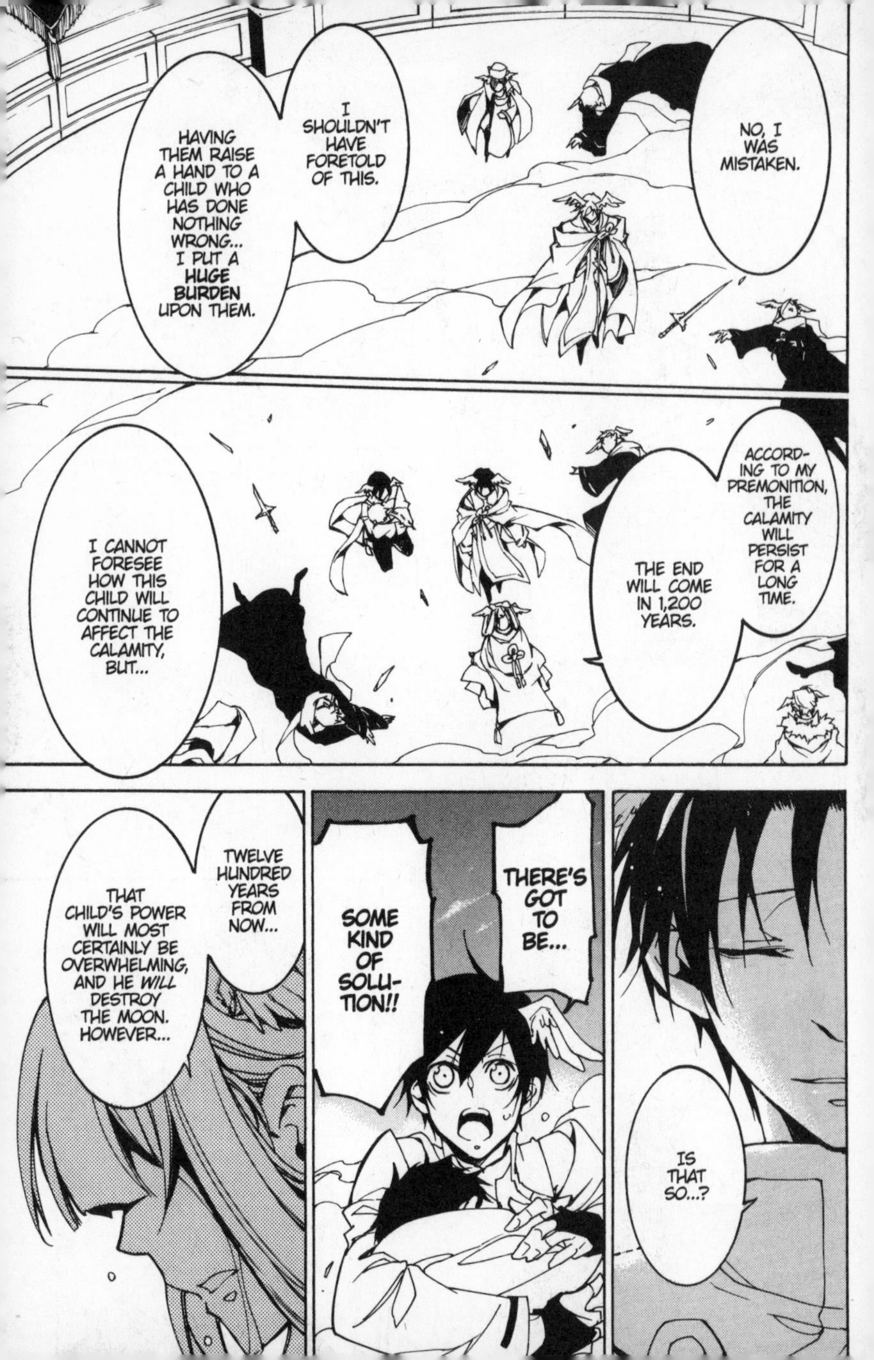
NO, I WAS MISTAKEN.
I SHOULDN'T HAVE FORETOLD OF THIS.
HAVING THEM RAISE A HAND TO A CHILD WHO HAS DONE NOTHING WRONG... I PUT A **HUGE BURDEN** UPON THEM.
ACCORDING TO MY PREMONITION, THE CALAMITY WILL PERSIST FOR A LONG TIME.
THE END WILL COME IN 1,200 YEARS.
I CANNOT FORESEE HOW THIS CHILD WILL CONTINUE TO AFFECT THE CALAMITY, BUT...
IS THAT SO...?
THERE'S GOT TO BE...
SOME KIND OF SOLUTION!!
TWELVE HUNDRED YEARS FROM NOW...
THAT CHILD'S POWER WILL MOST CERTAINLY BE OVERWHELMING, AND HE *WILL* DESTROY THE MOON. HOWEVER...

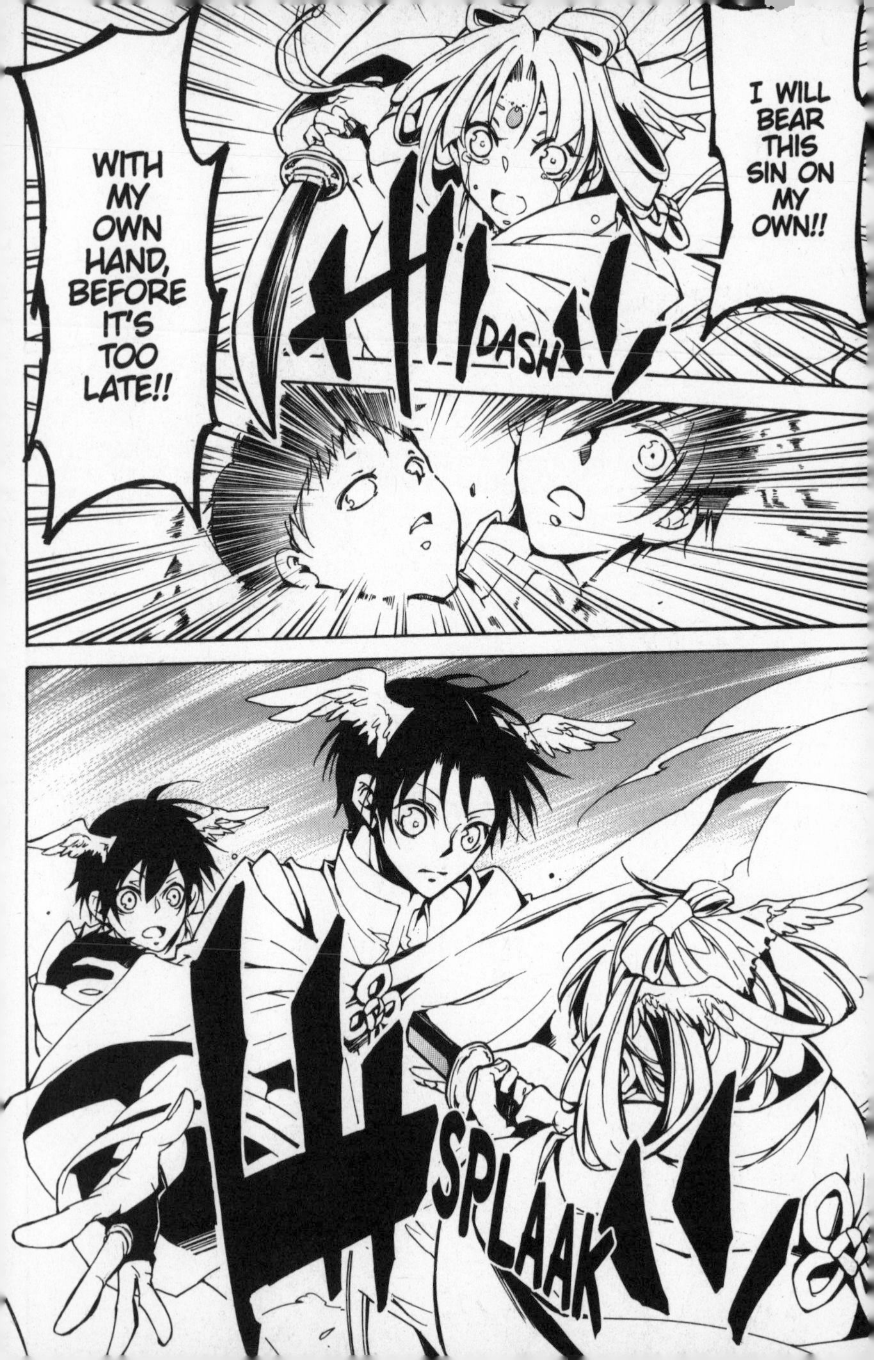
I WILL BEAR THIS SIN ON MY OWN!!
WITH MY OWN HAND, BEFORE IT'S TOO LATE!!
DASH
SPLAAK

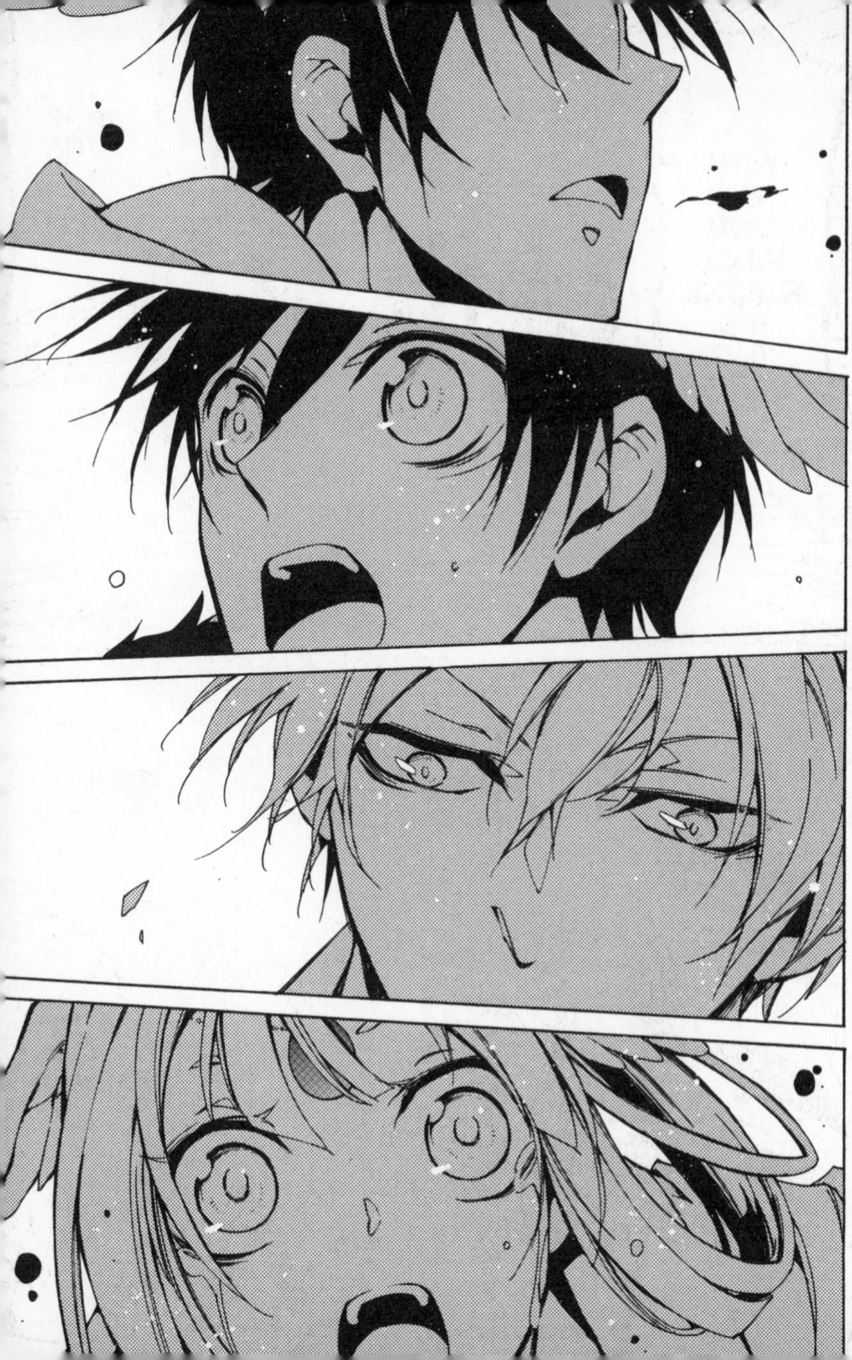

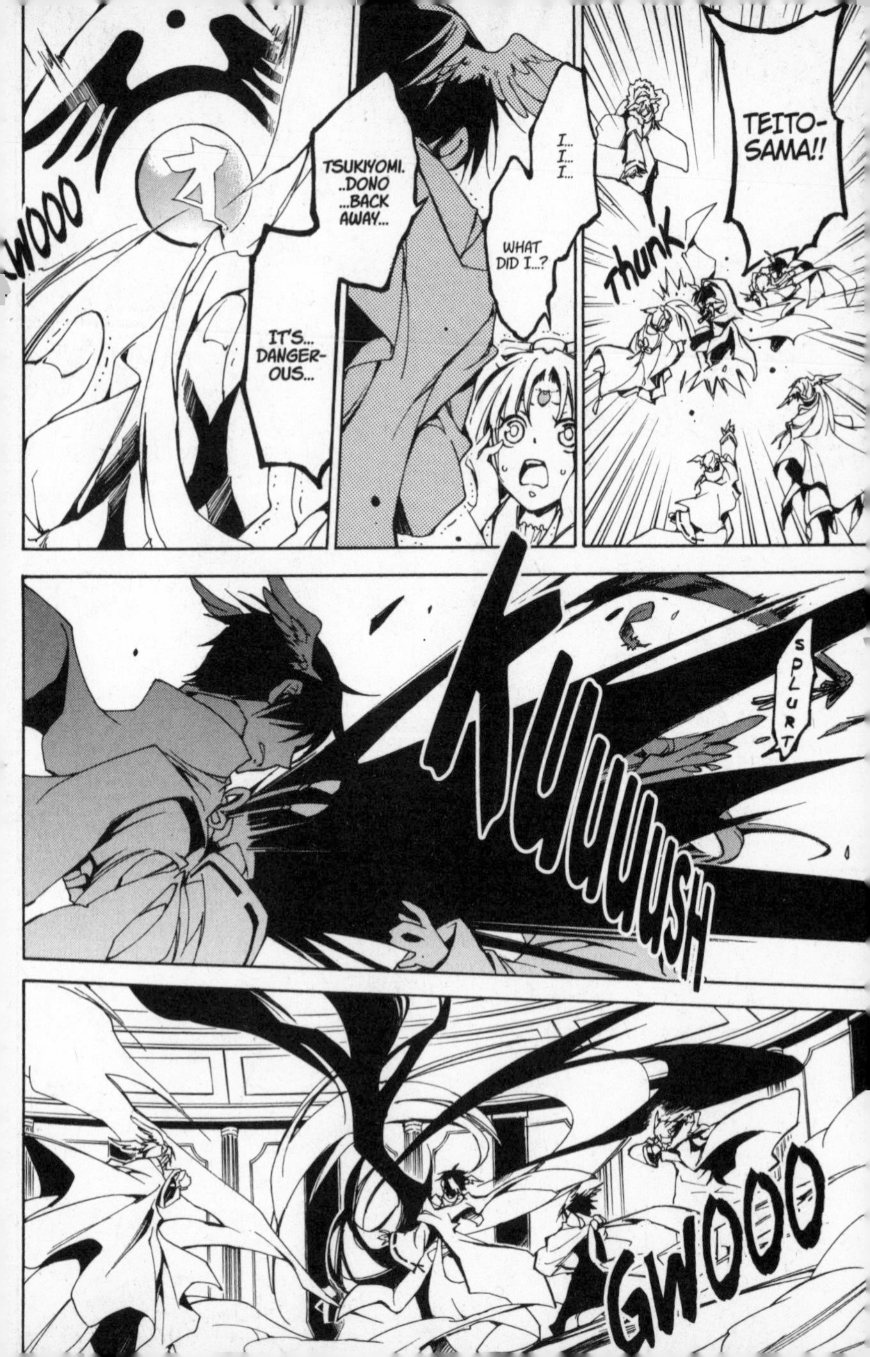
TEITO-SAMA!!
thunk
I... I... I...
WHAT DID I...?
TSUKIYOMI. ..DONO ...BACK AWAY...
IT'S... DANGER-OUS...
WOOO
SPLURT
XUUUUUSH
GWOOO

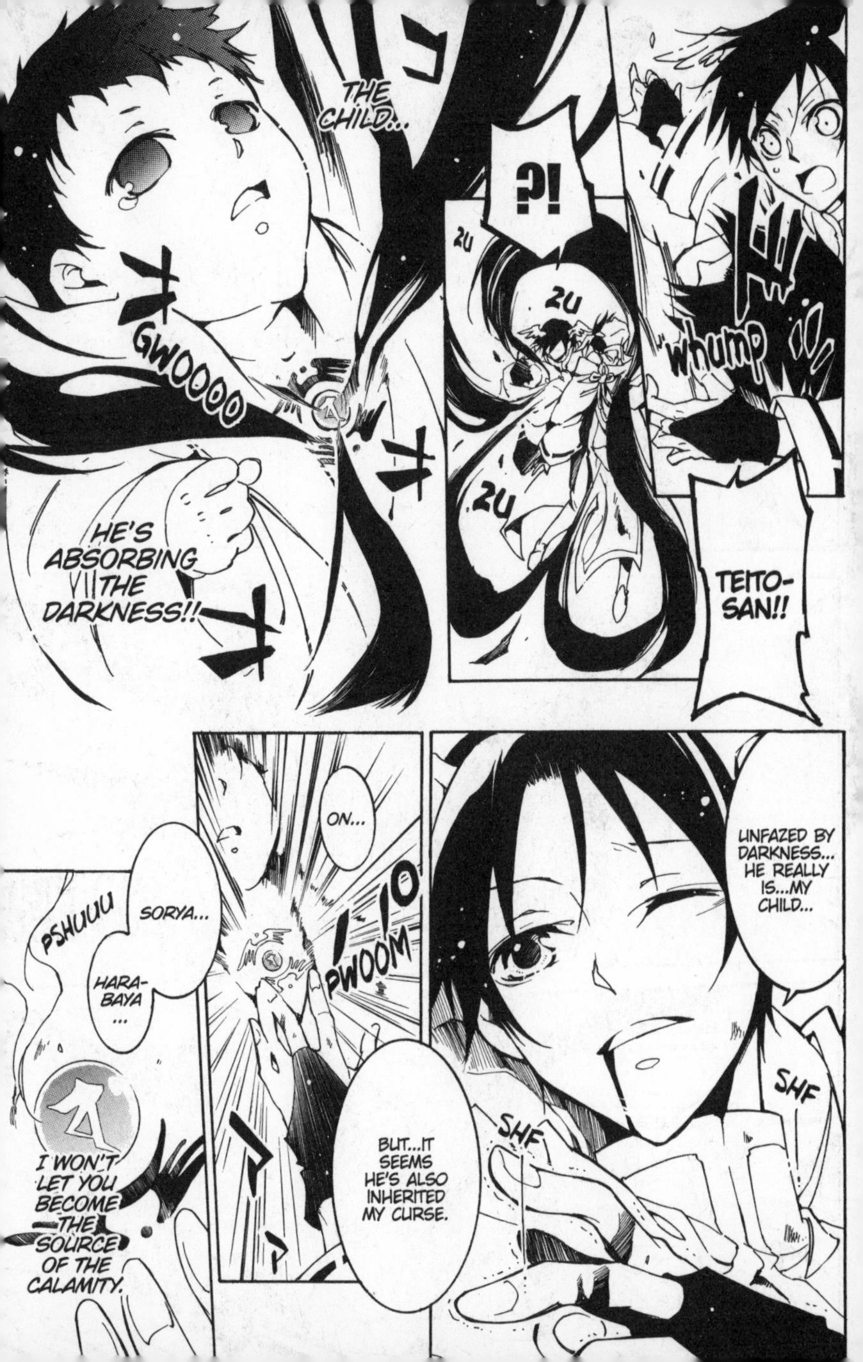
?!
H!!
whump
TEITO-SAN!!
ZU
ZU
ZU
THE CHILD...
GWOOOO
HE'S ABSORBING THE DARKNESS!!
UNFAZED BY DARKNESS... HE REALLY IS...MY CHILD...
SHF
SHF
BUT...IT SEEMS HE'S ALSO INHERITED MY CURSE.
ON...
PWOOM
SORYA...
HARA-BAYA ...
PSHUUU
I WON'T LET YOU BECOME THE SOURCE OF THE CALAMITY.

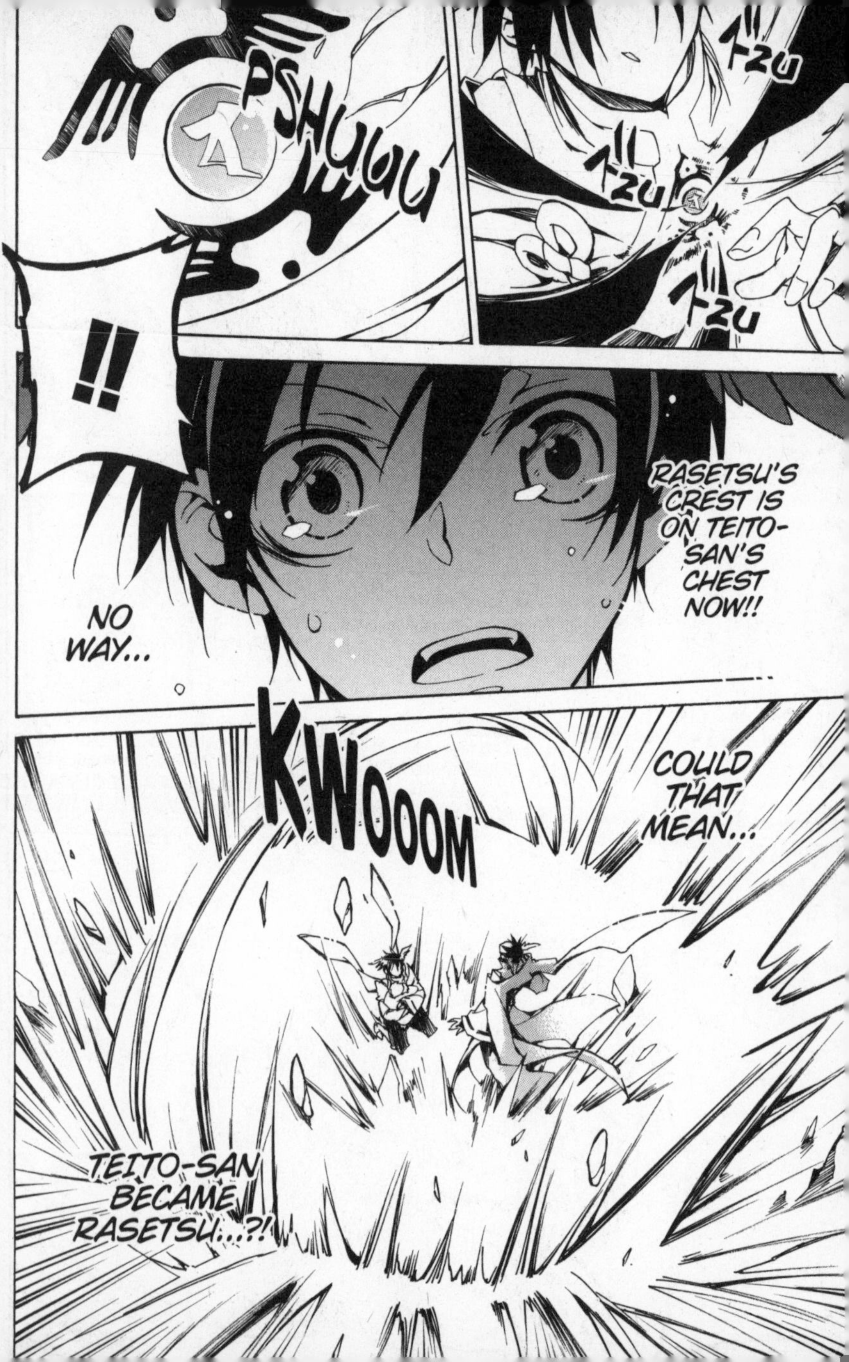
TZU
TZU
TZU
PSHUUU
!!
RASETSU'S CREST IS ON TEITO-SAN'S CHEST NOW!!
NO WAY...
KWOOOM
COULD THAT MEAN...
TEITO-SAN BECAME RASETSU...?!

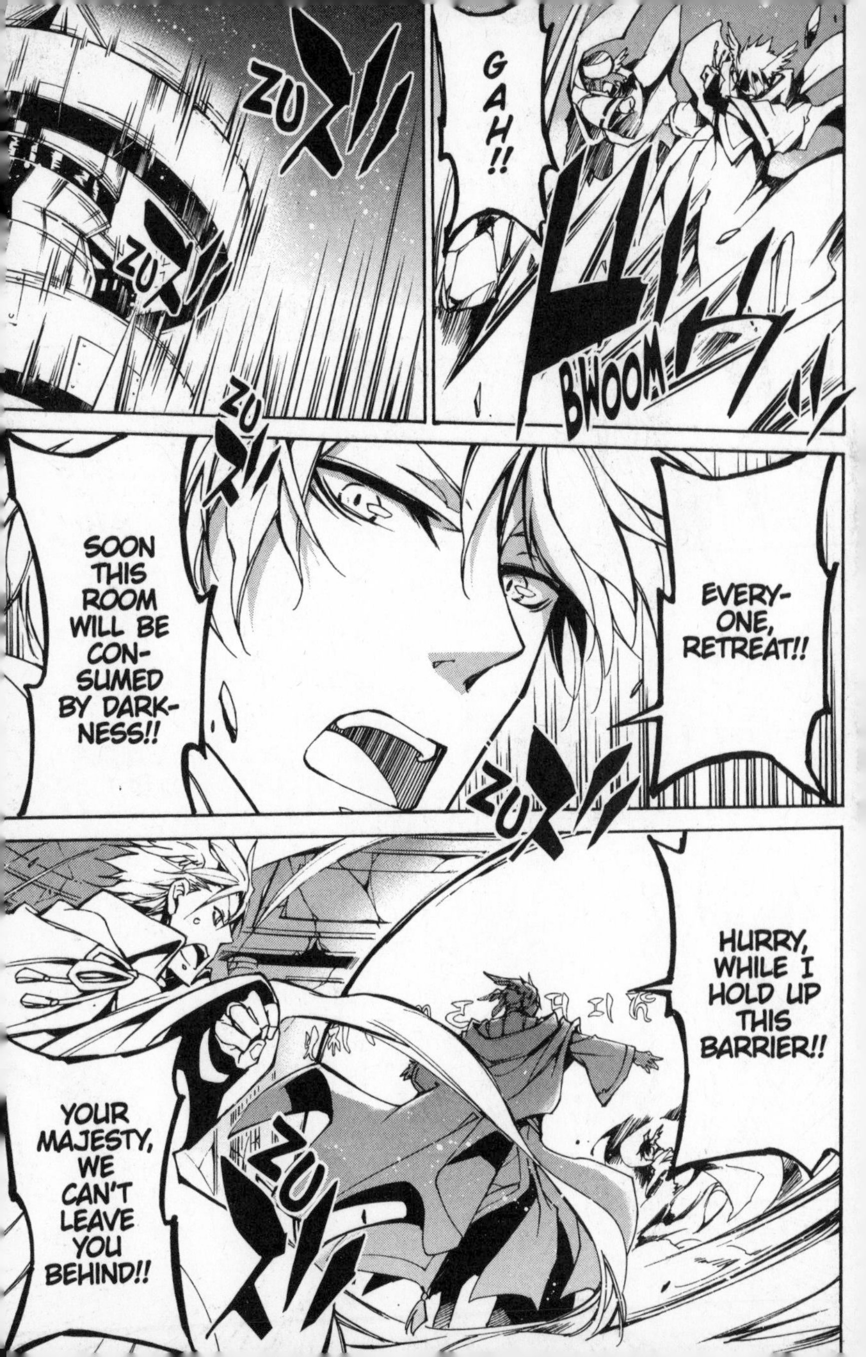
GAH!!
BWOOM
ZU
ZU
ZU
EVERYONE, RETREAT!!
SOON THIS ROOM WILL BE CONSUMED BY DARKNESS!!
ZU
HURRY, WHILE I HOLD UP THIS BARRIER!!
YOUR MAJESTY, WE CAN'T LEAVE YOU BEHIND!!
ZU

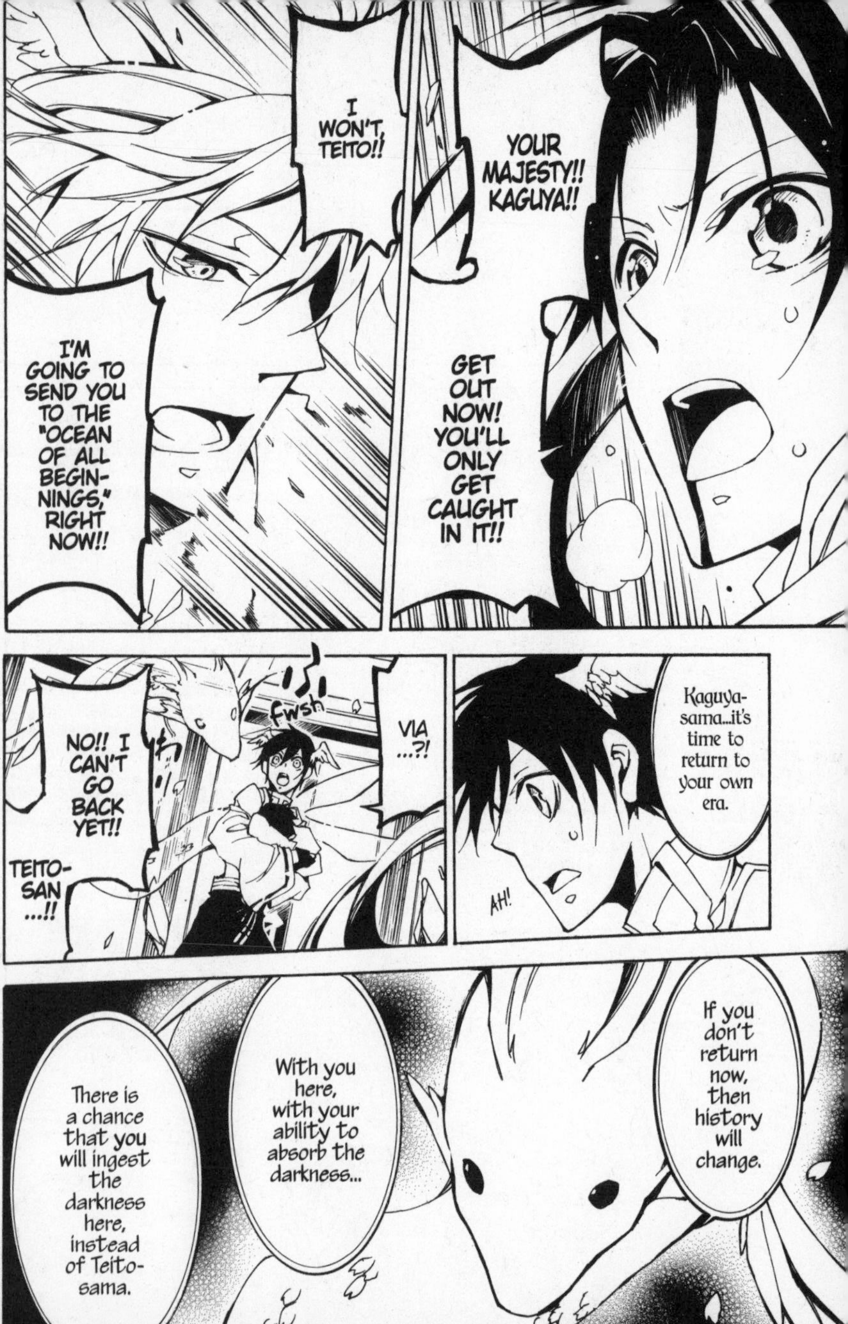
YOUR MAJESTY!! KAGUYA!!
GET OUT NOW! YOU'LL ONLY GET CAUGHT IN IT!!
I WON'T, TEITO!!
I'M GOING TO SEND YOU TO THE "OCEAN OF ALL BEGINNINGS," RIGHT NOW!!
Kaguya-sama...it's time to return to your own era.
AH!
VIA ...?!
fwsh
NO!! I CAN'T GO BACK YET!!
TEITO-SAN ...!!
If you don't return now, then history will change.
With you here, with your ability to absorb the darkness...
There is a chance that you will ingest the darkness here, instead of Teito-sama.

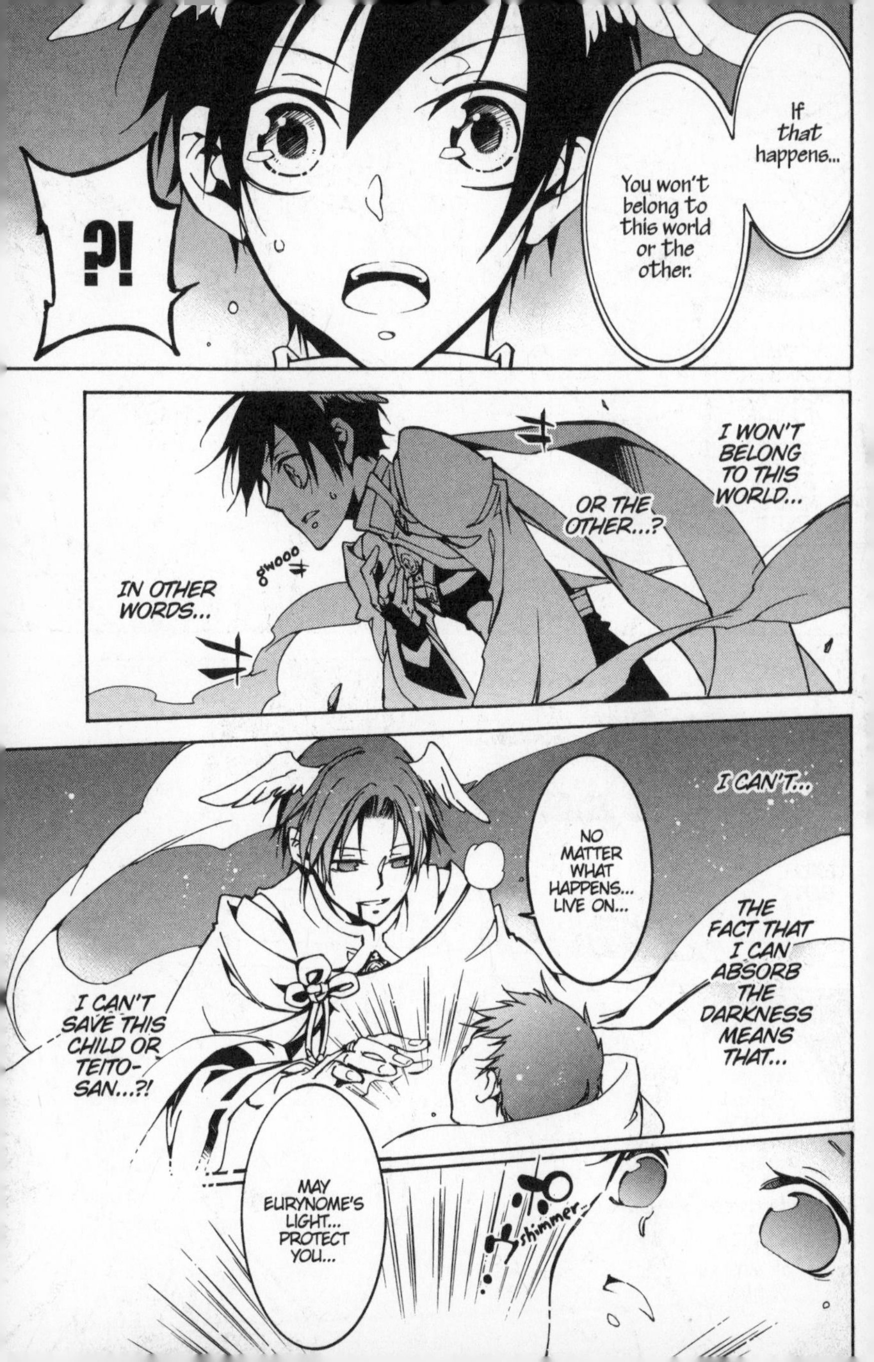
If that happens...
You won't belong to this world or the other.
?!
I WON'T BELONG TO THIS WORLD...
OR THE OTHER...?
gwooo
IN OTHER WORDS...
I CAN'T...
NO MATTER WHAT HAPPENS... LIVE ON...
THE FACT THAT I CAN ABSORB THE DARKNESS MEANS THAT...
I CAN'T SAVE THIS CHILD OR TEITO-SAN...?!
shimmer...
MAY EURYNOME'S LIGHT... PROTECT YOU...

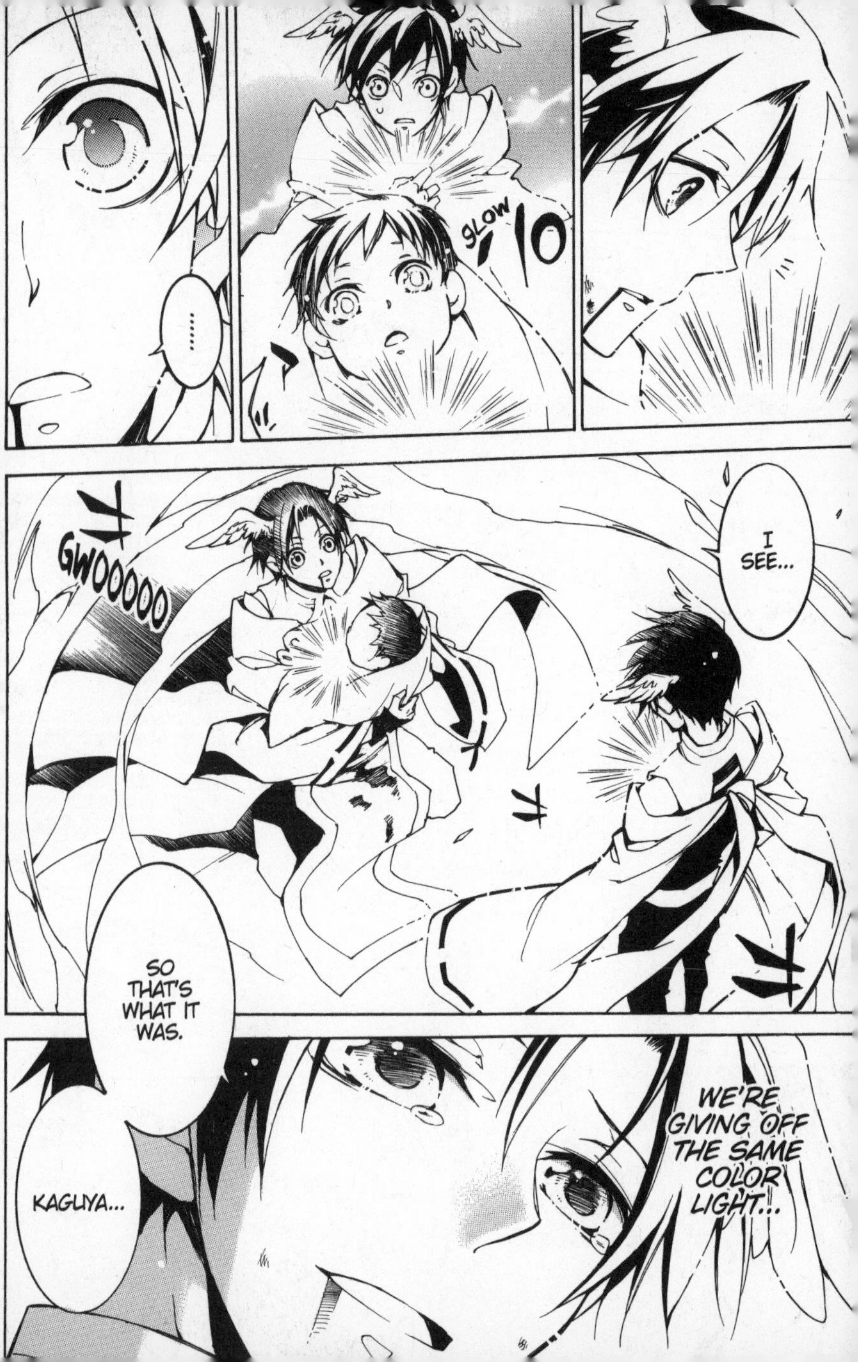
GLOW
......
I SEE...
GWOOOOO
SO THAT'S WHAT IT WAS.
WE'RE GIVING OFF THE SAME COLOR LIGHT...
KAGUYA...

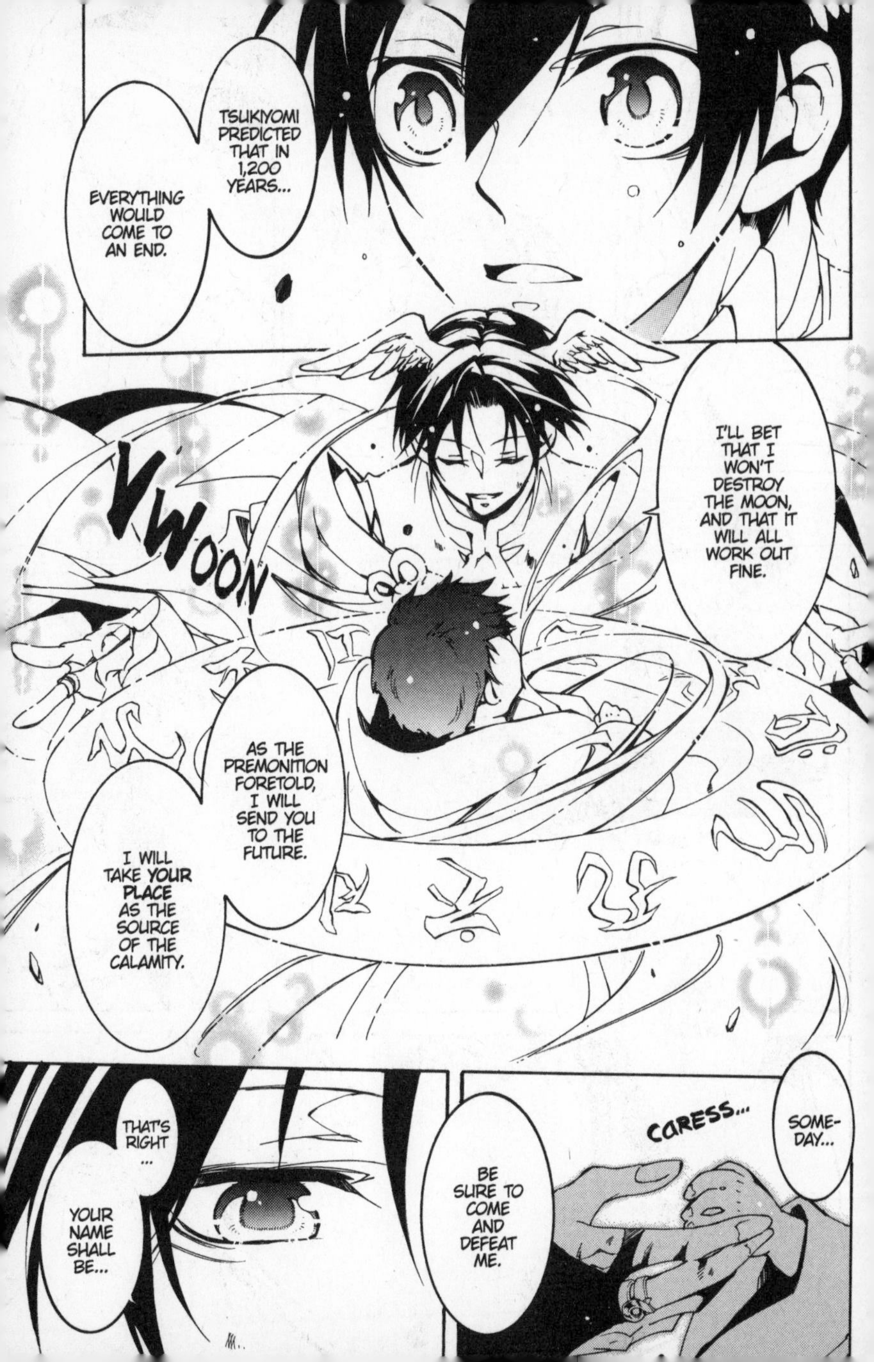
TSUKIYOMI PREDICTED THAT IN 1,200 YEARS...
EVERYTHING WOULD COME TO AN END.
I'LL BET THAT I WON'T DESTROY THE MOON, AND THAT IT WILL ALL WORK OUT FINE.
VWOON
AS THE PREMONITION FORETOLD, I WILL SEND YOU TO THE FUTURE.
I WILL TAKE YOUR PLACE AS THE SOURCE OF THE CALAMITY.
SOME-DAY...
CARESS...
BE SURE TO COME AND DEFEAT ME.
THAT'S RIGHT ...
YOUR NAME SHALL BE...

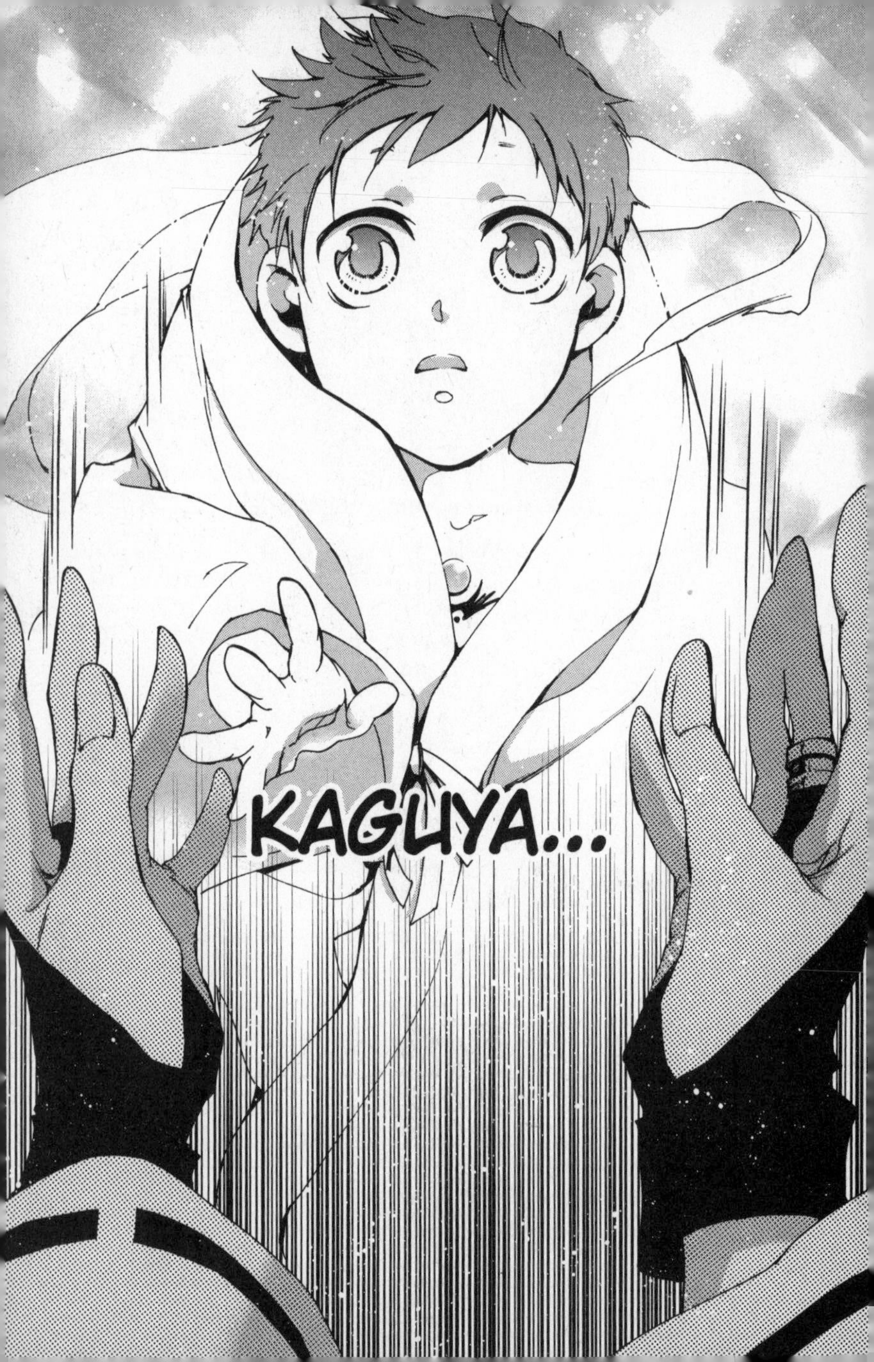
KAGUYA...

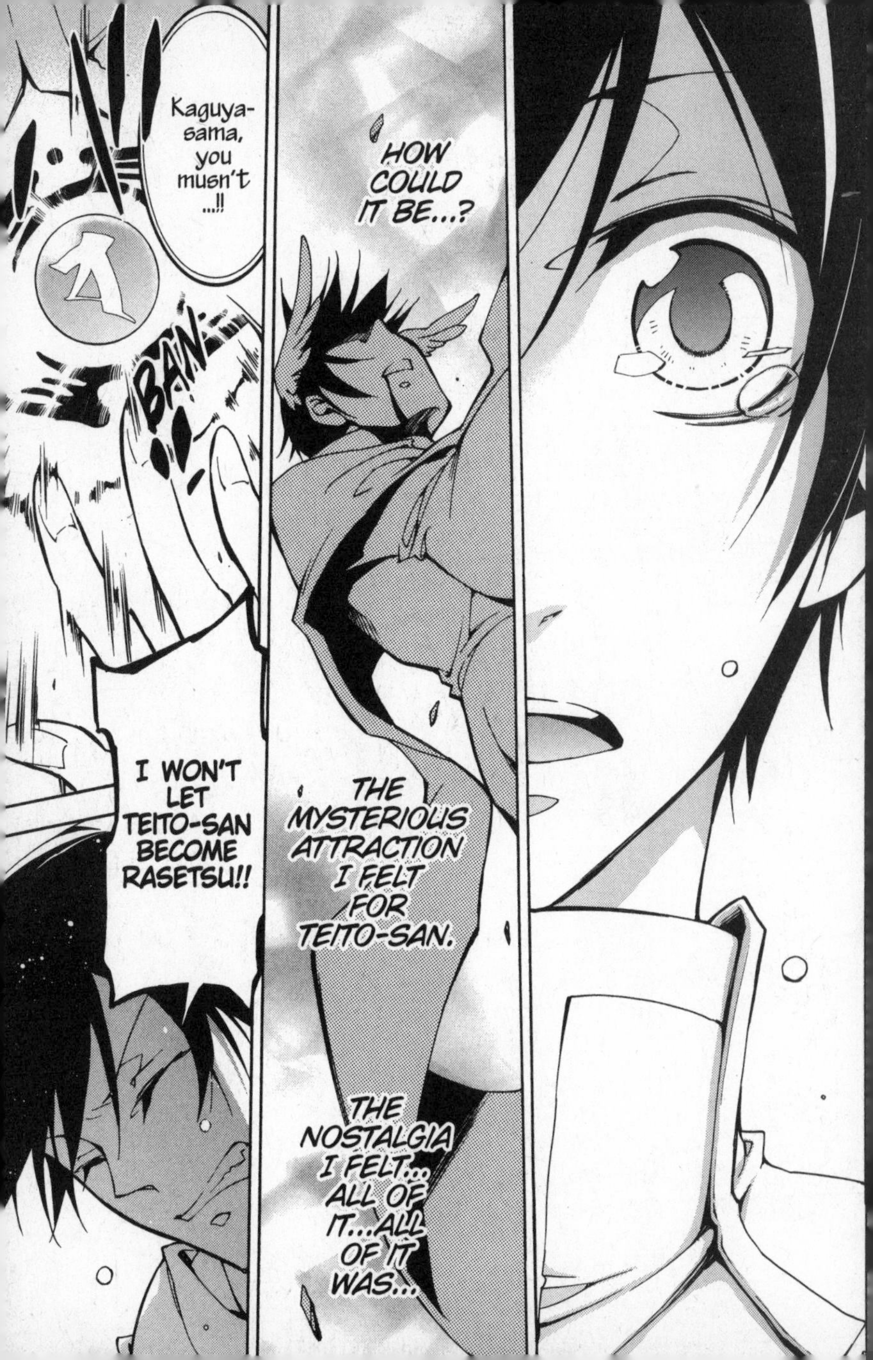
HOW COULD IT BE...?
THE MYSTERIOUS ATTRACTION I FELT FOR TEITO-SAN.
THE NOSTALGIA I FELT... ALL OF IT...ALL OF IT WAS...
Kaguya-sama, you musn't ...!!
BAN
I WON'T LET TEITO-SAN BECOME RASETSU!!

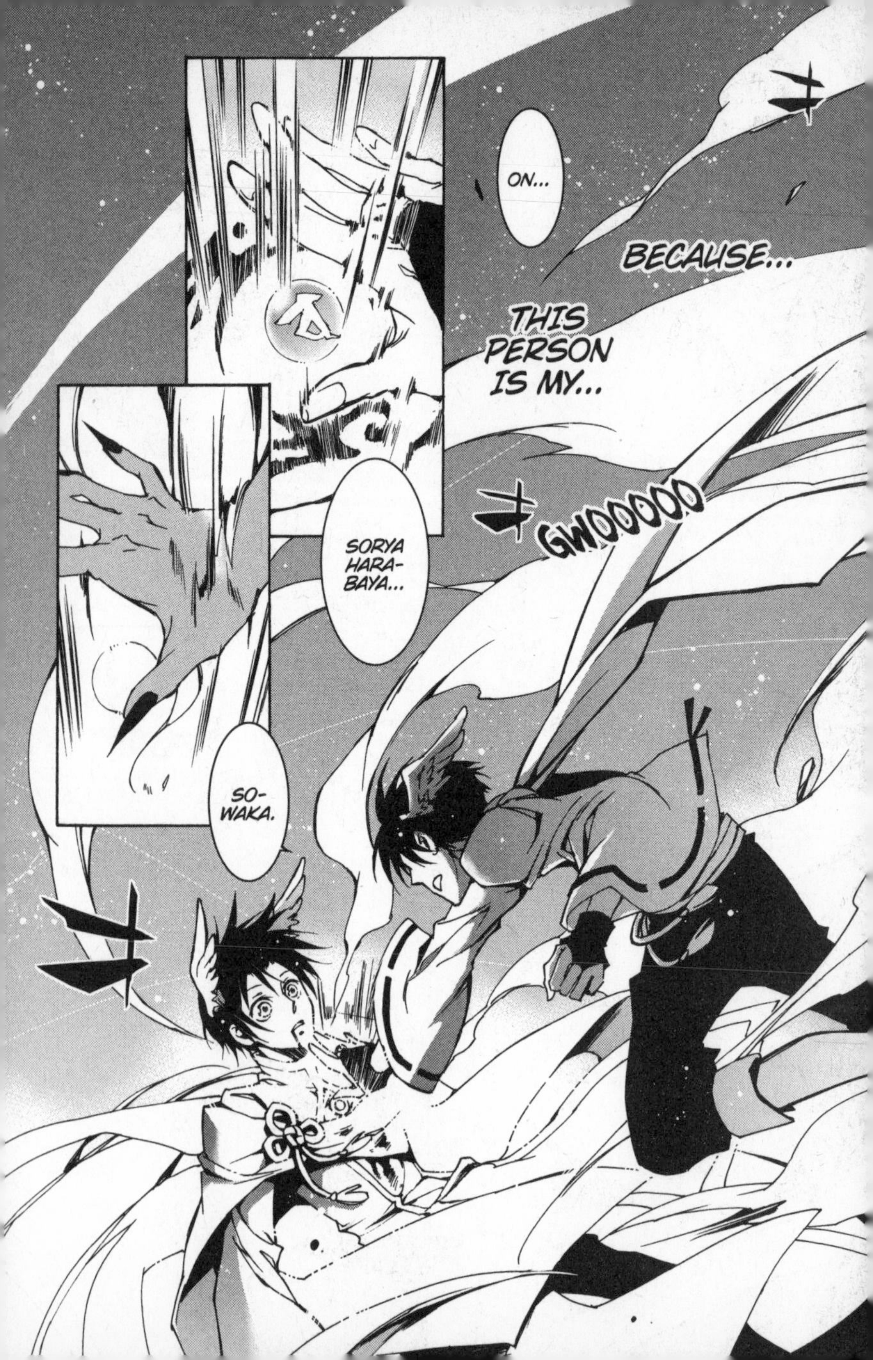
ON...
BECAUSE...
THIS PERSON IS MY...
GWOOOOO
SORYA HARA-BAYA...
SO-WAKA.

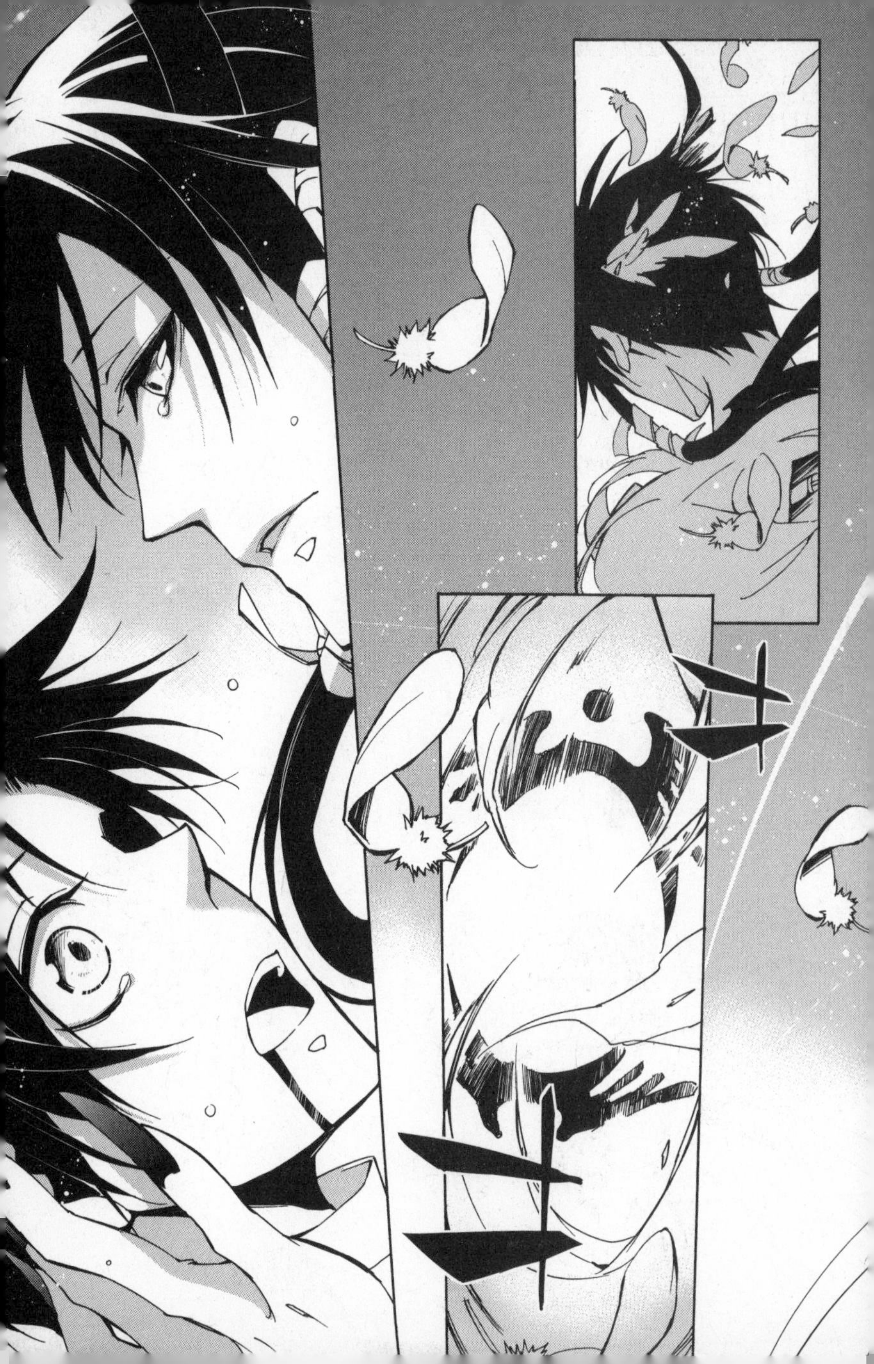

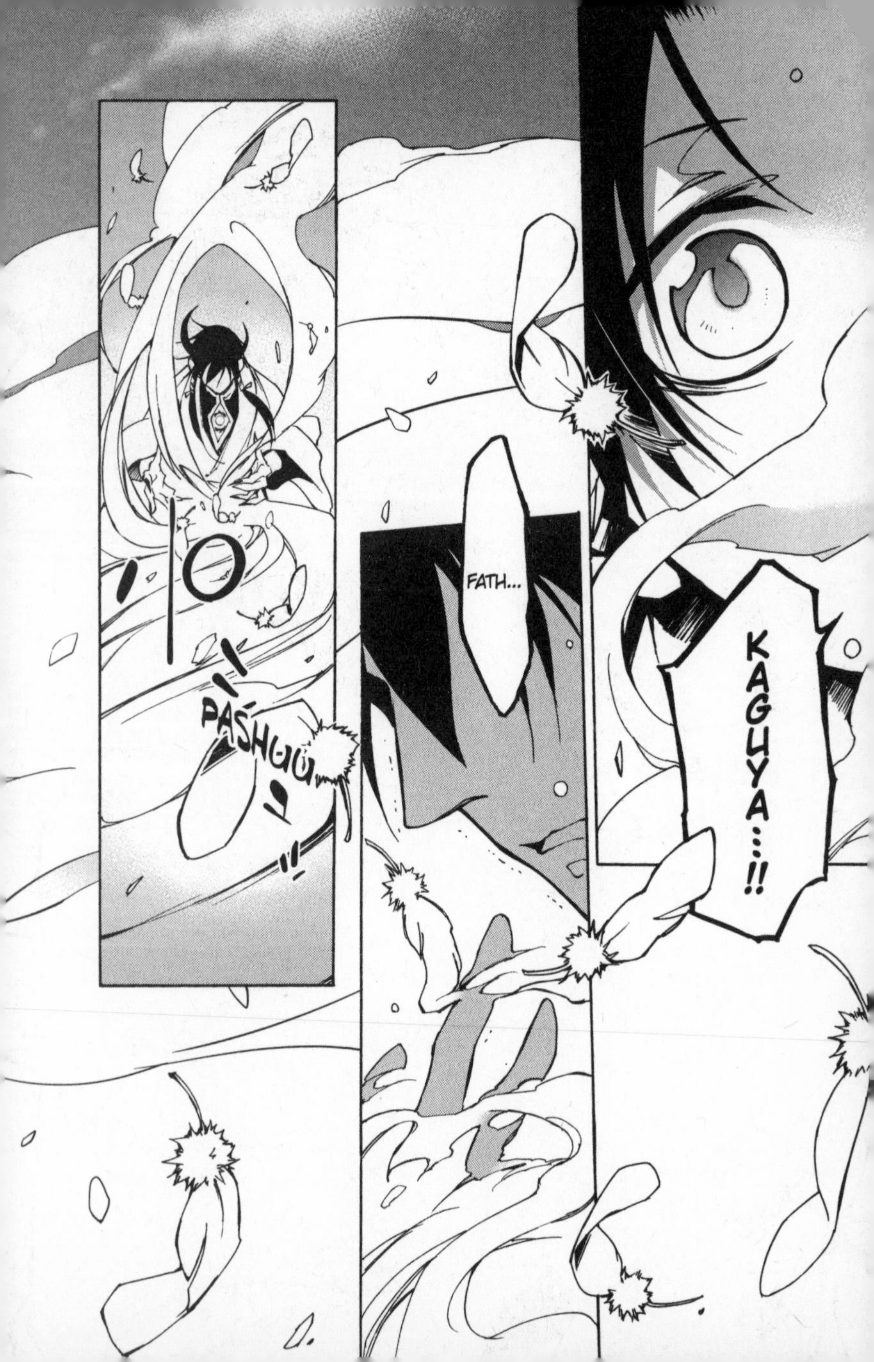
KAGUYA...!!
FATH...
PASHUU

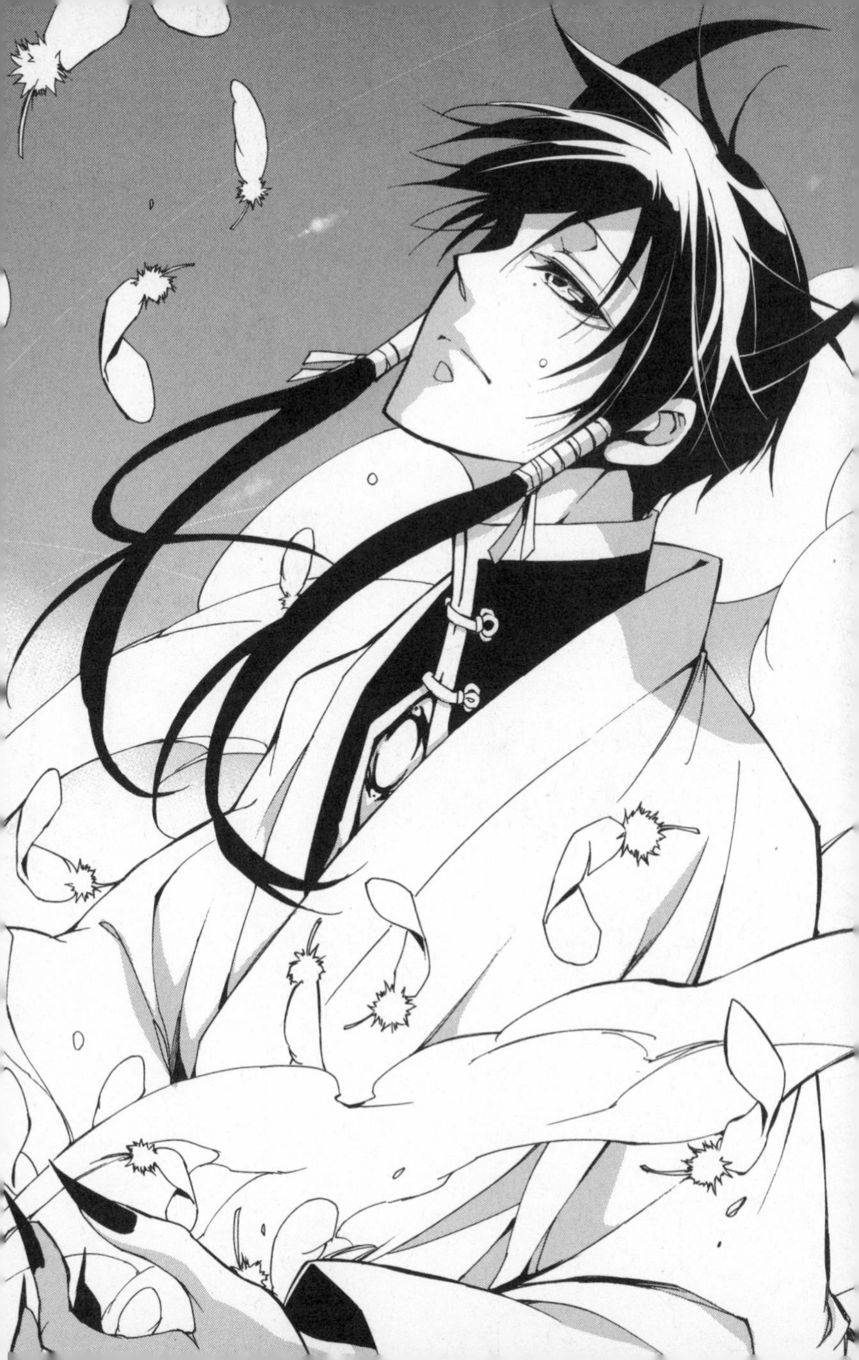

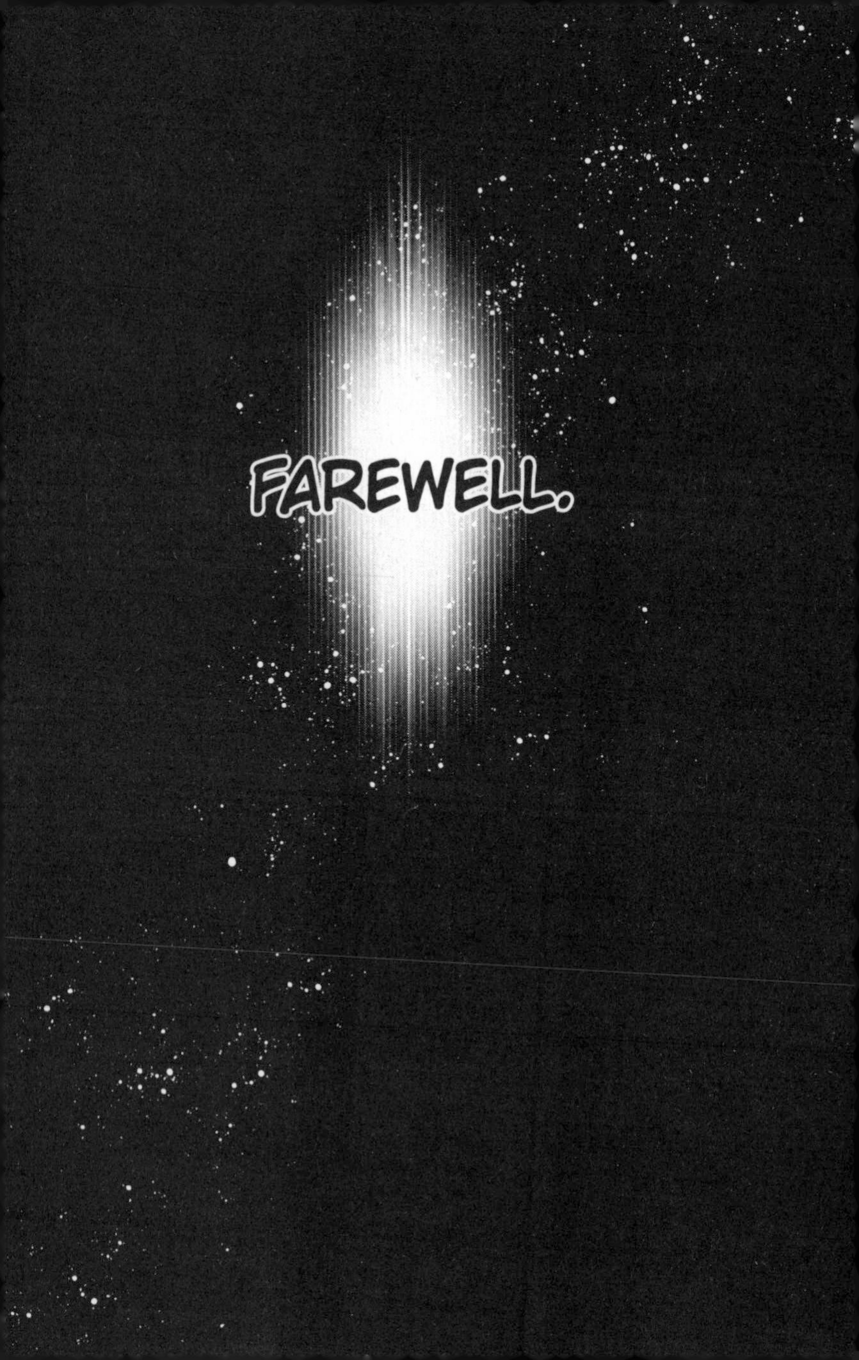
FAREWELL.

Chapter 20

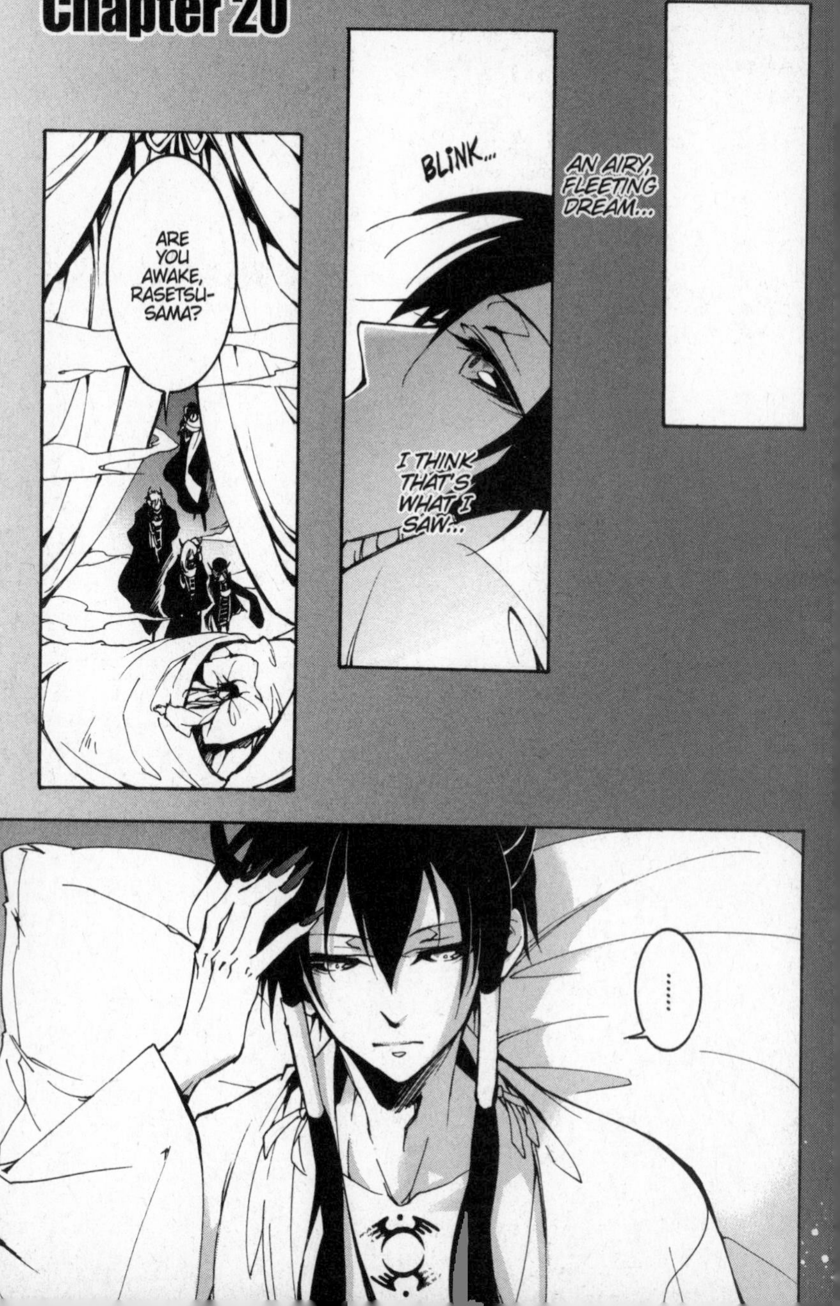
AN AIRY, FLEETING DREAM...
BLINK...
I THINK THAT'S WHAT I SAW...
ARE YOU AWAKE, RASETSU-SAMA?
......

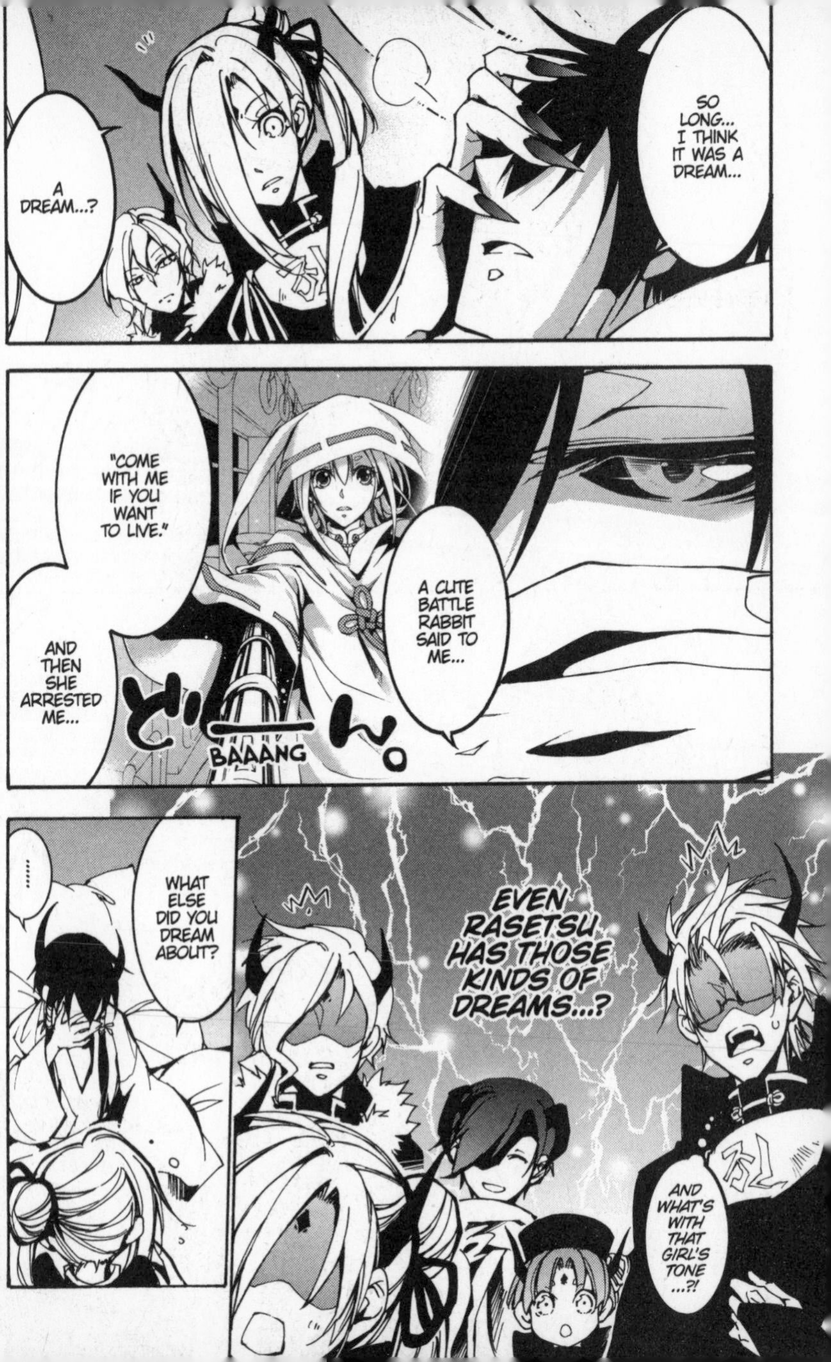
SO LONG... I THINK IT WAS A DREAM...
A DREAM...?
A CUTE BATTLE RABBIT SAID TO ME...
"COME WITH ME IF YOU WANT TO LIVE."
AND THEN SHE ARRESTED ME...
どーーん。
BAAANG
EVEN RASETSU HAS THOSE KINDS OF DREAMS...?
AND WHAT'S WITH THAT GIRL'S TONE ...?!
WHAT ELSE DID YOU DREAM ABOUT?
......

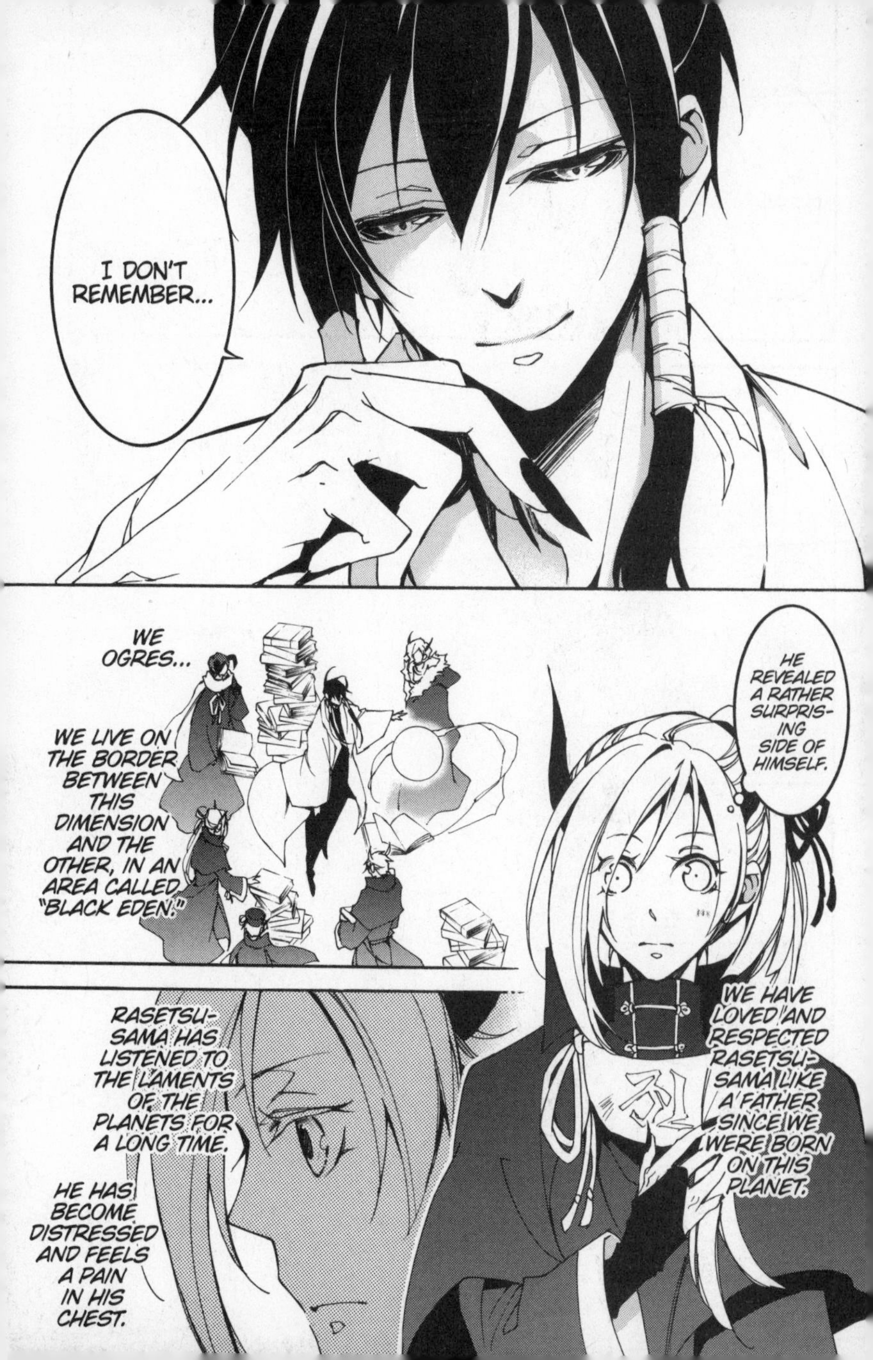
I DON'T REMEMBER...
HE REVEALED A RATHER SURPRISING SIDE OF HIMSELF.
WE HAVE LOVED AND RESPECTED RASETSU-SAMA LIKE A FATHER SINCE WE WERE BORN ON THIS PLANET.
WE OGRES...
WE LIVE ON THE BORDER BETWEEN THIS DIMENSION AND THE OTHER, IN AN AREA CALLED "BLACK EDEN."
RASETSU-SAMA HAS LISTENED TO THE LAMENTS OF THE PLANETS FOR A LONG TIME.
HE HAS BECOME DISTRESSED AND FEELS A PAIN IN HIS CHEST.

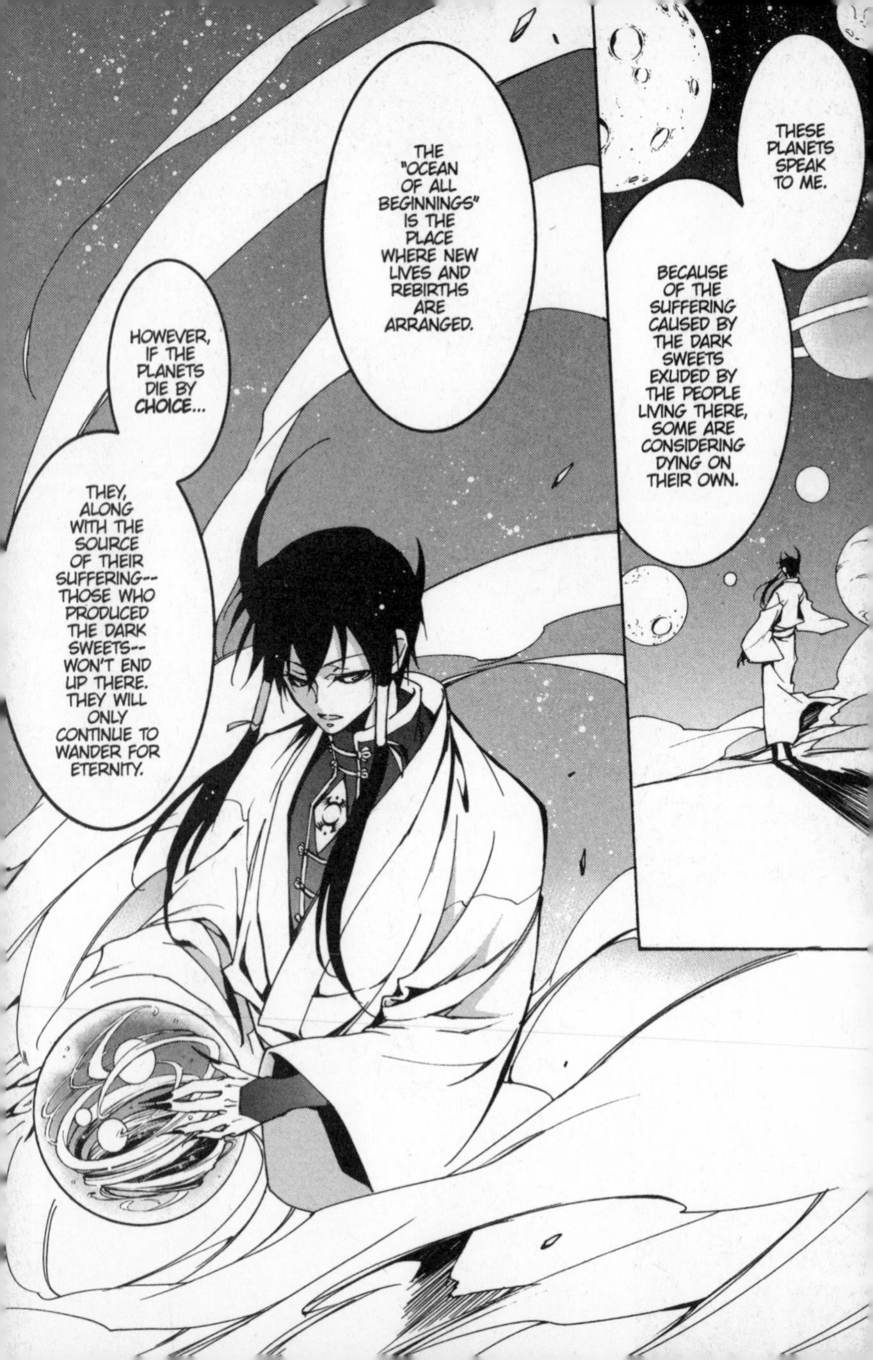
THESE PLANETS SPEAK TO ME.
BECAUSE OF THE SUFFERING CAUSED BY THE DARK SWEETS EXUDED BY THE PEOPLE LIVING THERE, SOME ARE CONSIDERING DYING ON THEIR OWN.
THE "OCEAN OF ALL BEGINNINGS" IS THE PLACE WHERE NEW LIVES AND REBIRTHS ARE ARRANGED.
HOWEVER, IF THE PLANETS DIE BY CHOICE...
THEY, ALONG WITH THE SOURCE OF THEIR SUFFERING-- THOSE WHO PRODUCED THE DARK SWEETS-- WON'T END UP THERE. THEY WILL ONLY CONTINUE TO WANDER FOR ETERNITY.

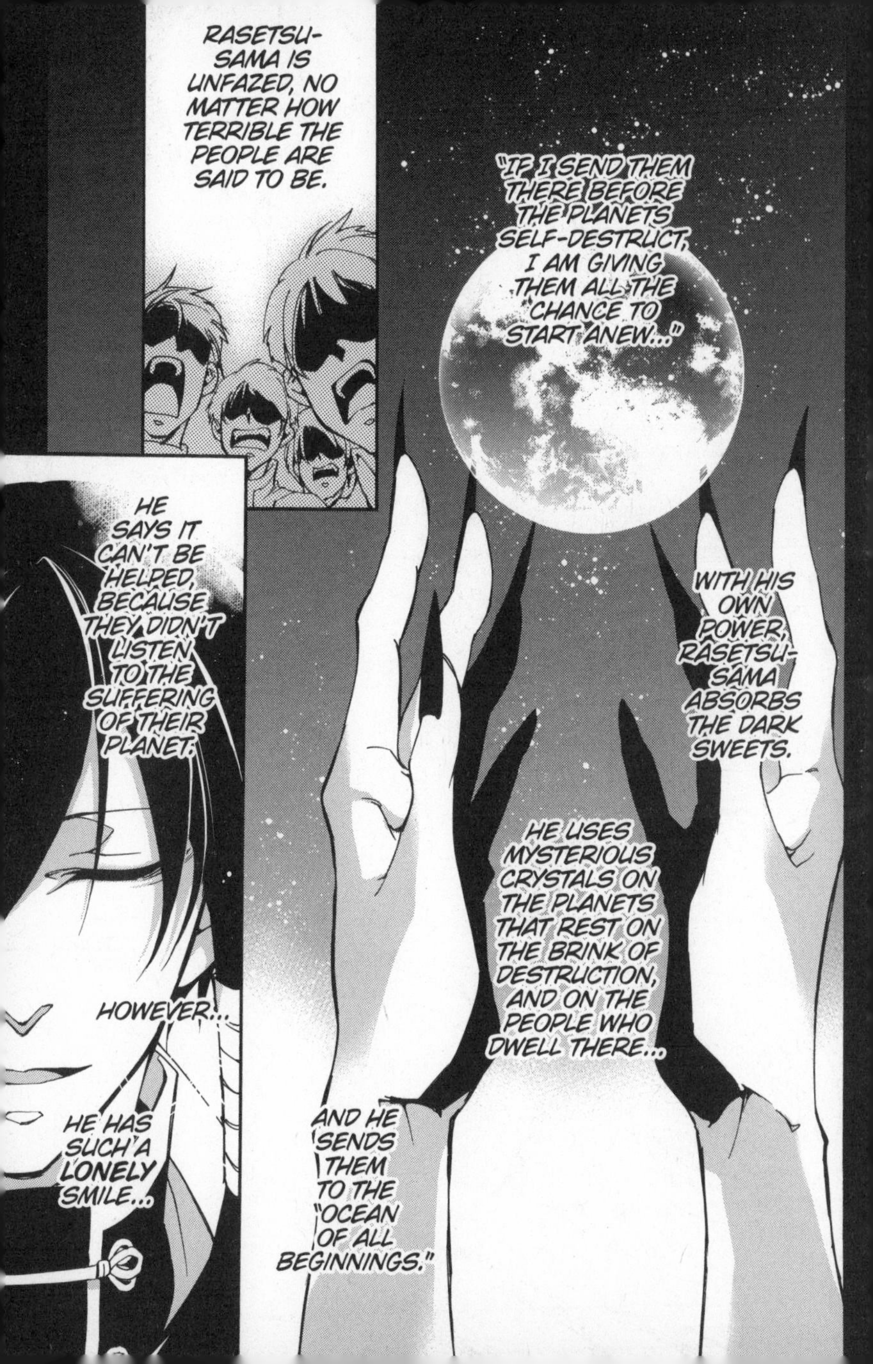
"IF I SEND THEM THERE BEFORE THE PLANETS SELF-DESTRUCT, I AM GIVING THEM ALL THE CHANCE TO START ANEW..."
WITH HIS OWN POWER, RASETSU-SAMA ABSORBS THE DARK SWEETS.
HE USES MYSTERIOUS CRYSTALS ON THE PLANETS THAT REST ON THE BRINK OF DESTRUCTION, AND ON THE PEOPLE WHO DWELL THERE...
AND HE SENDS THEM TO THE "OCEAN OF ALL BEGINNINGS."
RASETSU-SAMA IS UNFAZED, NO MATTER HOW TERRIBLE THE PEOPLE ARE SAID TO BE.
HE SAYS IT CAN'T BE HELPED, BECAUSE THEY DIDN'T LISTEN TO THE SUFFERING OF THEIR PLANET.
HOWEVER...
HE HAS SUCH A LONELY SMILE...

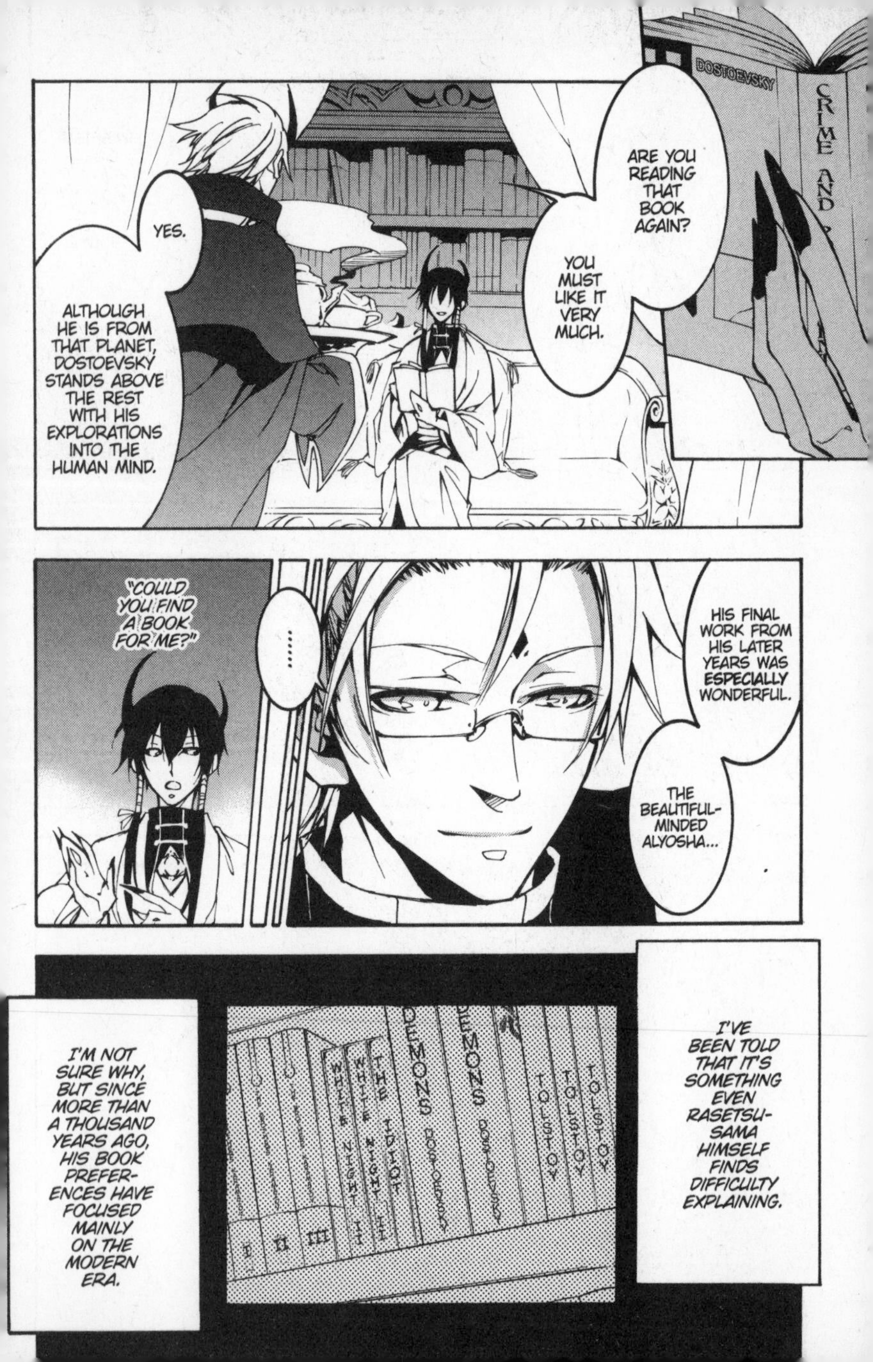
DOSTOEVSKY
CRIME AND
ARE YOU READING THAT BOOK AGAIN?
YOU MUST LIKE IT VERY MUCH.
YES.
ALTHOUGH HE IS FROM THAT PLANET, DOSTOEVSKY STANDS ABOVE THE REST WITH HIS EXPLORATIONS INTO THE HUMAN MIND.
……
HIS FINAL WORK FROM HIS LATER YEARS WAS ESPECIALLY WONDERFUL.
THE BEAUTIFUL-MINDED ALYOSHA...
"COULD YOU FIND A BOOK FOR ME?"
I'VE BEEN TOLD THAT IT'S SOMETHING EVEN RASETSU-SAMA HIMSELF FINDS DIFFICULTY EXPLAINING.
TOLSTOY
TOLSTOY
TOLSTOY
DEMONS DOSTOEVSKY
DEMONS DOSTOEVSKY
THE IDIOT
WHITE NIGHT
WHITE NIGHT
I'M NOT SURE WHY, BUT SINCE MORE THAN A THOUSAND YEARS AGO, HIS BOOK PREFERENCES HAVE FOCUSED MAINLY ON THE MODERN ERA.

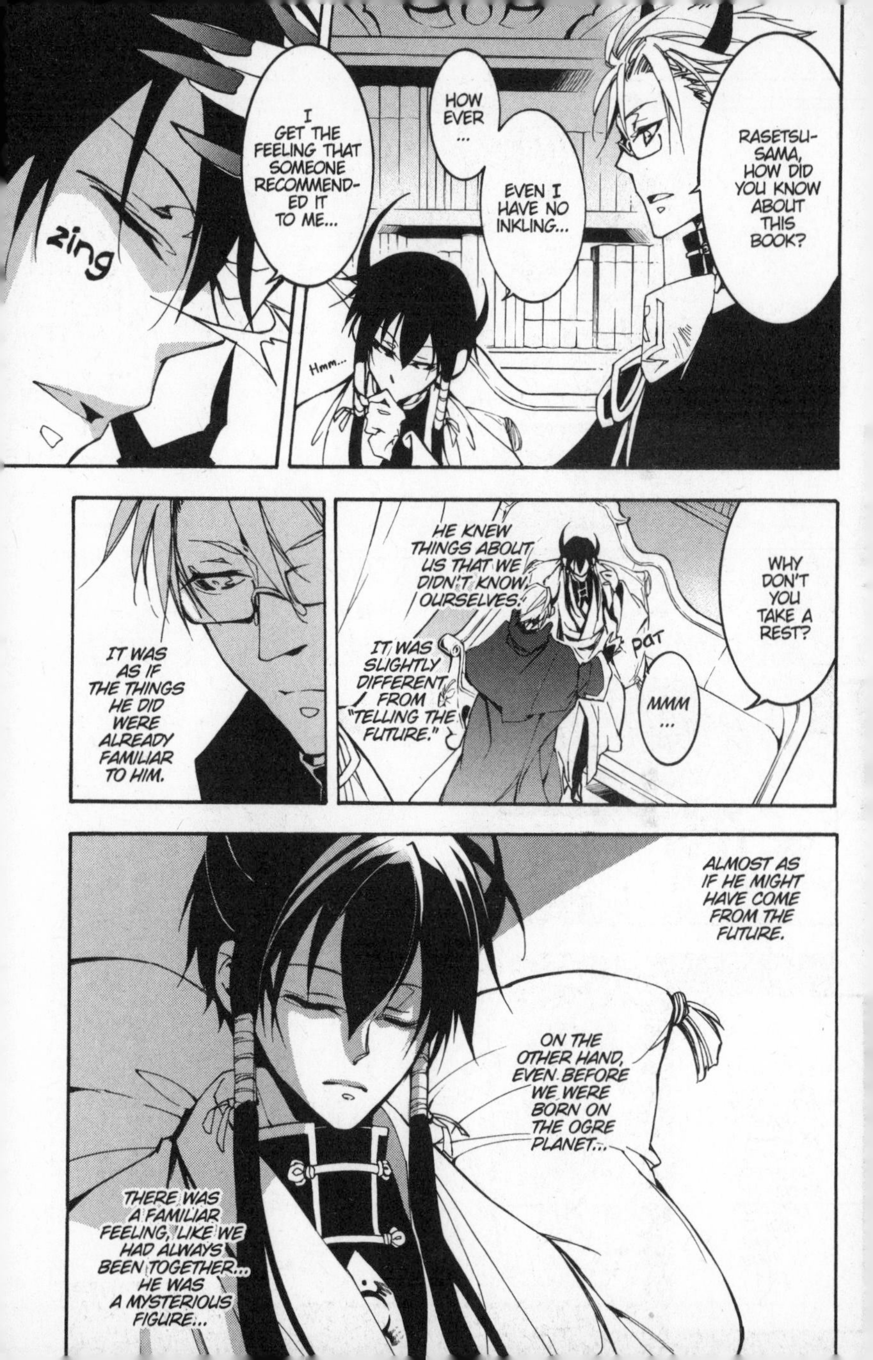
RASETSU-SAMA, HOW DID YOU KNOW ABOUT THIS BOOK?
HOW EVER ...
EVEN I HAVE NO INKLING...
I GET THE FEELING THAT SOMEONE RECOMMENDED IT TO ME...
Hmm...
zing
WHY DON'T YOU TAKE A REST?
pat
MMM ...
HE KNEW THINGS ABOUT US THAT WE DIDN'T KNOW OURSELVES.
IT WAS SLIGHTLY DIFFERENT FROM "TELLING THE FUTURE."
IT WAS AS IF THE THINGS HE DID WERE ALREADY FAMILIAR TO HIM.
ALMOST AS IF HE MIGHT HAVE COME FROM THE FUTURE.
ON THE OTHER HAND, EVEN BEFORE WE WERE BORN ON THE OGRE PLANET...
THERE WAS A FAMILIAR FEELING, LIKE WE HAD ALWAYS BEEN TOGETHER... HE WAS A MYSTERIOUS FIGURE...

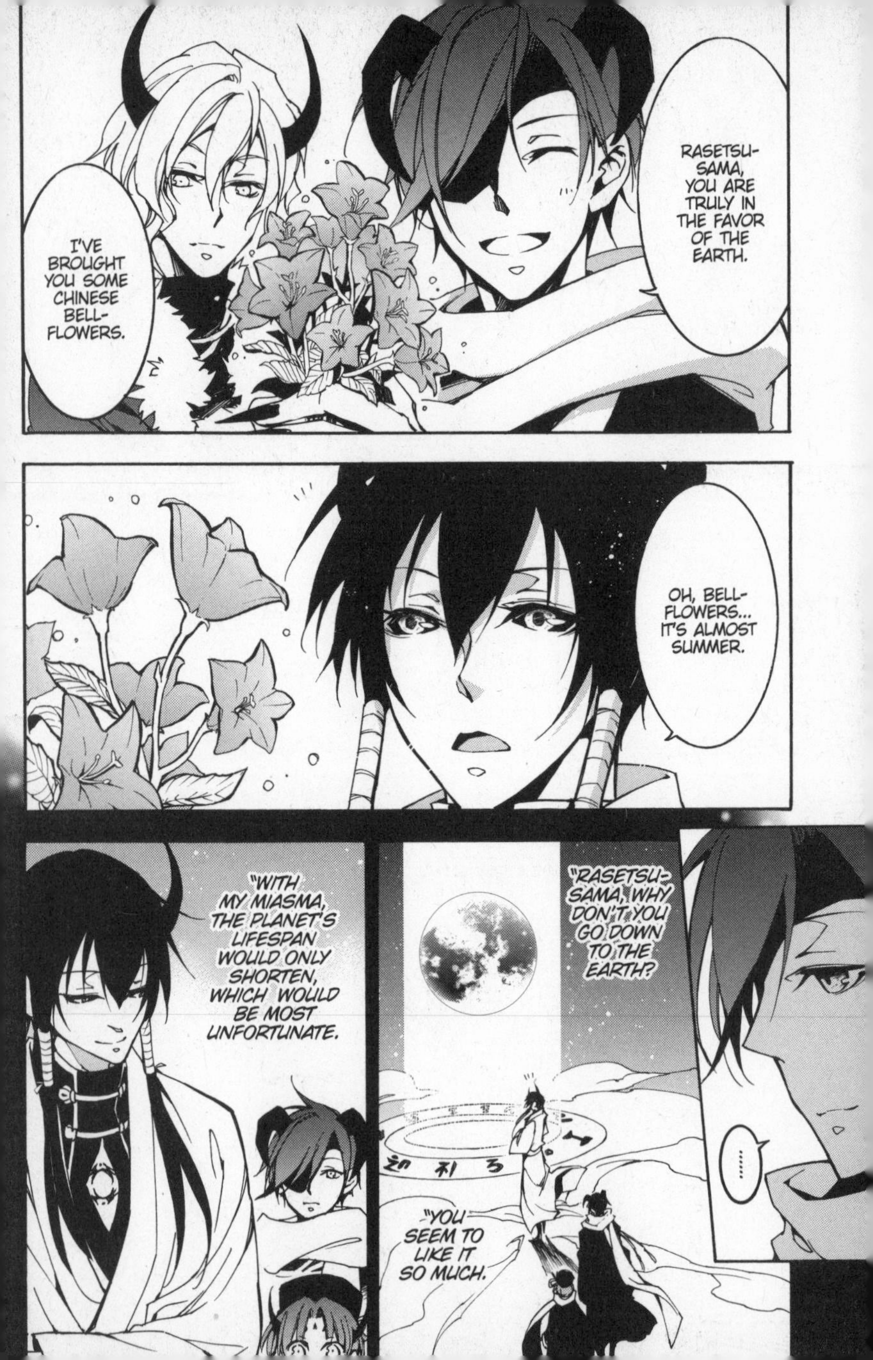
RASETSU-SAMA, YOU ARE TRULY IN THE FAVOR OF THE EARTH.
I'VE BROUGHT YOU SOME CHINESE BELL-FLOWERS.
OH, BELL-FLOWERS... IT'S ALMOST SUMMER.
......
"RASETSU-SAMA, WHY DON'T YOU GO DOWN TO THE EARTH?
"YOU SEEM TO LIKE IT SO MUCH.
"WITH MY MIASMA, THE PLANET'S LIFESPAN WOULD ONLY SHORTEN, WHICH WOULD BE MOST UNFORTUNATE.

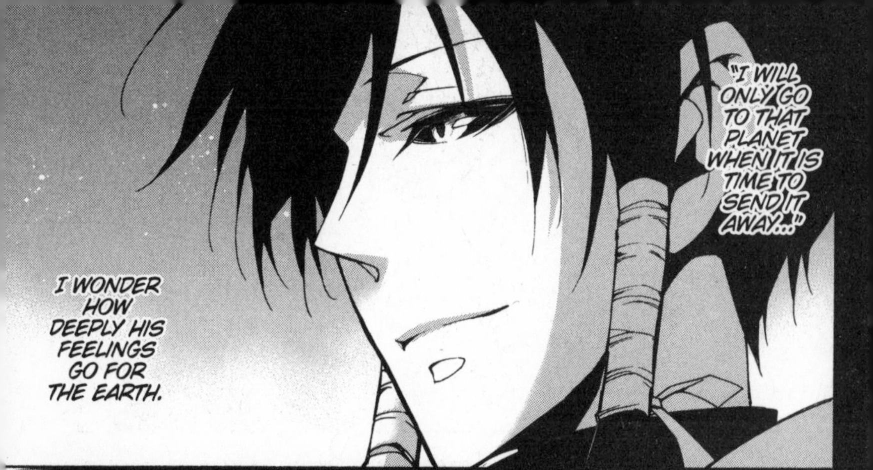
"I WILL ONLY GO TO THAT PLANET WHEN IT IS TIME TO SEND IT AWAY..."
I WONDER HOW DEEPLY HIS FEELINGS GO FOR THE EARTH.
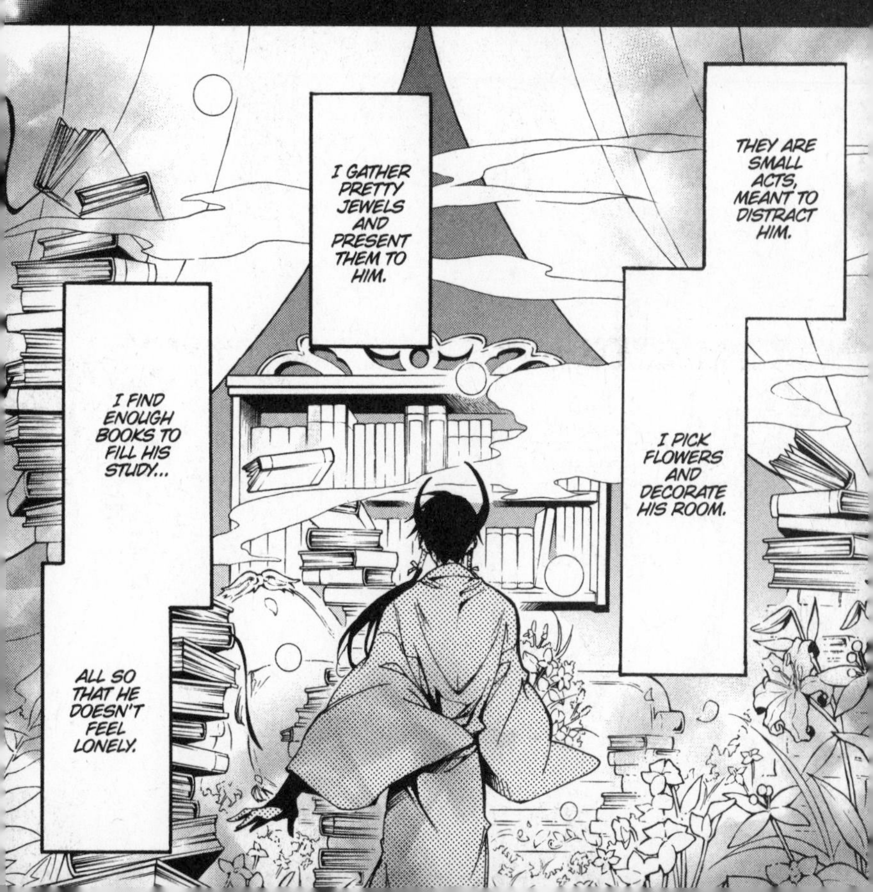
THEY ARE SMALL ACTS, MEANT TO DISTRACT HIM.
I GATHER PRETTY JEWELS AND PRESENT THEM TO HIM.
I PICK FLOWERS AND DECORATE HIS ROOM.
I FIND ENOUGH BOOKS TO FILL HIS STUDY...
ALL SO THAT HE DOESN'T FEEL LONELY.

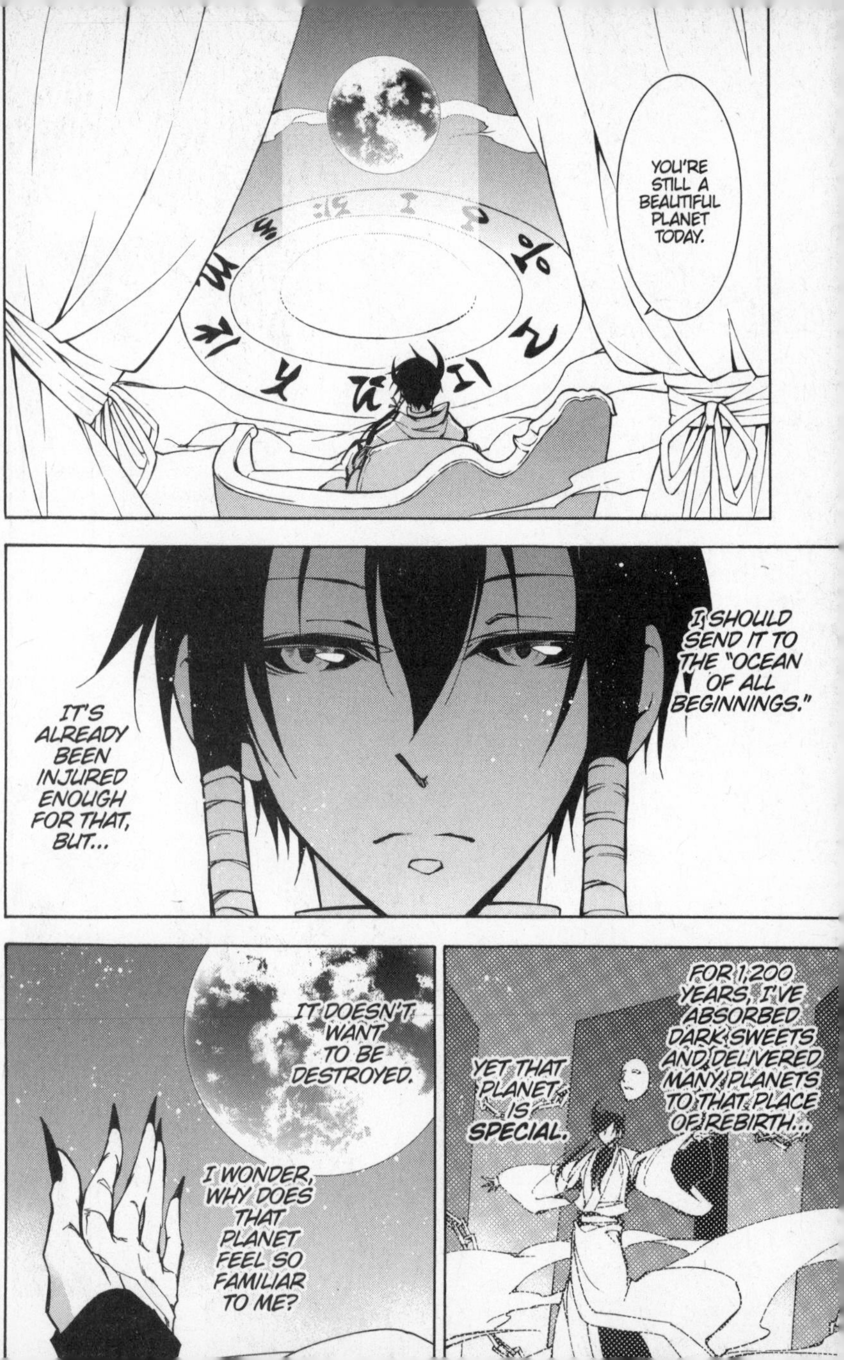
YOU'RE STILL A BEAUTIFUL PLANET TODAY.
I SHOULD SEND IT TO THE "OCEAN OF ALL BEGINNINGS."
IT'S ALREADY BEEN INJURED ENOUGH FOR THAT, BUT...
FOR 1,200 YEARS, I'VE ABSORBED DARK SWEETS AND DELIVERED MANY PLANETS TO THAT PLACE OF REBIRTH...
YET THAT PLANET IS SPECIAL.
IT DOESN'T WANT TO BE DESTROYED.
I WONDER, WHY DOES THAT PLANET FEEL SO FAMILIAR TO ME?

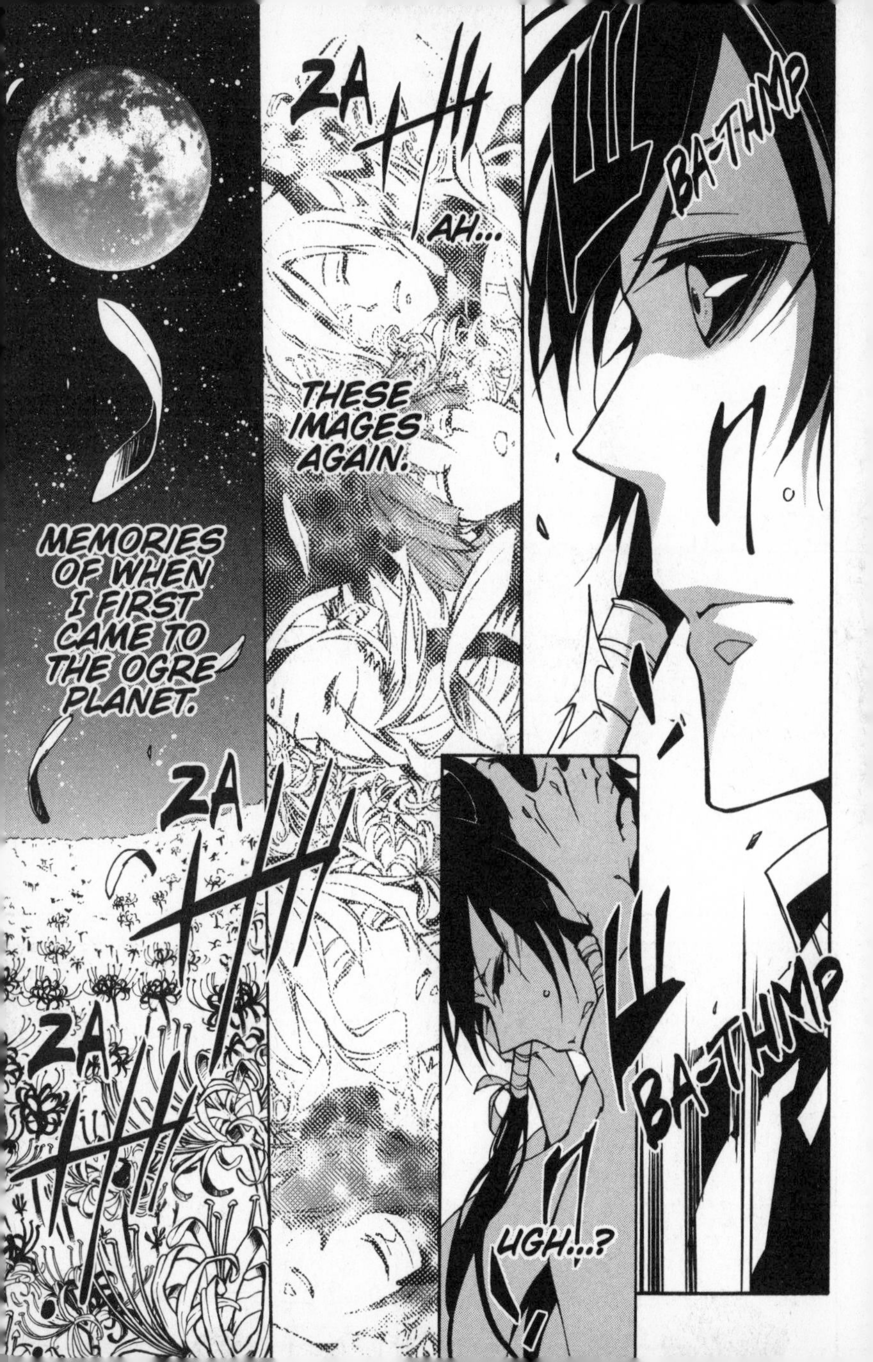
BA-THMP
BA-THMP
UGH...?
ZA
AH...
THESE IMAGES AGAIN.
MEMORIES OF WHEN I FIRST CAME TO THE OGRE PLANET.
ZA
ZA

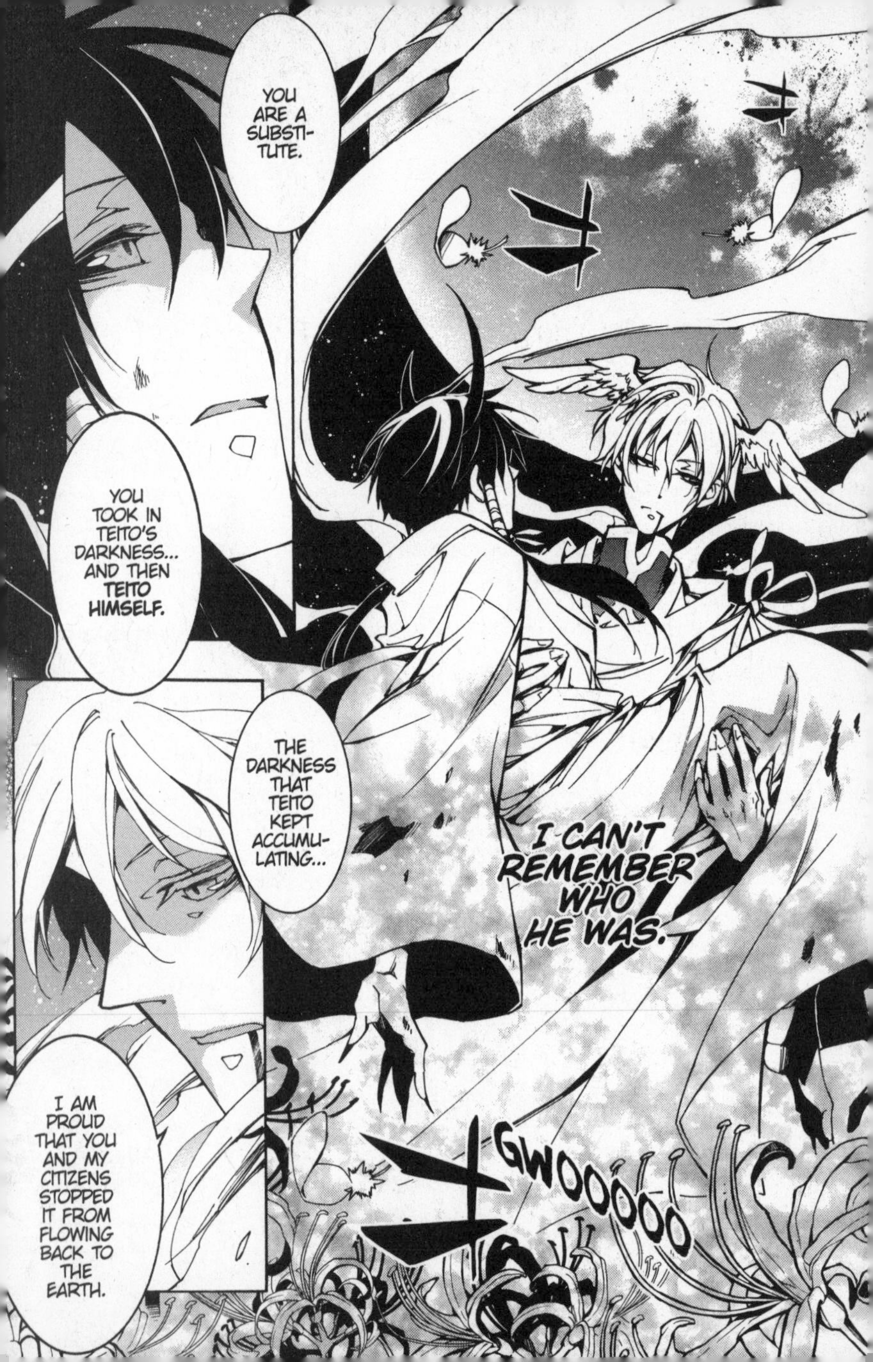
I CAN'T REMEMBER WHO HE WAS.
GWOOOOOO
YOU ARE A SUBSTI-TUTE.
YOU TOOK IN TEITO'S DARKNESS... AND THEN TEITO HIMSELF.
THE DARKNESS THAT TEITO KEPT ACCUMU-LATING...
I AM PROUD THAT YOU AND MY CITIZENS STOPPED IT FROM FLOWING BACK TO THE EARTH.

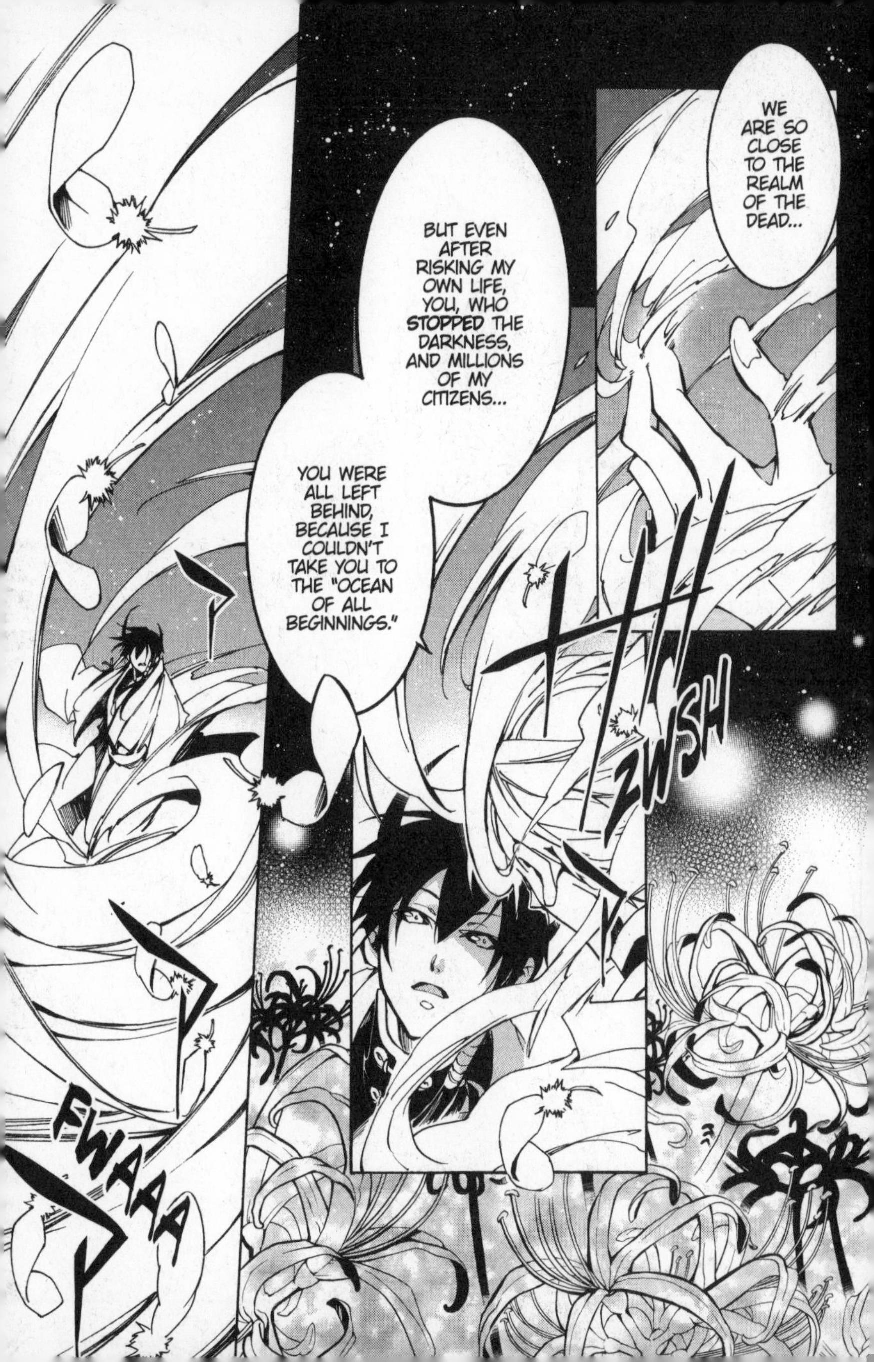
WE ARE SO CLOSE TO THE REALM OF THE DEAD...
BUT EVEN AFTER RISKING MY OWN LIFE, YOU, WHO STOPPED THE DARKNESS, AND MILLIONS OF MY CITIZENS...
YOU WERE ALL LEFT BEHIND, BECAUSE I COULDN'T TAKE YOU TO THE "OCEAN OF ALL BEGINNINGS."
ZWSH
FWAAA

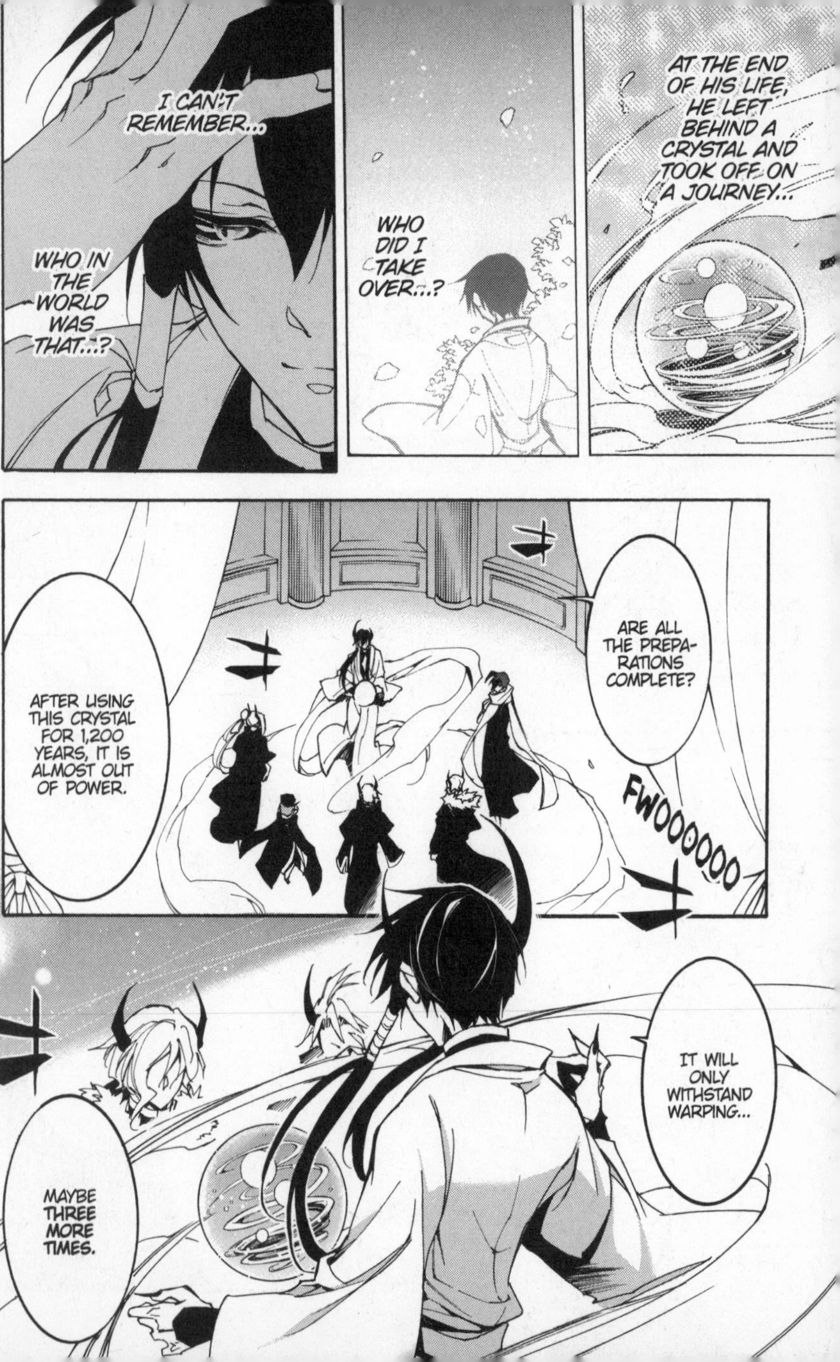
AT THE END OF HIS LIFE, HE LEFT BEHIND A CRYSTAL AND TOOK OFF ON A JOURNEY...
WHO DID I TAKE OVER...?
I CAN'T REMEMBER...
WHO IN THE WORLD WAS THAT...?
ARE ALL THE PREPARATIONS COMPLETE?
FWOOOOOO
AFTER USING THIS CRYSTAL FOR 1,200 YEARS, IT IS ALMOST OUT OF POWER.
IT WILL ONLY WITHSTAND WARPING...
MAYBE THREE MORE TIMES.

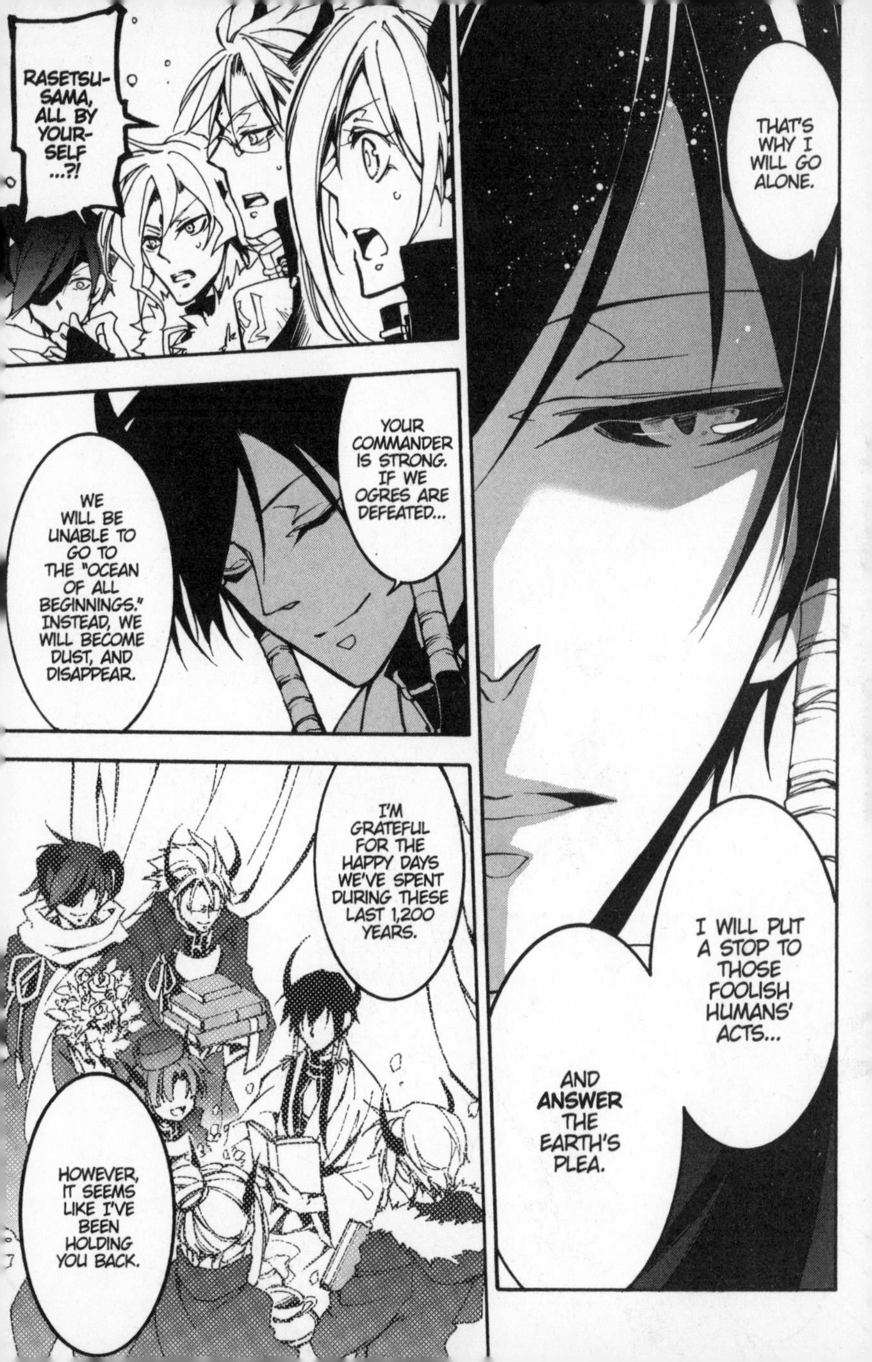
THAT'S WHY I WILL GO ALONE.
I WILL PUT A STOP TO THOSE FOOLISH HUMANS' ACTS...
AND ANSWER THE EARTH'S PLEA.
RASETSU-SAMA, ALL BY YOURSELF ...?!
YOUR COMMANDER IS STRONG. IF WE OGRES ARE DEFEATED...
WE WILL BE UNABLE TO GO TO THE "OCEAN OF ALL BEGINNINGS." INSTEAD, WE WILL BECOME DUST, AND DISAPPEAR.
I'M GRATEFUL FOR THE HAPPY DAYS WE'VE SPENT DURING THESE LAST 1,200 YEARS.
HOWEVER, IT SEEMS LIKE I'VE BEEN HOLDING YOU BACK.

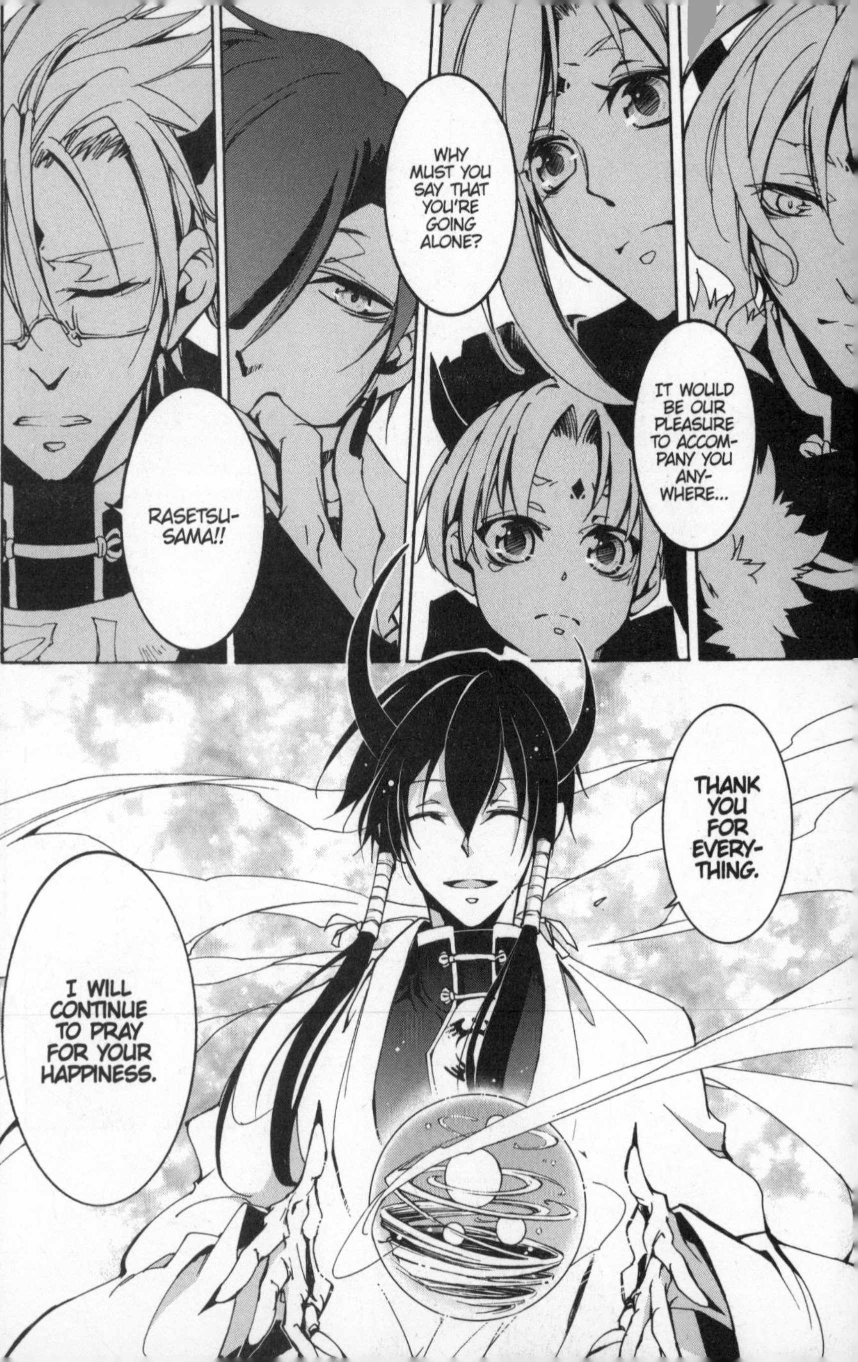
WHY MUST YOU SAY THAT YOU'RE GOING ALONE?
IT WOULD BE OUR PLEASURE TO ACCOMPANY YOU ANYWHERE...
RASETSU-SAMA!!
THANK YOU FOR EVERYTHING.
I WILL CONTINUE TO PRAY FOR YOUR HAPPINESS.

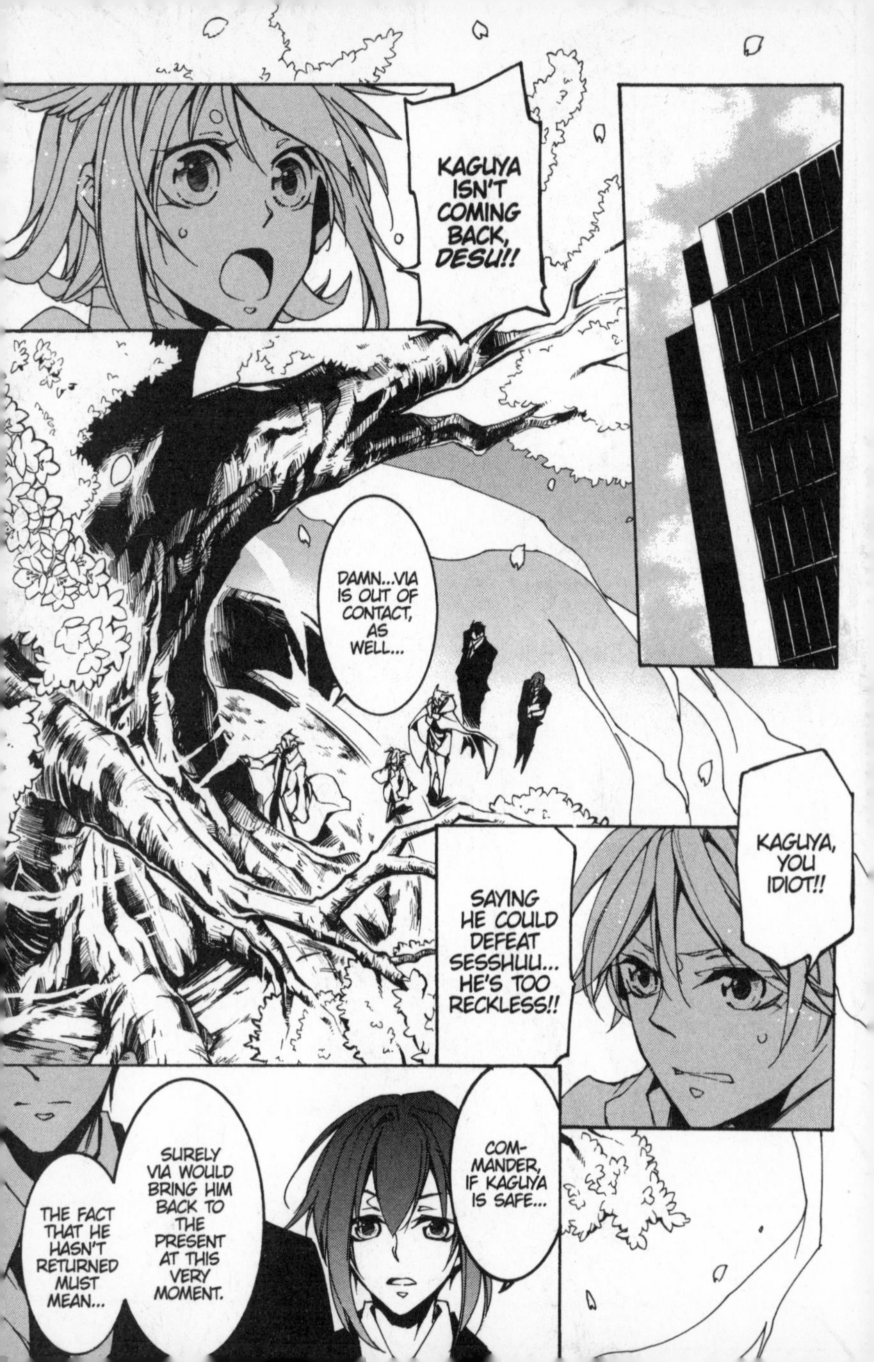
KAGUYA ISN'T COMING BACK, DESU!!
DAMN...VIA IS OUT OF CONTACT, AS WELL...
KAGUYA, YOU IDIOT!!
SAYING HE COULD DEFEAT SESSHUU... HE'S TOO RECKLESS!!
COM-MANDER, IF KAGUYA IS SAFE...
SURELY VIA WOULD BRING HIM BACK TO THE PRESENT AT THIS VERY MOMENT.
THE FACT THAT HE HASN'T RETURNED MUST MEAN...

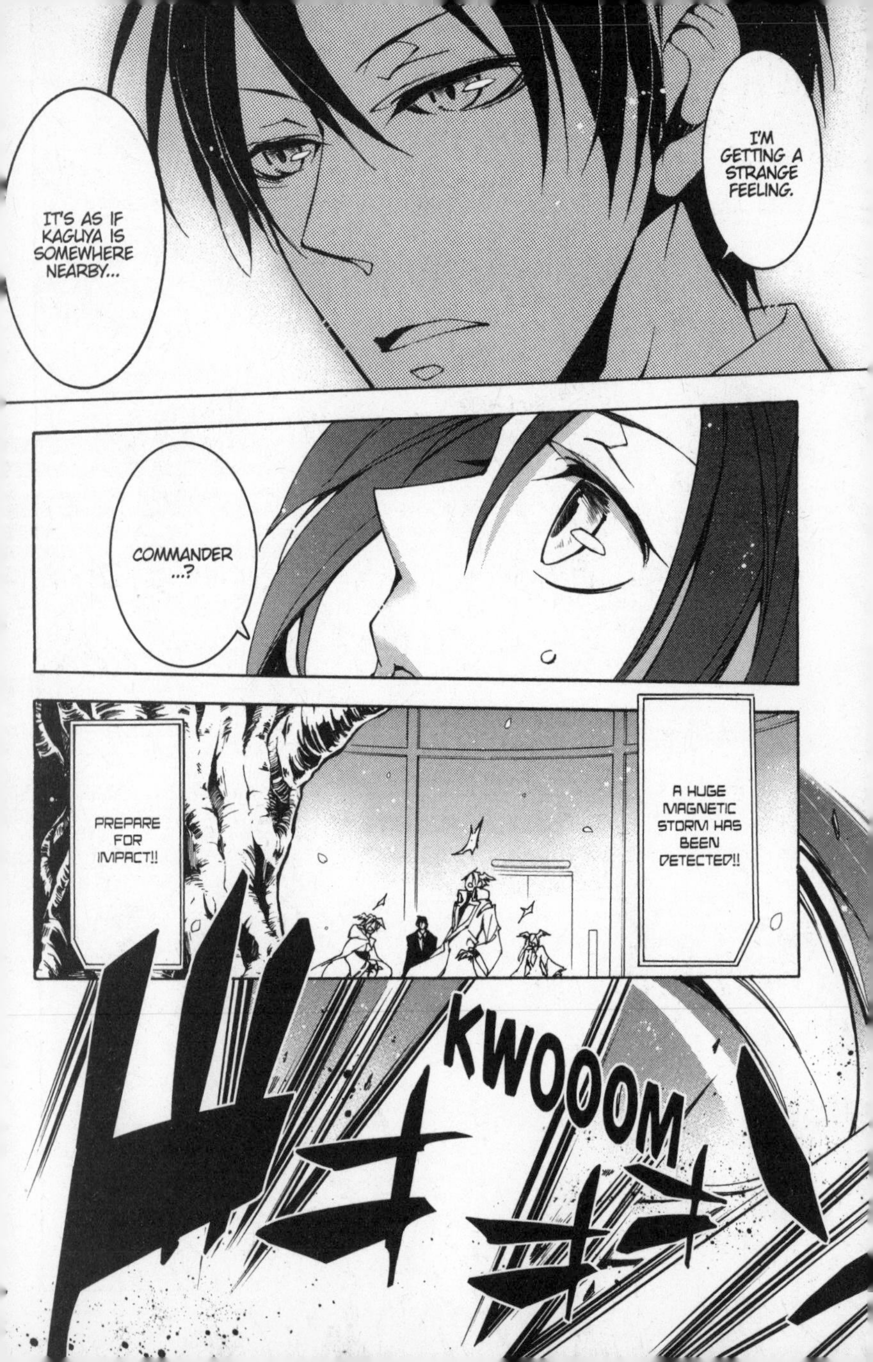
I'M GETTING A STRANGE FEELING.
IT'S AS IF KAGUYA IS SOMEWHERE NEARBY...
COMMANDER ...?
A HUGE MAGNETIC STORM HAS BEEN DETECTED!!
PREPARE FOR IMPACT!!
KWOOOM

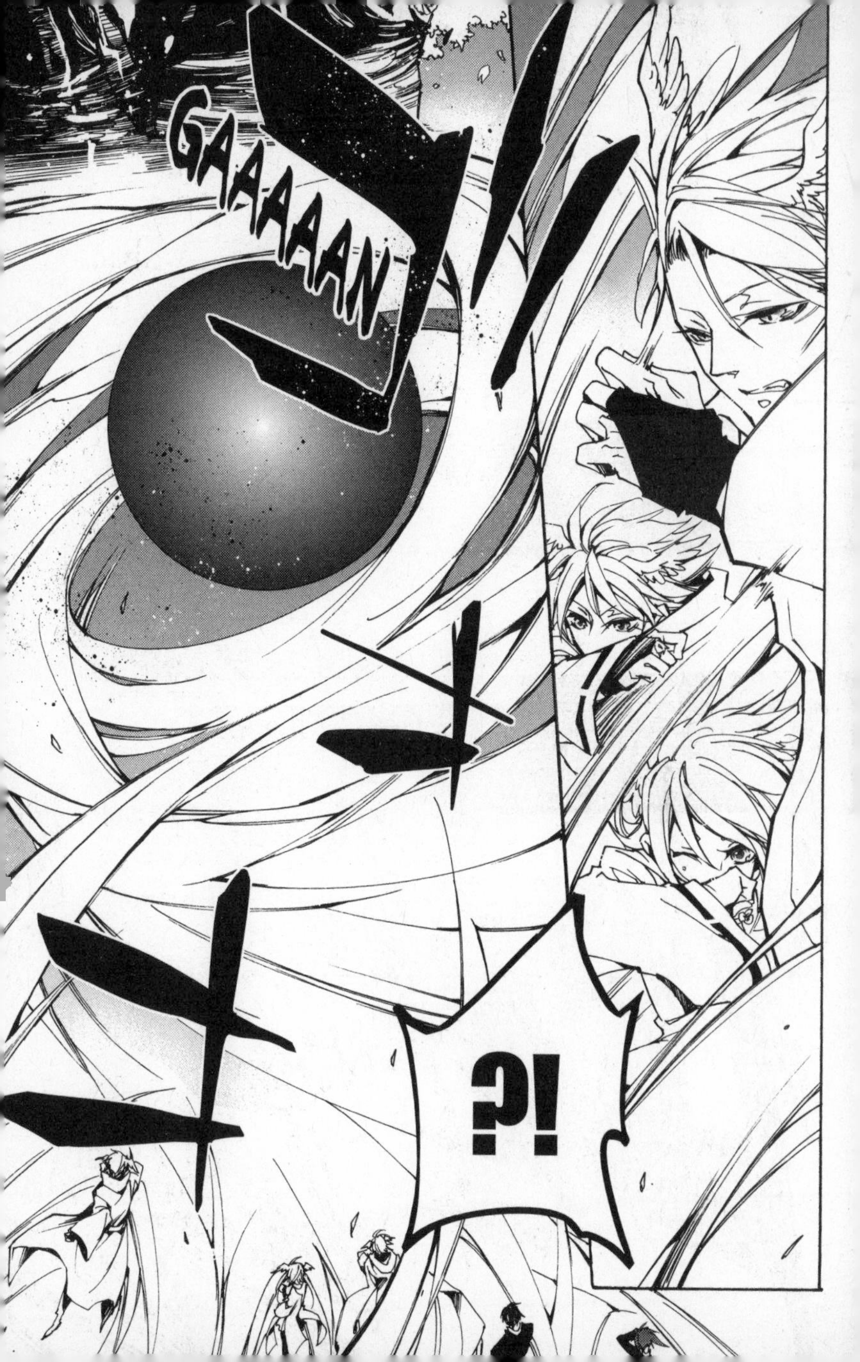
GAAAAAN
?!

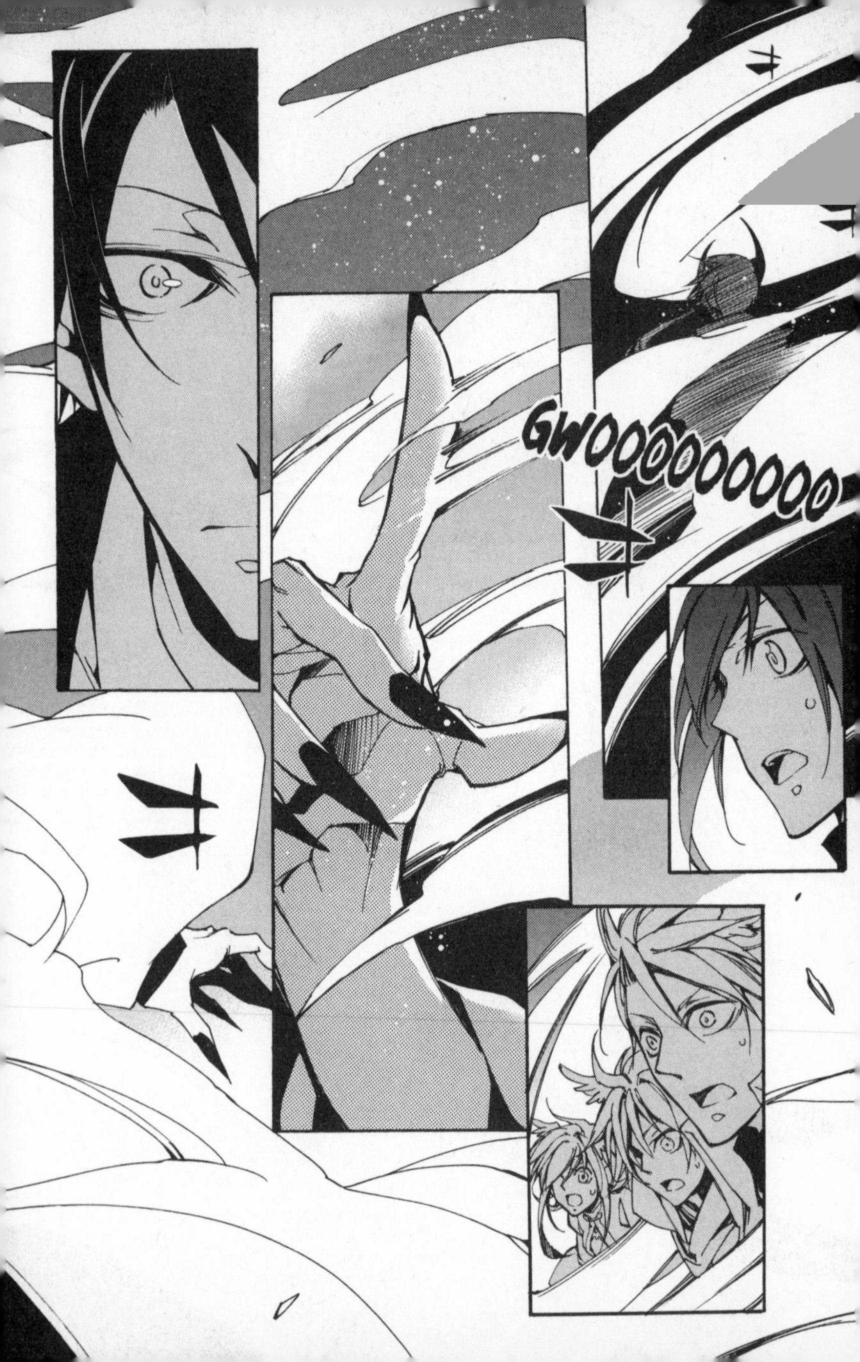
GWOOOOOOOOOO

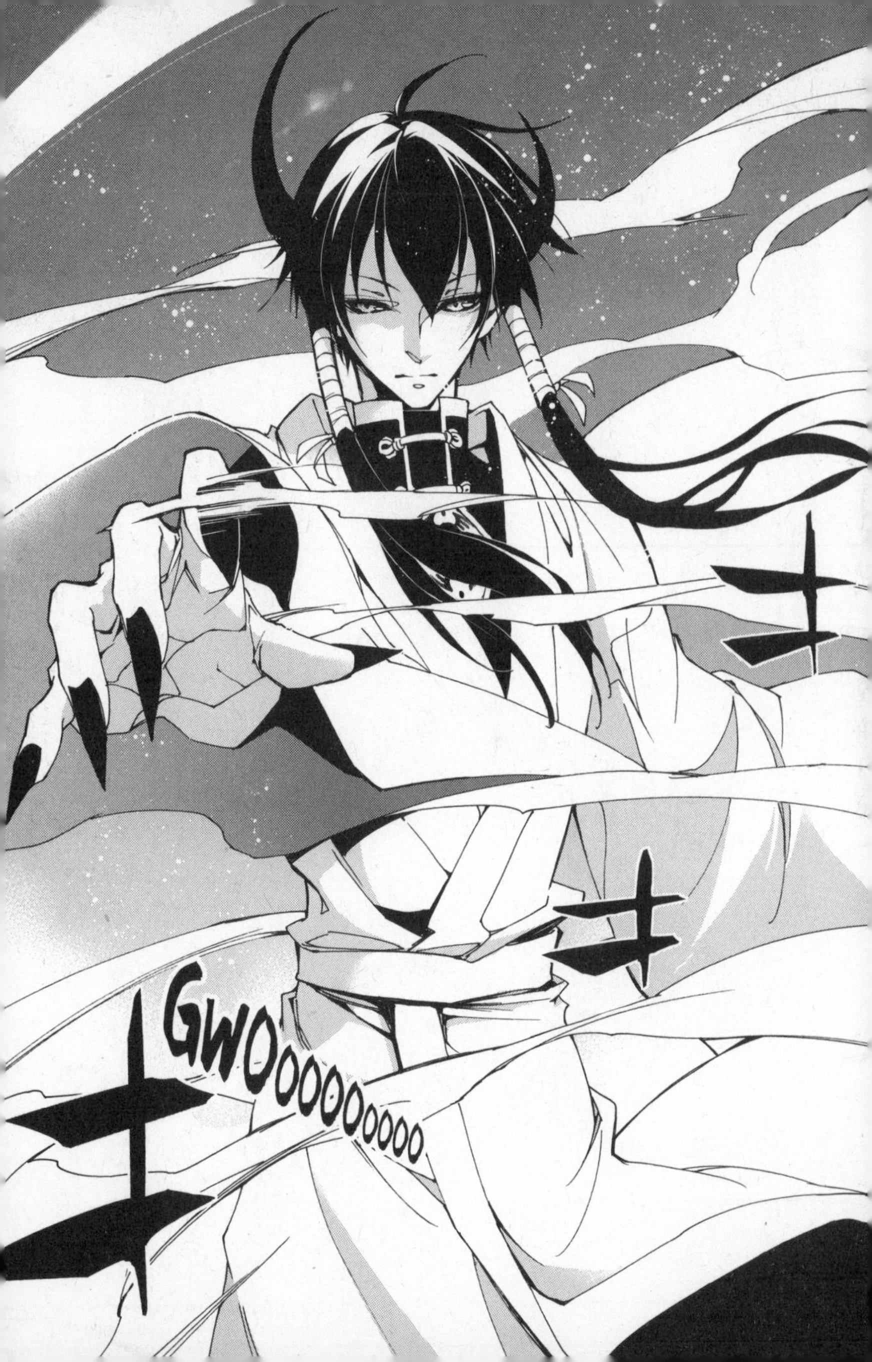
GWOOOOOOOOO

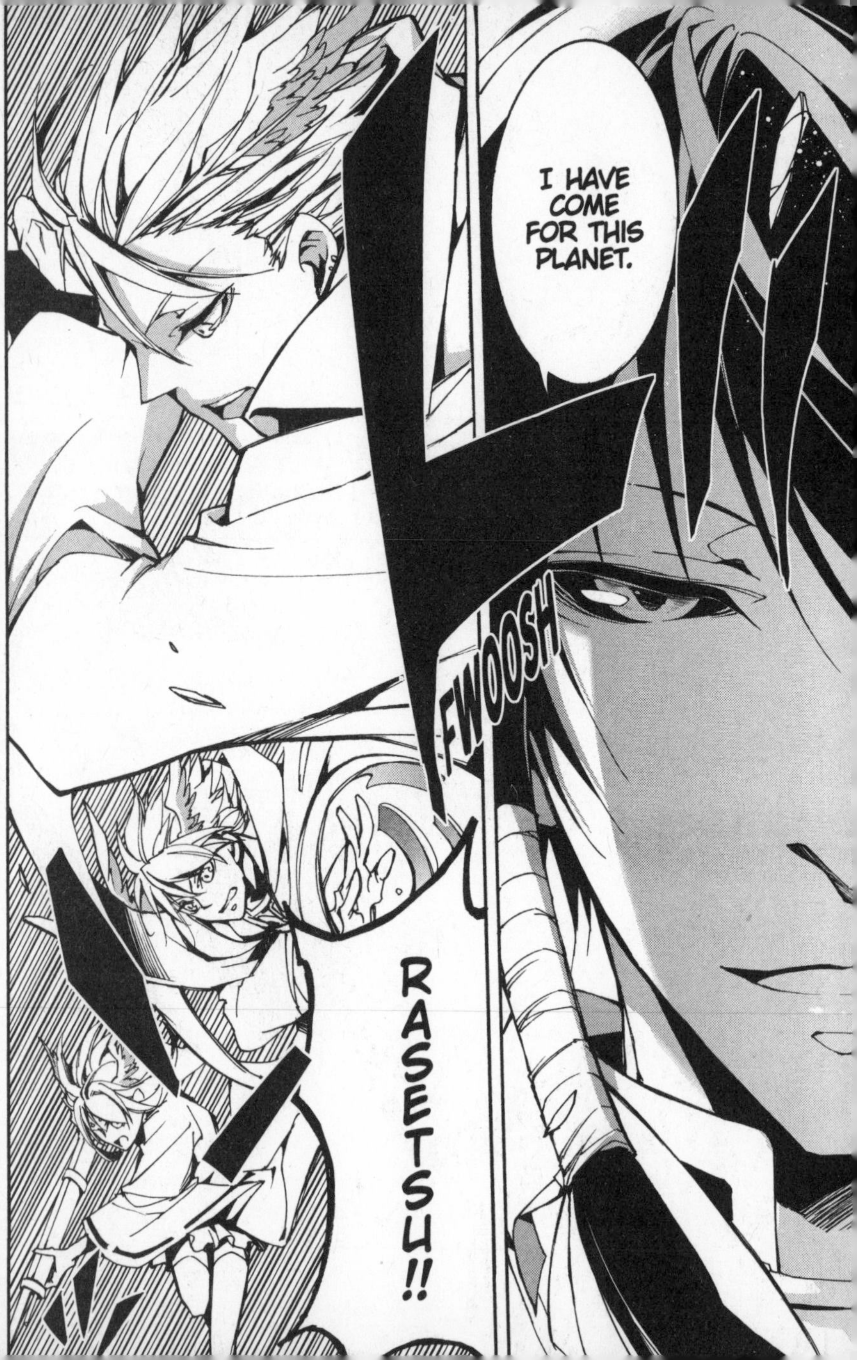
I HAVE COME FOR THIS PLANET.
FWOOSH
RASETSU!!

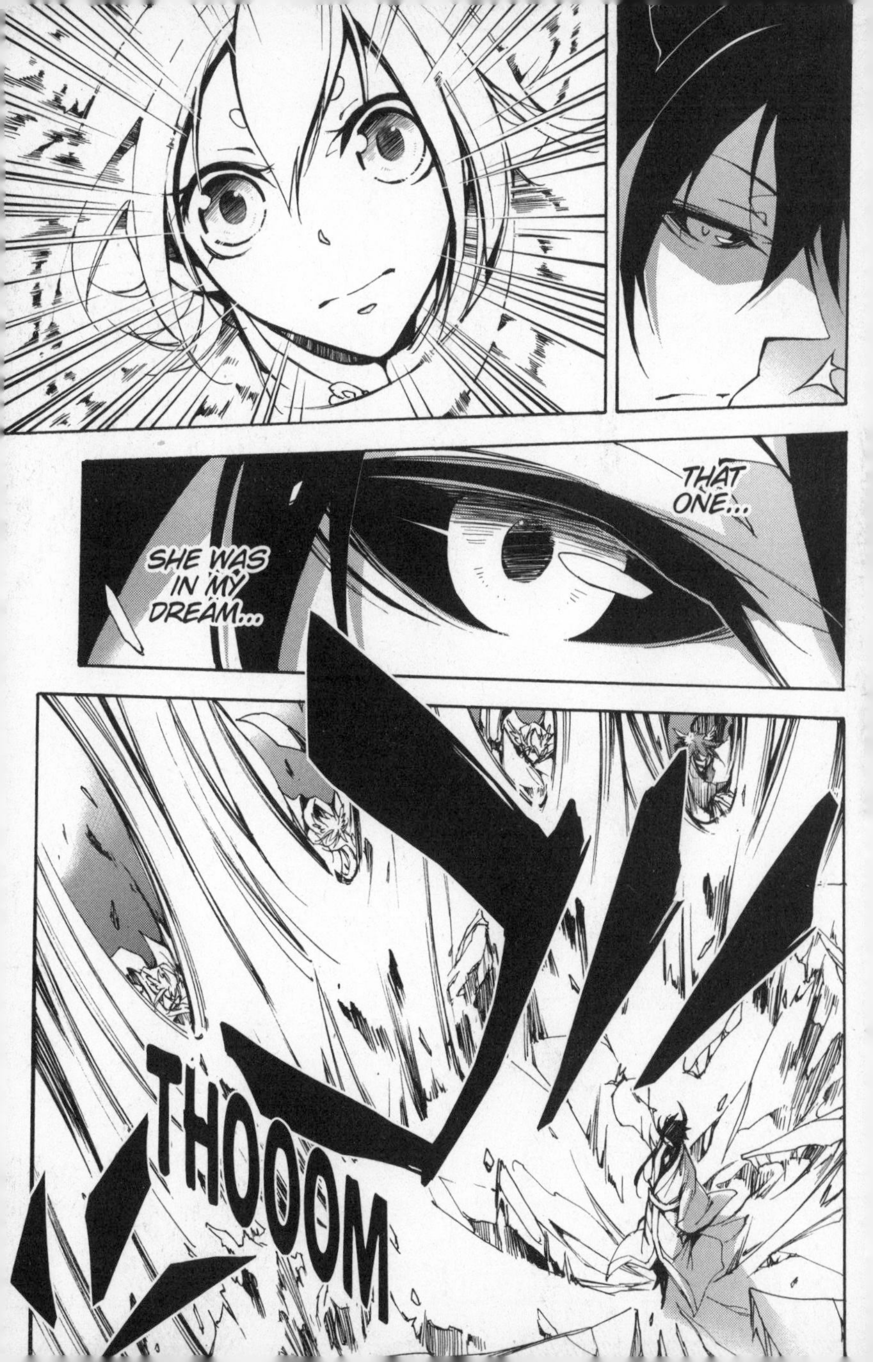
THAT ONE...
SHE WAS IN MY DREAM...
THOOOM

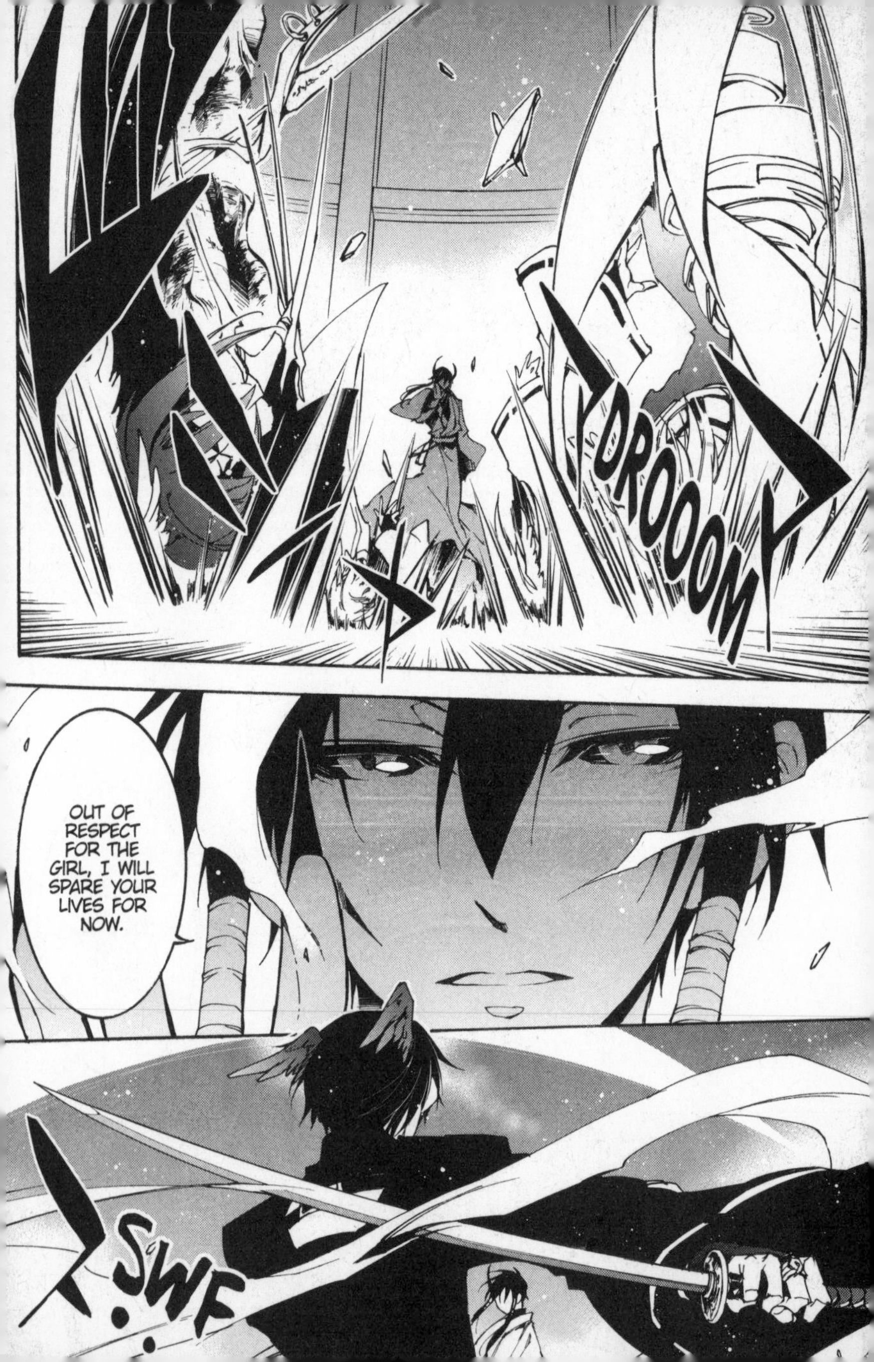
DROOOOM
OUT OF RESPECT FOR THE GIRL, I WILL SPARE YOUR LIVES FOR NOW.
SWF

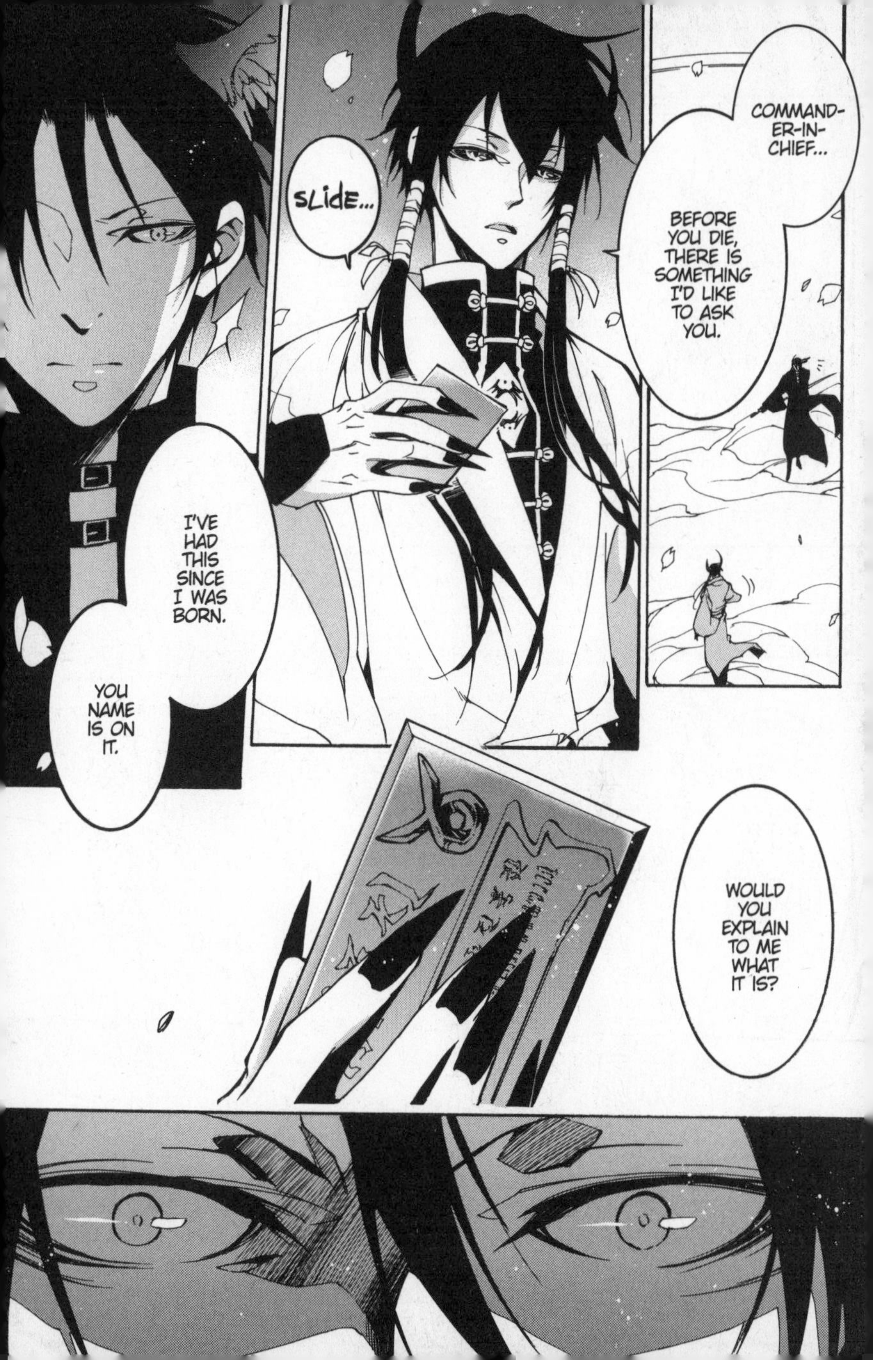
COMMANDER-IN-CHIEF...
BEFORE YOU DIE, THERE IS SOMETHING I'D LIKE TO ASK YOU.
SLIDE...
I'VE HAD THIS SINCE I WAS BORN.
YOU NAME IS ON IT.
WOULD YOU EXPLAIN TO ME WHAT IT IS?

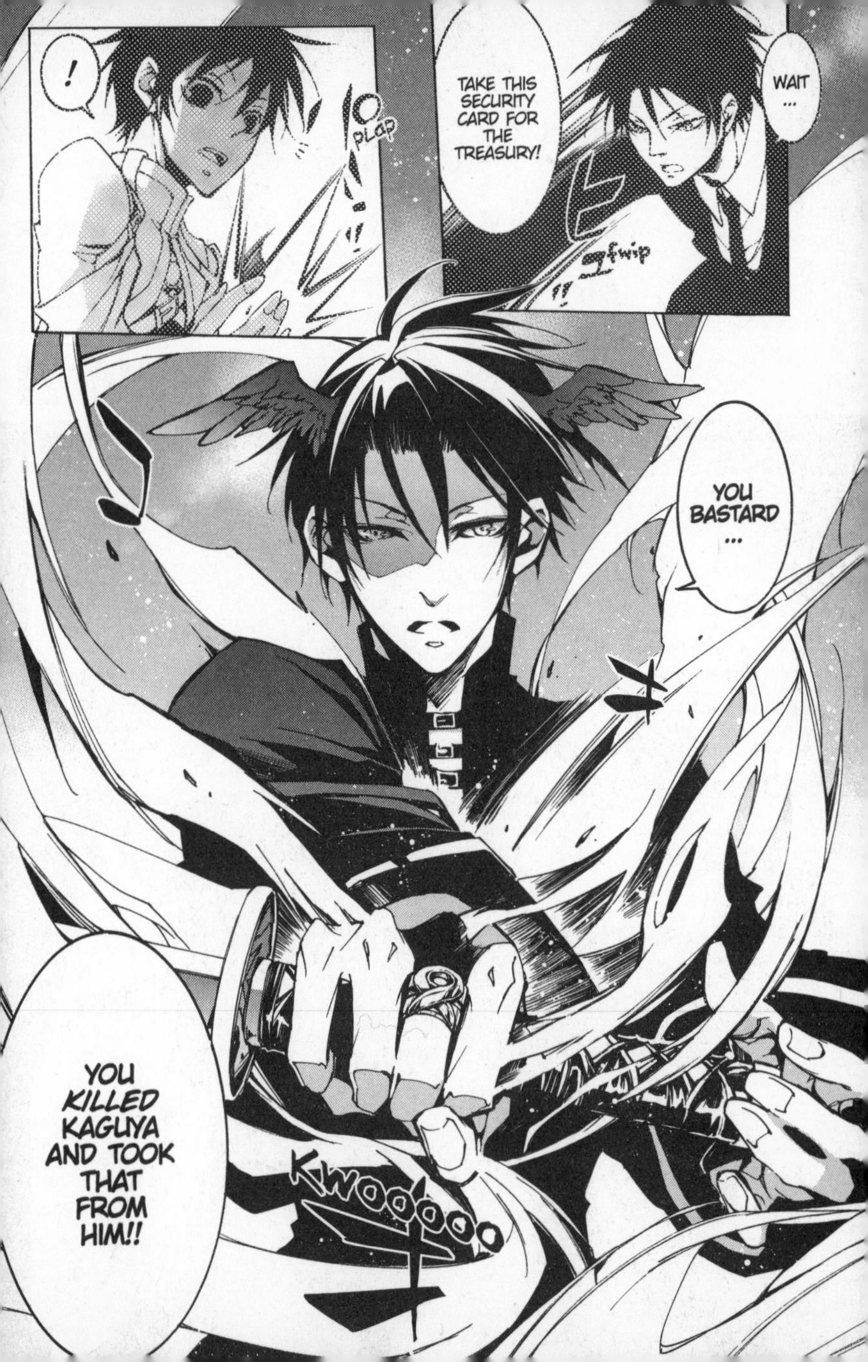
WAIT ...
TAKE THIS SECURITY CARD FOR THE TREASURY!
fwip
!
plap
YOU BASTARD ...
YOU KILLED KAGUYA AND TOOK THAT FROM HIM!!
KWOOOOOO

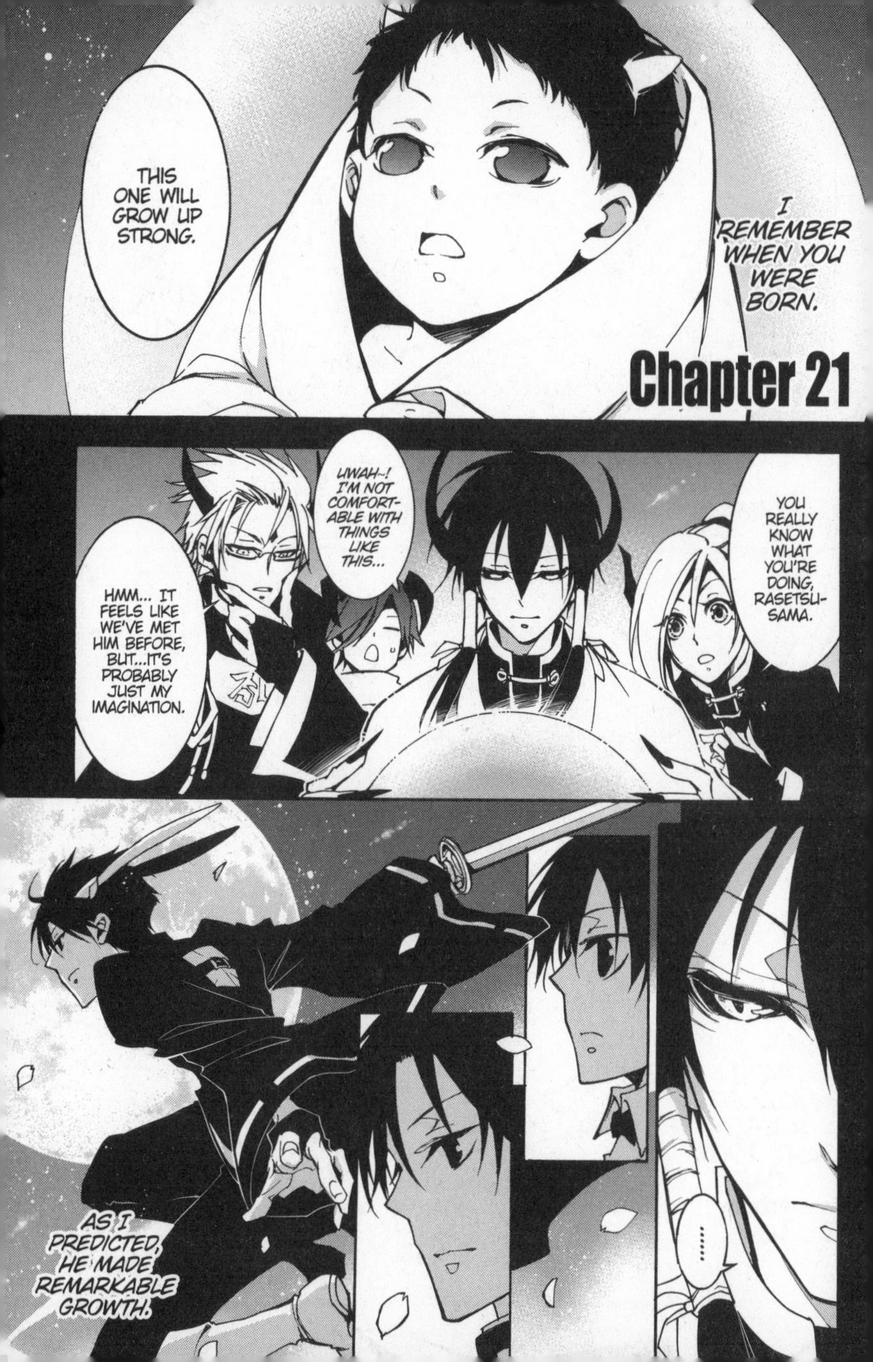
I REMEMBER WHEN YOU WERE BORN.
THIS ONE WILL GROW UP STRONG.
Chapter 21
YOU REALLY KNOW WHAT YOU'RE DOING, RASETSU-SAMA.
UWAH~! I'M NOT COMFORTABLE WITH THINGS LIKE THIS...
HMM... IT FEELS LIKE WE'VE MET HIM BEFORE, BUT...IT'S PROBABLY JUST MY IMAGINATION.
......
AS I PREDICTED, HE MADE REMARKABLE GROWTH.

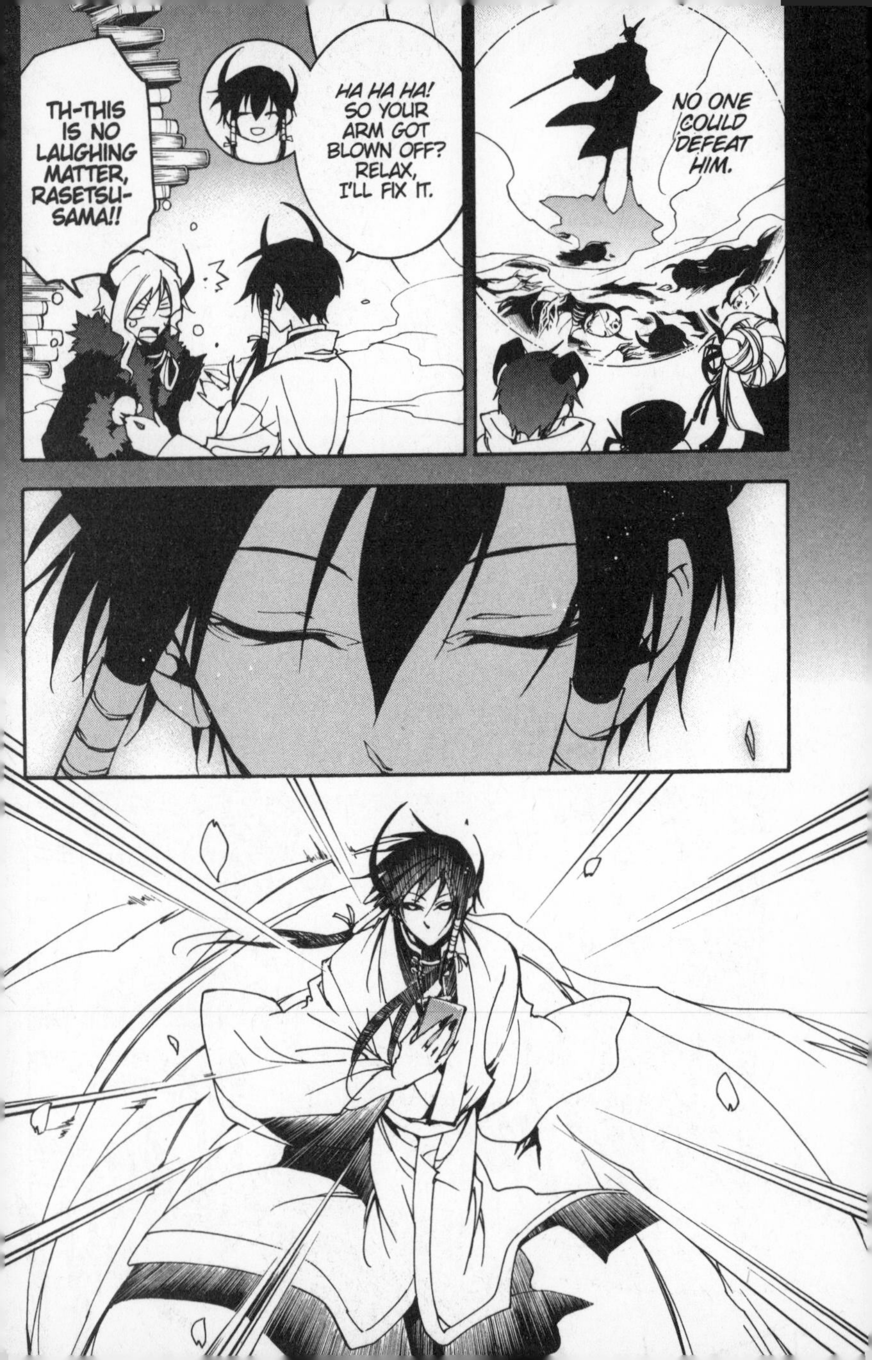
NO ONE COULD DEFEAT HIM.
HA HA HA! SO YOUR ARM GOT BLOWN OFF? RELAX, I'LL FIX IT.
TH-THIS IS NO LAUGHING MATTER, RASETSU-SAMA!!

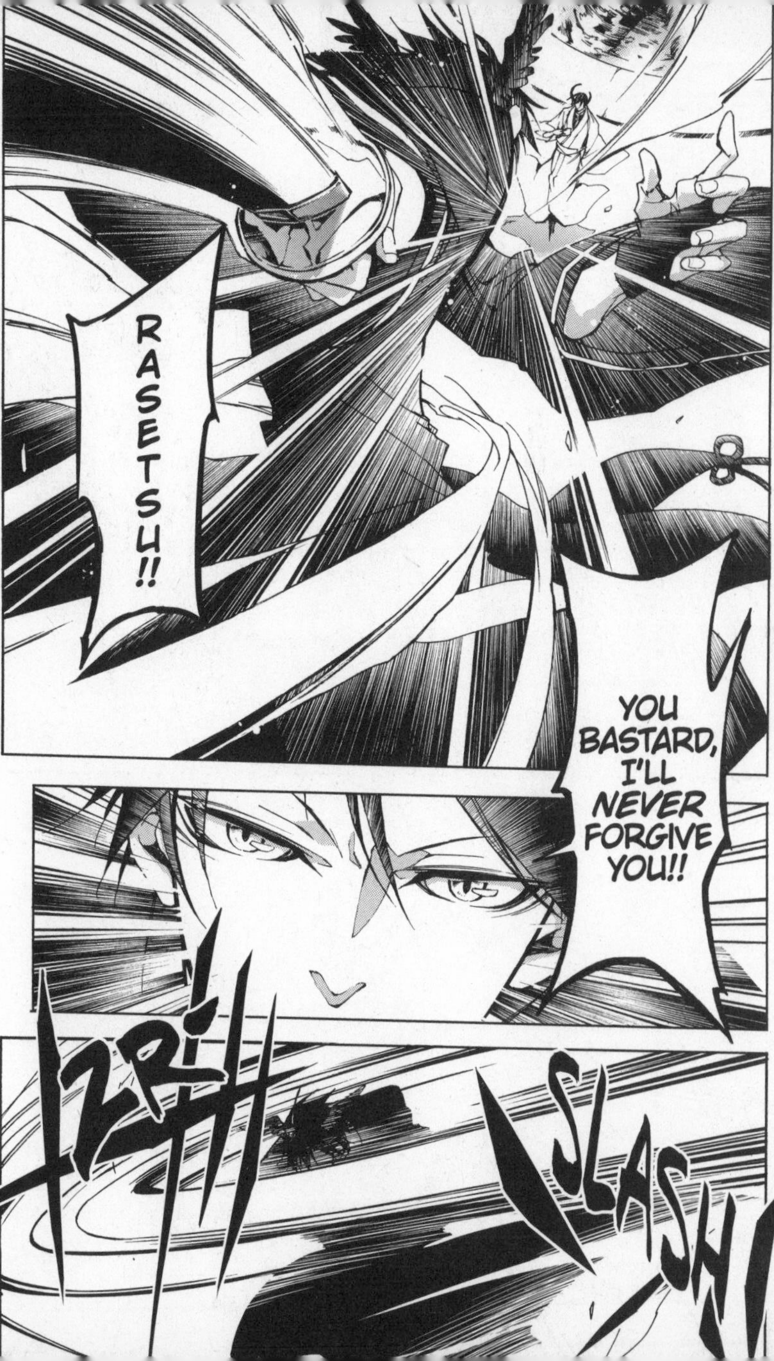
RASETSU!!
YOU BASTARD, I'LL NEVER FORGIVE YOU!!
SLASH!

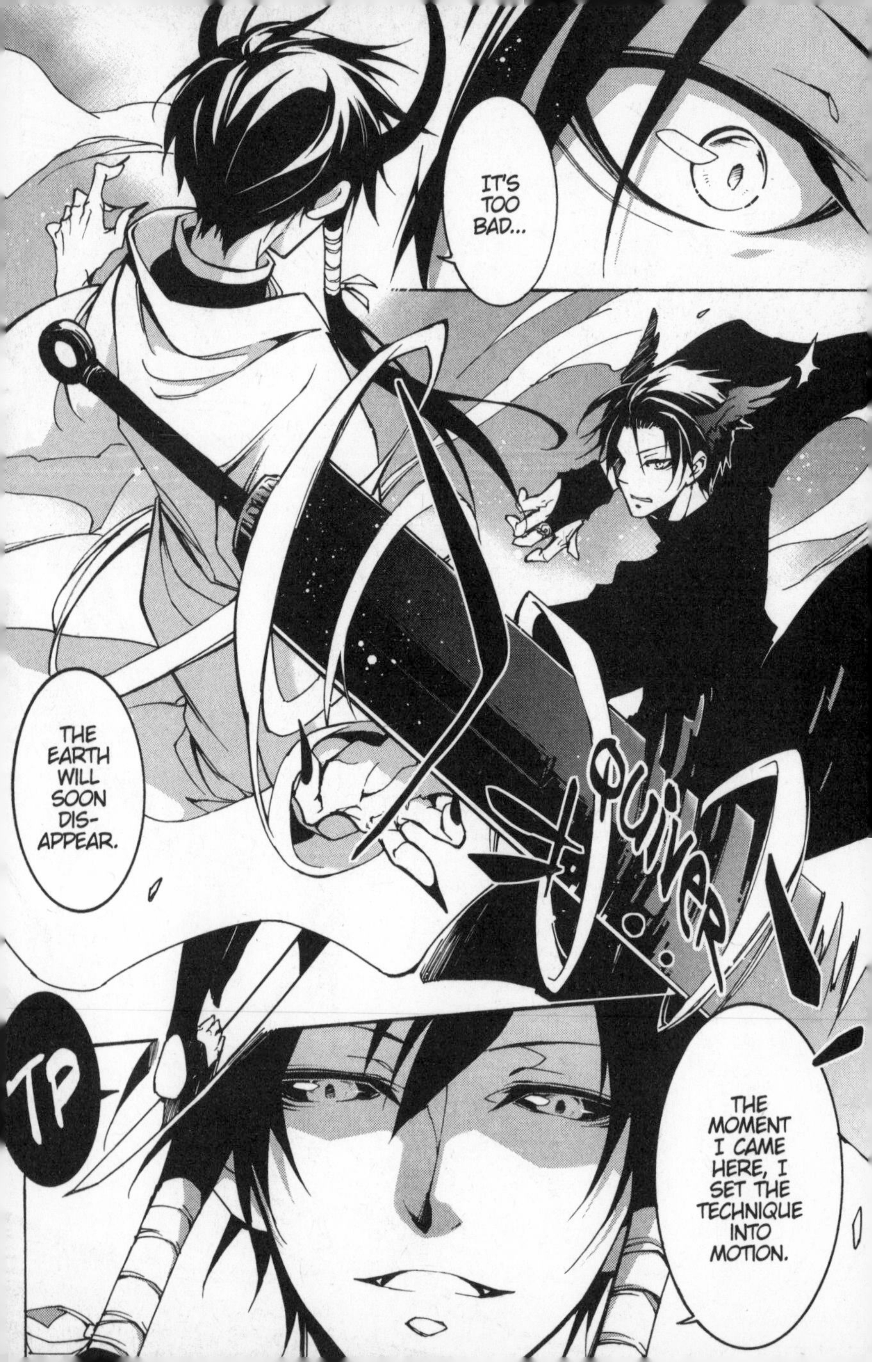
IT'S TOO BAD...
THE EARTH WILL SOON DIS- APPEAR.
QUIVER
THE MOMENT I CAME HERE, I SET THE TECHNIQUE INTO MOTION.
TP

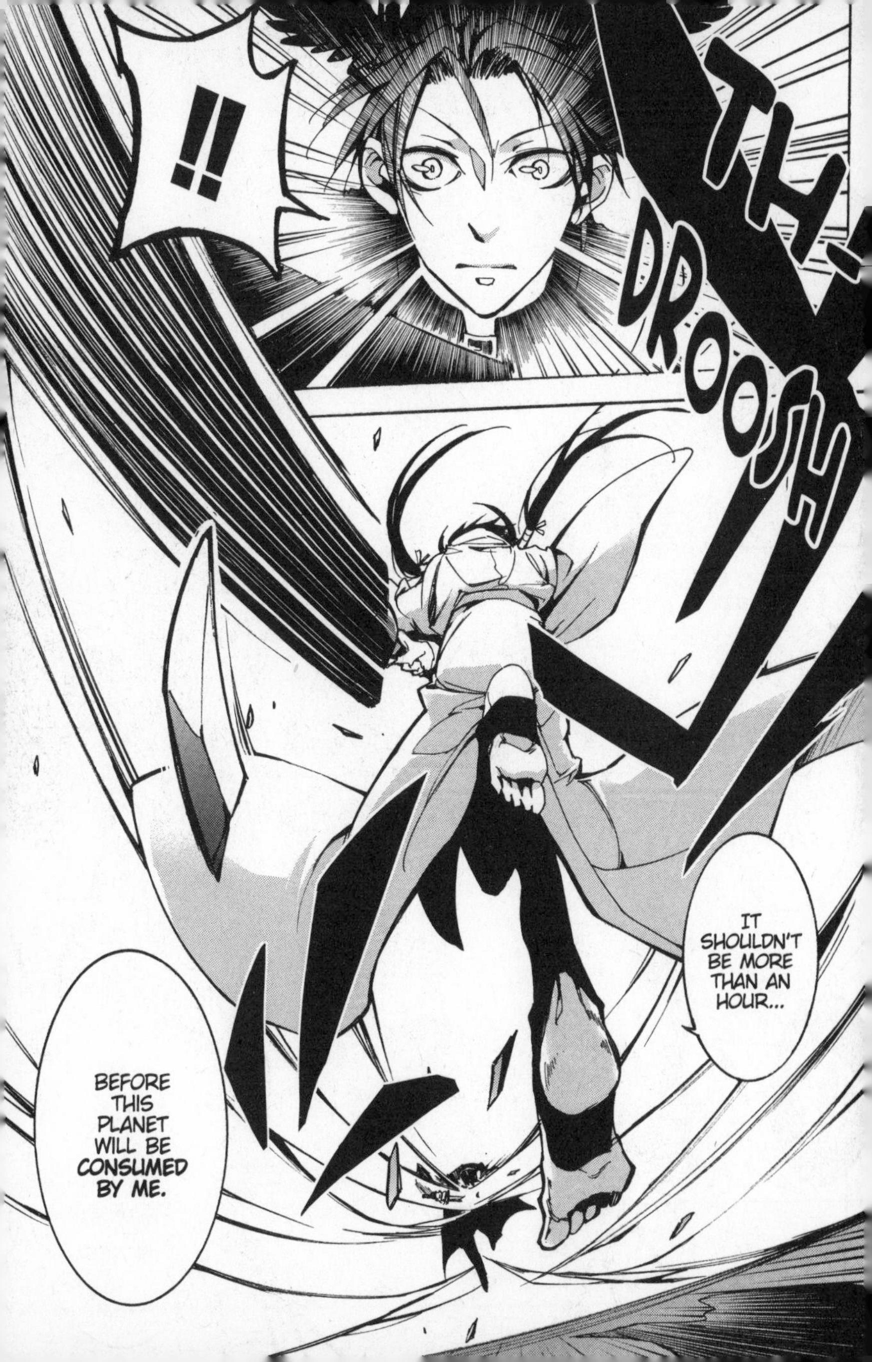
THA-
!!
DROOSH
IT SHOULDN'T BE MORE THAN AN HOUR...
BEFORE THIS PLANET WILL BE CONSUMED BY ME.

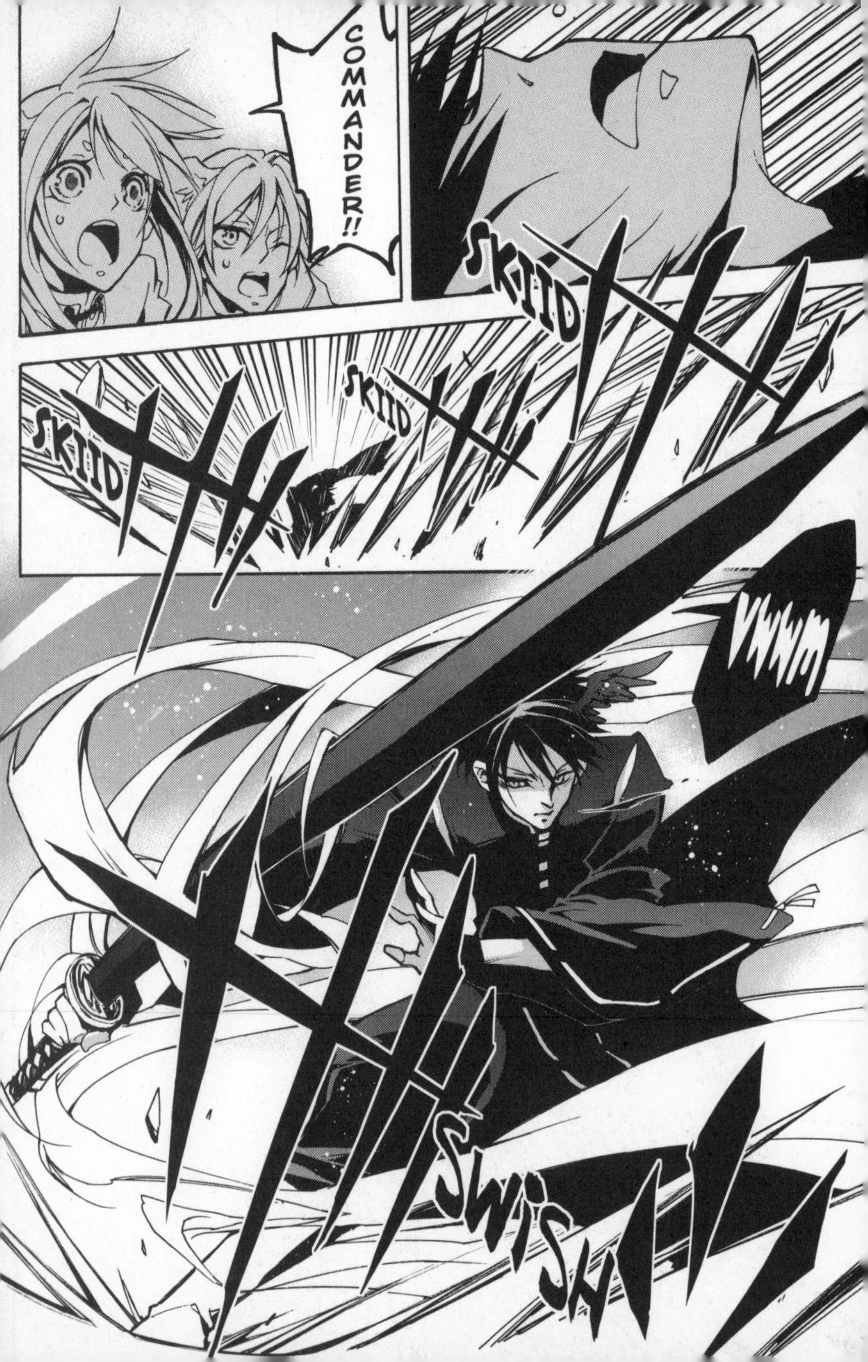
SKIID
COMMANDER!!
SKIID
SKIID
SWISH

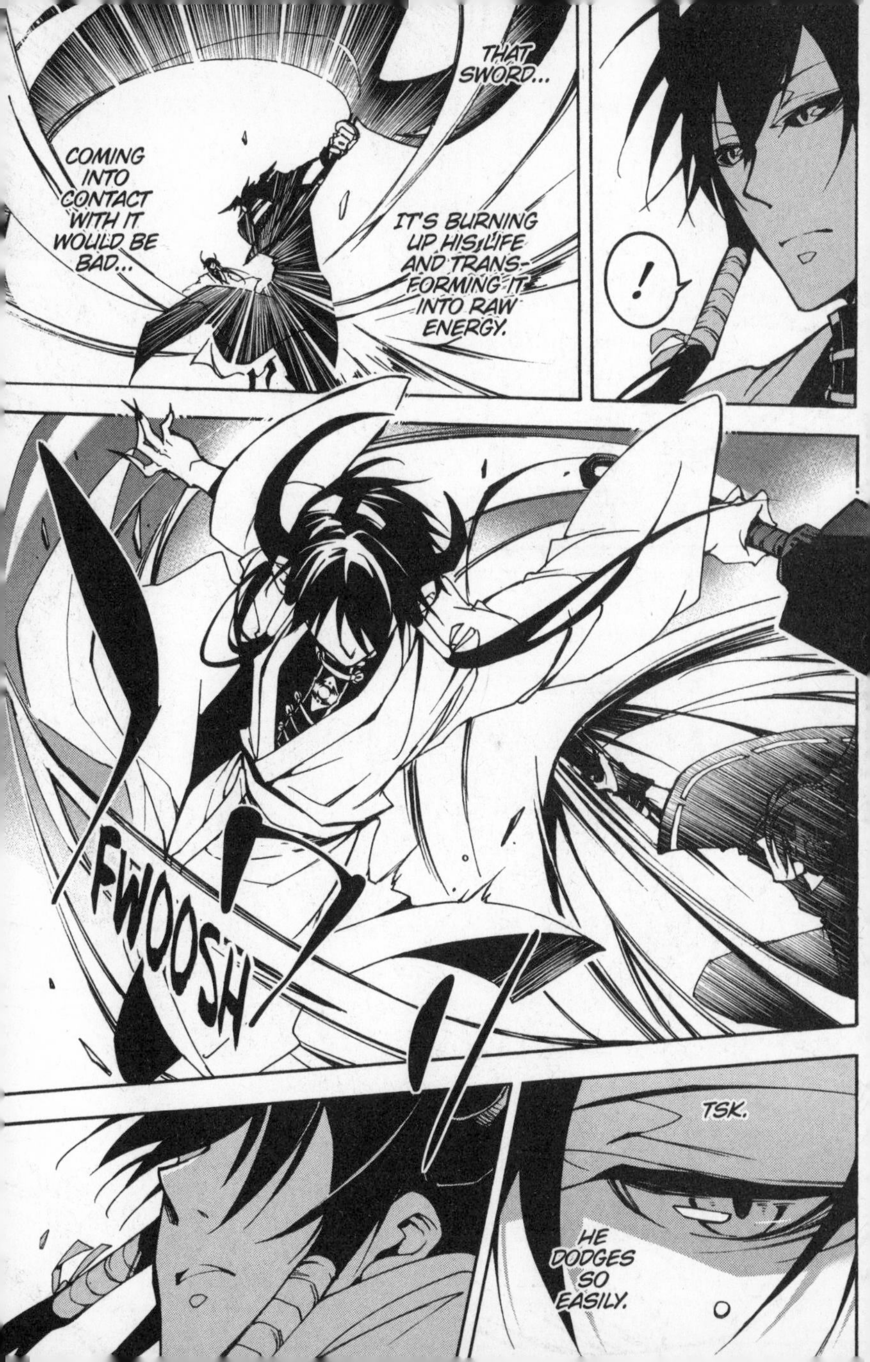
!
THAT SWORD...
IT'S BURNING UP HIS LIFE AND TRANS-FORMING IT INTO RAW ENERGY.
COMING INTO CONTACT WITH IT WOULD BE BAD...
FWOOSH
TSK.
HE DODGES SO EASILY.

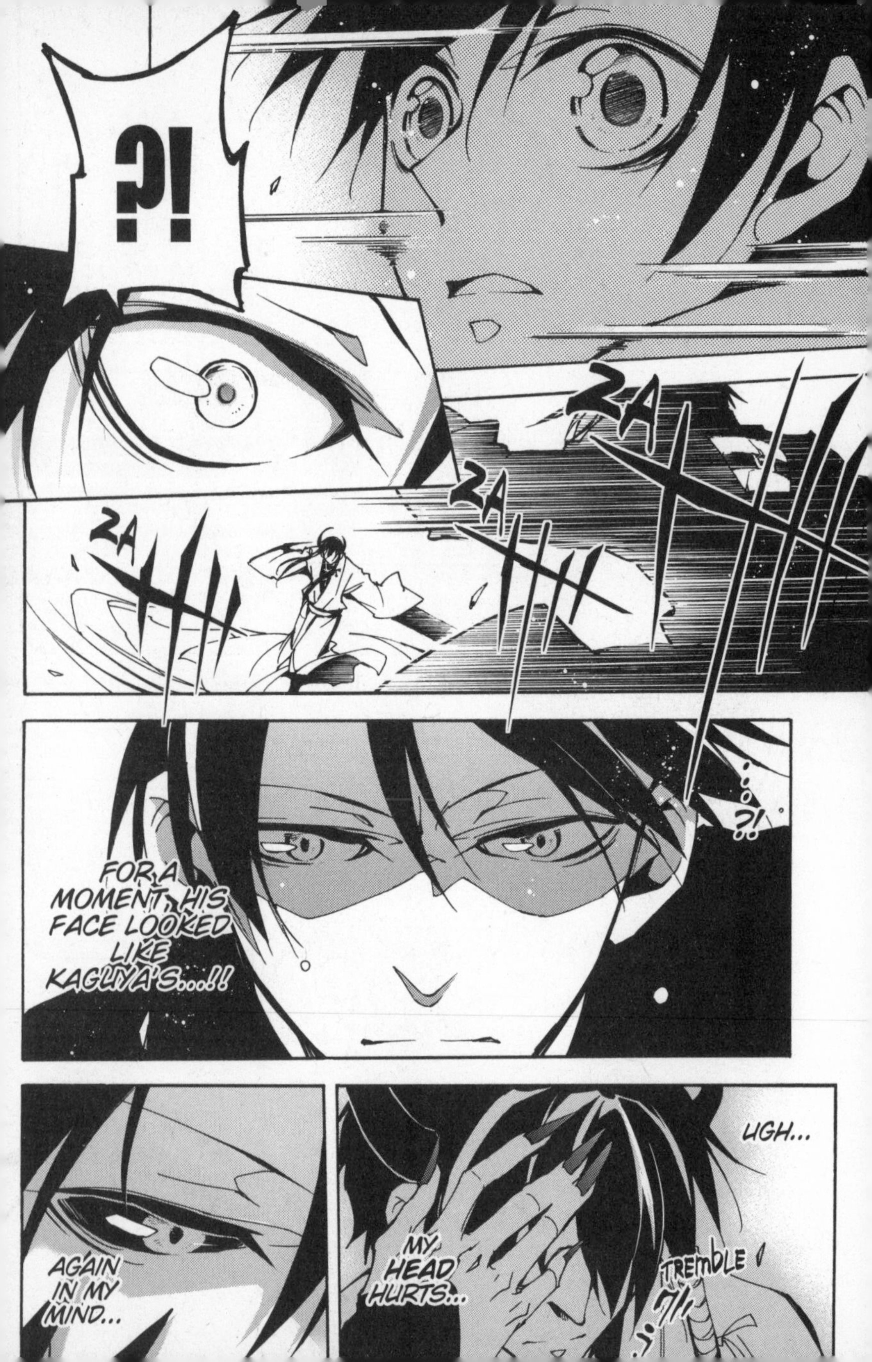
?!
ZA
ZA
ZA
...?!
FOR A MOMENT, HIS FACE LOOKED LIKE KAGUYA'S...!!
UGH...
MY HEAD HURTS...
TREMBLE
AGAIN IN MY MIND...

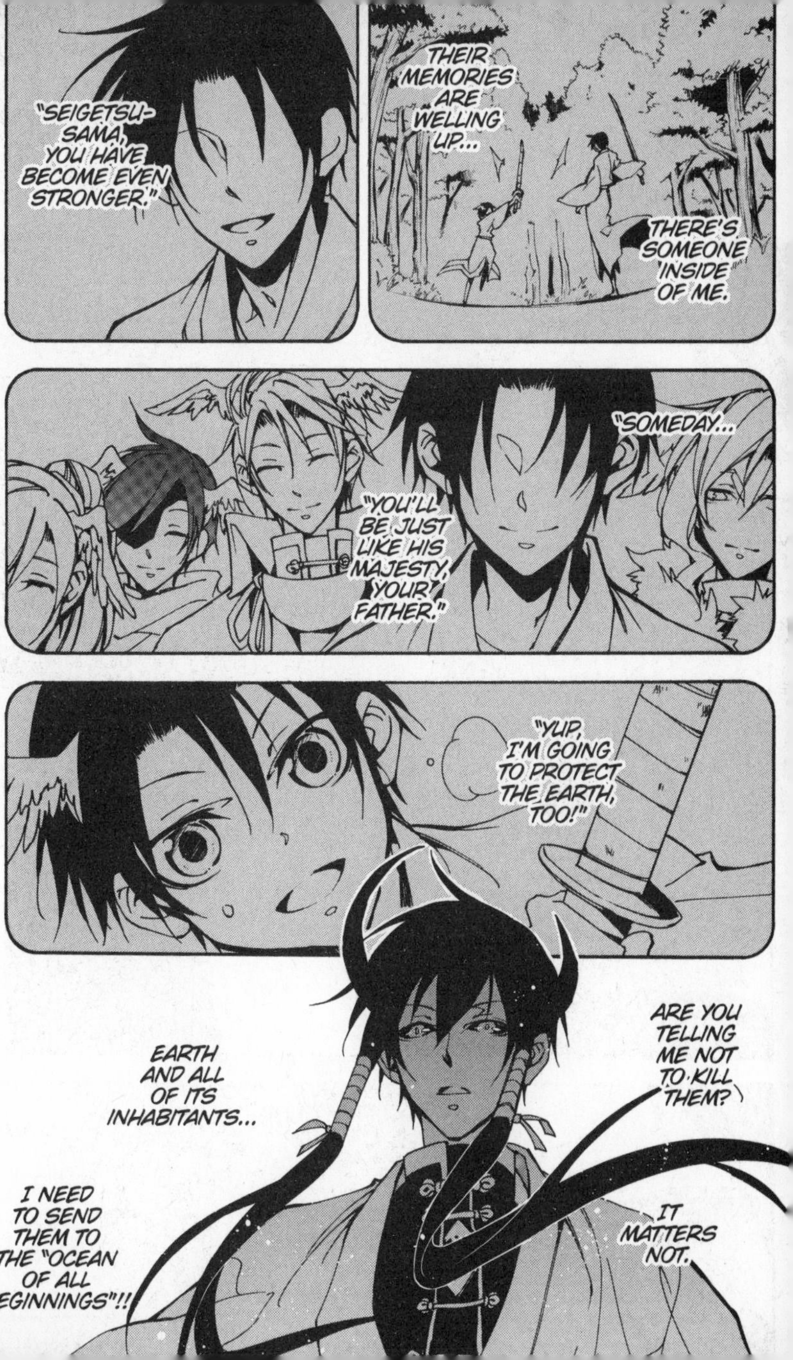
THEIR MEMORIES ARE WELLING UP...
THERE'S SOMEONE INSIDE OF ME.
"SEIGETSU-SAMA, YOU HAVE BECOME EVEN STRONGER."
"SOMEDAY...
"YOU'LL BE JUST LIKE HIS MAJESTY, YOUR FATHER."
"YUP, I'M GOING TO PROTECT THE EARTH, TOO!"
ARE YOU TELLING ME NOT TO KILL THEM?
IT MATTERS NOT.
EARTH AND ALL OF ITS INHABITANTS...
I NEED TO SEND THEM TO THE "OCEAN OF ALL BEGINNINGS"!!

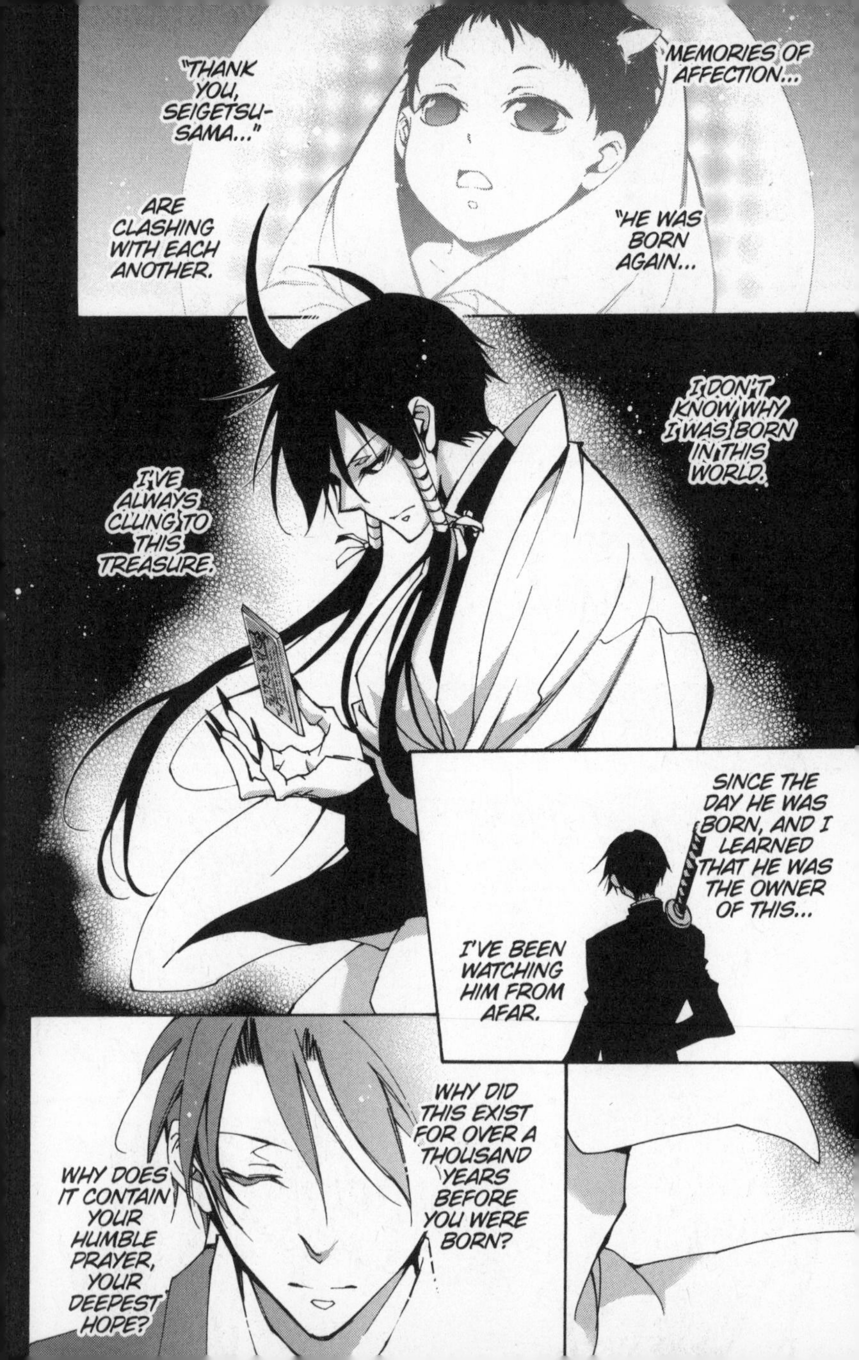
MEMORIES OF AFFECTION...
"THANK YOU, SEIGETSU-SAMA..."
"HE WAS BORN AGAIN...
ARE CLASHING WITH EACH ANOTHER.
I DON'T KNOW WHY I WAS BORN IN THIS WORLD.
I'VE ALWAYS CLUNG TO THIS TREASURE.
SINCE THE DAY HE WAS BORN, AND I LEARNED THAT HE WAS THE OWNER OF THIS...
I'VE BEEN WATCHING HIM FROM AFAR.
WHY DID THIS EXIST FOR OVER A THOUSAND YEARS BEFORE YOU WERE BORN?
WHY DOES IT CONTAIN YOUR HUMBLE PRAYER, YOUR DEEPEST HOPE?

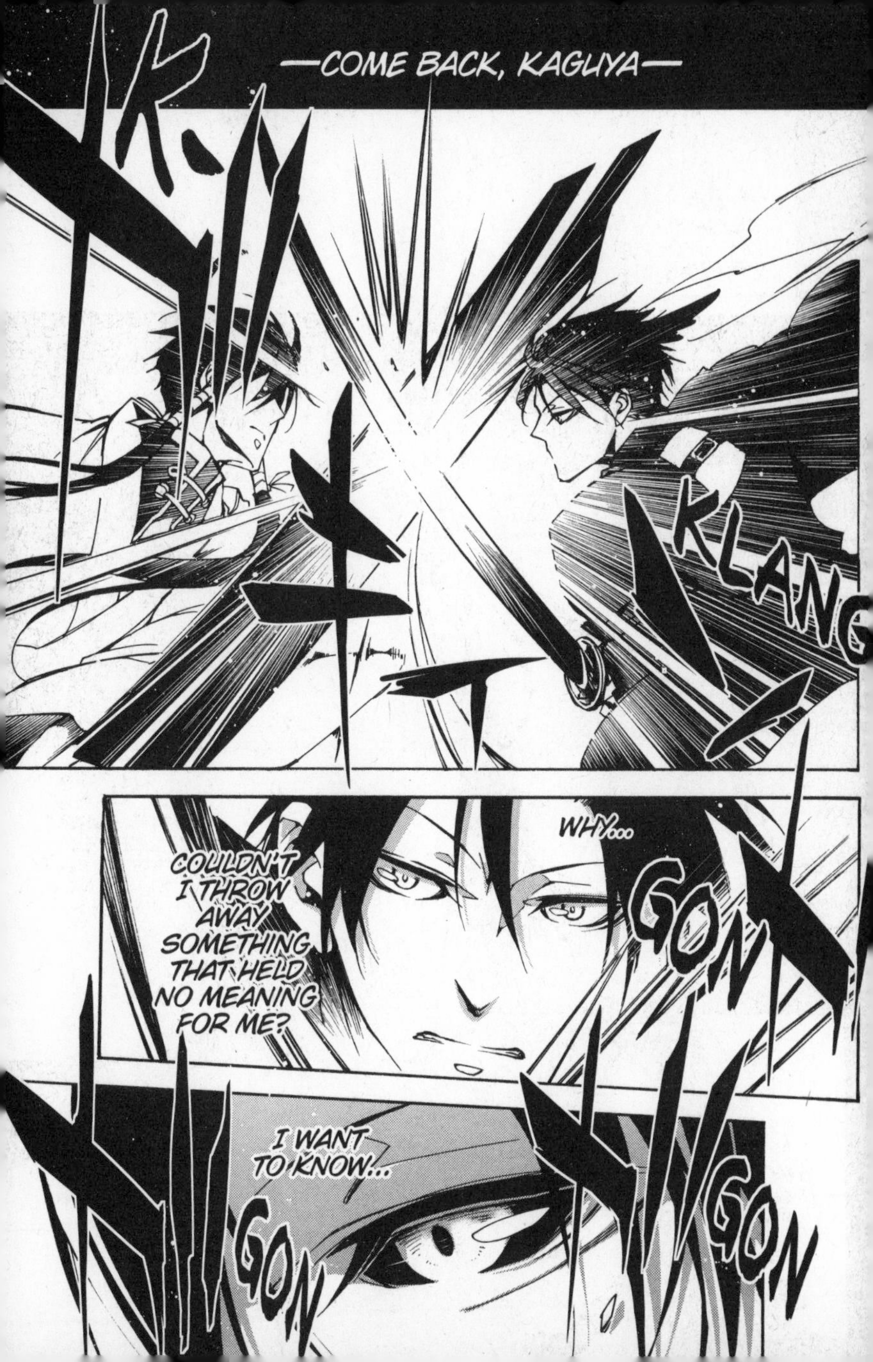
—COME BACK, KAGUYA—
KLANG
GON
WHY...
COULDN'T I THROW AWAY SOMETHING THAT HELD NO MEANING FOR ME?
GON
I WANT TO KNOW...
GON

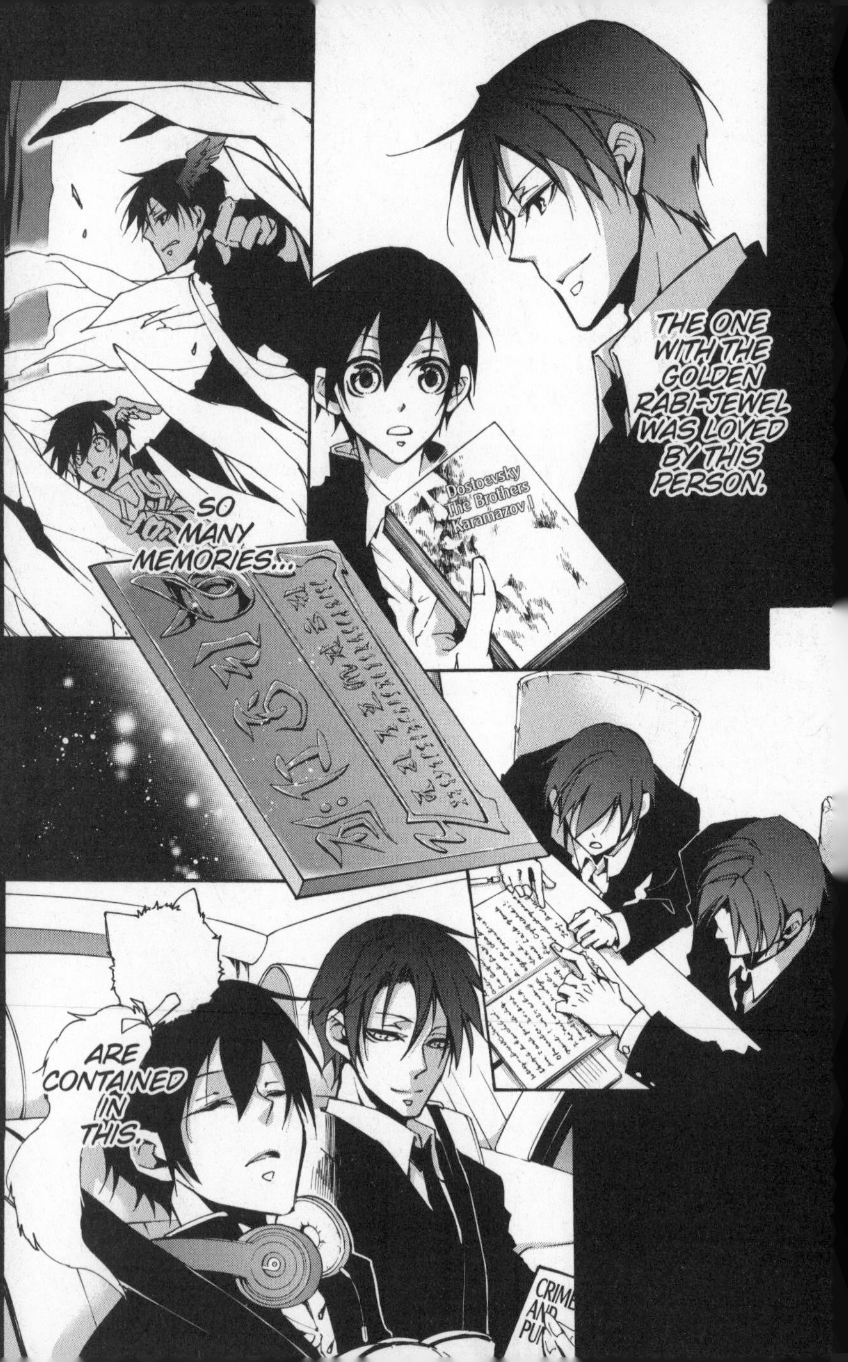
THE ONE WITH THE GOLDEN RABI-JEWEL WAS LOVED BY THIS PERSON.
Dostoevsky The Brothers Karamazov I
SO MANY MEMORIES...
ARE CONTAINED IN THIS.
CRIME AND PU

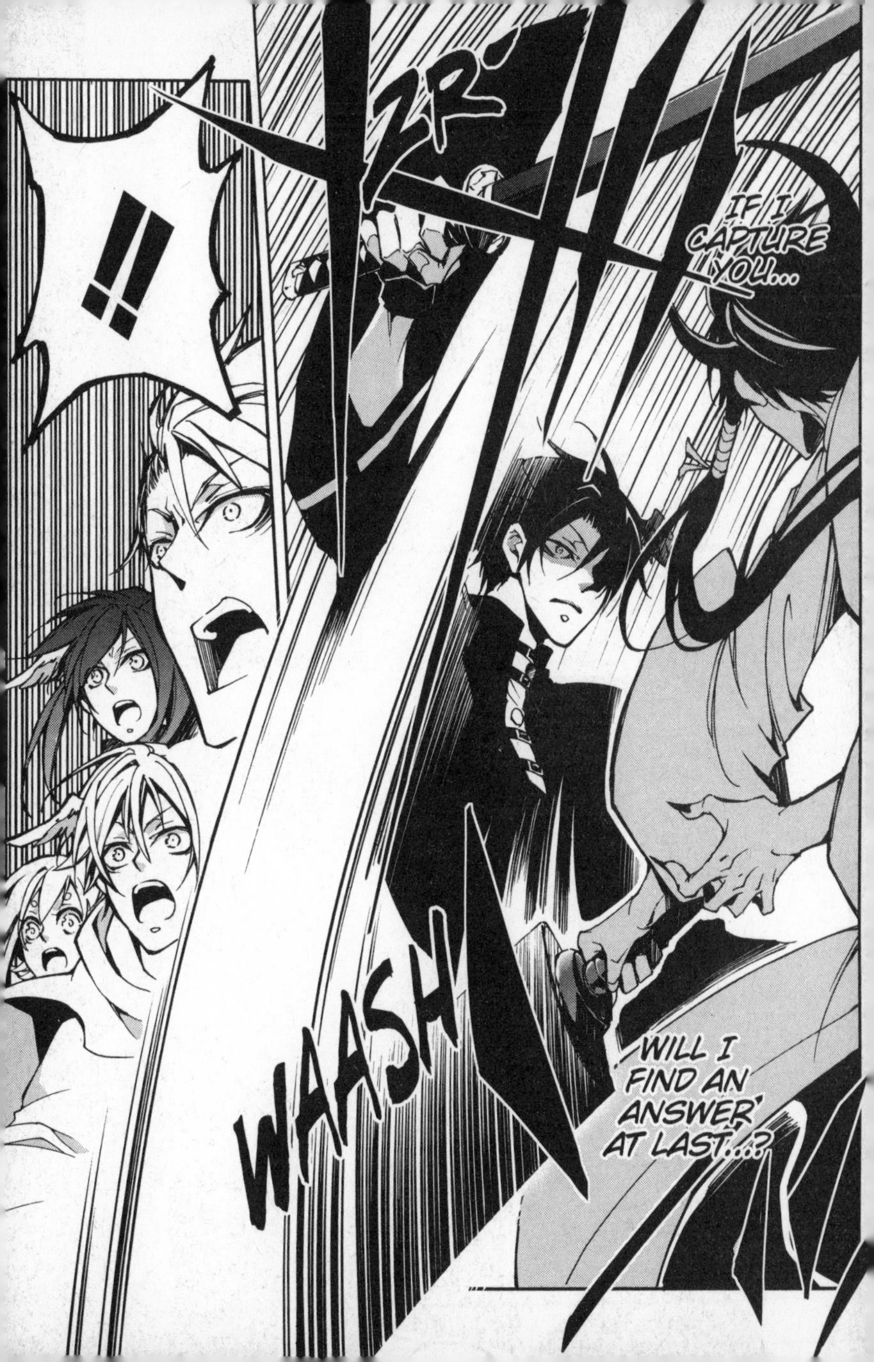
IF I CAPTURE YOU...
ZR
!!
WILL I FIND AN ANSWER AT LAST...?
WAASH

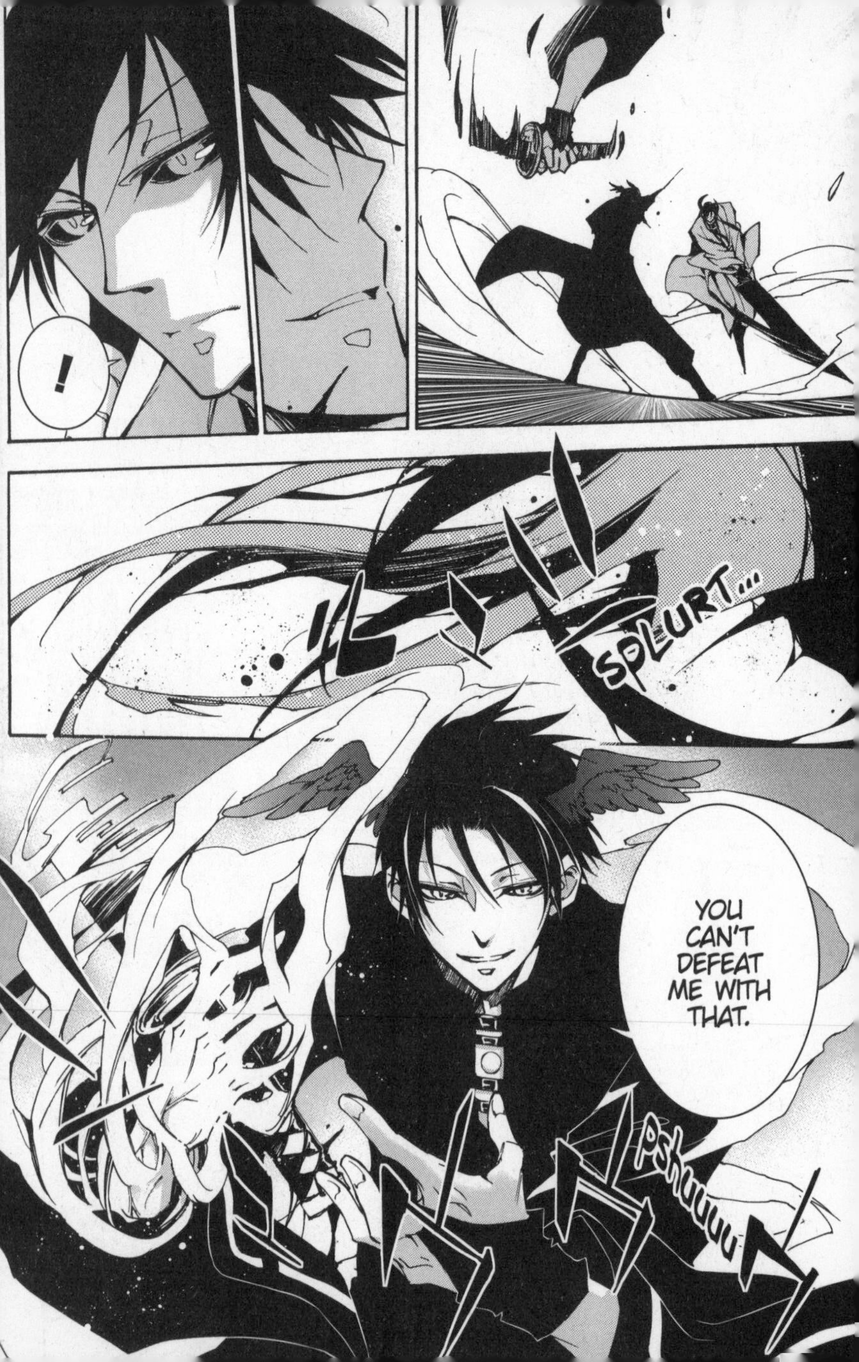
!
SPLURT...
YOU CAN'T DEFEAT ME WITH THAT.
pshuuuu

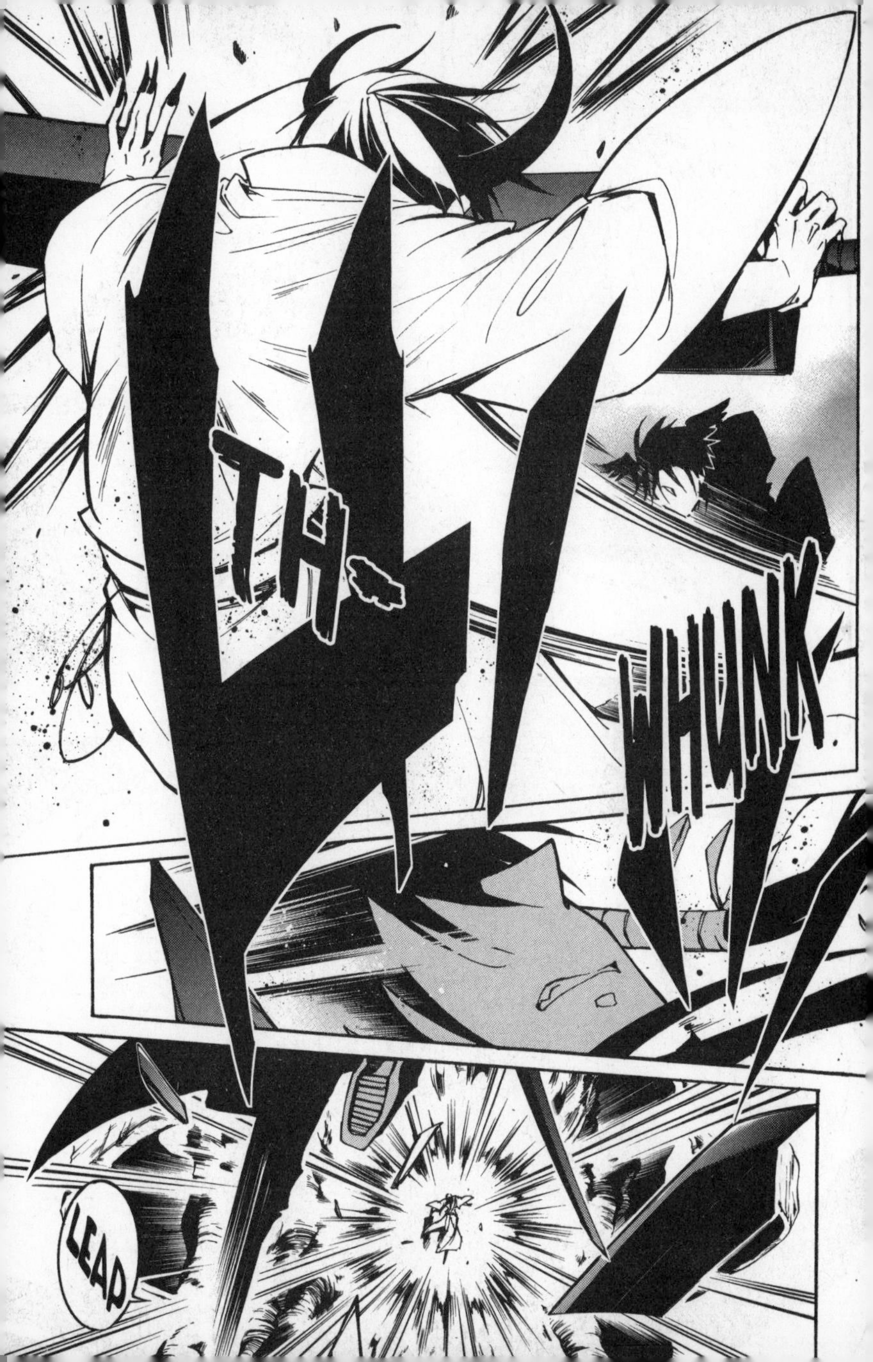
WHUNK
TH-
LEAP

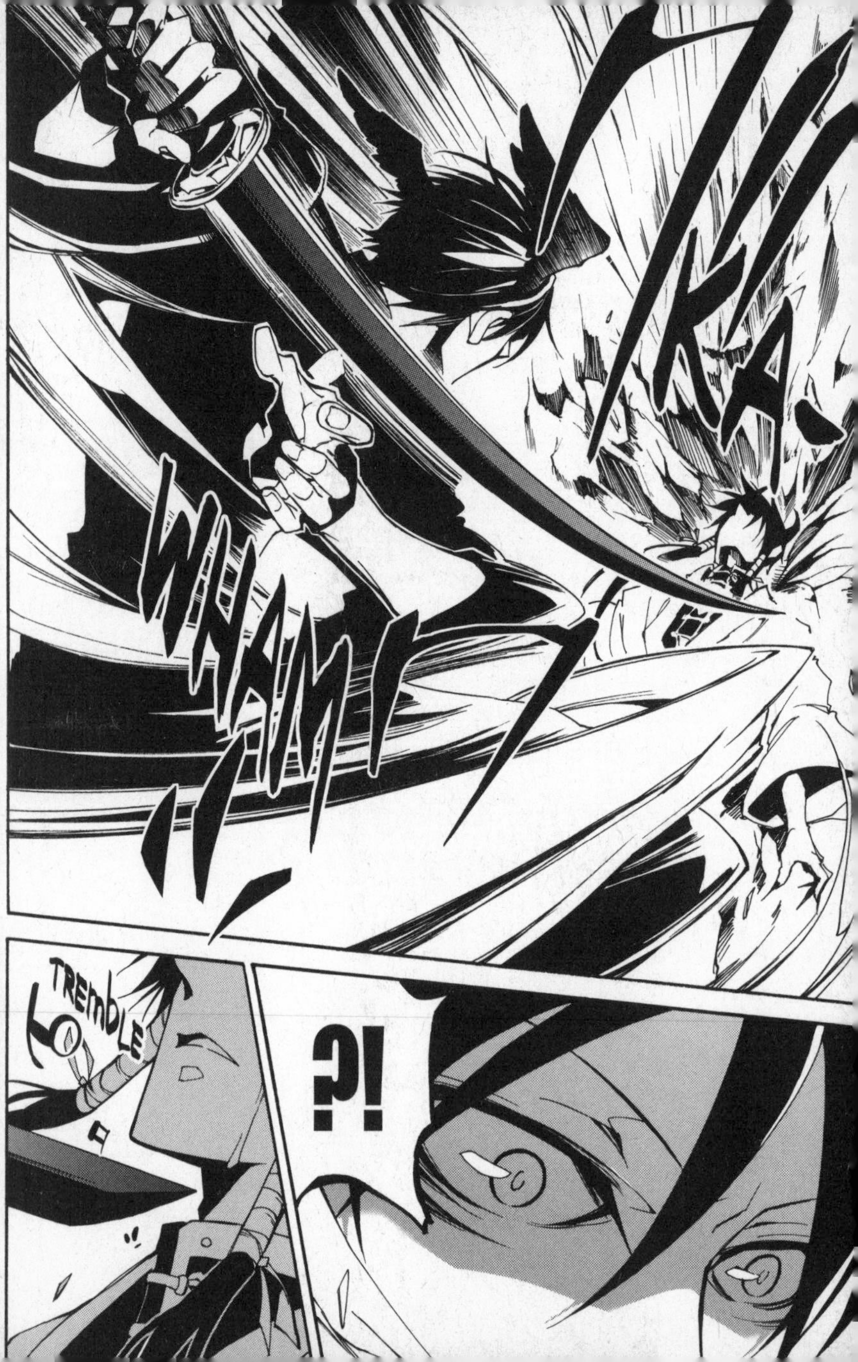
KA-
WHAM!!
?!
TREMBLE

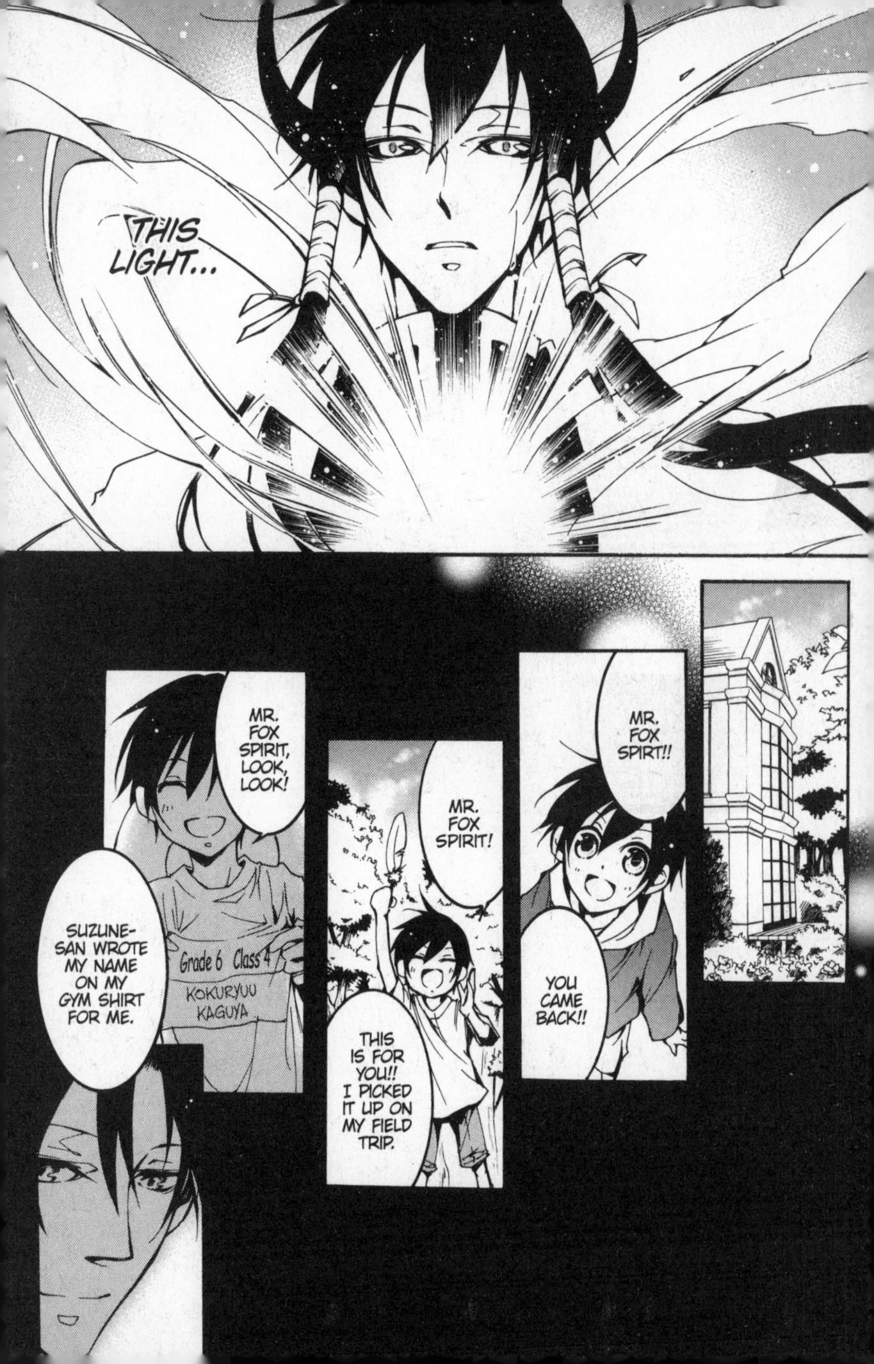
THIS LIGHT...
MR. FOX SPIRT!!
YOU CAME BACK!!
MR. FOX SPIRIT!
THIS IS FOR YOU!! I PICKED IT UP ON MY FIELD TRIP.
MR. FOX SPIRIT, LOOK, LOOK!
SUZUNE-SAN WROTE MY NAME ON MY GYM SHIRT FOR ME.
Grade 6 Class 4
KOKURYUU KAGUYA

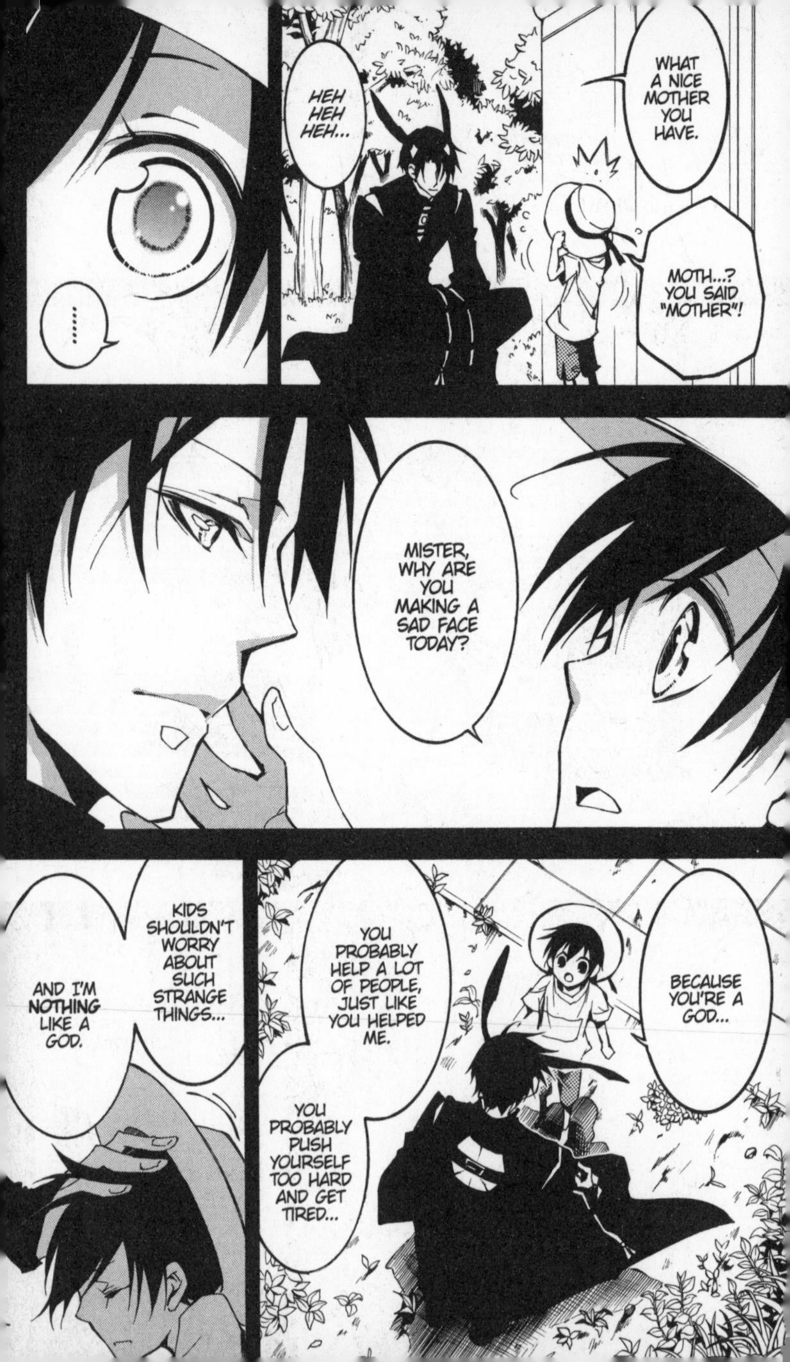

WHAT A NICE MOTHER YOU HAVE.
HEH HEH HEH...
MOTH...? YOU SAID "MOTHER"!
......
MISTER, WHY ARE YOU MAKING A SAD FACE TODAY?
BECAUSE YOU'RE A GOD...
YOU PROBABLY HELP A LOT OF PEOPLE, JUST LIKE YOU HELPED ME.
YOU PROBABLY PUSH YOURSELF TOO HARD AND GET TIRED...
KIDS SHOULDN'T WORRY ABOUT SUCH STRANGE THINGS...
AND I'M NOTHING LIKE A GOD.

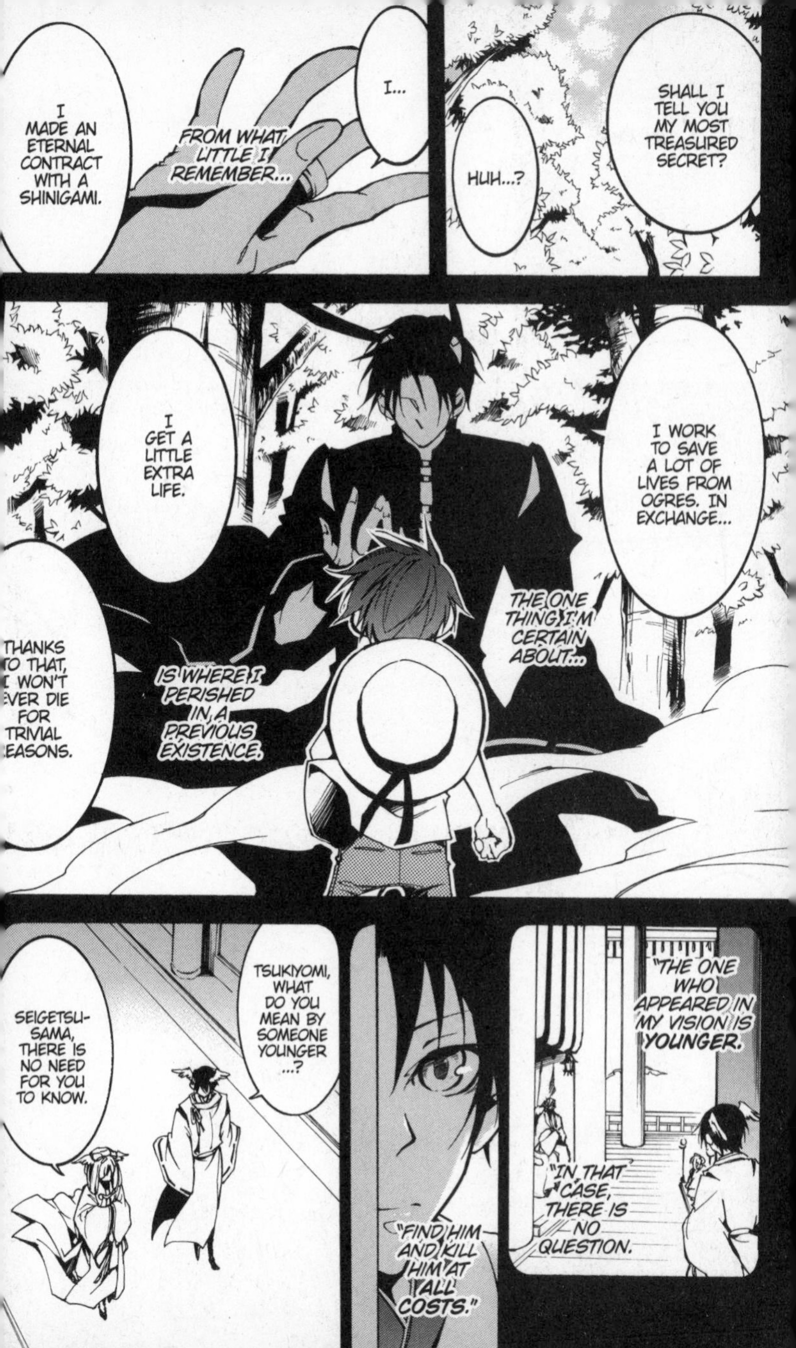
SHALL I TELL YOU MY MOST TREASURED SECRET?
HUH...?
I...
FROM WHAT LITTLE I REMEMBER...
I MADE AN ETERNAL CONTRACT WITH A SHINIGAMI.
I WORK TO SAVE A LOT OF LIVES FROM OGRES. IN EXCHANGE...
I GET A LITTLE EXTRA LIFE.
THE ONE THING I'M CERTAIN ABOUT...
IS WHERE I PERISHED IN A PREVIOUS EXISTENCE.
THANKS TO THAT, I WON'T EVER DIE FOR TRIVIAL REASONS.
"THE ONE WHO APPEARED IN MY VISION IS **YOUNGER.**
"IN THAT CASE, THERE IS NO QUESTION.
"FIND HIM AND KILL HIM AT ALL COSTS."
TSUKIYOMI, WHAT DO YOU MEAN BY SOMEONE YOUNGER ...?
SEIGETSU-SAMA, THERE IS NO NEED FOR YOU TO KNOW.

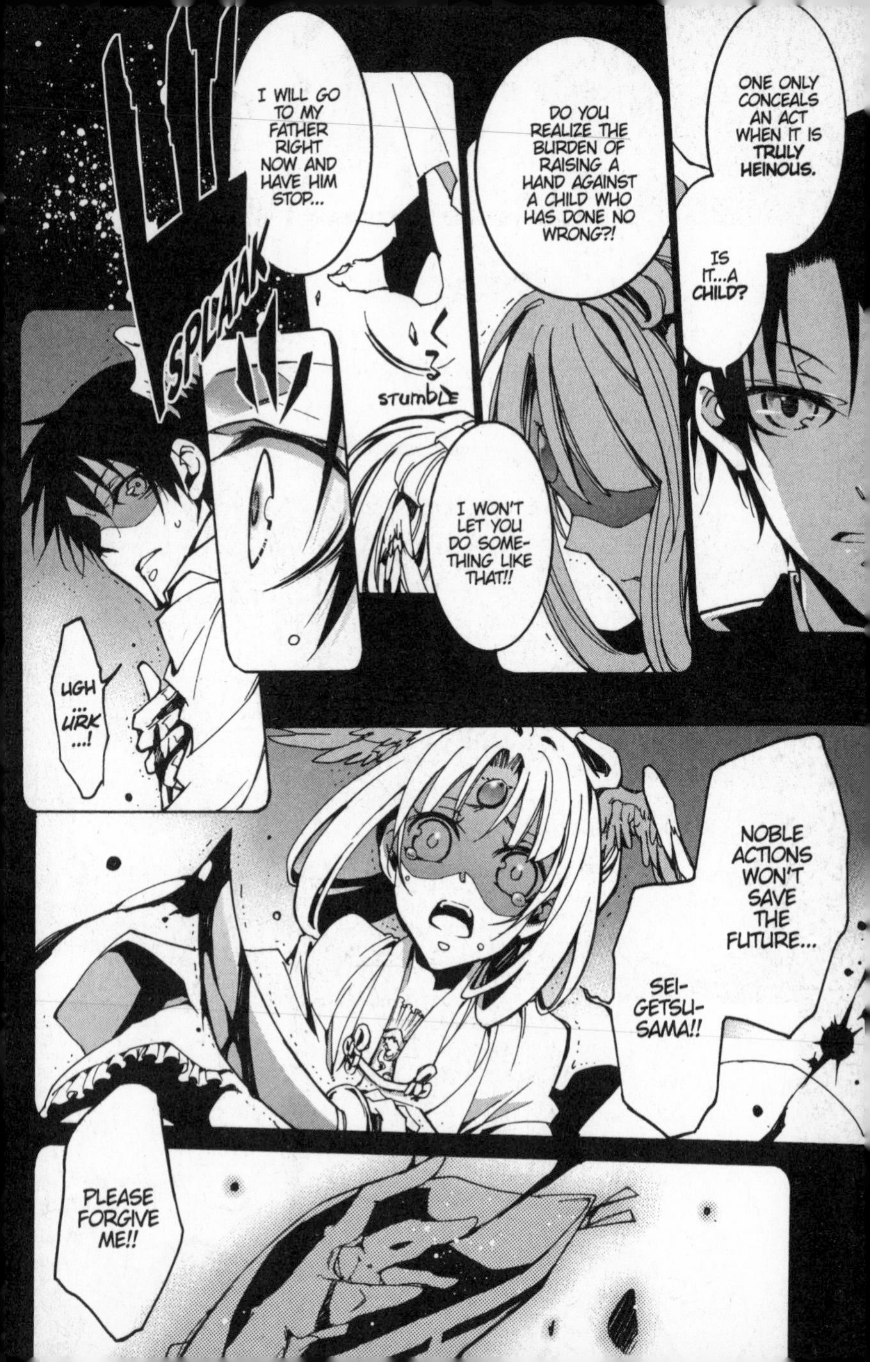
ONE ONLY CONCEALS AN ACT WHEN IT IS TRULY HEINOUS.
IS IT...A CHILD?
DO YOU REALIZE THE BURDEN OF RAISING A HAND AGAINST A CHILD WHO HAS DONE NO WRONG?!
I WON'T LET YOU DO SOMETHING LIKE THAT!!
I WILL GO TO MY FATHER RIGHT NOW AND HAVE HIM STOP...
STUMBLE
SPLAAK
UGH ... URK ...!
NOBLE ACTIONS WON'T SAVE THE FUTURE...
SEI-GETSU-SAMA!!
PLEASE FORGIVE ME!!

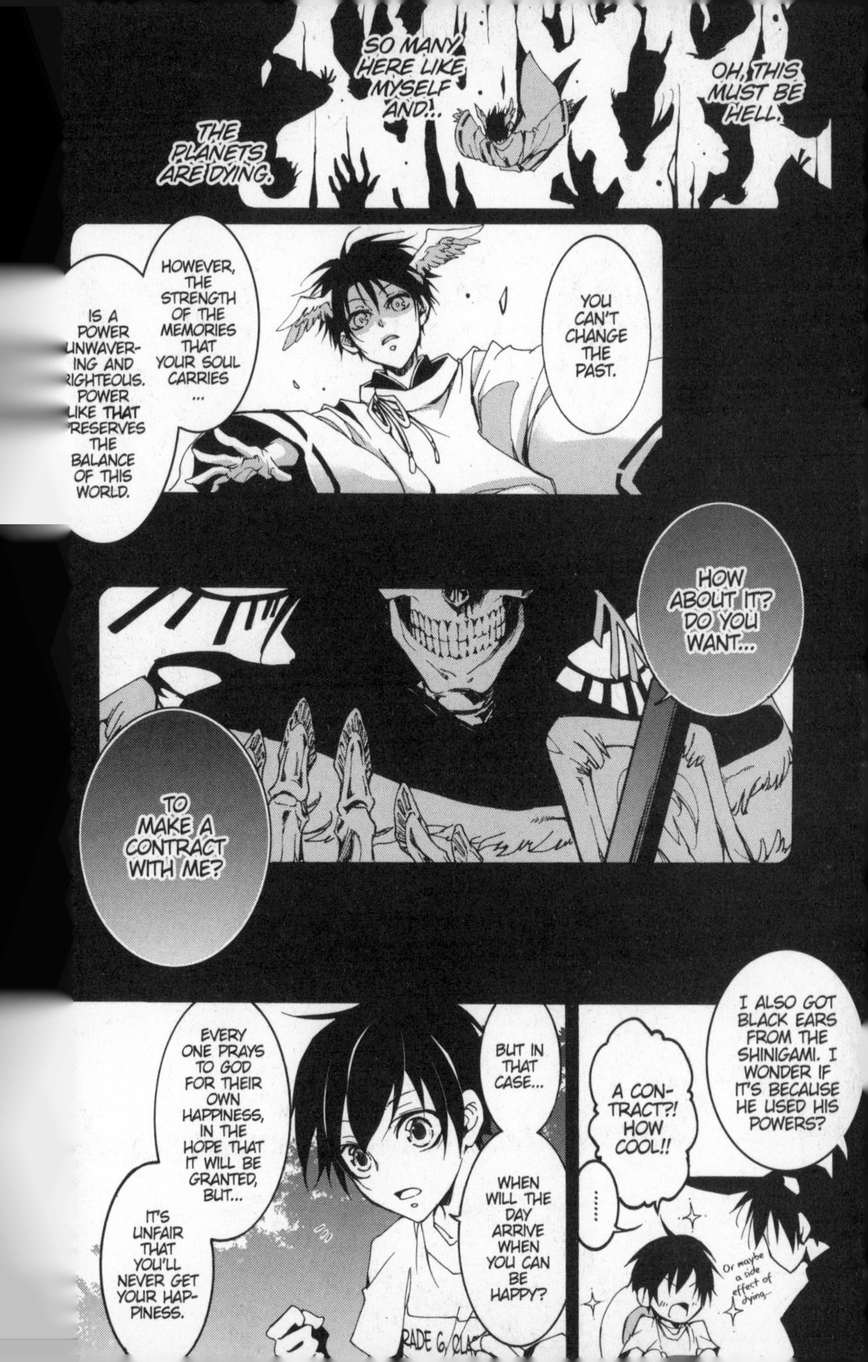

OH, THIS MUST BE HELL.
SO MANY HERE LIKE MYSELF AND...
THE PLANETS ARE DYING.
YOU CAN'T CHANGE THE PAST.
HOWEVER, THE STRENGTH OF THE MEMORIES THAT YOUR SOUL CARRIES ...
IS A POWER UNWAVER- ING AND RIGHTEOUS. POWER LIKE THAT PRESERVES THE BALANCE OF THIS WORLD.
HOW ABOUT IT? DO YOU WANT...
TO MAKE A CONTRACT WITH ME?
I ALSO GOT BLACK EARS FROM THE SHINIGAMI. I WONDER IF IT'S BECAUSE HE USED HIS POWERS?
A CON- TRACT?! HOW COOL!!
......
Or maybe a side effect of dying...
BUT IN THAT CASE...
EVERY ONE PRAYS TO GOD FOR THEIR OWN HAPPINESS, IN THE HOPE THAT IT WILL BE GRANTED, BUT...
WHEN WILL THE DAY ARRIVE WHEN YOU CAN BE HAPPY?
IT'S UNFAIR THAT YOU'LL NEVER GET YOUR HAP- PINESS.

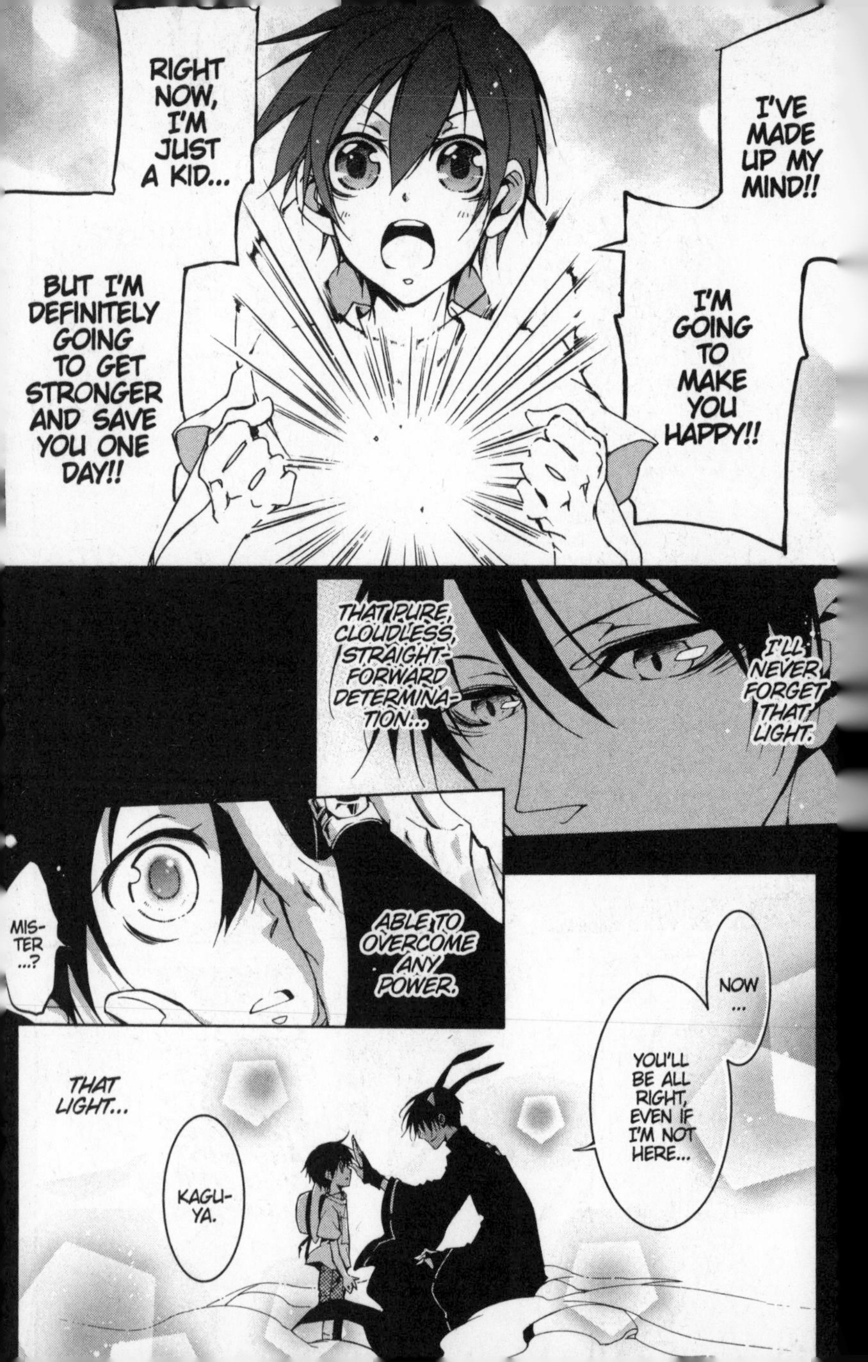
I'VE MADE UP MY MIND!!
RIGHT NOW, I'M JUST A KID...
BUT I'M DEFINITELY GOING TO GET STRONGER AND SAVE YOU ONE DAY!!
I'M GOING TO MAKE YOU HAPPY!!
THAT PURE, CLOUDLESS, STRAIGHT-FORWARD DETERMINA-TION...
I'LL NEVER FORGET THAT LIGHT.
ABLE TO OVERCOME ANY POWER.
MIS-TER ...?
NOW ...
YOU'LL BE ALL RIGHT, EVEN IF I'M NOT HERE...
KAGU-YA.
THAT LIGHT...

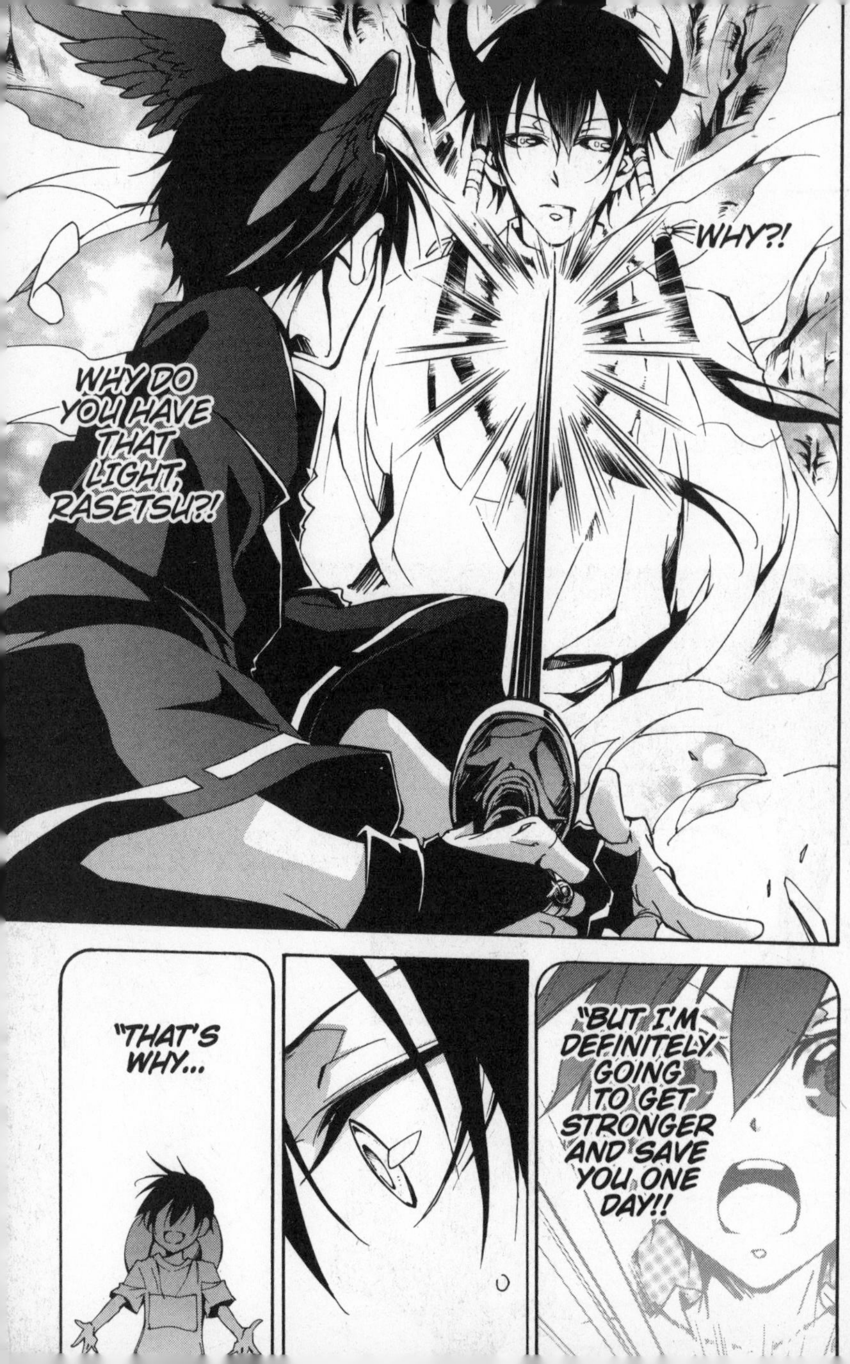
WHY?!
WHY DO YOU HAVE THAT LIGHT, RASETSU?!
"BUT I'M DEFINITELY GOING TO GET STRONGER AND SAVE YOU ONE DAY!!
"THAT'S WHY...

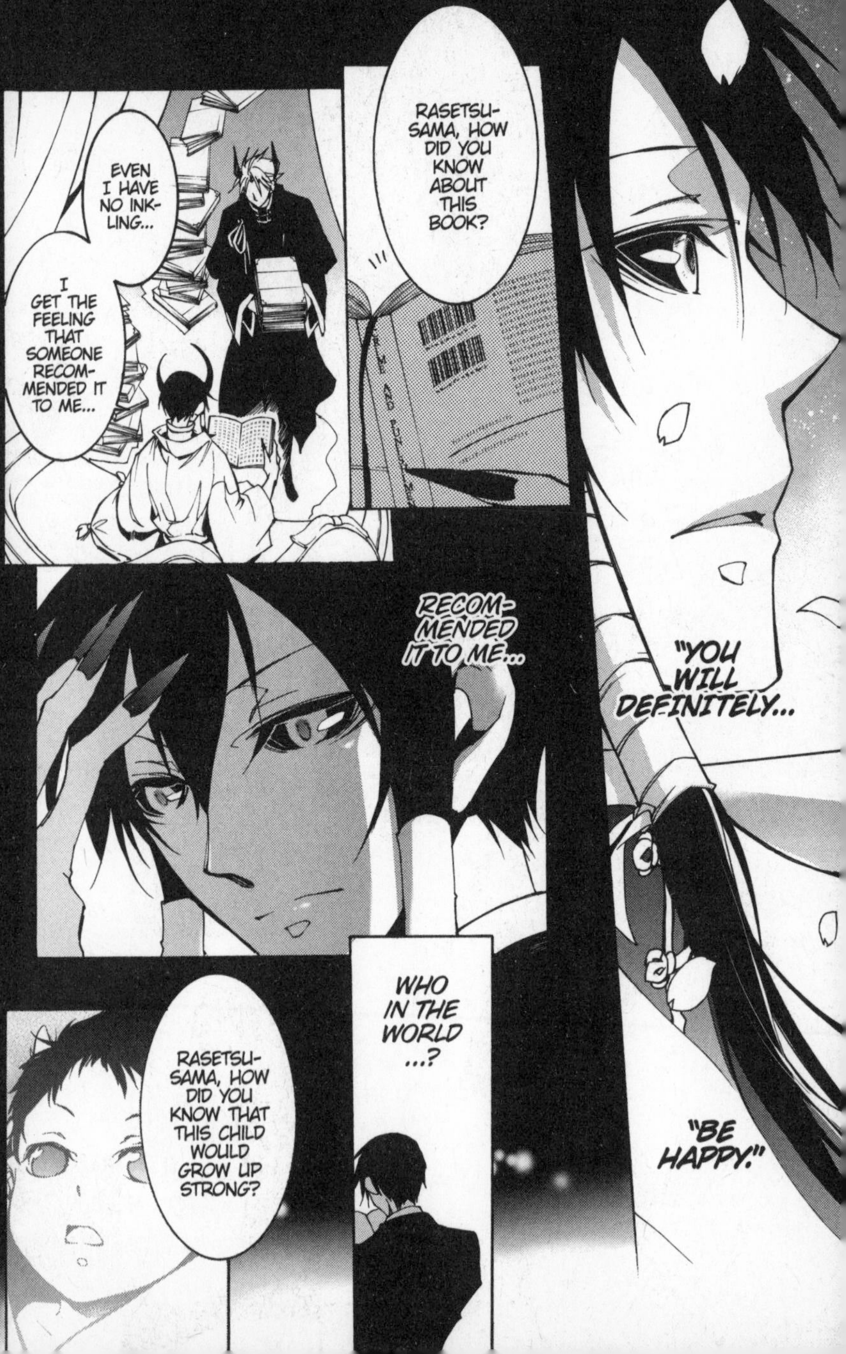
"YOU WILL DEFINITELY...
"BE HAPPY."
RASETSU-SAMA, HOW DID YOU KNOW ABOUT THIS BOOK?
EVEN I HAVE NO INK-LING...
I GET THE FEELING THAT SOMEONE RECOM-MENDED IT TO ME...
RECOM-MENDED IT TO ME...
WHO IN THE WORLD ...?
RASETSU-SAMA, HOW DID YOU KNOW THAT THIS CHILD WOULD GROW UP STRONG?

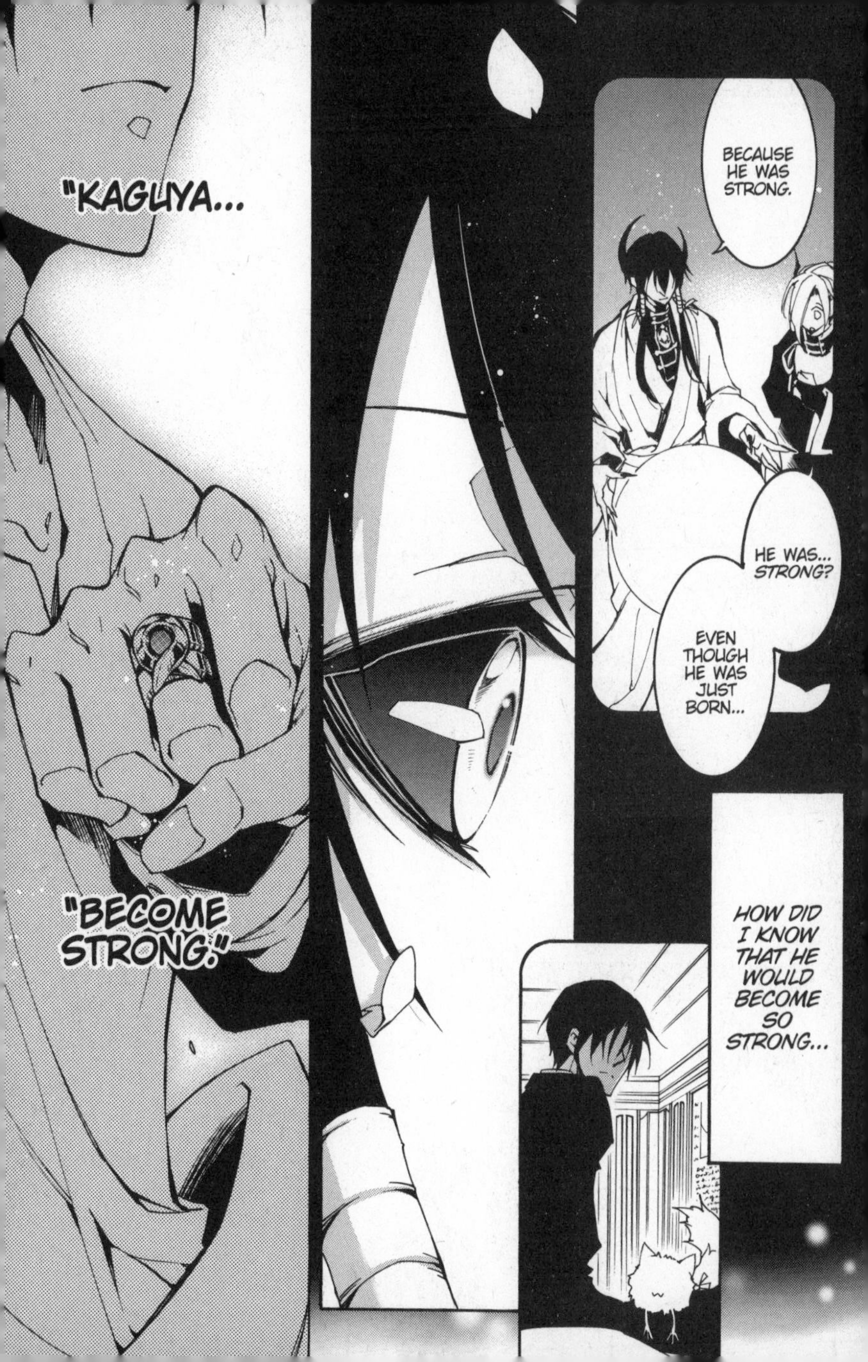
BECAUSE HE WAS STRONG.
HE WAS... STRONG?
EVEN THOUGH HE WAS JUST BORN...
HOW DID I KNOW THAT HE WOULD BECOME SO STRONG...
"KAGUYA...
"BECOME STRONG."

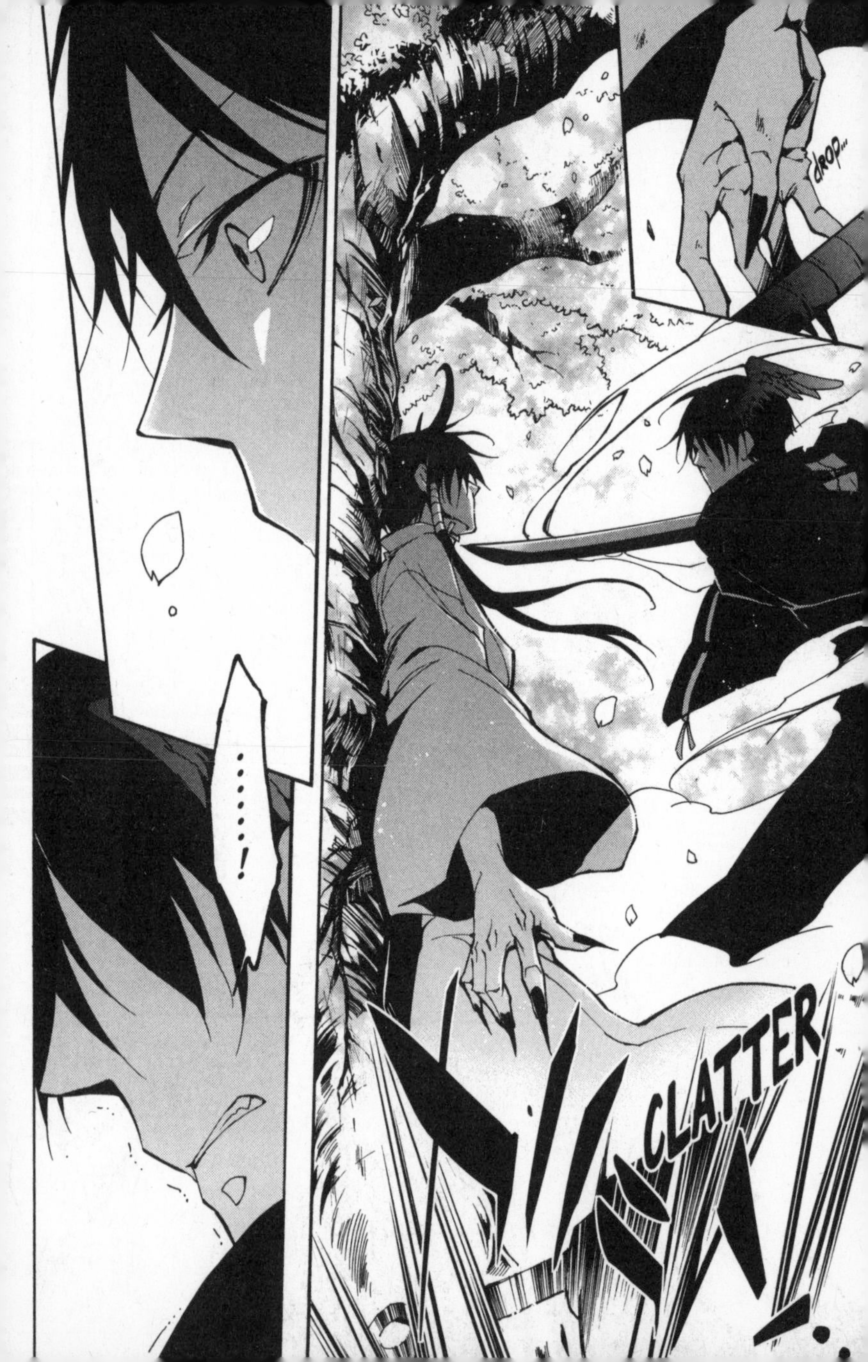
drop...
...CLATTER!
......!

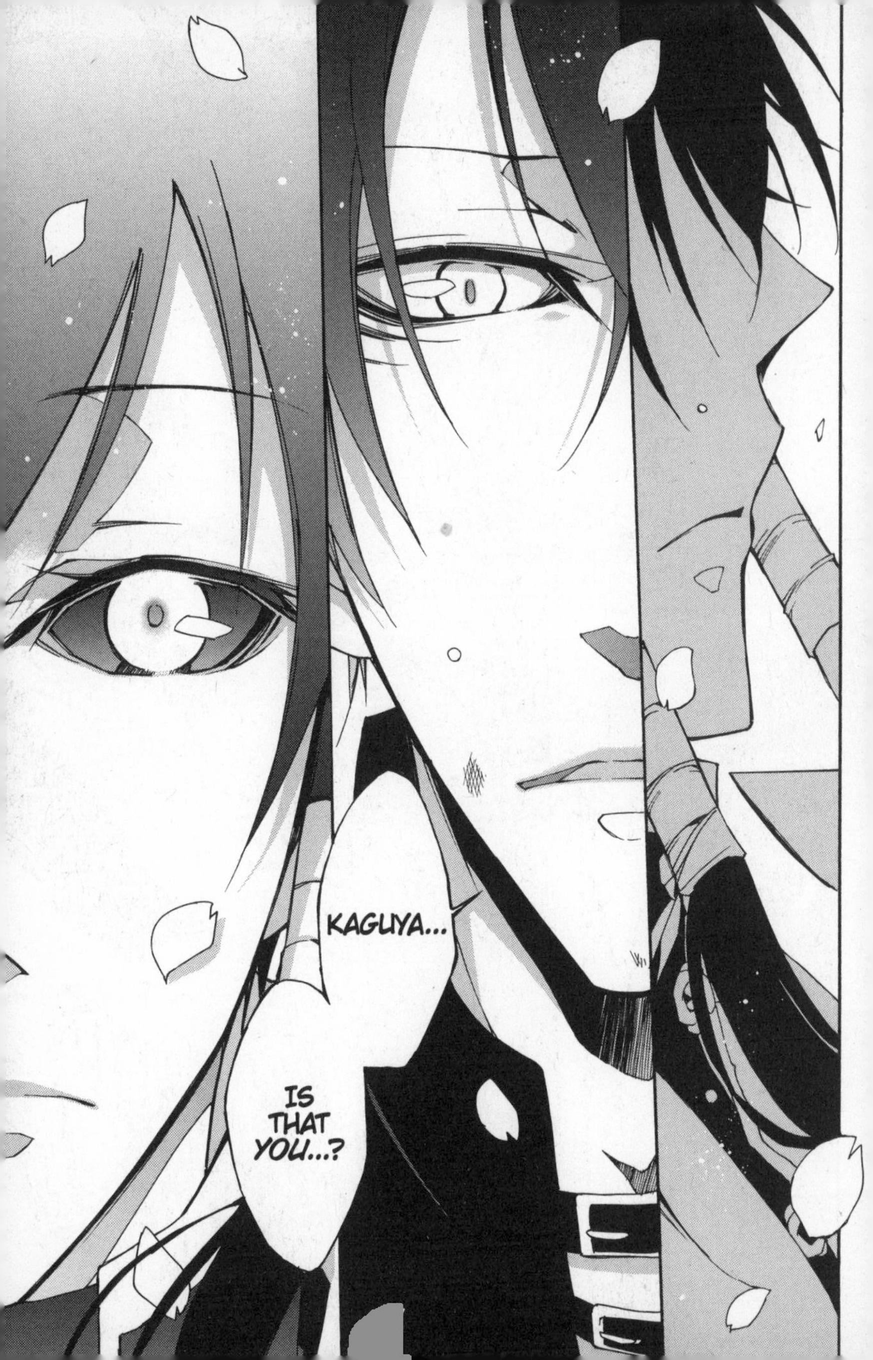
KAGUYA...
IS THAT YOU...?

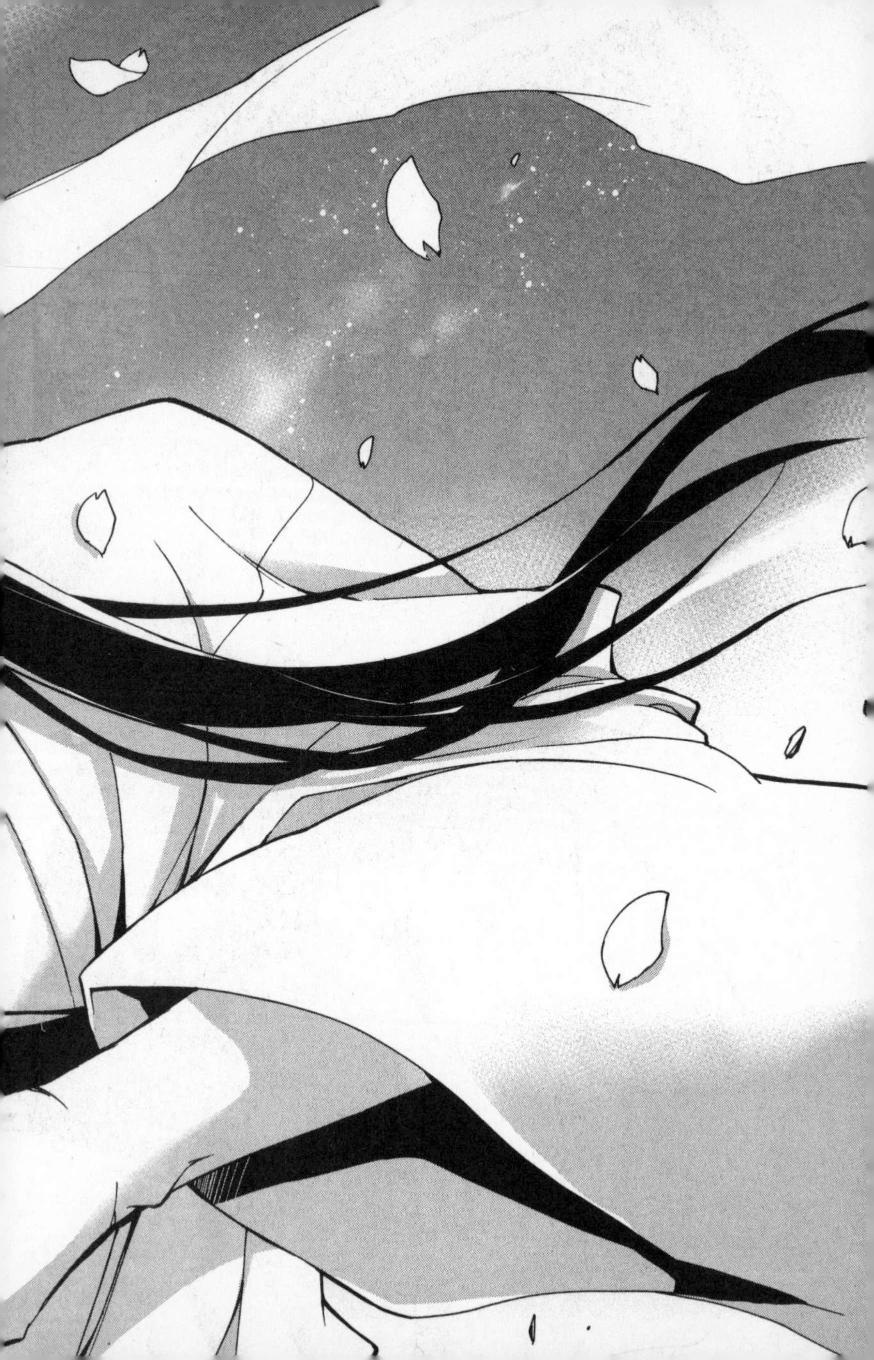

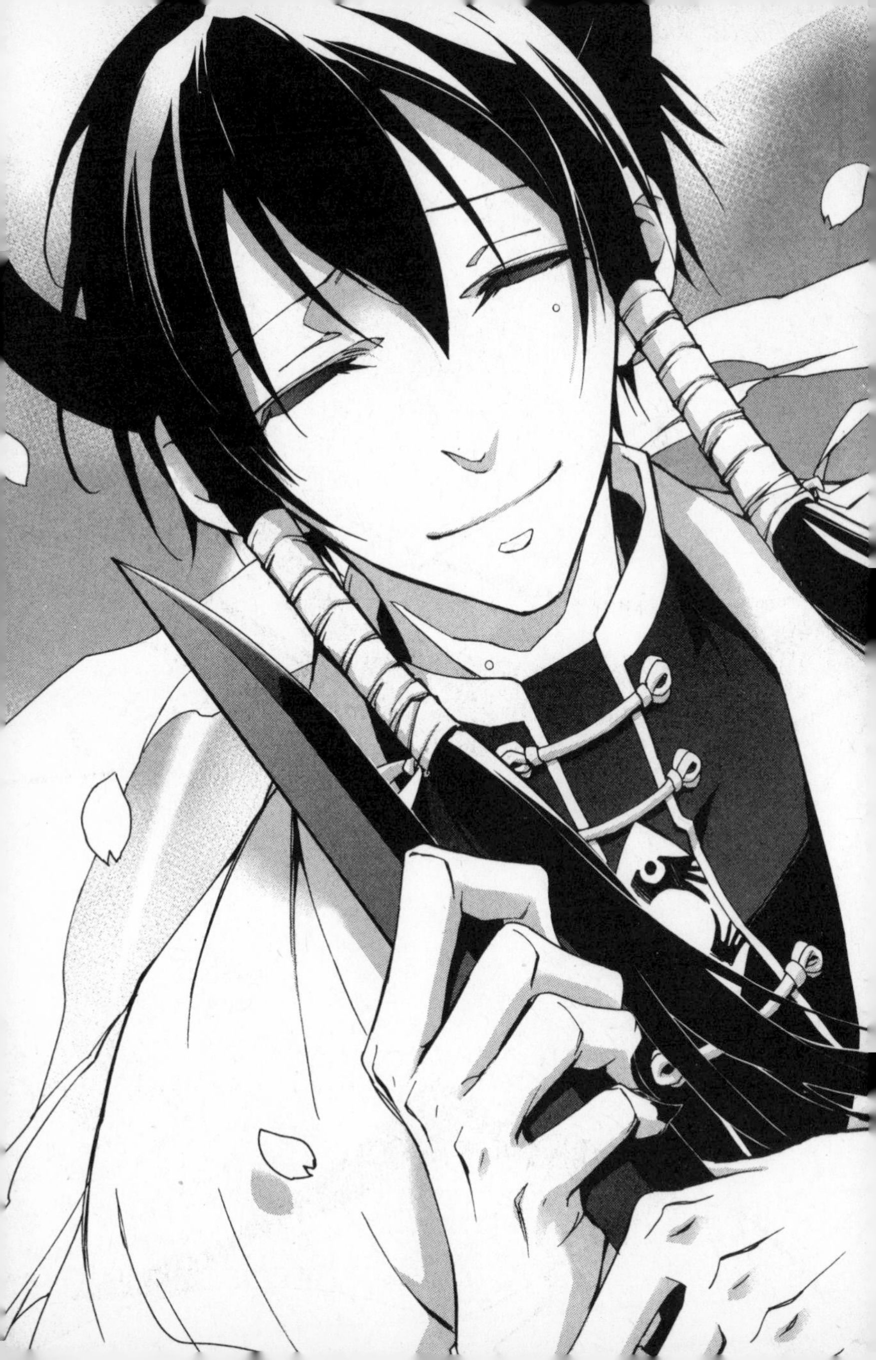

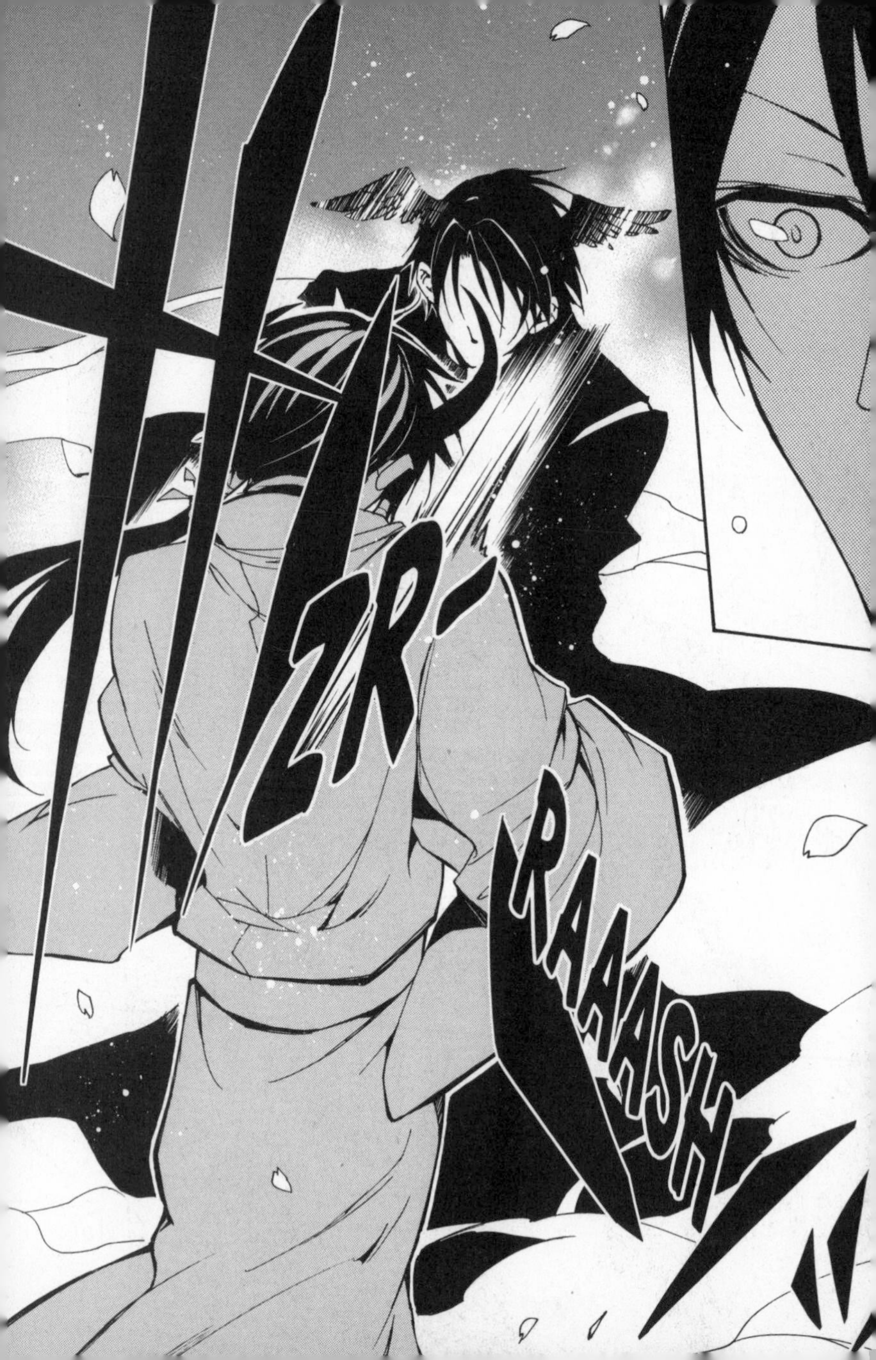
ZR-
RAAASH

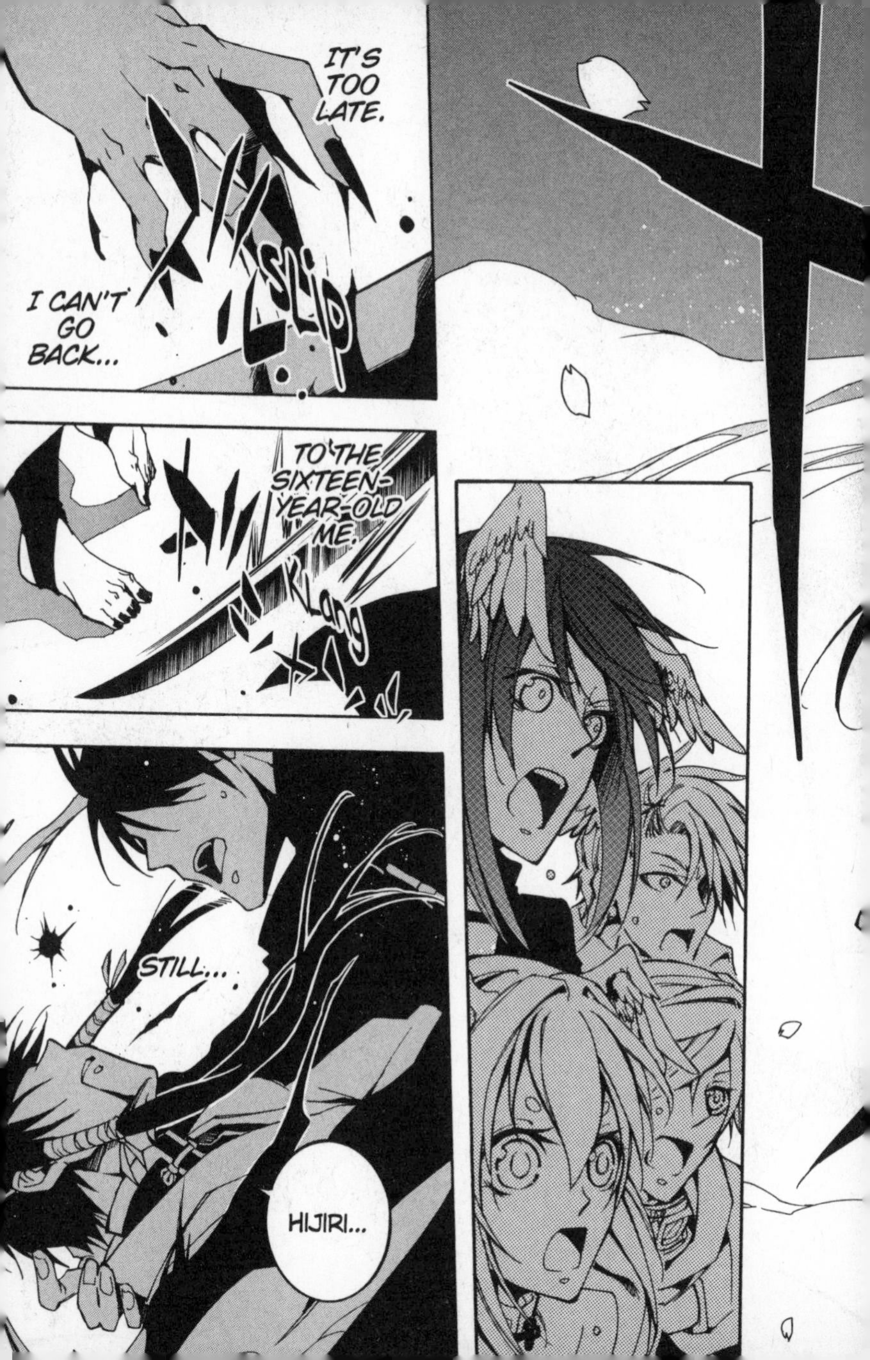
IT'S TOO LATE.
I CAN'T GO BACK...
SLIP
TO THE SIXTEEN-YEAR-OLD ME.
KLANG
STILL...
HIJIRI...

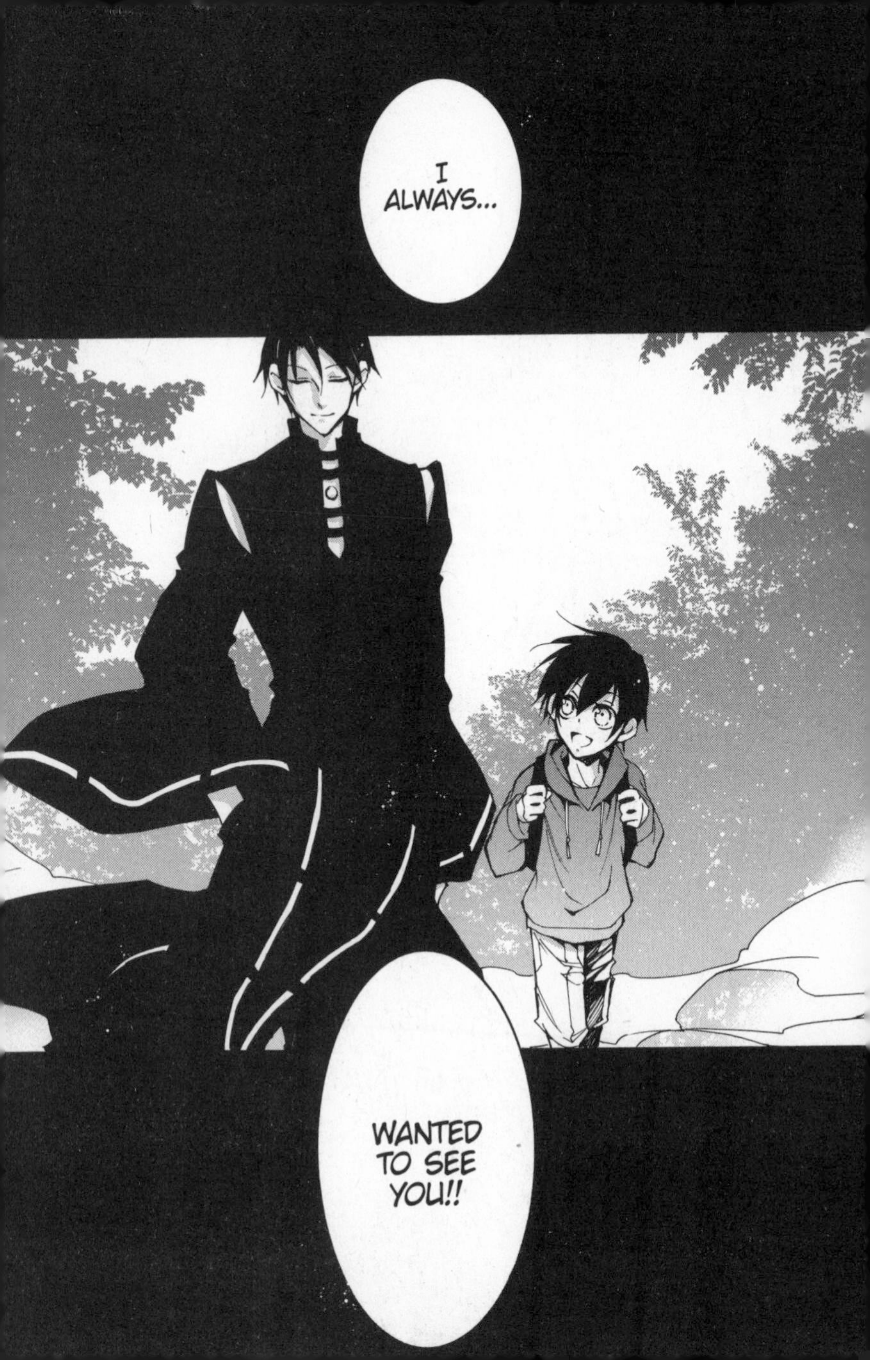
I ALWAYS...
WANTED TO SEE YOU!!

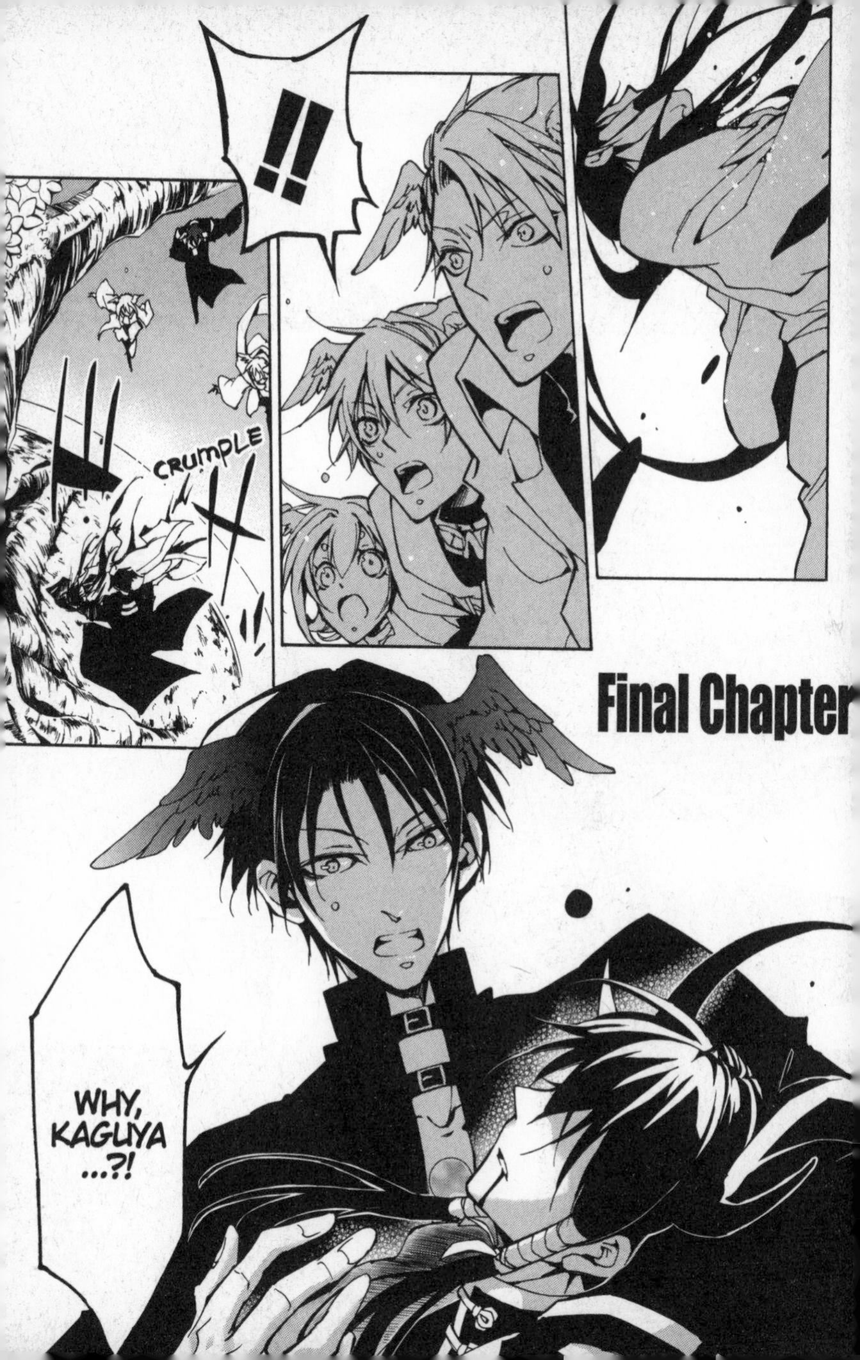
!!
CRUMPLE
Final Chapter
WHY, KAGUYA ...?!

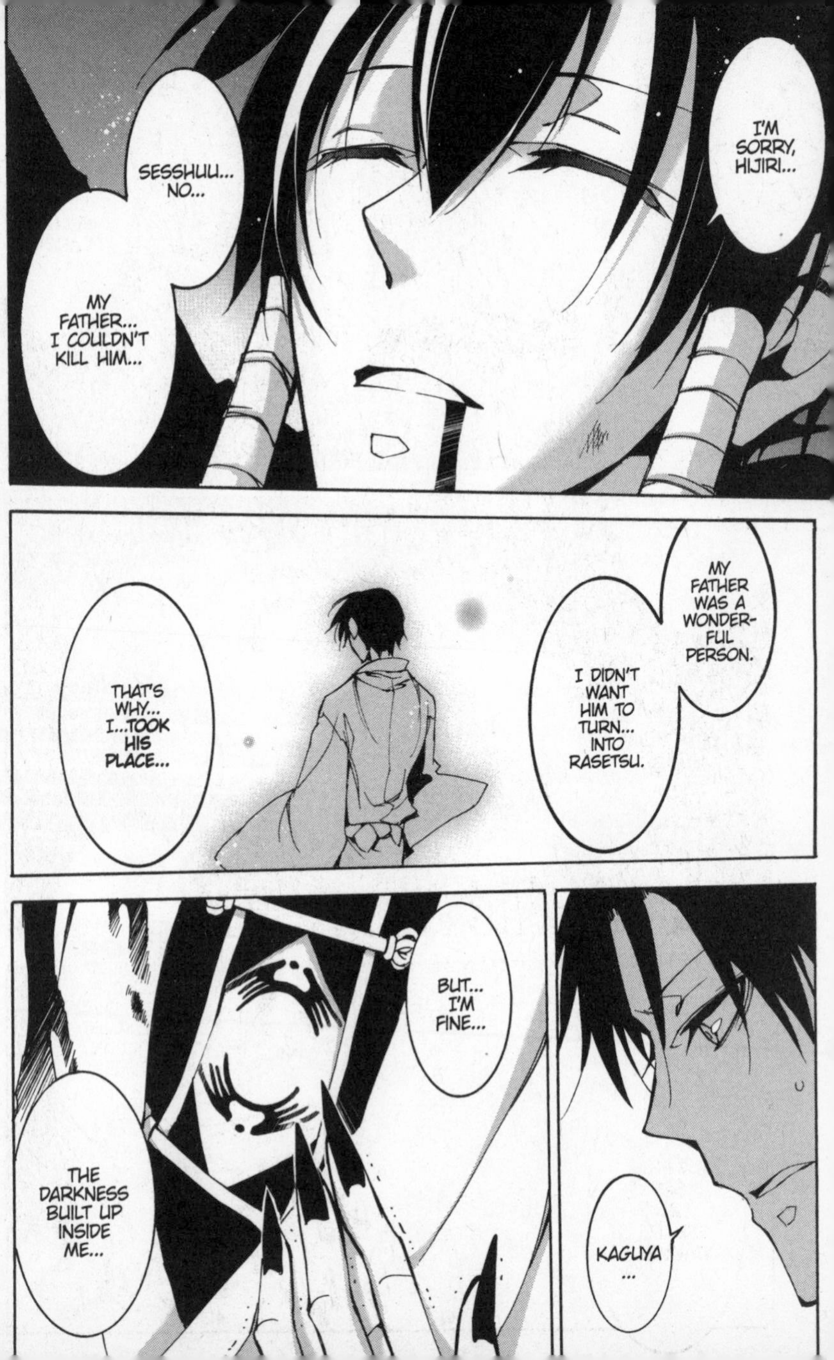
I'M SORRY, HIJIRI...
SESSHUU... NO...
MY FATHER... I COULDN'T KILL HIM...
MY FATHER WAS A WONDERFUL PERSON.
I DIDN'T WANT HIM TO TURN... INTO RASETSU.
THAT'S WHY... I...TOOK HIS PLACE...
KAGUYA ...
BUT... I'M FINE...
THE DARKNESS BUILT UP INSIDE ME...

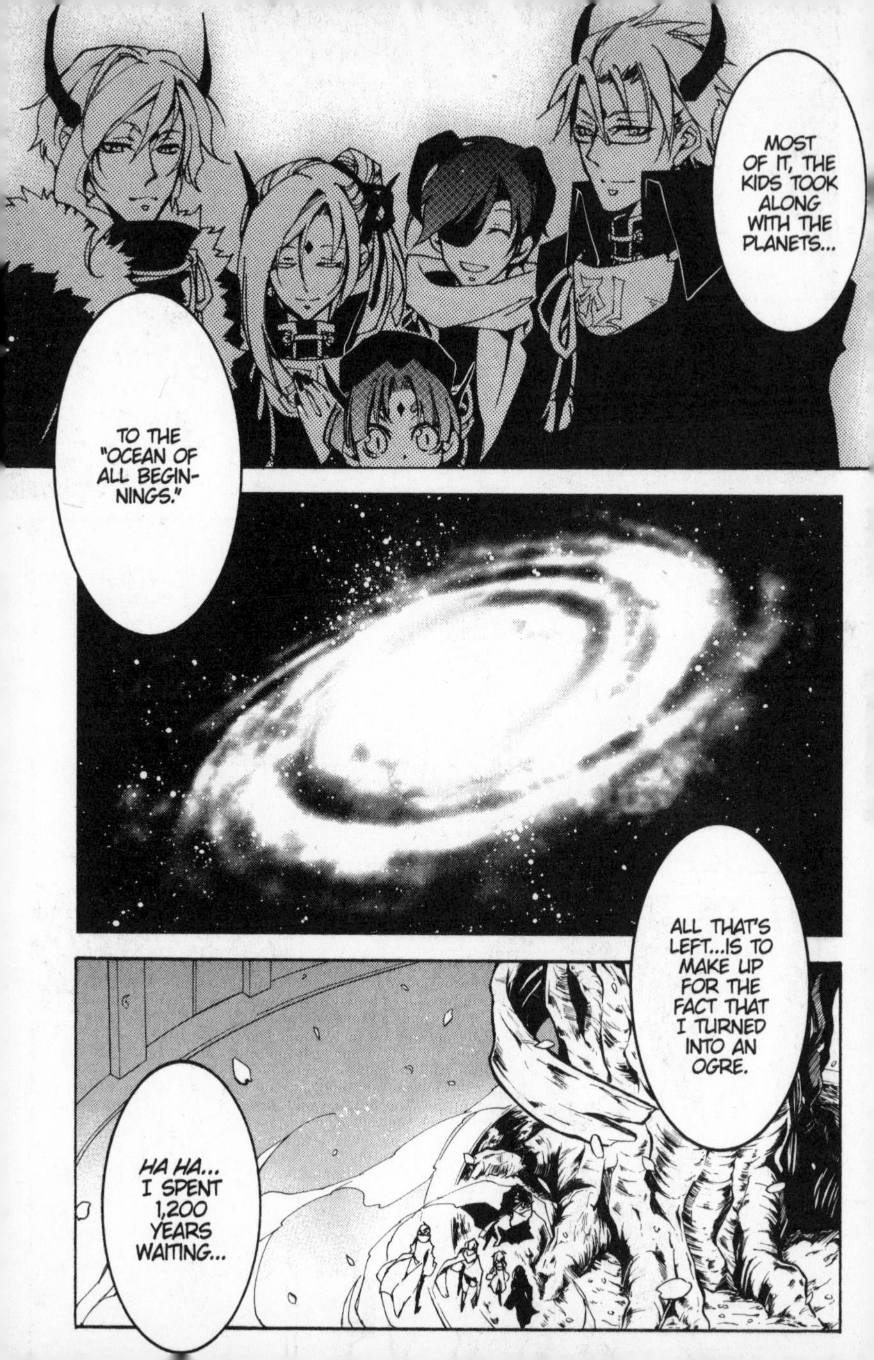
MOST OF IT, THE KIDS TOOK ALONG WITH THE PLANETS...
TO THE "OCEAN OF ALL BEGIN-NINGS."
ALL THAT'S LEFT...IS TO MAKE UP FOR THE FACT THAT I TURNED INTO AN OGRE.
HA HA... I SPENT 1,200 YEARS WAITING...

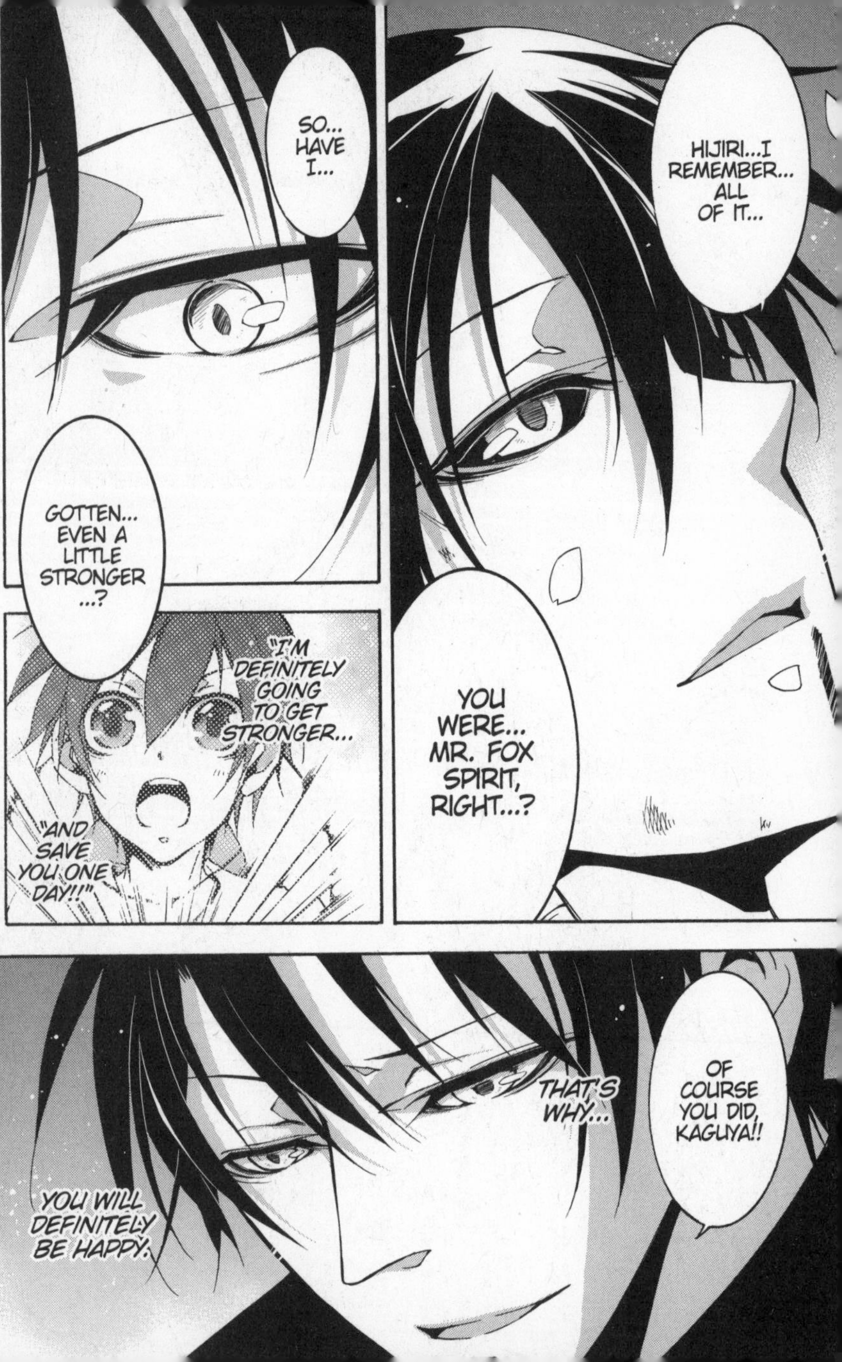
HIJIRI...I REMEMBER... ALL OF IT...
YOU WERE... MR. FOX SPIRIT, RIGHT...?
SO... HAVE I...
GOTTEN... EVEN A LITTLE STRONGER ...?
"I'M DEFINITELY GOING TO GET STRONGER...
"AND SAVE YOU ONE DAY!!"
OF COURSE YOU DID, KAGUYA!!
THAT'S WHY...
YOU WILL DEFINITELY BE HAPPY.

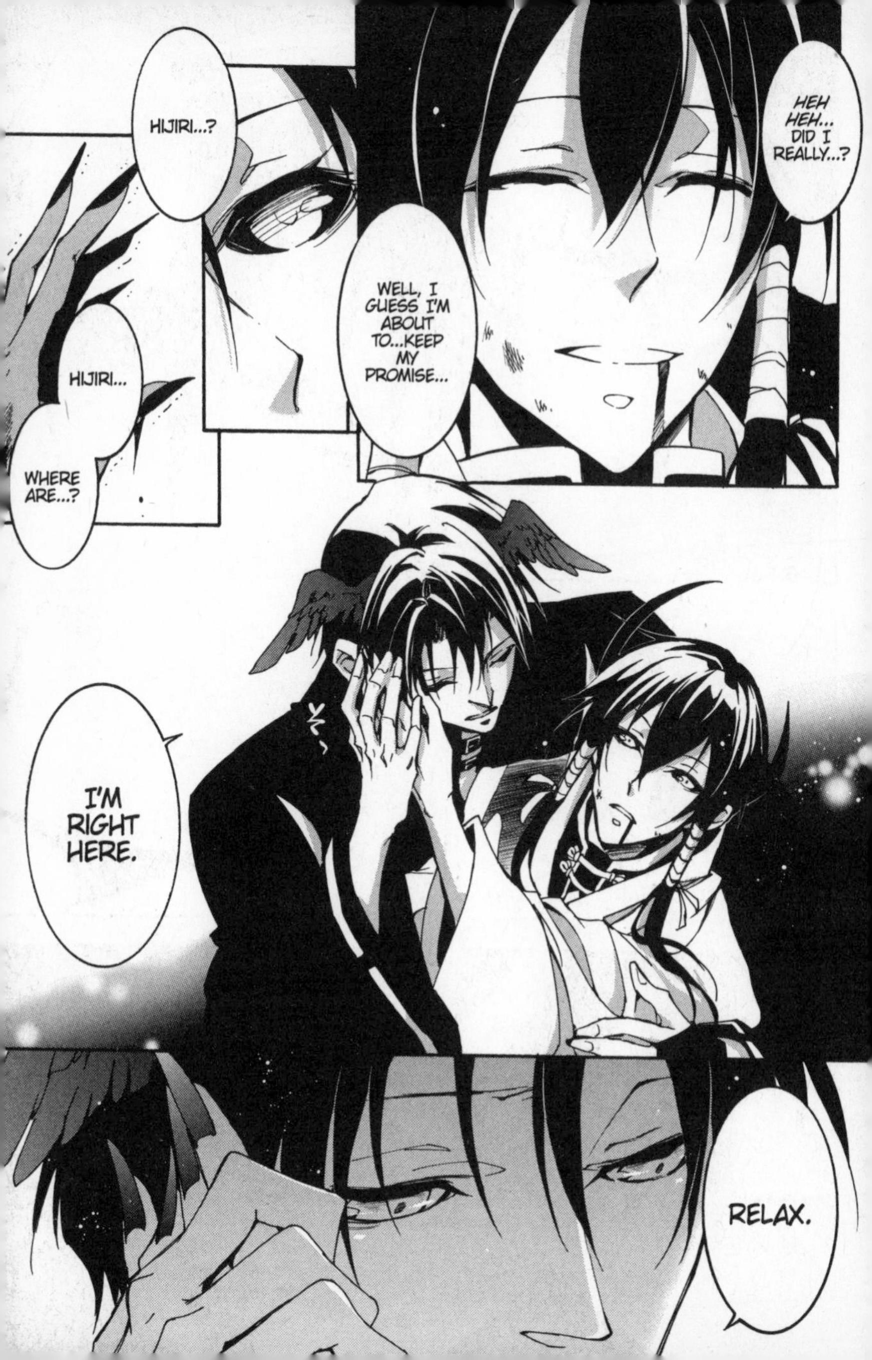
HEH HEH... DID I REALLY...?
WELL, I GUESS I'M ABOUT TO...KEEP MY PROMISE...
HIJIRI...?
HIJIRI...
WHERE ARE...?
I'M RIGHT HERE.
RELAX.

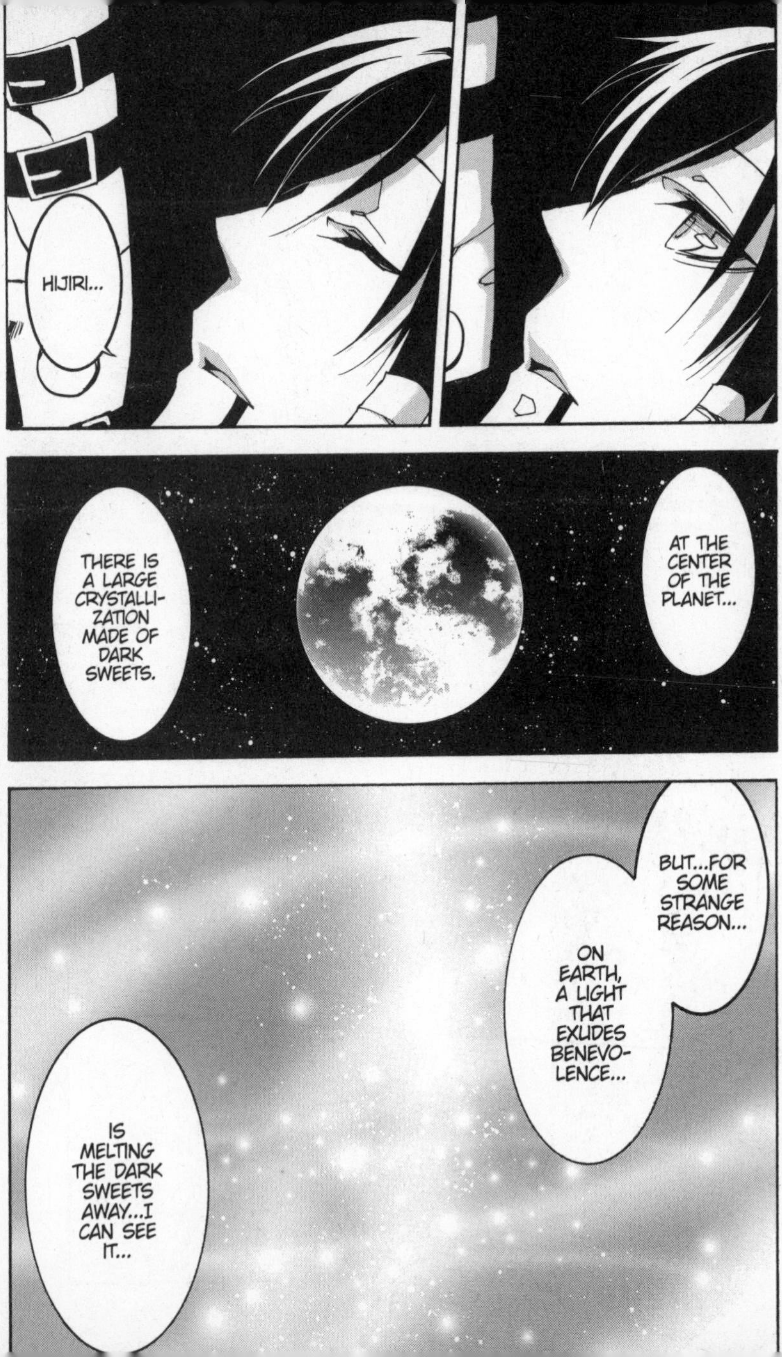
HIJIRI...
AT THE CENTER OF THE PLANET...
THERE IS A LARGE CRYSTALLI-ZATION MADE OF DARK SWEETS.
BUT...FOR SOME STRANGE REASON...
ON EARTH, A LIGHT THAT EXUDES BENEVO-LENCE...
IS MELTING THE DARK SWEETS AWAY...I CAN SEE IT...

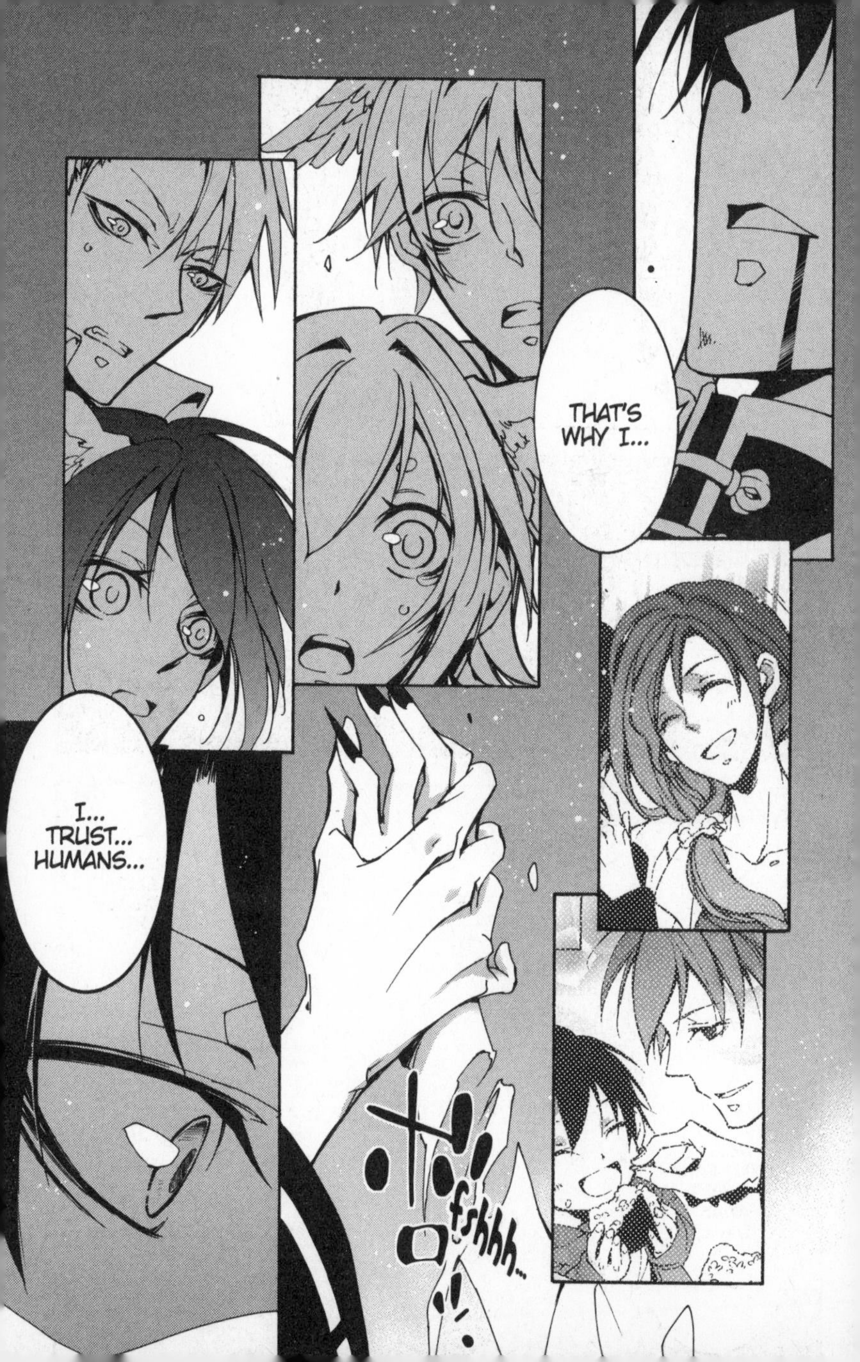
THAT'S WHY I...
I... TRUST... HUMANS...
fshhh...

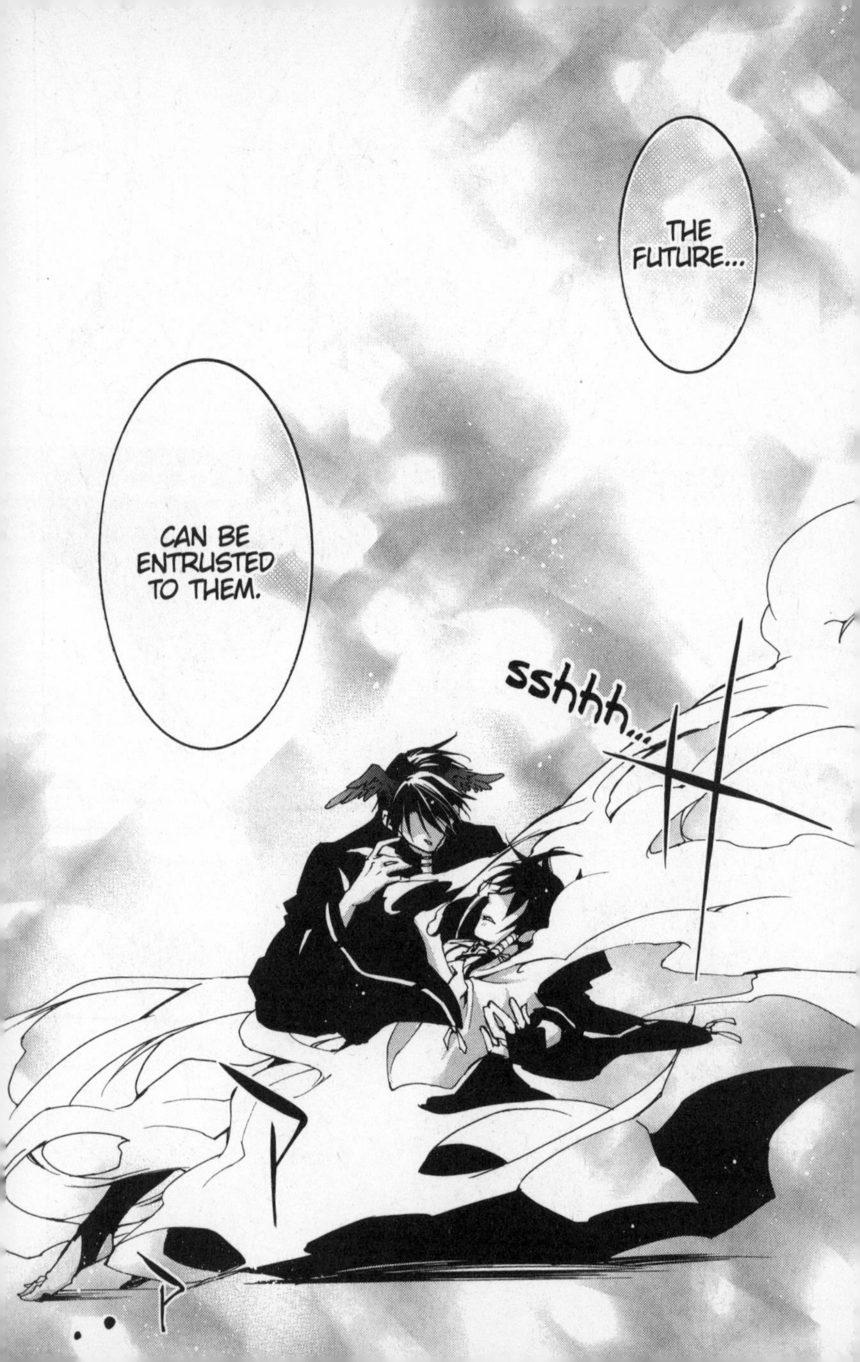
THE FUTURE...
CAN BE ENTRUSTED TO THEM.
sshhh...

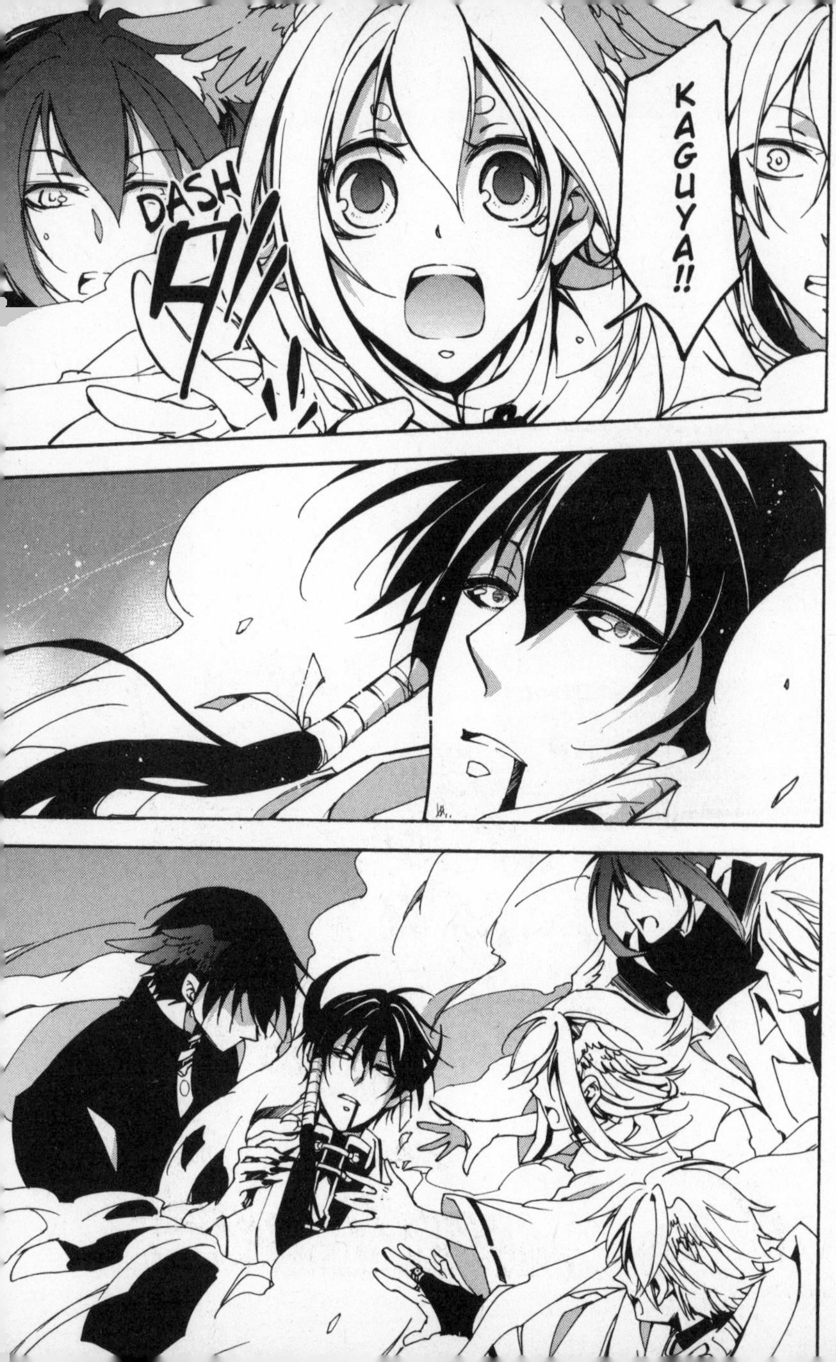
KAGUYA!!
DASH

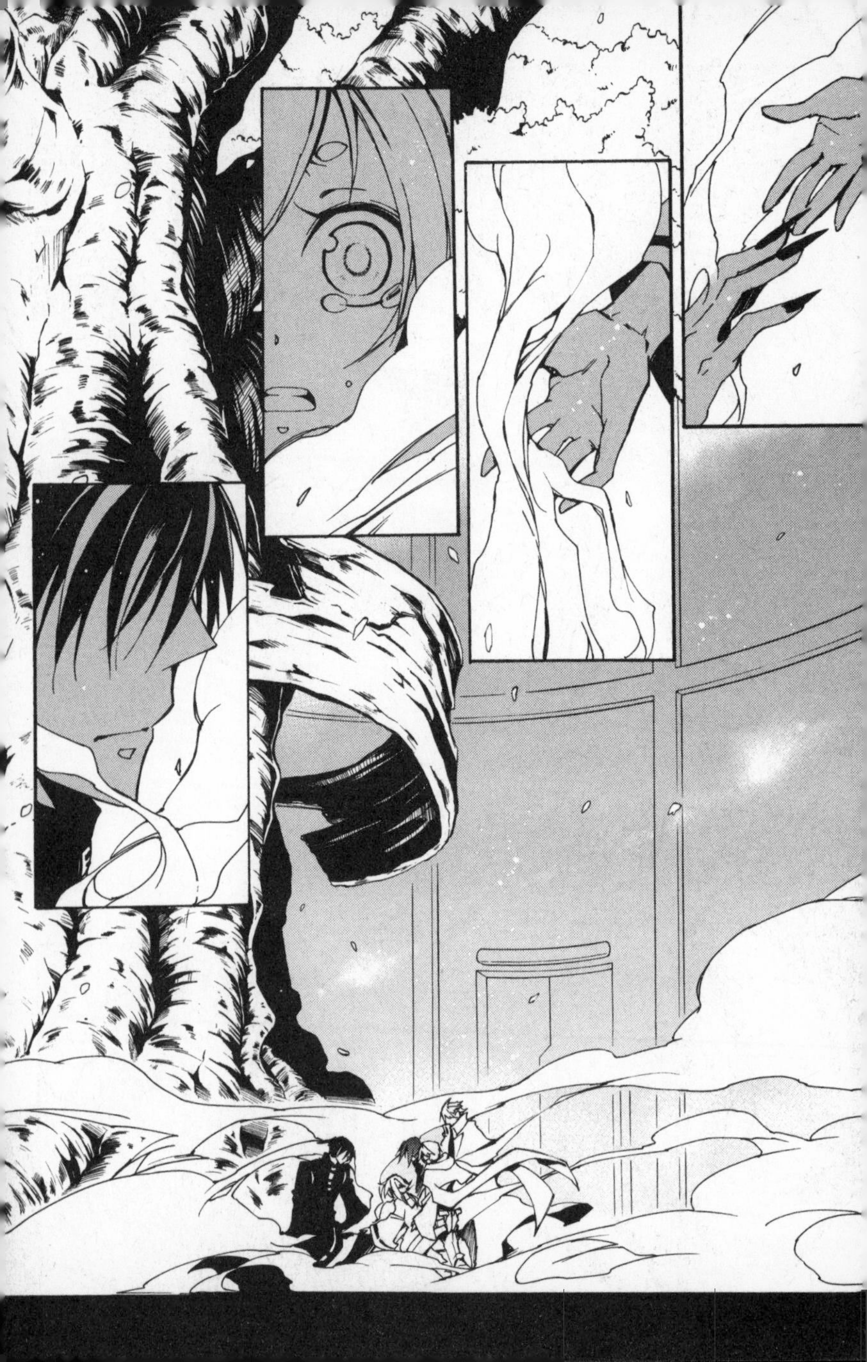

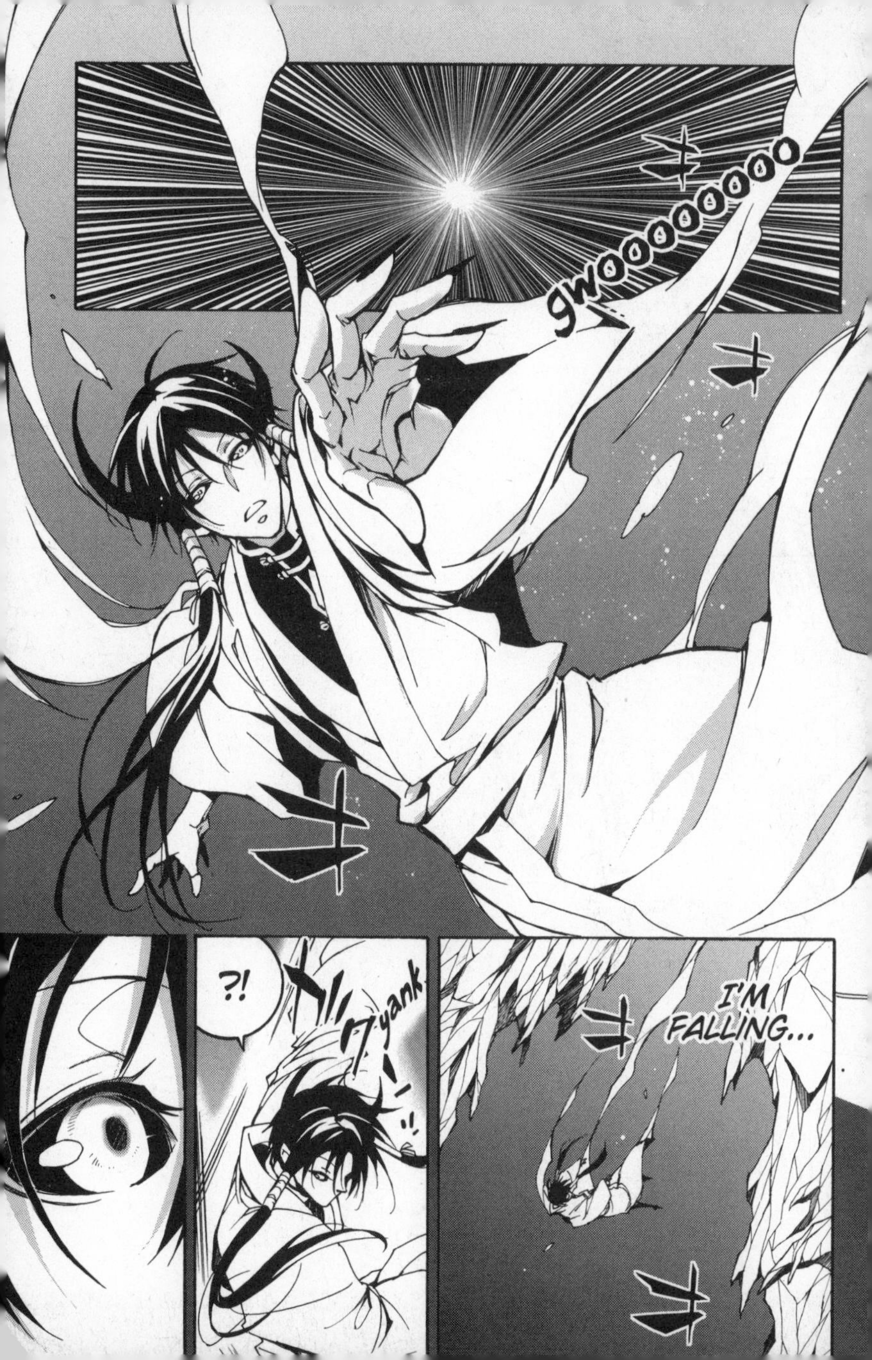
gwoooooooo
I'M FALLING...
?!
yank

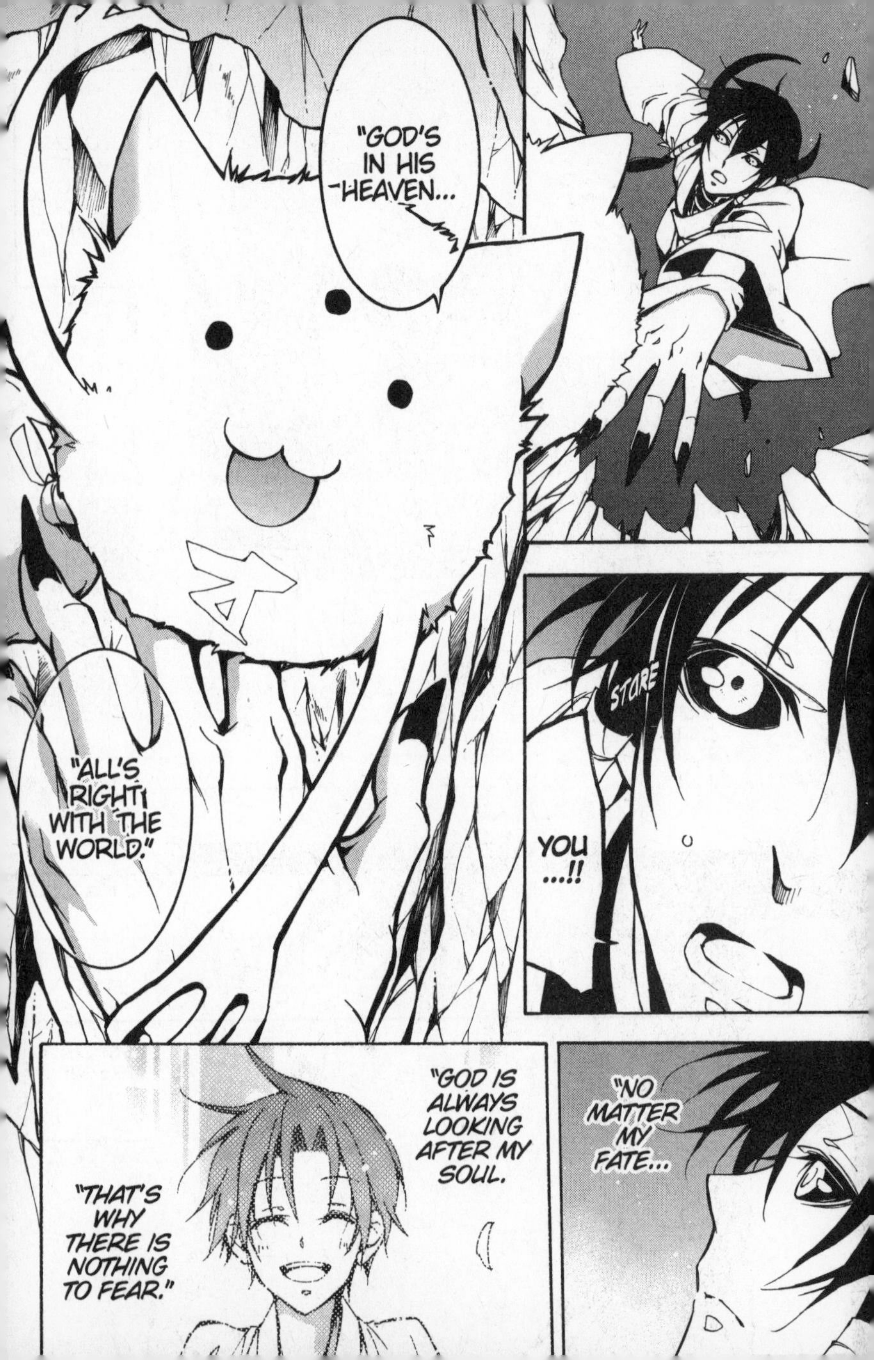
STARE
YOU ...!!
"GOD'S IN HIS HEAVEN...
"ALL'S RIGHT WITH THE WORLD."
"NO MATTER MY FATE...
"GOD IS ALWAYS LOOKING AFTER MY SOUL.
"THAT'S WHY THERE IS NOTHING TO FEAR."

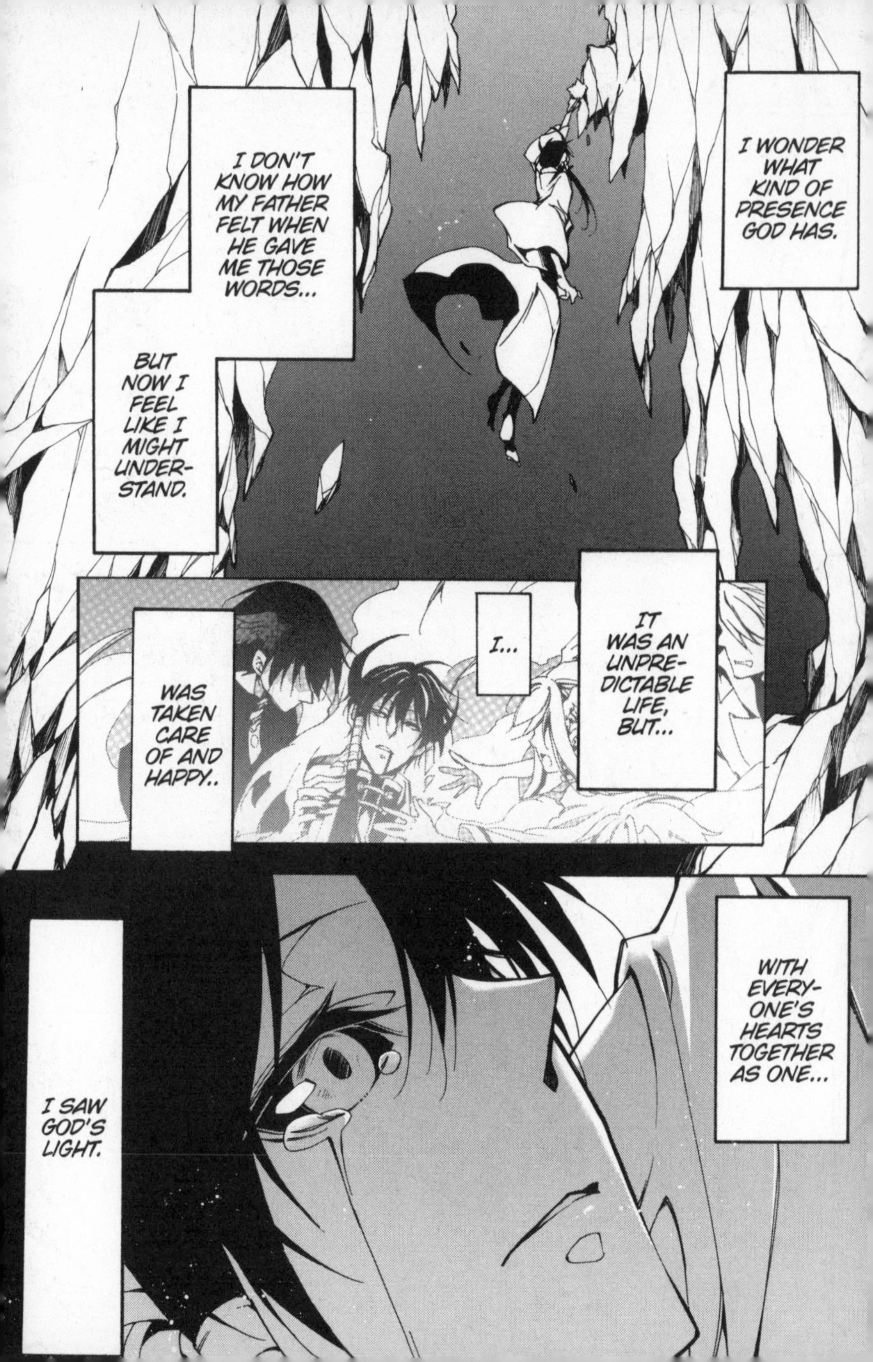
I WONDER WHAT KIND OF PRESENCE GOD HAS.
I DON'T KNOW HOW MY FATHER FELT WHEN HE GAVE ME THOSE WORDS...
BUT NOW I FEEL LIKE I MIGHT UNDER-STAND.
IT WAS AN UNPRE-DICTABLE LIFE, BUT...
I...
WAS TAKEN CARE OF AND HAPPY..
WITH EVERY-ONE'S HEARTS TOGETHER AS ONE...
I SAW GOD'S LIGHT.

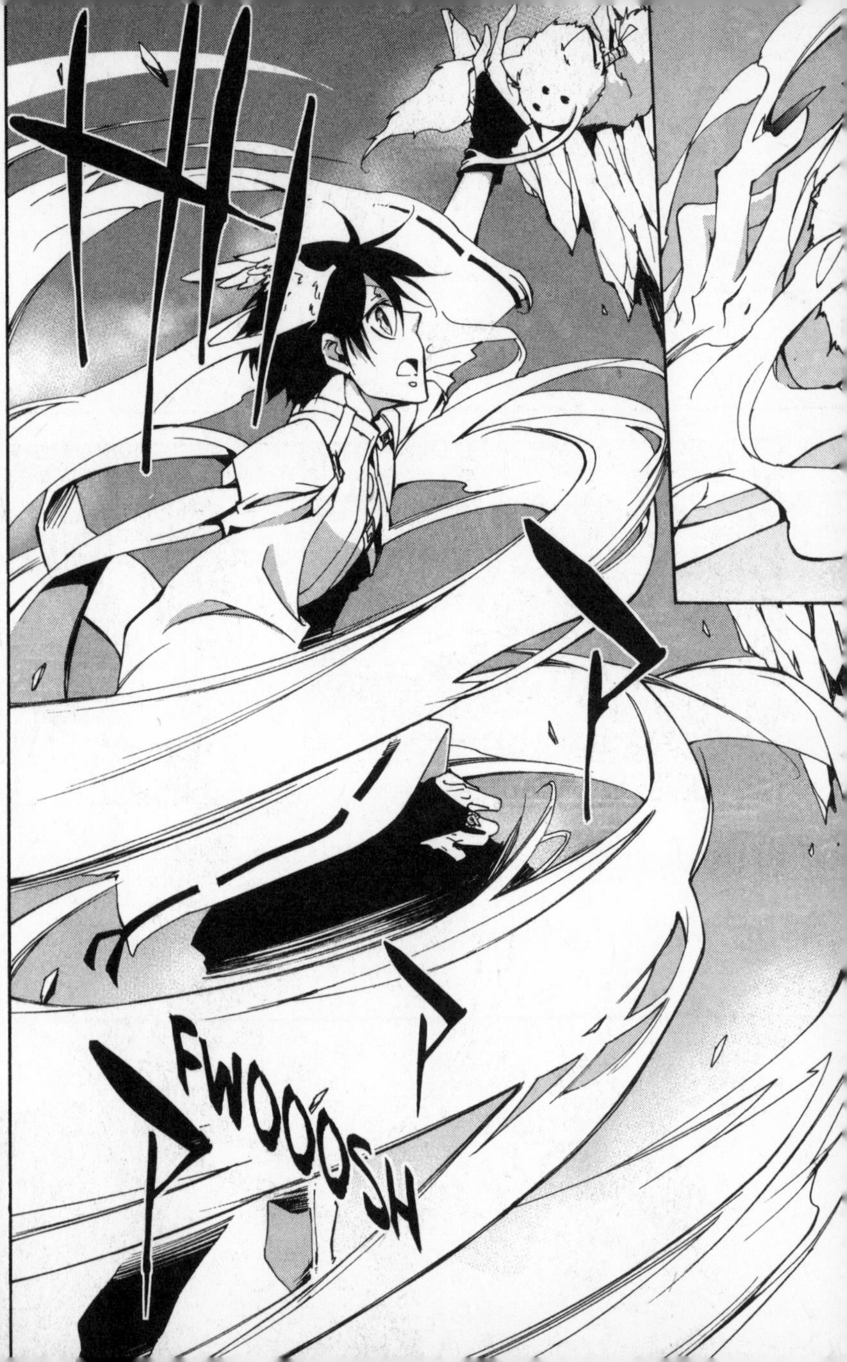
FWOOOSH

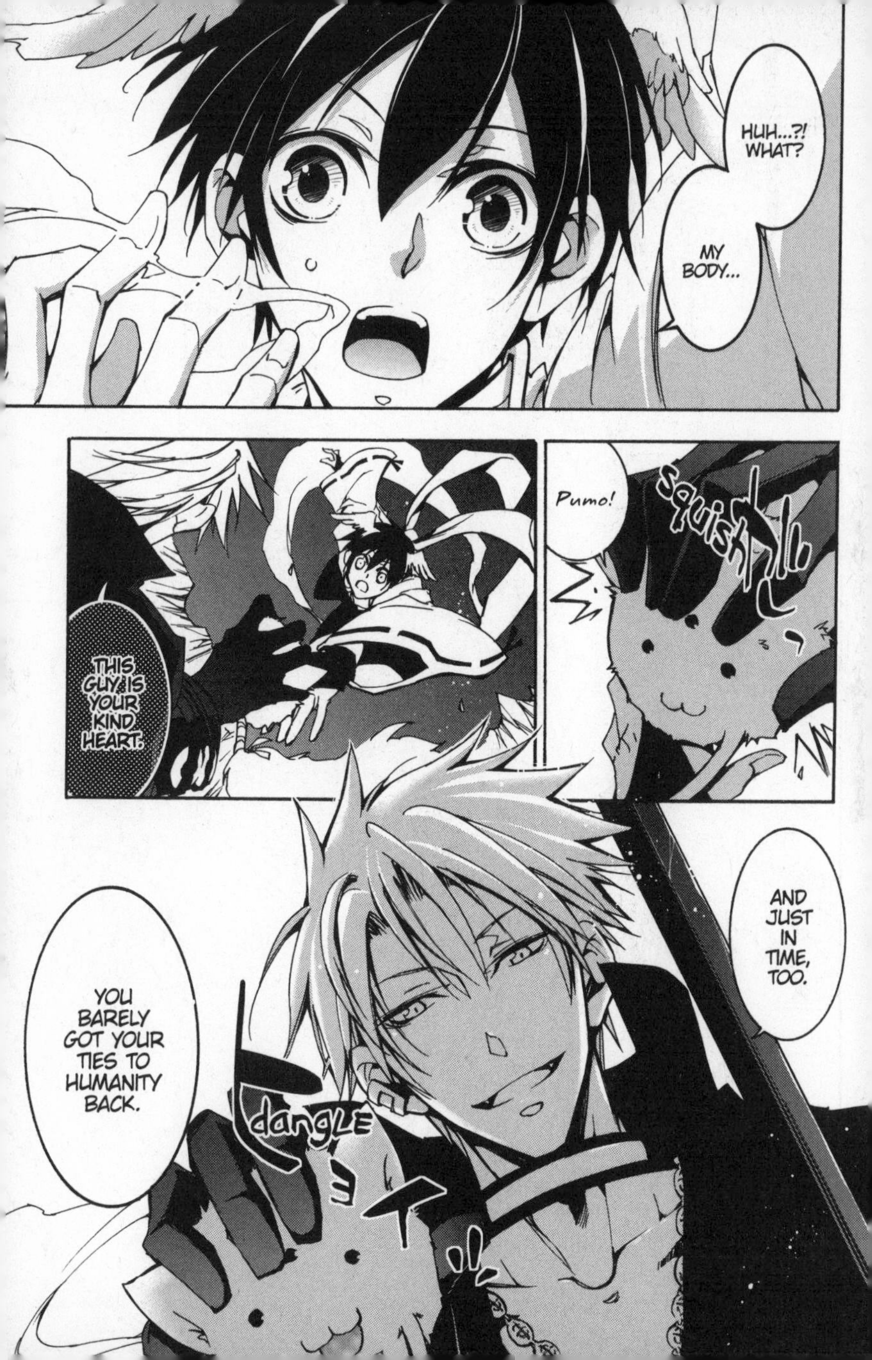
HUH...?! WHAT?
MY BODY...
Pumo!
squish
THIS GUY IS YOUR KIND HEART.
AND JUST IN TIME, TOO.
YOU BARELY GOT YOUR TIES TO HUMANITY BACK.
dangLE

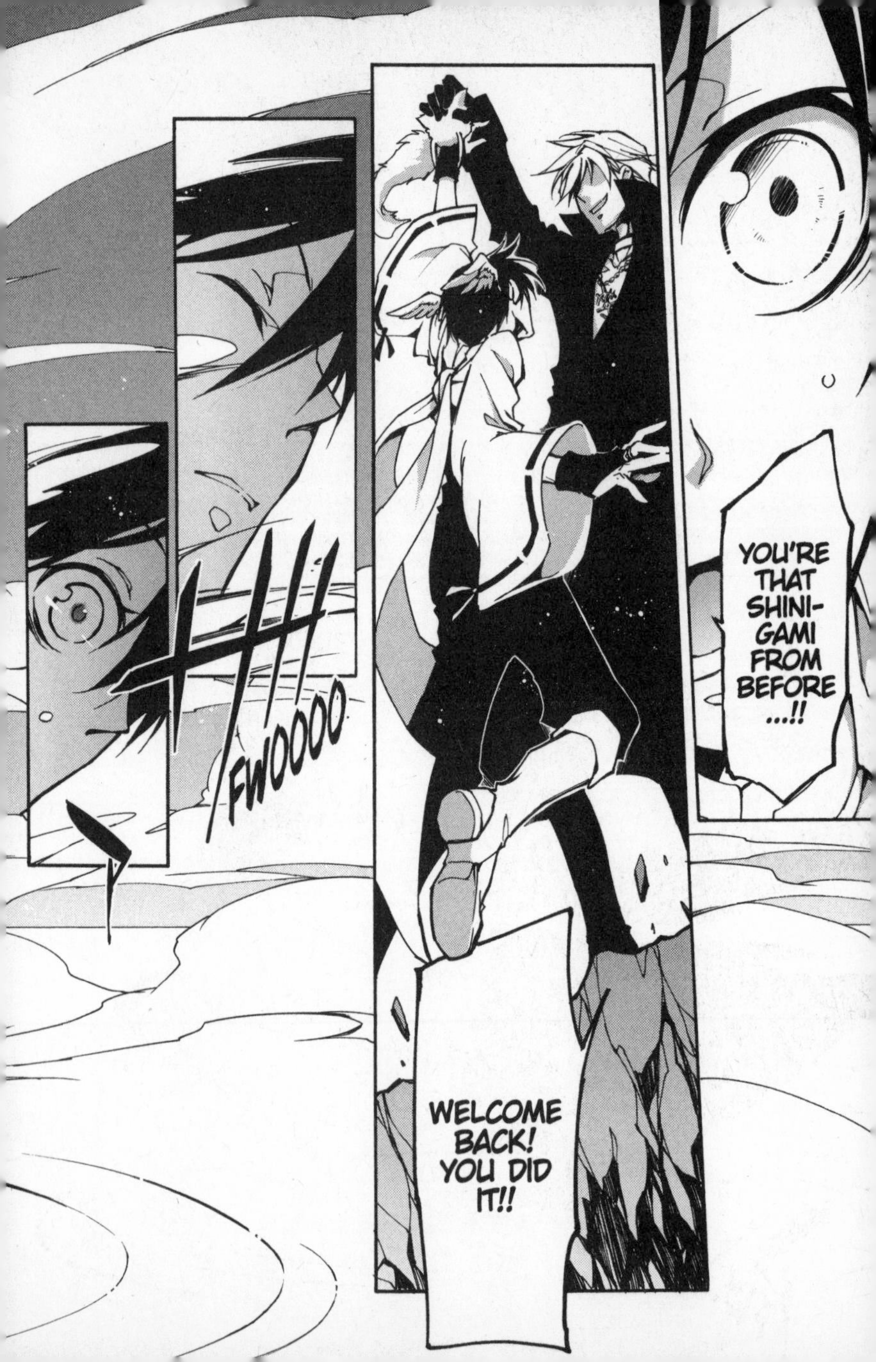
YOU'RE THAT SHINI-GAMI FROM BEFORE ...!!
WELCOME BACK! YOU DID IT!!
FWOOOO

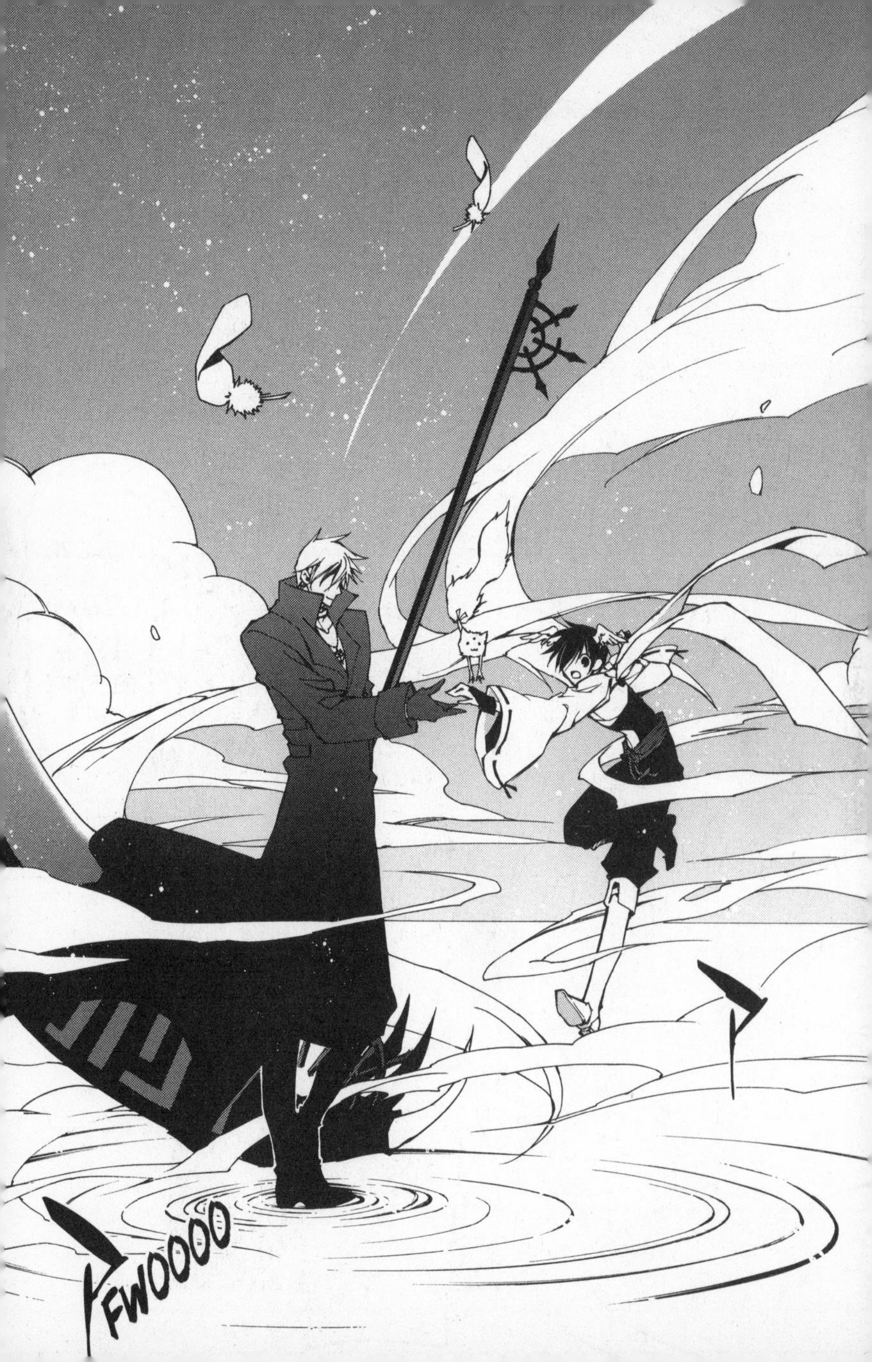
FWOOOO

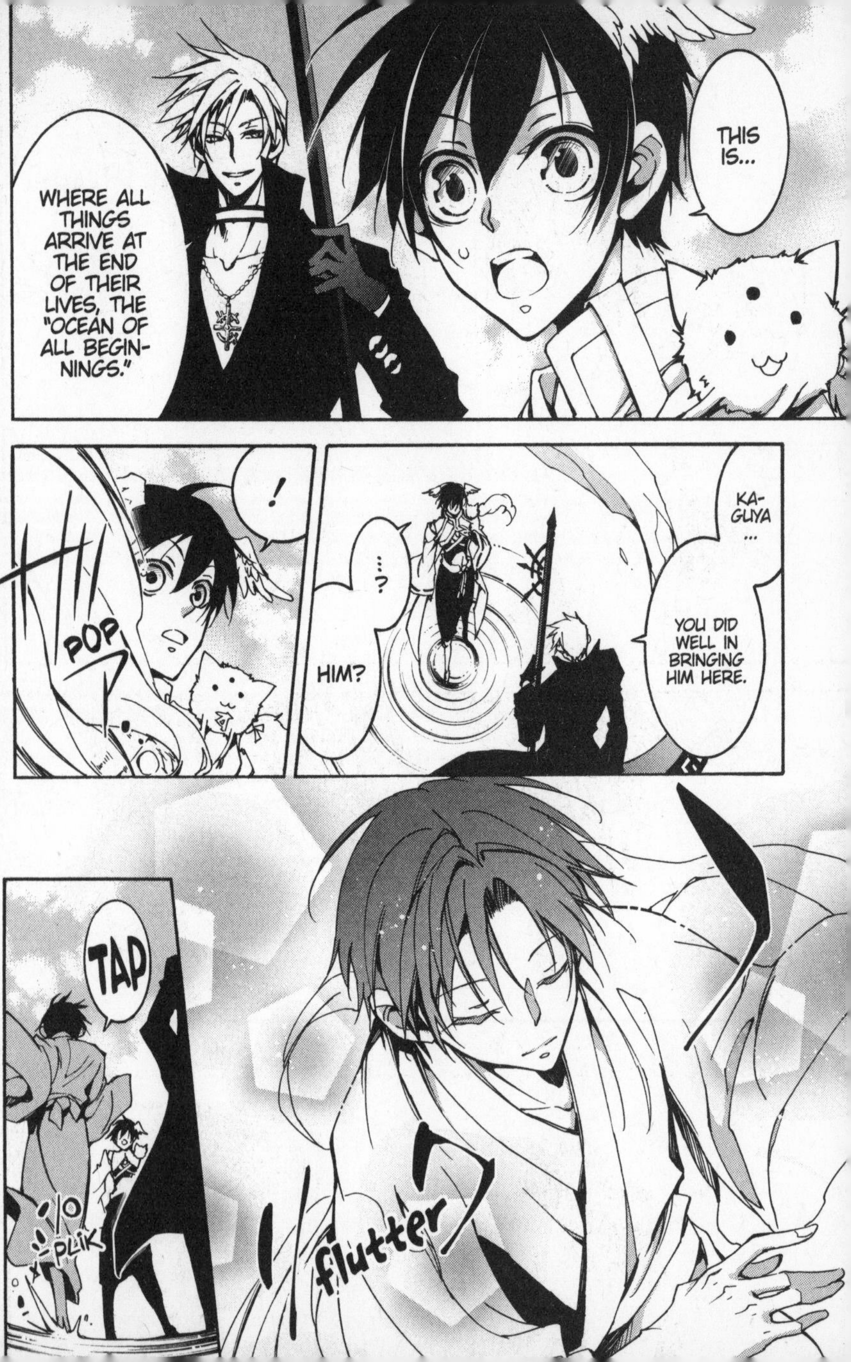
THIS IS...
WHERE ALL THINGS ARRIVE AT THE END OF THEIR LIVES, THE "OCEAN OF ALL BEGINNINGS."
KA-GUYA ...
YOU DID WELL IN BRINGING HIM HERE.
...?
HIM?
!
POP
flutter
TAP
PLIK

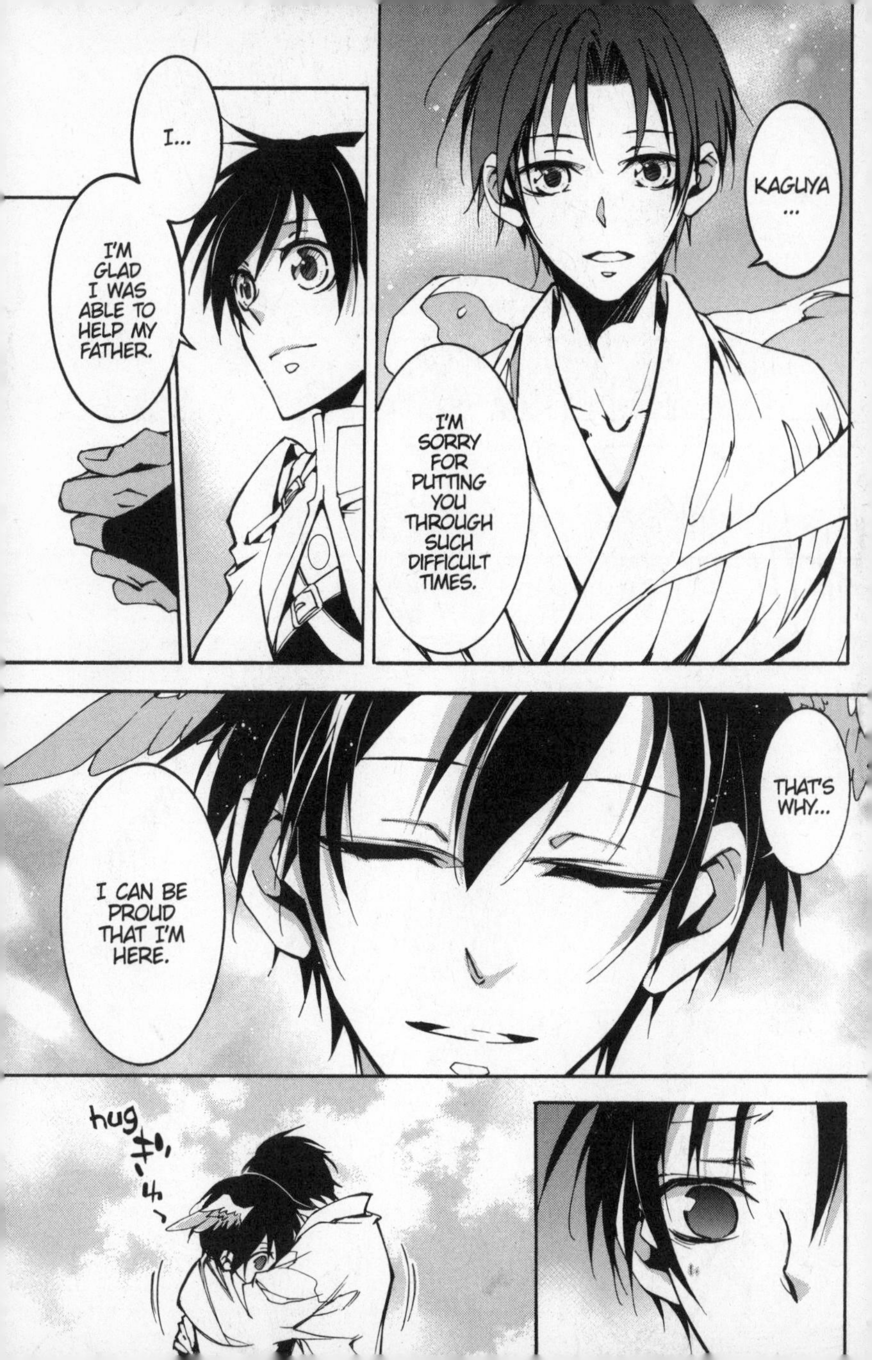
KAGUYA ...
I'M SORRY FOR PUTTING YOU THROUGH SUCH DIFFICULT TIMES.
I...
I'M GLAD I WAS ABLE TO HELP MY FATHER.
THAT'S WHY...
I CAN BE PROUD THAT I'M HERE.
hug

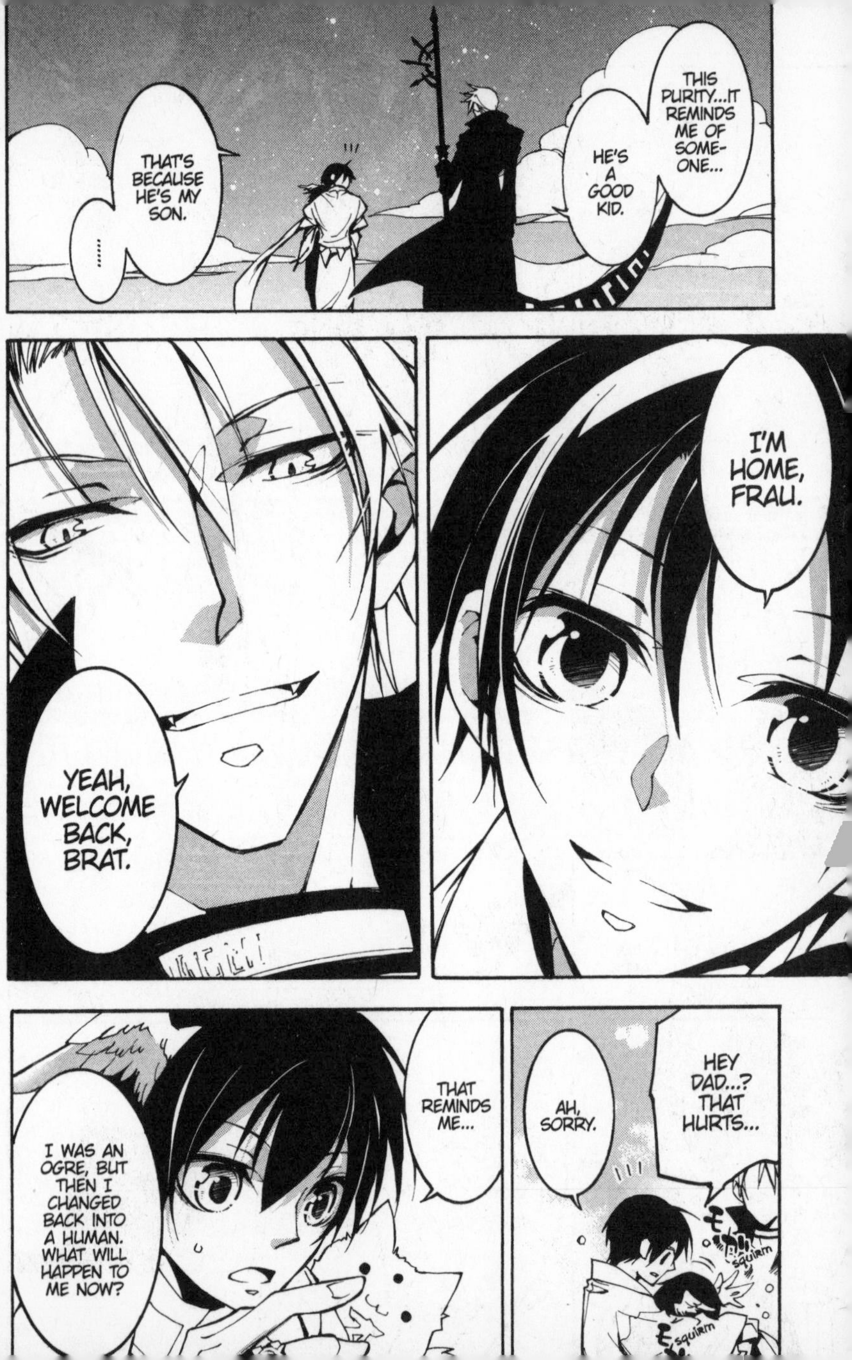
THIS PURITY...IT REMINDS ME OF SOME-ONE...
HE'S A GOOD KID.
THAT'S BECAUSE HE'S MY SON.
......
I'M HOME, FRAU.
YEAH, WELCOME BACK, BRAT.
HEY DAD...? THAT HURTS...
AH, SORRY.
squirm
squirm
THAT REMINDS ME...
I WAS AN OGRE, BUT THEN I CHANGED BACK INTO A HUMAN. WHAT WILL HAPPEN TO ME NOW?

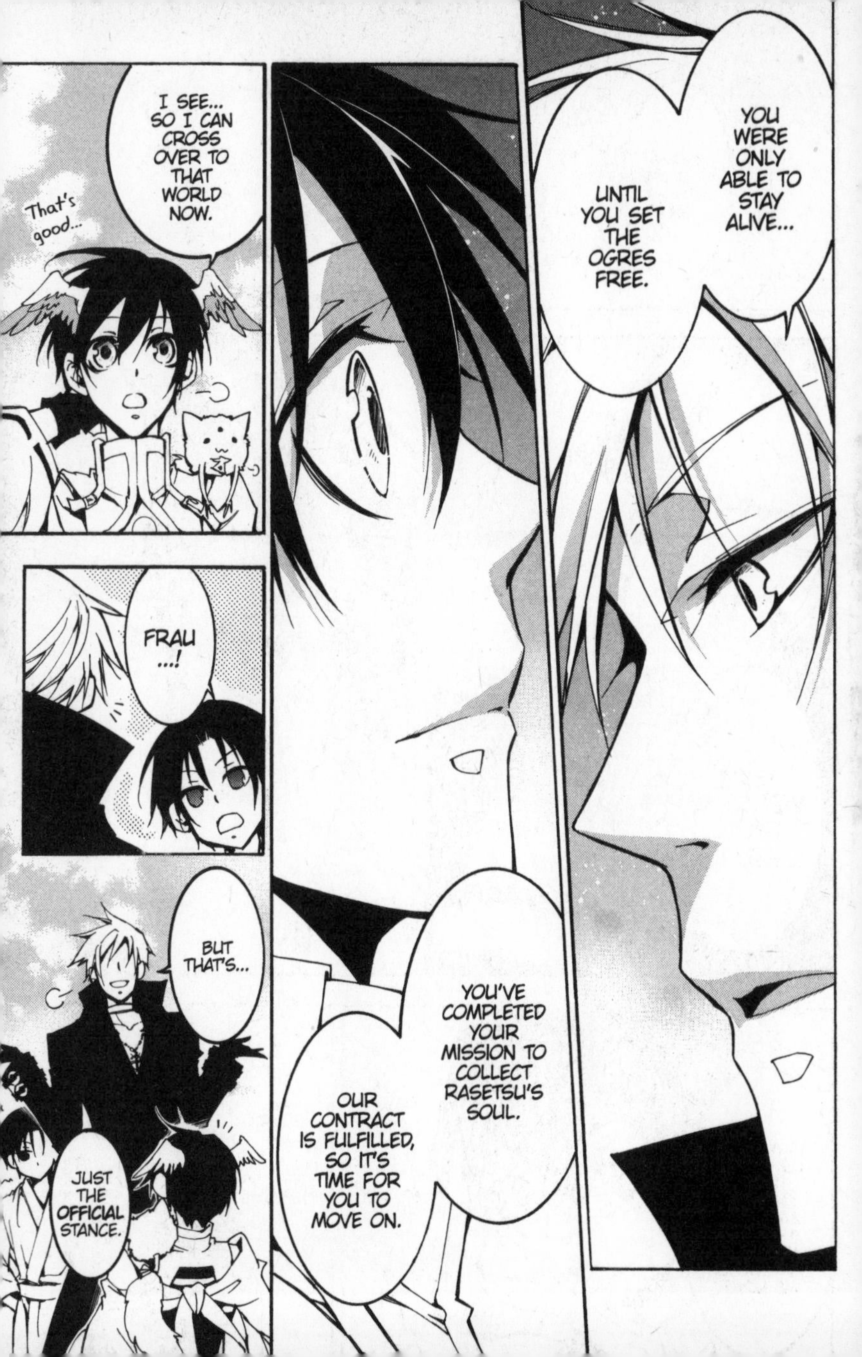
YOU WERE ONLY ABLE TO STAY ALIVE...
UNTIL YOU SET THE OGRES FREE.
YOU'VE COMPLETED YOUR MISSION TO COLLECT RASETSU'S SOUL.
OUR CONTRACT IS FULFILLED, SO IT'S TIME FOR YOU TO MOVE ON.
I SEE... SO I CAN CROSS OVER TO THAT WORLD NOW.
That's good...
FRAU ...!
BUT THAT'S...
JUST THE OFFICIAL STANCE.

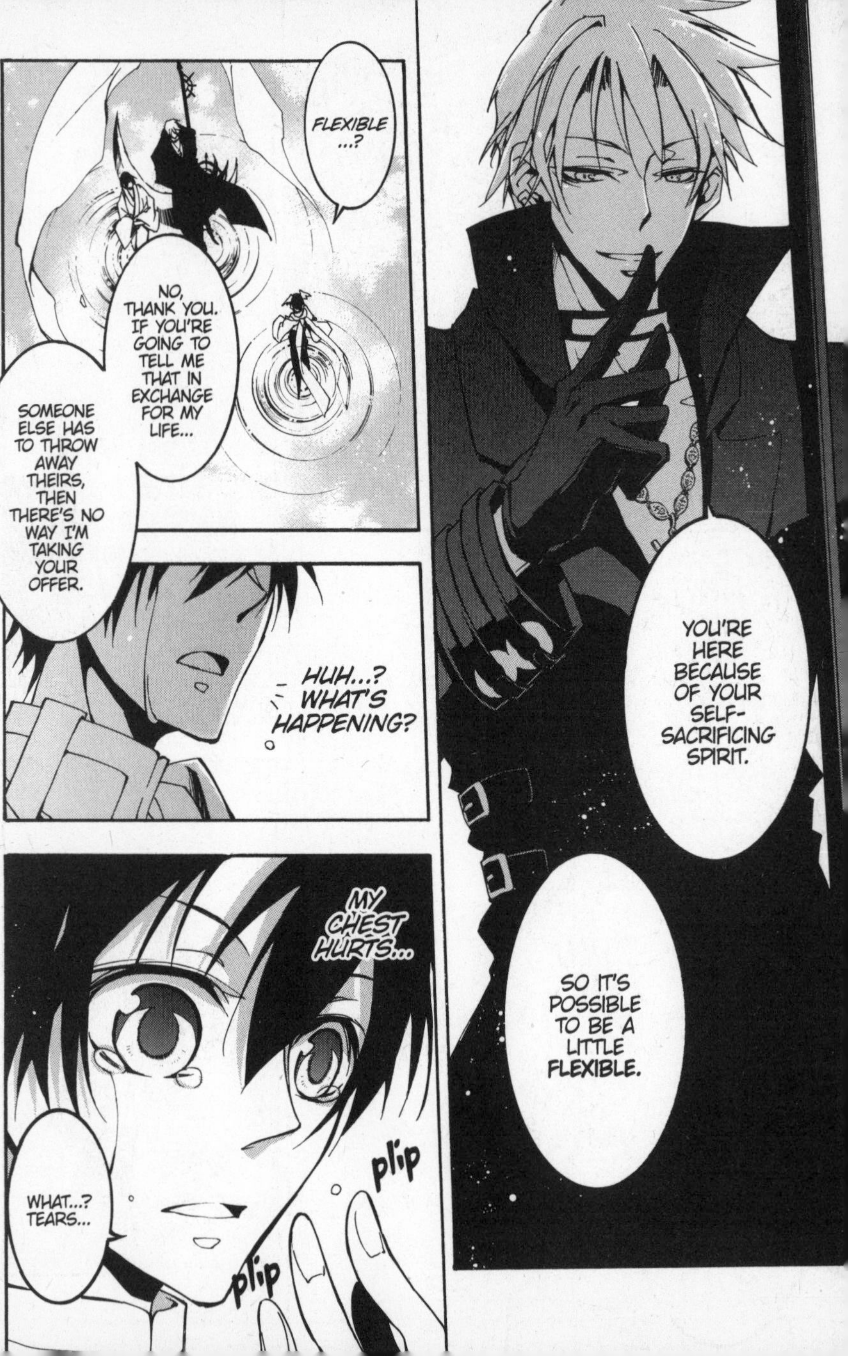
YOU'RE HERE BECAUSE OF YOUR SELF-SACRIFICING SPIRIT.
SO IT'S POSSIBLE TO BE A LITTLE FLEXIBLE.
FLEXIBLE ...?
NO, THANK YOU. IF YOU'RE GOING TO TELL ME THAT IN EXCHANGE FOR MY LIFE...
SOMEONE ELSE HAS TO THROW AWAY THEIRS, THEN THERE'S NO WAY I'M TAKING YOUR OFFER.
HUH...? WHAT'S HAPPENING?
MY CHEST HURTS...
plip
WHAT...? TEARS...
plip

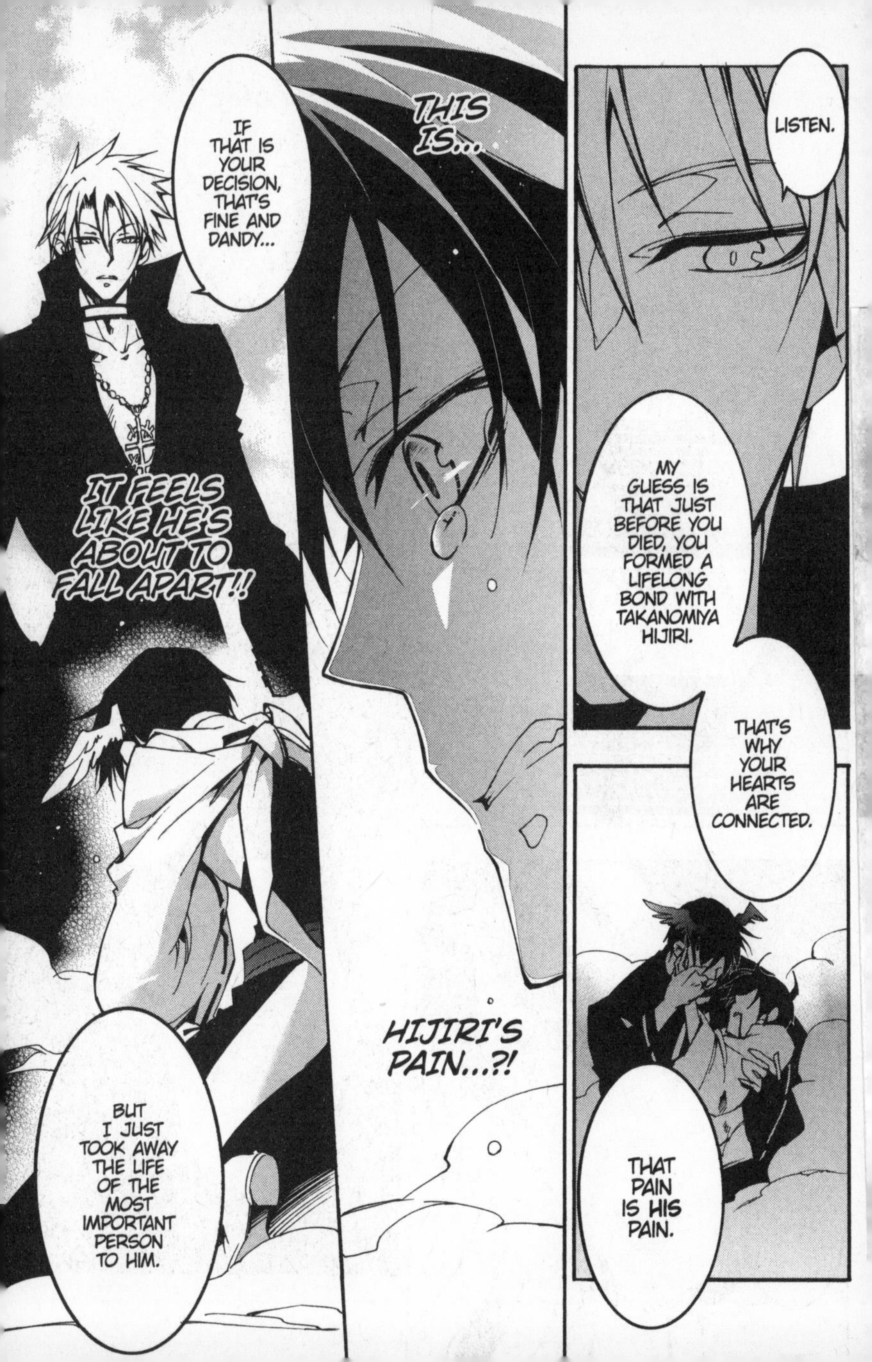
LISTEN.
MY GUESS IS THAT JUST BEFORE YOU DIED, YOU FORMED A LIFELONG BOND WITH TAKANOMIYA HIJIRI.
THAT'S WHY YOUR HEARTS ARE CONNECTED.
THAT PAIN IS HIS PAIN.
THIS IS...
HIJIRI'S PAIN...?!
IF THAT IS YOUR DECISION, THAT'S FINE AND DANDY...
IT FEELS LIKE HE'S ABOUT TO FALL APART!!
BUT I JUST TOOK AWAY THE LIFE OF THE MOST IMPORTANT PERSON TO HIM.

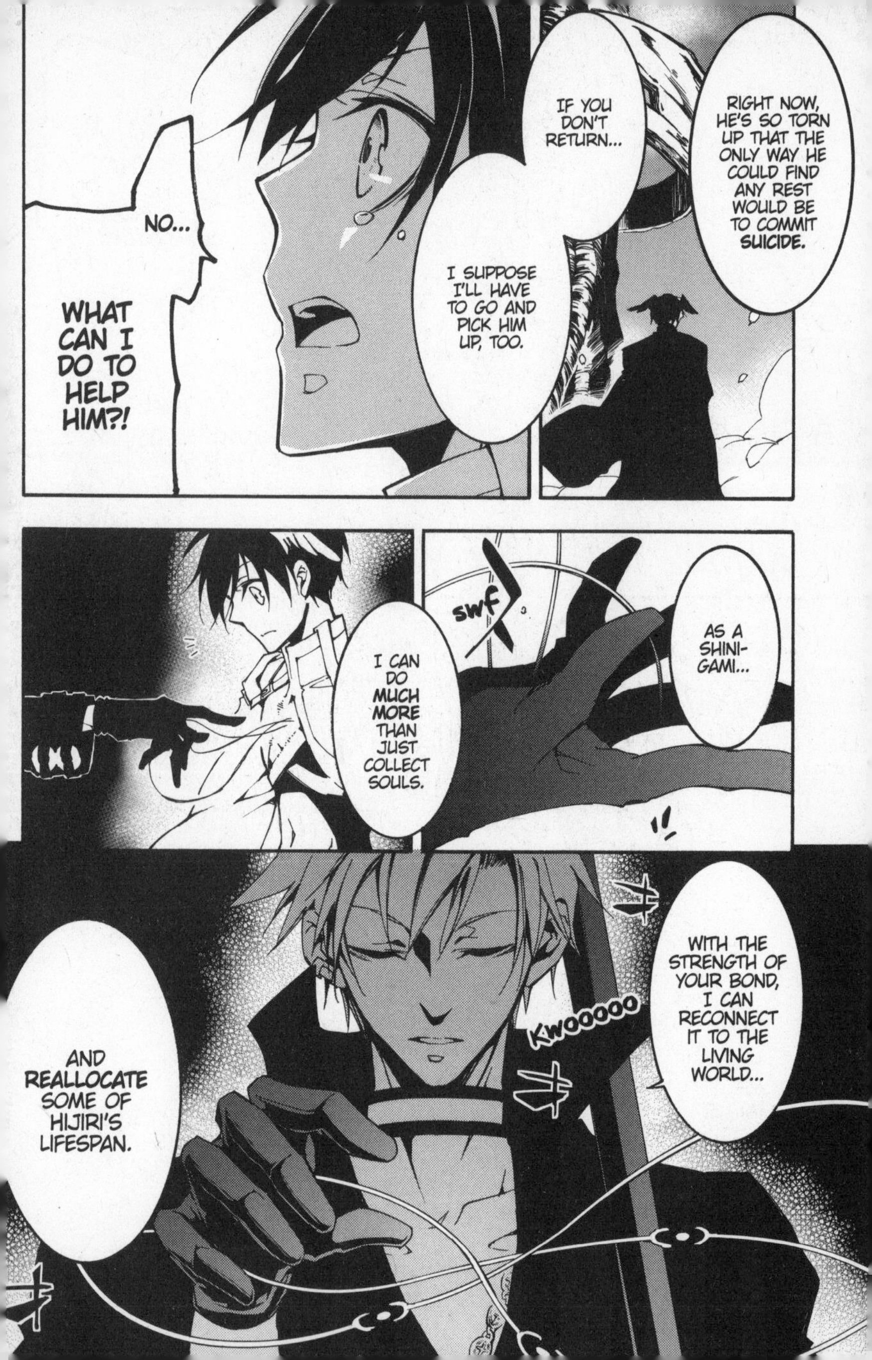
RIGHT NOW, HE'S SO TORN UP THAT THE ONLY WAY HE COULD FIND ANY REST WOULD BE TO COMMIT **SUICIDE.**
IF YOU DON'T RETURN...
I SUPPOSE I'LL HAVE TO GO AND PICK HIM UP, TOO.
NO...
WHAT CAN I DO TO HELP HIM?!
AS A SHINIGAMI...
swf
I CAN DO **MUCH MORE** THAN JUST COLLECT SOULS.
!!
WITH THE STRENGTH OF YOUR BOND, I CAN RECONNECT IT TO THE LIVING WORLD...
KWOOOOO
AND REALLOCATE SOME OF HIJIRI'S LIFESPAN.

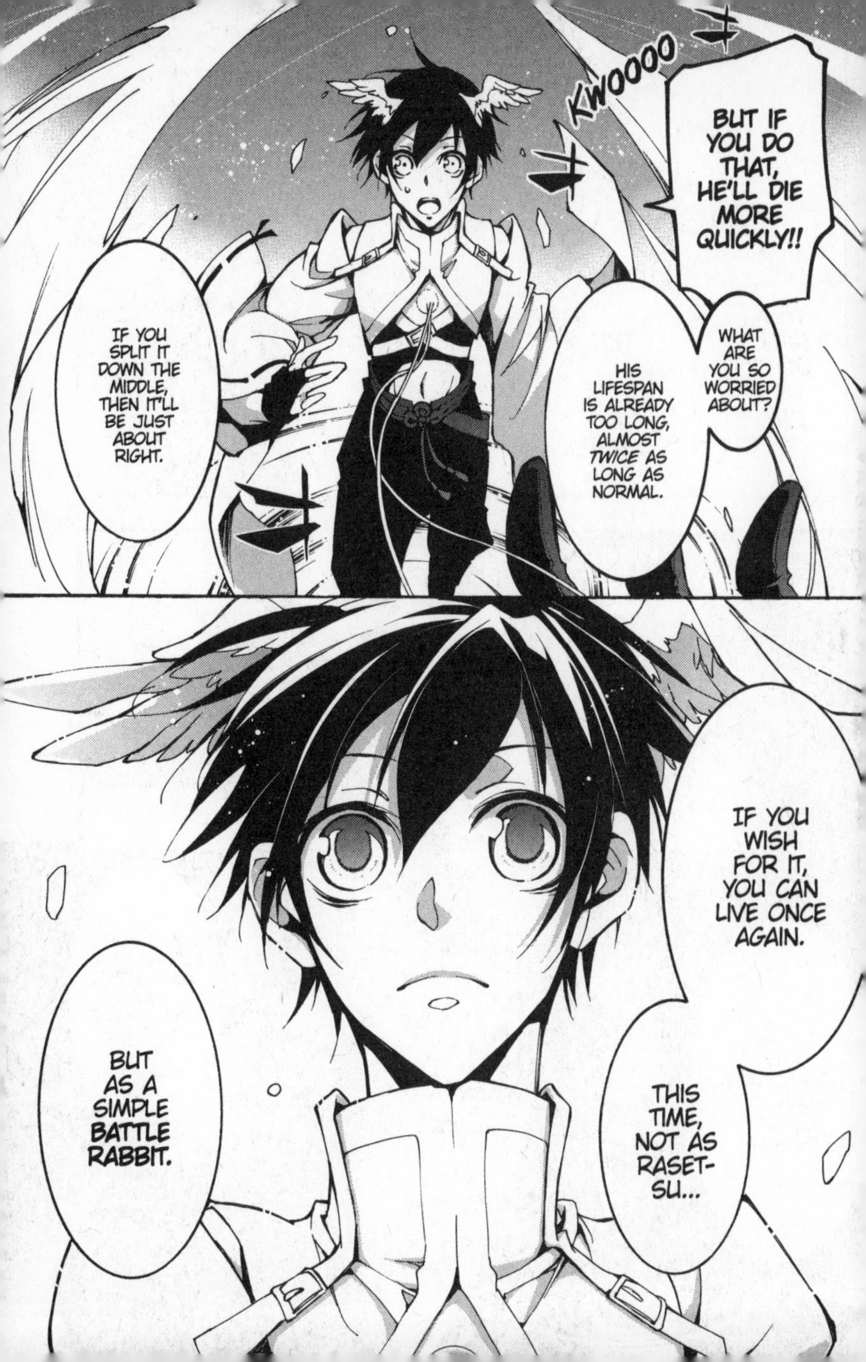
KWOOOO
BUT IF YOU DO THAT, HE'LL DIE MORE QUICKLY!!
WHAT ARE YOU SO WORRIED ABOUT?
HIS LIFESPAN IS ALREADY TOO LONG, ALMOST *TWICE* AS LONG AS NORMAL.
IF YOU SPLIT IT DOWN THE MIDDLE, THEN IT'LL BE JUST ABOUT RIGHT.
IF YOU WISH FOR IT, YOU CAN LIVE ONCE AGAIN.
THIS TIME, NOT AS RASET-SU...
BUT AS A SIMPLE BATTLE RABBIT.

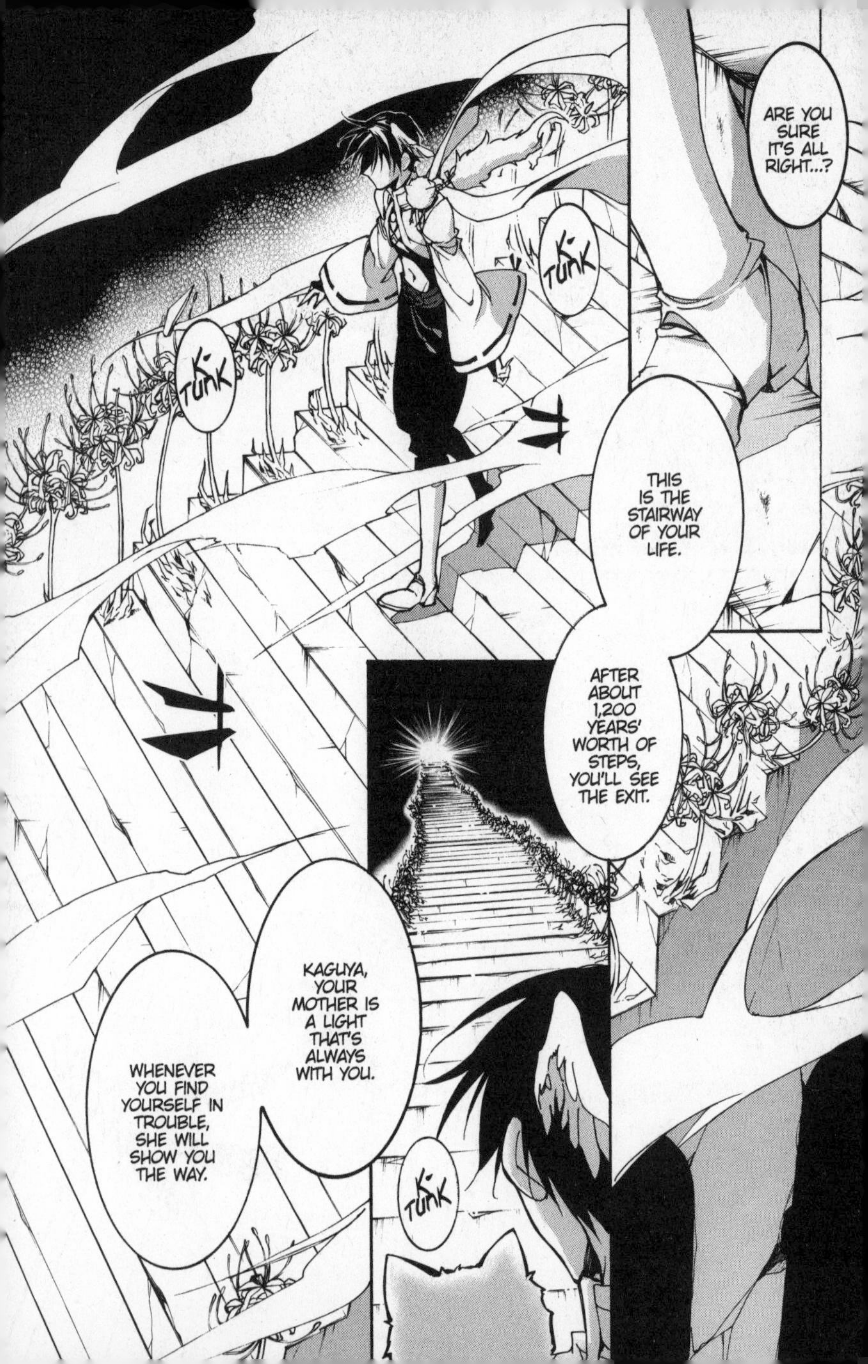
ARE YOU SURE IT'S ALL RIGHT...?
K-TUNK
K-TUNK
THIS IS THE STAIRWAY OF YOUR LIFE.
AFTER ABOUT 1,200 YEARS' WORTH OF STEPS, YOU'LL SEE THE EXIT.
KAGUYA, YOUR MOTHER IS A LIGHT THAT'S ALWAYS WITH YOU.
WHENEVER YOU FIND YOURSELF IN TROUBLE, SHE WILL SHOW YOU THE WAY.
K-TUNK

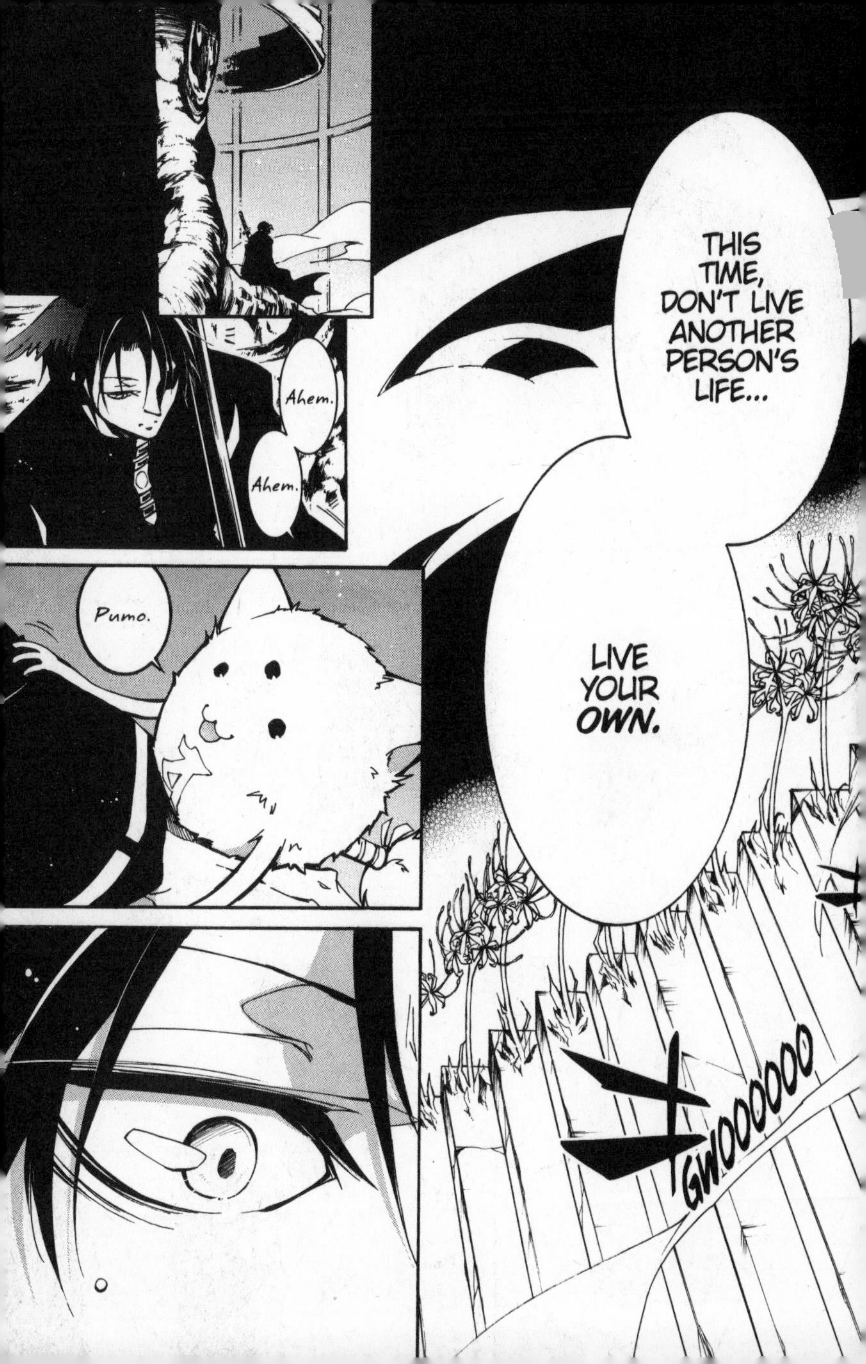
THIS TIME, DON'T LIVE ANOTHER PERSON'S LIFE...
LIVE YOUR OWN.
GWOOOOOO
Ahem.
Ahem.
Pumo.

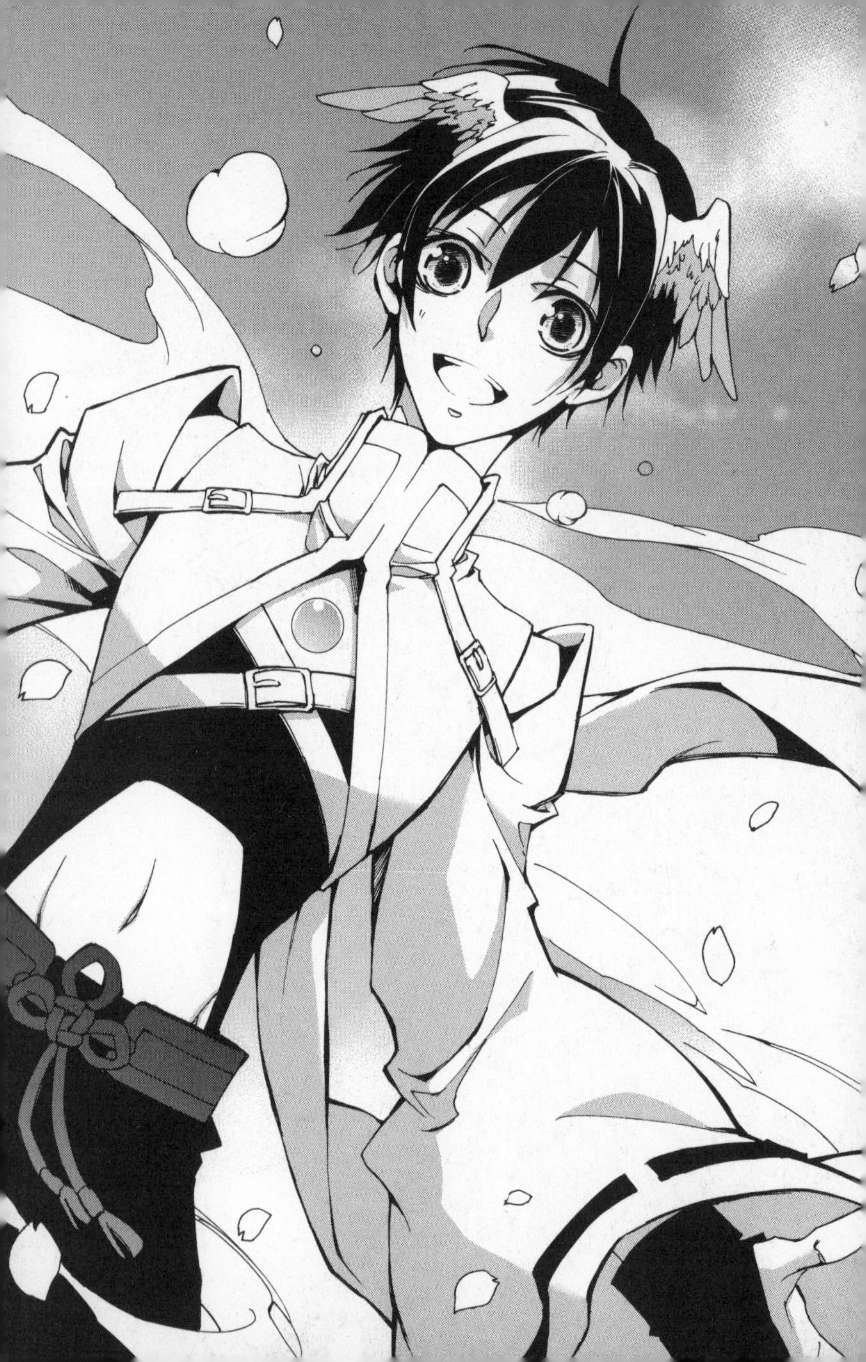

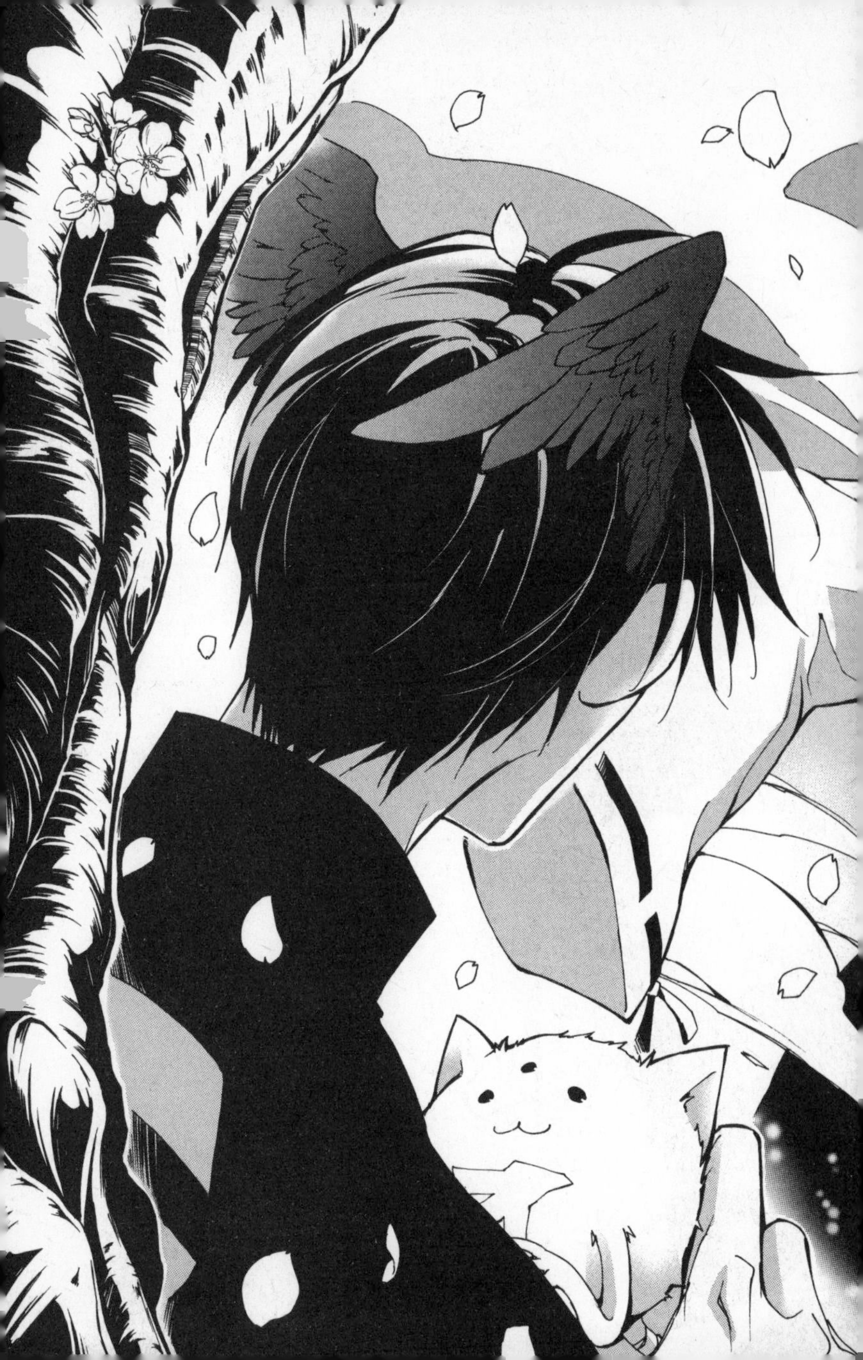

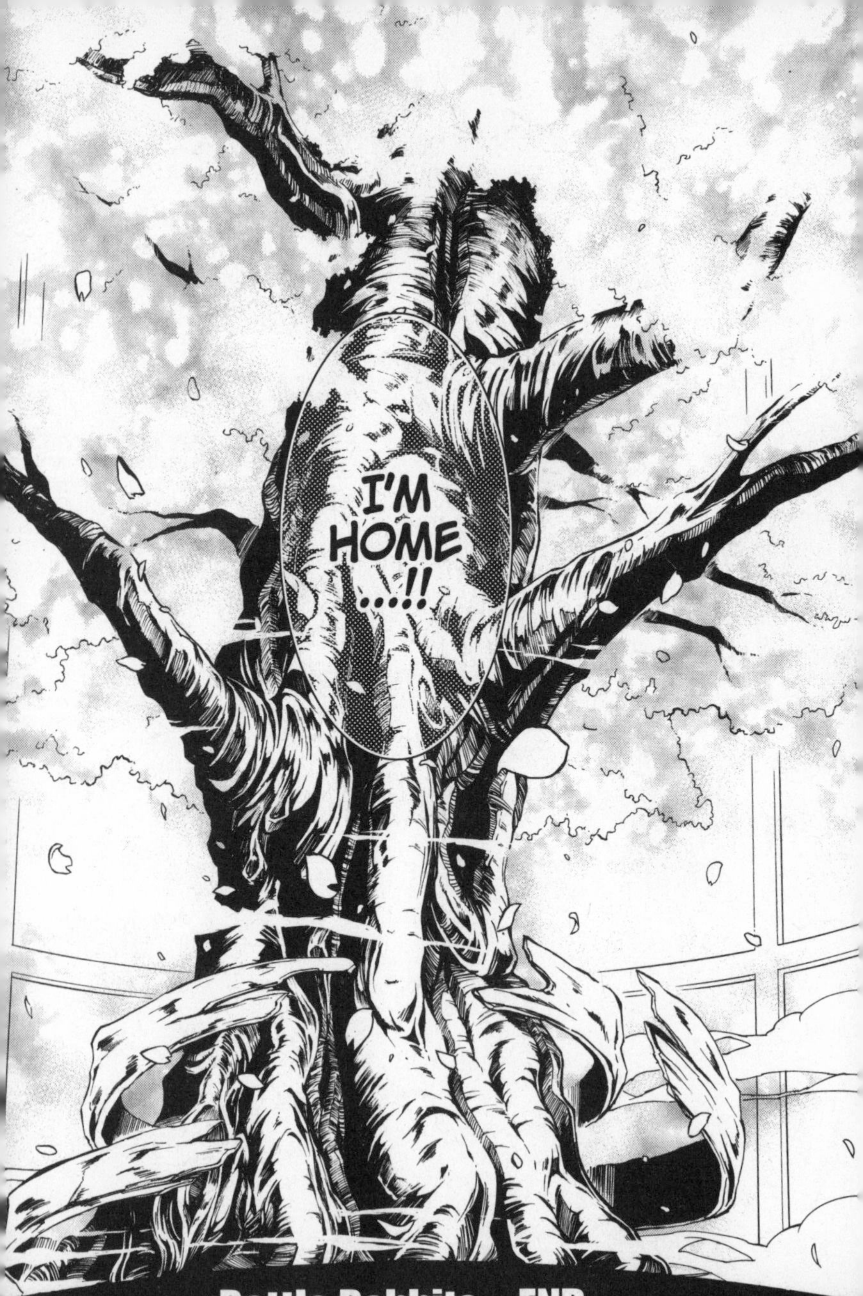
I'M HOME ...!!

Battle Rabbits – END

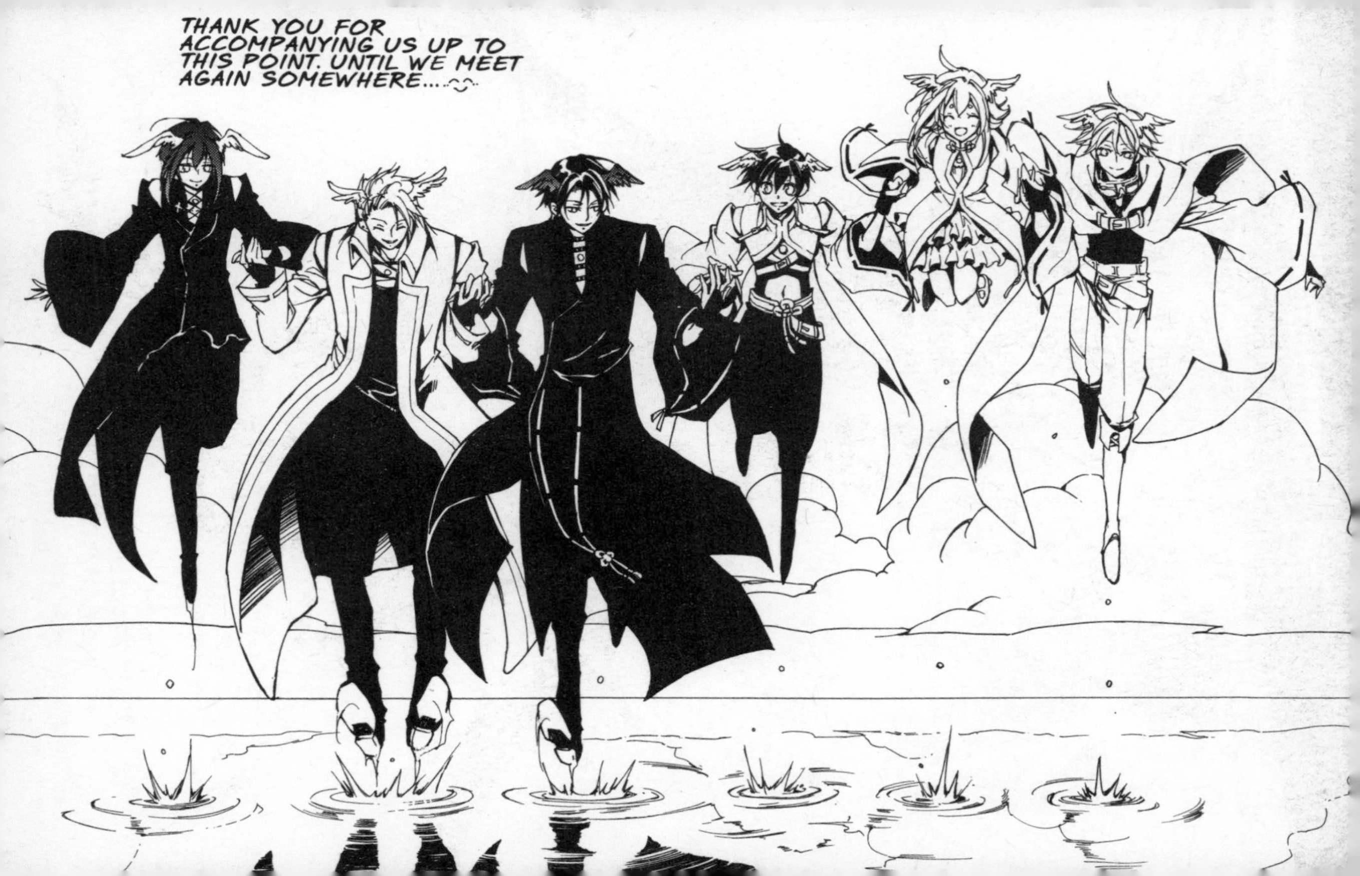
THANK YOU FOR ACCOMPANYING US UP TO THIS POINT. UNTIL WE MEET AGAIN SOMEWHERE...

SEVEN SEAS ENTERTAINMENT PRESENTS

BATTLE RABBITS

story and art by AMEICHI

VOLUME 4

TRANSLATION
Jill Morita

ADAPTATION
Janet Houck

LETTERING AND RETOUCH
Meaghan Tucker

LOGO DESIGN
Karis Page

COVER DESIGN
Nicky Lim

PROOFREADER
Danielle King

ASSISTANT EDITOR
Jenn Grunigen

PRODUCTION ASSISTANT
CK Russell

PRODUCTION MANAGER
Lissa Pattillo

EDITOR-IN-CHIEF
Adam Arnold

PUBLISHER
Jason DeAngelis

BATTLE RABBITS VOL. 4
© AMEICHI 2016
First published in Japan in 2016 by ICHIJINSHA Inc., Tokyo.
English translation rights arranged with ICHIJINSHA Inc., Tokyo, Japan.

Seven Seas books may be purchased in bulk for promotional, educational, or business use. Please contact your local bookseller or the Macmillan Corporate and Premium Sales Department at 1-800-221-7945, extension 5442, or by e-mail at MacmillanSpecialMarkets@macmillan.com.

ISBN: 978-1-626924-49-9

Printed in Canada

First Printing: July 2017

10 9 8 7 6 5 4 3 2 1

FOLLOW US ONLINE: *www.gomanga.com*

READING DIRECTIONS

This book reads from *right to left*, Japanese style. If this is your first time reading manga, you start reading from the top right panel on each page and take it from there. If you get lost, just follow the numbered diagram here. It may seem backwards at first, but you'll get the hang of it! Have fun!!

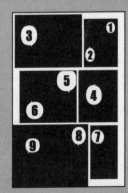